NATIVE AMERICAN

Bozeman's Trail to Destiny

PROMISE

Bozeman's Trail

to Destiny

SERLE L. CHAPMAN

BOZEMAN
TRAIL RUTS

PROMISE
Bozeman's Trail to D

Written & Photographed by

SERLE L. CHAPMAN

Foreword by

RICK INGOLDSBY
PRESIDENT - FORT PHIL KEARNY/BOZEMAN TRAIL ASSOCIATION

GEORGE MAGPIE
WOLF CHIEF - BOWSTRINGS MILITARY SOCIETY, CHEYENNE NATION

Introduction by

DR. HENRIETTA MANN

Featuring the Art of

DONALD MONTILEAUX
KEVIN RED STAR

With contributions from

DR. SUSAN BADGER DOYLE
JACK BAILEY
LEONA BUCKMAN
ISAAC DOG EAGLE
JOHNSON HOLY ROCK
TIM LAME WOMAN
DR. JOSEPH MEDICINE CROW
WILMER STAMPEDE MESTETH
ALFRED RED CLOUD
ELMER 'SONNY' REISCH
DOUGLAS SPOTTED EAGLE
RICHARD TALL BULL JR
ROBERT C. WILSON

Postscript by

HAROLD SALWAY & HERB PAVEY

for Tashiya and the medicine people of both science and ceremony who gave her life,

and to her aunt Jackie who gave her the name A-me'ha'e (Flying Butterfly) on Noaha-vose,

and for her uncle Ryck and aunt Tracey for being there for her.

All photography copyright © 2002/2003/2004 by Serle L. Chapman except where indicated.

Design by Serle L. Chapman.

Digital Artwork Manager and Creative Consultant: John Parker.
Project Coordinator: Sarah Gilbertson-Chapman.
Proofreaders: Jasmine Star/Beth Parker.
Photographic Services: G. King Photo Color Ltd., Vancouver, Canada, and The Photo Factory, San Diego, California.

Printed in Hong Kong by MANTEC.

Pavey Western Publishing, PO Box 982020, Park City, UT 84098 USA. 435-615-7900.
www.gonativeamerica.com
www.serlechapman.com
info@gonativeamerica.com

Distributed by Mountain Press Publishing Company, 1301 S. Third Street W, PO Box 2399, Missoula, MT 59806 USA. 800-234-5308.
www.mtnpress.com

FIRST EDITION 2004

ISBN 0-9528607-9-1

Library of Congress Control Number: 2004091471

Cover: Nupa White Plume (Oglala Sioux) by Serle L. Chapman. Chief Red Cloud (Denver Public Library, Western History Collection, X-31824). William T. Sherman (Little Bighorn Battlefield National Monument, Western National Parks Association). William J. Fetterman (Fort Laramie National Historic Site, National Park Service). Iron Bull (Joe Medicine Crow Collection). Jim Bridger (Kansas State Historical Society, Topeka, Kansas). John Bozeman (Montana Historical Society, Helena). Ledger art by Don Montileaux. Frontispiece: Nupa White Plume. Bozeman Trail wagon ruts on the Fetterman Battlefield. Title page: Jasmine Pickner (Crow Creek Sioux) by Serle L. Chapman.

CONTENTS

THE JOURNEY

BY SERLE L. CHAPMAN

There is nothing easy about leaving, I thought, as my friend became lost in the dark shapes of a cluster of mountains that clouds and my rear view mirror took behind my back. I don't know if she stood there waving until there was only wondering. I don't know if she was there at all. But I know that she had been. Not even the words "I'll see you soon" made it out from the rubble of emotions. A promise isn't a promise just because it has the same sound. We talked on the phone later, not saying how we really felt, but in a code that is universal, a code that let's friends leave without the scrutiny of love or good or bye. I felt better, but not about leaving. Amarillo came quickly out of the distance of thinking and New Mexico. I'd never been in Texas before when it rained like this. Neon bled into the night and the puddles, and the puddles seethed between speed and wheels, and the Hemphill county line didn't seem so far so I kept driving.

The sun rearranged the earth in dawn and made the world again from darkness. This was a day to know the unknown, or to at least reach out for its meaning. I am a stranger here, I thought, as I crossed the Sweetwater and graveyards of rusting farm machinery, the iron limbs of earth diggers laying on buffalo bones, the skeletal remains and incantations of the dreamers and the dreamed, each foreign to the other but all decaying. I drove on through small towns where you can find breakfast, a haircut, and Jesus if you stay past noon, until eventually I arrived at Gageby Creek. This is the kind of place where the only other people you see are lost. The plains unravel to infinity in great dunes carpeted in threadbare sod, and there is ritual to the earth's rendezvous with sky for between their acts and ceremonies lies the world, but most men do not see it and recognize only the making of their own hand, that which they name, that which they call to. Here there is not another man to listen. Leaves rattled on a ragged stand of timber and I read, "Stand silent! Heroes here have been who cleared the way for other men."

Hidden within the folds of this land I counted six names on the monument but returned to only one, Amos Chapman. I wondered about this man whose last name I share. One immigrant described him as being around six feet tall with dark, piercing eyes, "a quiet, rawboned man who slightly resembles an Indian," they noted, adding that he rode "a pure white horse." Another settler scarred his face with a bullet because he mistook him for an Indian. Somewhere a part of him and a part of me came down the same bloodstream in the passage of stone to fish to human. He bled where I stood. This was an awful place to fight, I thought, so easily is the eye deceived. These waves are shallow until they surround you and you cannot see over one to what awaits behind another. So it was on September 12, 1874, when indigo was frayed by flame and that first light anointed a Kiowa war party who

Top: Shield-style petroglyph, Castle Gardens, Wyoming. Cheyenne shield, circa 1870.

rode out of the horizon in vestments of sunrise like a body of impassioned saints. To the six staked to the plain by isolation they were unhallowed and kin to demons risen, but the canonized and the damned were one, they were men, and each was the other's prophesy that filled the void between life and death. These plains owe little to infinity. The distance amidst near and far is mortality and then as now that place is unreckoned. Between the Kiowa and that place, Amos Chapman saw a buffalo wallow a hundred yards away and Billy Dixon, who killed buffalo for a living, ran for its refuge. Amos and three of the Sixth Cavalry troopers, Sergeant Woodall and Privates Rath and Harrington, reached Dixon in the wallow. Smith, their comrade, lay dead or dying. The Kiowa collected six new American horses. *They will appear, may you behold them! A horse nation will appear*, foretold a Kiowa song. Chapman and Dixon clawed and hacked at the buffalo wallow with Bowie knives and their hands.

The Panhandle was a long way from the stench of the world that drifted up the River Thames to the grime of peasants and nobility slopped into the gutters of London's cobbled streets. "When I was a young boy I just wandered out west," Amos told Mrs. Morgan Thomas, a diarist on Charley Biggers 1867 wagon train, when London can't have been much more to him than a city where they had a queen. From the docks of London, the Chapmans made it to Collier's Harbor near Fort Drummond, the last British stronghold in

Mrs. Amos Chapman, Mary Long Neck

the United States. The fort loomed over the Straits of Mackinac, the economic heartland of the tribes on the Upper Great Lakes, where the fur trade was the king's until 1828. Some say Amos was born and raised there in Michigan and then left for Missouri, but it seems that the draw of commerce from the two great rivers took his family down one to profit from the other, and Amos was born between the Mississippi and the Missouri on March 15, 1837. Of all the goods loaded on and off the keel boats, story must have held a special value to the boy, the storytellers wrapped in their hides and furs and blankets and tales, weathered by brutality and wonder. Across the Missouri River the stories and the tellers were alive, and at sixteen Amos left Chillicothe and crossed the river into Kansas. "I became a teamster and later a scout. I don't know much of anything else, and if I had to do it over, I'd do the same thing. I reckon it gets in your blood," he explained to Mrs. Thomas as they crossed the Cheyenne's Smoky Hill River country on the way to Trinidad, Colorado.

"I reckon it gets in your blood." The phrase kept turning over in my mind. An ant, then another six or seven, scuttled across my hand as I laid in the dirt that the buffalo had once pawed and rubbed into a wallow. Dogs do this, I thought, when they roll in a scent that is instinct, that is remembered, that is in the blood. I reckon Amos did know what that was. Amos was acquainted with Lieutenant Colonel George A. Custer, "they embraced like long lost brothers," Mrs. Thomas noted in her diary after the Biggers' train had reached Fort Wallace on Independence Day, 1867. Not two weeks earlier Mrs. Thomas had written, "As Chapman stood talking to Roman Nose I brazenly walked out and asked Chapman to introduce me to the famous chief." Roman Nose was not a chief, he was a people's dream. He was born to die. He was consecrated with blood and sweat and tears and pain, theirs and his and those of his enemies. If Roman Nose saw any contradiction between life and death nobody ever said. "Amos is a good man, he'll guide you safe," Roman Nose told the white woman in the white tongue he'd learned from a white boy. He let another woman, a Mrs. Baxter, sketch him, and to this stranger who embodied much of what he had vowed to repel he handed the burden of belief, for in her culture belief was the burden of seeing. Roman Nose was simply a believer. For two months Generals Hancock and Custer had pursued what they could not see. They said he was a Dog Soldier Chief but he wasn't, he carried one of the Crooked Lances of the Elk Horn Scrapers military society. They said his name before any others, but he didn't even know theirs; Hancock was just the Officer-Who-Burned-the-Dog-Soldier-Camp-on-Red-Arm-Creek. After Mrs. Baxter gave Roman Nose his likeness and kept the other for herself, the immigrants and the Cheyenne departed for the same destination. The Cheyenne got there first, and their attack on Fort Wallace ended a moon in which the nonbelievers saw for 170-miles east and west of the post, along the Smoky Hill Road and Kansas Pacific. Roman Nose understood the language of blood and that blood is the most ancient of currencies, and in Chapman he saw a fellow believer who knew the debt and how to pay.

Not a day's ride to the east of this buffalo wallow, Chapman's wife's family and her people purchased the Washita in such a way. In the fall of 1868 Roman Nose was sacrificed at Beecher Island, and Amos was scouting for the Seventh Cavalry under Major Joel Elliott as the regimental band honed the 'Garryowen' for winter. "Here goes for a brevet or a coffin," Elliott is said to have bellowed as he charged after bewildered Cheyennes while Custer's battalions sacked Chief Black Kettle's village along the Washita River at dawn on November 27, 1868. The hooves of Roman-Nose-Thunder's pony and those of the Arapaho flat-club owner, Tobacco, made an old song new on the backs of Elliott and his men, and Man-Riding-on-a-Cloud ensured that a brevet wouldn't be Elliott's destiny. To sit by the Washita is to wait in the silence of passing. There are two knolls to the south of where the village stood, and it was towards those that Magpie and Pushing Bear crawled and then ran that morning. Magpie had seen Chief Black Kettle and his wife Medicine Woman Later shot down at the ford, and the boy himself had been lamed. A soldier crashed through the brush on a big brown horse and hacked at Magpie with a saber. He missed. The boy shoved a black-powder pistol into the bluecoat's gut and fired. I have walked where Magpie stumbled through breaking bones and branches and the screams of mothers and children and dancing horses dying in dull thuds as they patterned the snow with afterbirth and death. The band played on. "To follow this way of life is a hard way to live," one of his grandsons has reminded me many times. The next day Magpie dragged the body of Long Neck's grandfather from the river and helped return the chief to the earth. Mrs. Chapman had lost her grandfather, and the Southern Cheyennes had lost their most willing peace-talker, Chief Black Kettle. The riverbank, the prairie and the mounds that boil from it are dusted with pipestone. Beneath snow that orange dirt must ooze red. It gets in your blood.

The Washita brought warfare that until then was uncontested, but it was still war and in it such men found the communion of body and soul. Six years passed, and Amos and his fellow hostages were laying on their bellies in the dried piss of buffaloes and knots of auburn hair where the great beasts had churned the ground to sand and dust and in which brown-headed birds had feasted and whistled and then flown back to the herd because the war wasn't over. Their lips were cracked and swollen and blistered and dirt whipped into their eyes and clicked in their teeth or where they used to be. Their canteens had gone with the horses. The sun was ripening and peeling back their skin. There were no clouds nor anything to sully the cobalt blue save the fatigue of the day welling in the west and the cries of the Kiowas loosed upon the waste. I leaned against the sterile railing within which the buffalo wallow is now encased in concrete and weighted down by the marbled marker. It was the same sky as on that day, but the cries were echoes in the sighs of grass as brittle as life beneath one foot, one hoof, and then the others. A hundred yards didn't seem far to me, but I wasn't running toward a man whose life was seeping through his chest as he lay crumpled, dark and malformed. The men in the buffalo wallow needed the dead man's rounds, then Chapman saw the dead man writhe. "He's still alive, we can't leave him out there," he said, and they didn't. Amos Chapman ran from the wallow to Smith, and hauled him up and carried him, the 170-pound half-dead trooper flopping gently like a grotesque stole hanging over Chapman's shoulders. "Amos! Amos! We have got you now!" Chapman said fifteen of the Kiowas shouted as they rode him down. Smith slumped to the ground as Amos drew his revolver and the horsemen toyed with him and then wheeled away from the fire. Chapman again wrestled Smith on to his back and staggered to within twenty yards of the buffalo wallow when a bullet sliced into his left leg just above the ankle and Smith fell on top of him as an amorous drunk might a whore in a bar, and the shattered leg snapped. Amos dragged himself out from beneath Smith, then lugged himself and the dying trooper closer to the wallow, his foot sliding behind his leg with the bone protruding from his boot as his shank made a furrow to the buffalo wallow in the manner of some rudimentary gothic plow. "Amos, you're bad hit," said Dixon, whose widow later credited him with the rescue of Smith in his 1914 autobiography.

Amos described the Kiowa combatant who shot him as, "A little old scoundrel I had fed fifty times." In the two decades that had passed since he first crossed the Missouri, Chapman had learned many of the ways and the languages of the Kiowa and Cheyenne, a cultural apprenticeship that began when members of each tribe were his primary trading partners and mentors in plains-craft. Aside from the debate Olive Dixon fostered as to who rescued Private Smith, historians have also bickered over whether the besiegers were Kiowa, Comanche, Cheyenne, or a combination of the three, and if there actually were 125 warriors in the Buffalo Wallow Fight as Colonel Nelson A. Miles reported on September 24, 1874. Perhaps few were better qualified than Amos Chapman to identify the tribesmen. Cheyenne oral history indicates that after the June 27, 1874 fight with the Anglo buffalo hunters at Adobe Walls, the Cheyenne were reluctant to participate in any action that involved the Comanches, the Kiowa war faction's principal allies in the Red River War. "We quit because we had been fooled about the medicine charm being so strong that the white men's guns would not fire," Short Nose explained to Amos's son, Frank Chapman. Short Nose was referring to Esa-taí, a Comanche spiritual leader, who was known as "son of the wolf." Esa-taí's people, the Quahada Comanche, bore witness to his journey to the sun where he had been blessed with mystery and power, and upon his return they had watched as he vomited cartridges, a gift he had received for his people, a gift to protect them from the bullets of the white men's guns. "Esa-taí make big talk that time," recounted Quanah Parker, the legendary Quahada chief, in an interview with Captain Hugh Scott in 1897. "Lots of white men, I stop the bullets in guns. Bullets not penetrate shirts. We kill them like old women. God told me truth," said Quanah of Esa-taí as they planned the attack on Adobe Walls. "My power is strong, the hunters' bullets will not harm us," Esa-taí chanted as the Comanches, Kiowa, Cheyenne and Arapaho counciled on Elk Creek. "Those white men will not fire a shot, we shall kill them all," he predicted, and some four hundred men were converted and under the new moon rode to the rhythm of this would-be Messiah, learning a dance akin to that of the ghosts.

Esa-taí, Quanah Parker, He Bear and Tabananaka led the Comanches away from Elk Creek and the coils of the column that swayed behind them held Lone Wolf of the Kiowa, and Gray Beard, Bull Bear, Red Moon, Eagle Head and Medicine Water of the Cheyenne. What the Comanches' moon did not tell was that the white men had been warned, for as Esa-taí imparted his revelation, Amos Chapman had arrived at Adobe Walls. Rumors of the attack had reached Camp Supply and the post traders, Lee and Reynolds, requested a messenger to carry the news to the merchants who had set up shop around the Bent brothers' old trading post at Adobe Walls. Billy Dixon had guided the entrepreneurs and their buffalo-skinning clientele west from Dodge City, Kansas and on the afternoon of June 25 Amos gave the time and date of the impending attack to Charles Rath, Charlie Myers and saloon proprietor, Jim Hanrahan. The merchants were reluctant to inform the buffalo hunters and their skinners for fear that their already tenuous business venture would collapse with the threat alone. "The Indians around Fort Supply told us they were going down to Adobe Walls to kill the buffalo hunters," recalled James McAllister, an employee of Lee and Reynolds who accompanied Amos and seven troopers to Adobe Walls. "We told the hunters what the Indians had said, and that they were coming, but they wouldn't believe us." Evidently a couple did, as Amos left with the Mooar brothers. Of the merchants, Myers and Rath took their leave, but Jim Hanrahan stayed and took the opportunity to go into business with Billy Dixon who was a crack shot and relentless buffalo slayer, attractive attributes for the best or worst of times to come on the Canadian. Chapman said the attack would come early morning June 27, and it did.

Esa-taí set his pony on a butte above Adobe Walls and to any of the twenty-eight men and one woman huddled in the saloon and two stores the yellow figure wreathed in sage atop a yellow horse must have glowed in the breaking day as an incubus or centaur ablaze and freed from some myth or fable they had heard but long since forgotten. By noon he was just a painted man on a painted horse with nothing to silence the Sharps .50 caliber rifles that boomed from inside the walls. Esa-taí had painted Quanah so no bullet could hit him, but when one did and he fell even the Comanches lost faith and they withdrew with the Kiowa and Cheyenne. Five Cheyennes, Horse Road, Stone Teeth, Coyote, Spotted Feathers and Walks-on-the-Ground, lay dead around the outpost, and the next afternoon as the Cheyenne derided Esa-taí a buffalo hunter's slug cracked open his pony's skull. The Cheyenne looked down at the bulletproof Comanche in a mess of bloody horseflesh, and they saw him again in the blind and sagging faces of their fallen men whose heads the buffalo hunters had nailed to stakes around the corral after the siege of Adobe Walls ended. It was as Short Nose said, and the Cheyenne didn't fight with the Comanches and Kiowa against Lyman's supply train or at the buffalo wallow because they had been deceived by Esa-taí. "The Cheyennes were pretty mad at Esa-taí," remembered Quanah Parker. When Amos was trying to stem the bleeding from the wreckage of his leg in the buffalo wallow, the Cheyenne's then most effective force, the Bowstrings military society, was in Kansas.

As Amos had been acquainted with Roman Nose it is reasonable to assume that he was familiar with Roman Nose's closest friend, the Dog Soldier,

Quanah Parker

BUFFALO WALLOW BATTLE GROUND
HERE ON SEPTEMBER 12TH 1874 TWO SCOUTS
AND FOUR SOLDIERS DEFEATED 125 KIOWA
AND COMANCHE INDIANS
SCOUTS
WILLIAM DIXON
AMOS CHAPMAN
SOLDIERS

Buffalo Wallow Battle Ground marker near Gageby Creek, Hemphill County, Texas

Gray Beard. In 1870 Gray Beard succeeded his father-in-law, Black Shin, as chief of the southern So'taaeo'o band that Roman Nose associated with before his death. Had Gray Beard been at the buffalo wallow, Chapman would have known. Along with Many Magpies, Eagle Head, Sand Hill and Stone Forehead – the Keeper of the Four Sacred Arrows, Gray Beard saw no alternative but to fight in the Red River War to protect what buffalo remained on the southern plains from the hide hunters who General Philip Sheridan had identified as the empire's most potent force in settling "the vexed Indian question." Sheridan, the commander of U.S. troops on the southern plains, advocated exterminating the buffalo to starve the tribes into submission. After Adobe Walls, the Cheyennes on the Staked Plains were harried by Colonel Nelson A. Miles' Fifth Infantry and Sixth Cavalry, and only parties from the Bowstrings and Dog Soldiers military societies were able to break-out of the Panhandle. Both groups headed back to the Cheyenne's old buffalo ranges in the Smoky Hill country of Kansas. White Horse and Bull Bear led the remnants of the Dog Soldiers, but the Bowstrings under Medicine Water were at the height of their power. The Bowstrings targeted the Smoky Hill Road, and on the way they wiped out Oliver Short's surveying crew, and killed ranchers' cattle in retribution for the slaughter of the buffalo. A matter of hours before Amos Chapman, Billy Dixon and the four cavalrymen were trapped in the buffalo wallow by Gageby Creek, the Bowstrings were still in Kansas. Medicine Water's party were about a day's ride from Fort Wallace when, on September 11, 1874, they devastated John German's troupe, killing five of the family and taking German's four surviving daughters captive.

Among Medicine Water's men were some of Amos Chapman's future in-laws. His wife, Mary Long Neck Chapman, was three years old when Colonel John Chivington's mob of "100-daysers" and First Colorado Cavalry slaughtered the Cheyenne at Sand Creek. Long Neck's father, Sleeping Bear, was head chief of the Ivists'tsi-nih'pah, the Aorta band, who were camped downstream at the eastern extremity of that village. Sleeping Bear passed on nine days before the massacre, so when Chivington attacked on November 29, 1864, Sand Hill was the Aorta band's chief. Mary Long Neck Chapman's grandfather, Chief Black Kettle, survived the Sand Creek Massacre, as did Chief Sand Hill. Ten years later, Sand Hill's son, Yellow Horse, and Sleeping Bear's son, Lame Man, rode with Medicine Water. Lame Man was Mary Long Neck Chapman's brother, and at the close of the Red River War he was with Gray Beard's people when they surrendered at Darlington Agency on March 6, 1875. A month later Lame Man, Medicine Water, Gray Beard, Many Magpies and Eagle Head were among the 33 Cheyenne, 27 Kiowa, 9 Comanche, 2 Arapaho, and 1 Caddo who were arrested, shackled and exiled to Fort Marion, Florida, for their roles in the Red River War. On the list of prisoners Lame Man is entered as Cohoe, derived from 'cojo,' the Spanish for lame. Under that name, Amos Chapman's brother-in-law conceived a parade out of longing. Angular men with heads crowned in jagged warbonnets sat astride elongated mounts that galloped and floated across the prairie and sky and heart and mind like colossal seahorses jerking on the current of remembrance in the grand pursuit of staccato buffalo, antelope and elk in a stampede of primary colors that lifted Cohoe from the dungeon and the ocean when he released them in his ledgerbook and they carried him back home. He sent his heart back over the years and painted for the reasons that he fought, so his people would not forget. I am reminded of what my friend always tells me: "To follow this way of life is a hard way to live." And it is.

When Cohoe was released and he returned to the plains he never painted in a white man's book again. A scout, a buffalo hunter and four bluecoats being drained of life in a buffalo wallow would have been a worthy subject to record, I thought, had any of the Cheyenne warrior-artists been here. Loneliness and I crouched together, me on my haunches and loneliness wherever lonely pleased. I stared over at the buffalo wallow now resting beneath the concrete and a gust of dun-colored finches blew by and teetered wing-to-wing on a blackened line of straggly barbed wire that hee-hawed with the breeze and beneath the birds in the way of certain old men in these parts who have watched everything that has passed before them but see only what remains. The displaced trees withered and bowed just a little more and the birds burst from the fence into rumpled shadows that were melting onto the plains and then the birds were gone in the sweep of the sky and country that any-which-way you look when you're on your knees in the buffalo wallow rolls away to the edge of the world. Between here and there the Kiowas fanned over the plain when Amos, Billy Dixon and the four troopers were down on their knees. "This is our country. We have always lived in it. We always had plenty to eat because the land was full of buffalo. We were happy. Then you came," the redoubtable Kiowa chief Set-t'ainte once explained. "You want to work the land. That is not all right. Land doesn't want to be worked. Land gives you what you need if you are smart enough to take it. This is good land but it is our land. . . . We have to save our country," he said. Whether they knew him as Set-t'ainte, Satanta, or White Bear, he was not a stranger to the land or the men in the buffalo wallow. As a child I was fascinated with his photograph, this robust man with a face made up of questions whose startled eyes follow me still, when as at the buffalo wallow his picture visits my mind.

Set-t'ainte was not alone in what he saw. Horned owls with throbbing hearts and eagles ascending out of redbirds and bison in the shape of the sun were with him, and these priests of the plains looked down on the accursed in the wallow from rawhide discs carved out of buffalo humps and setting suns and dreams reborn. Men from the Kiowa Owl Doctor Society and Buffalo Doctor Society, the seers and the healers, nurtured the blessed on their shields with the Kiowa's ten bravest warriors, the Koiet-senko, of which Set-t'ainte was one. It was not Set-t'ainte, Ado-eete (Big Tree), Guipahgo (Lone Wolf) or Mammedaty, Guipahgo's grandson, who chose if and when the men in the buffalo wallow would surrender life, it was the screech owl who came to Maman-ti, for Maman-ti had been to the dead men's village and he knew the things of which men wondered and feared. Private Smith was hunched over and wheezing and saying goodbye in damp bloody whispers. The raw meat that was Amos Chapman's leg was swelling around the bare white stick of splintered bone. All but Private Rath were wounded and the flies crooned and the magpies and turkey vultures would squabble soon. They couldn't shoot without bullets and all they had left was God. "It's a hazardous undertaking," Colonel Miles had cautioned Chapman and Dixon before they left McClellan Creek with a dispatch to be delivered at Camp Supply that warned of attack and his need for aid, the men under his command having been reduced to opening their own veins to moisten desiccated mouths with their own blood.

Miles' unrelenting advance across the Staked Plains on the hunt for Gray Beard's and Eagle Head's Cheyenne had strained to breaking his supply line, and on September 1 he had sent Major Wyllys Lyman with thirty-six empty wagons to intercept a train from Camp Supply. On Commission Creek the trains met, and Lyman restocked and then turned back to McClellan Creek with a detachment of 104 men. On the way they encountered Lieutenant Frank Baldwin and three scouts who had in their custody a Kiowa from Lone Wolf's band. Baldwin left the Kiowa boy, Tehan, with Lyman, believing Miles would benefit from any intelligence he could provide. Tehan was born white, but he had been captured by the Kiowa and adopted by Maman-ti. The owl found Maman-ti's son and on September 9, as Lyman's wagon train crossed the divide between the Canadian and the Washita, Maman-ti saw him and Lyman corralled his wagons on the north bank of the Washita and dug in for a siege. By September 10, Lyman's return was overdue and Chapman and Dixon received their orders and a four-man escort and resolved to ride by night. Before first light on September 12, Amos suggested that if they made it to the Washita they could travel by day. "Let's risk it," Billy Dixon agreed. With the sun they met Lone Wolf, Maman-ti, Set-t'ainte and those who followed. Big Bow and Tohauson had not cared to relinquish the hold that they and the Comanches had on Lyman's wagons and so they stayed. Tehan had escaped from Lyman on September 10, and the day after Maman-ti urged the Kiowa to heed the owl and find safety in Palo Duro Canyon. Each act in the world has before it another from which there is no going back and no alternative. Here was yet another, without choice, that was given, and in such a way that dawn and the world may be formed.

I waited by the buffalo wallow, for what I did not know, or even if it came. There was a certain order to life on Llano Estacado, I thought, although not a regimented order of rigid routine, more a ritual order draped in mystery over which

Set-t'ainte (Satanta) – White Bear

Mary Long Neck Chapman holding Benjamin Chapman

Amos Chapman

presided the sun. There are days that we all carry of which the memory escapes us, but if we could remember one thing it would be a reverence for the sun. The sun's child was raised amongst the Kiowa and the wilful boy, Tah'-lee, was also the bringer of gifts, of teachings, of miracles. As was his way and that of curiosity, one day the 'half-boy' disobeyed his grandmother and the consequence was that one became two, and the sun's child was no longer the 'half-boy' but 'half-boys,' the mortal and immortal halves of Tah'-lee. On Llano Estacado, the Staked Plains, the half-boys are sacrifice and sacred. Here on September 12, 1874, were six enemies discovered by the sun, men who killed the buffalo, a symbol of life, as was the sun. And what kind of men would kill the sun? To the watchers Set-t'ainte could have been made of dusk and dawn, the sun-man's breast and face and hair painted with vermillion, his flesh and bone a red orb settled on daylight's tapered sky. To the Kiowa it seems that this was not just war, it was part of the eternal procession of life and death, and such sacrifice invested their land with the sacred. Tah'-lee gave of himself and the pieces of his body became the ten sacred bundles of the Kiowa. Without sacrifice where was the sacred, and without sacred where was belief? This was the ritual and order, and the fight at the buffalo wallow was no more about killing than singing is about making noise. The song placed upon the silence breathes, and these six men, who to some would have been no more than crippled birds in a nest of sorts, would have been remembered in song, in deed, in story, and their lives and their passing would have been celebrated, and their power harnessed and not forgotten in the transition from broken to vivid of life, their revival to be painted upon buffalo robes and the men and the story of them kept alive in imagination. Such is immortality and the oral tradition.

Those who have written of the Buffalo Wallow Fight record that "the Indians made sport of the affair," and describe daring feats of horsemanship as preceding each assault on the men in the wallow. The Kiowa were supposed to have taken severe casualties, but George Bent, the Cheyenne son of the legendary trader William, stated, "Amos Chapman told me that they did not kill any Indians." Whether they did or did not, it is clear that the Kiowa could have ended the fight at any moment with the passing of noon, if that had been their purpose. As brave as they were, and as skilled a marksman as Billy Dixon was, six incapacitated men without water or any expendable rounds could not have resisted a party nearly a hundred strong if that time had come. Standing at the buffalo wallow I was not reminded of sport, but of ceremony. When the Kiowa held their Sun Dance, a buffalo bull had to be sacrificed in a prescribed way and then its hide was draped over the sacred tree and its head impaled at the zenith of the branches and belief, watching for the sun to rise over the ceremony and the pledgers as it gazed upon the east. Before the Sun Dance began, there were six days of preparation, and on the third day warriors adorned in their finery rode their best mounts in a choreographed battle against a cluster of foot soldiers. To the winners was given the honor of the sacred tree, but for the warriors to prevail they must dislodge the foot soldiers who had fortified themselves behind clumps of brush around the tree. When the mounted warriors were victorious in this holy duty, the sacred tree was then cut down and around it the dance and prayers were made and the world renewed. This was the tree of Tai-me, and Tai-me brought the Sun Dance to the Kiowa and in form became the embodiment of the divine. Set-t'ainte had carried one of the sacred shields that were hung before Tai-me, the sun and its corona and that of the moon fringed by red cloth and feathers into which gazed a crane during the ceremony, and during peace and war. The Sun Dance the Kiowa held that year on the North Fork of the Red River was the last Set-t'ainte and Maman-ti experienced. Or may be it wasn't. Maybe here was the end or the beginning of letting go. Do I know this to be true, I thought, still waiting. Whose truth? I asked myself. This is faith. *They will appear, may you behold them! A thunder-being nation will appear. They will appear, behold!* The Kiowa song ends. When the wind rushed in with the storm that day the Kiowa left the men in the buffalo wallow, the ochre smeared warlords and aristocrats and priests and poor sketched in lightning licking at the plain as they withdrew into the night and history to search again.

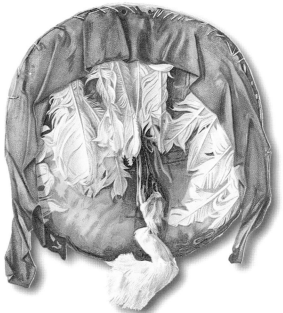

"Set-t'ainte had carried one of the sacred shields that were hung before Tai-me, the sun and its corona and that of the moon fringed by red cloth and feathers into which gazed a crane during the ceremony, and during peace and war."

The rain soaked the buffalo wallow and the men guzzled from the acrid puddles until there was one shallow pool that they lapped from, the sludge rank with their own phlegm and sweat and curdled by their blood and the corpse of their comrade. Half-crazed with dehydration, pain, hunger, relief and fear that the Kiowa or their brethren may be somewhere concealed, they scooped up tumbleweeds that flailed in the 'norther' battering the plains and they bedded down on the spiny squabs like watchful strays without trust of the night or its callers. Rath was the first to set out for help, but he couldn't find the trail and so Billy Dixon had to leave the wounded to whatever mercy there was. Within half a mile Dixon found the Camp Supply trail and soon came across a detachment from Lyman's train under Major Price, but other than scratching around for some dried beef and hardtack Price offered the men little comfort save his promise to report their condition to Colonel Miles. They sat alone in the wallow on Llano Estacado through the remains of that day, then another, and into a second night before the faint strains of a distant bugle brought a certain salvation. "It made us swallow a big lump in our throats and bite our lips," recounted Dixon. They used their knives to scrape a grave in the buffalo wallow for Private Smith, and when the relief column arrived Amos's leg was reported to have swelled "as big as a beer keg." Regardless, he rode a hundred miles or more to Camp Supply with the useless limb dangling from the saddle like some crude appendage that had no function, or none that could be explained. The surgeon amputated Amos's left leg below the knee and within a week he was wanting to get back in the field.

"Satanta the Kiowa chief came into Darlington some time after this fight and told us about it," remembered George Bent. As a thirteen-year-old boy Set-t'ainte watched the Kiowa's world change. On a November night in 1833 the stars fell and kept falling. In the streams of white light were seen the ghosts of the living and the forms of the dismayed witnesses flashed from dark to light in that false dawn on the Red River. Surely nothing could ever be the same, and it wasn't. "I have heard that you intend to set apart a reservation near the mountains. I don't want to settle. I love to roam over the prairie. There I feel free and happy, but when we settle down we get pale and die," Set-t'ainte told the treaty commissioners thirty-four years later. The Kiowa were pale in the light of the falling of stars. Set-t'ainte became one of those stars when he fell to earth. Days of freedom were few after the Buffalo Wallow Fight, and Set-t'ainte and Ado-eete were rearrested and charged with violating parole after previously being incarcerated for the 1871 Henry Warren wagon-train affair. On October 11, 1878, at the Texas State Penitentiary in Huntsville, the prison superintendent said Set-t'ainte committed suicide when he threw himself from a second floor landing. *No matter where my enemies destroy me, do not mourn for me, because this is the end all great warriors face,* was Set-t'ainte's Koiet-senko death song. The jailers didn't understand that he had seen the stars fall. Maman-ti died in Fort Marion, and Guipahgo passed on near Fort Sill, soon after he was returned from Florida. Amos Chapman returned to duty. "He was soon back in the government employ, as useful and as ready for a fight as any two-legged scout," reported Colonel Richard I. Dodge, who described Amos as "a remarkable man." The six men from the buffalo wallow were each awarded the Congressional Medal of Honor for, according to Colonel Miles, "indomitable courage, skill and true heroism," but in accordance with a 1913 regulation, Amos and Billy Dixon were officially removed from the Medal-of-Honor list in 1916 as they were not military personnel. After seventy-three years their names were restored to that list.

In December 1877 Amos reported that the exiled Northern Cheyenne were in a starving state, "so hungry that they readily ate dead horseflesh." Throughout 1878 he protested the conditions the Northern Cheyenne were being kept in and warned that Little Wolf and Morning Star would not stand by while their people wasted away. On September 9, 1878, the authorities listened when Little Wolf and Dull Knife left confinement in Indian Territory and began their journey home. Amos followed them, as a scout for the Fourth Cavalry. For the next twelve years, both in the employ of the military and as a deputy U.S. marshal, Amos Chapman waged what some believed was a personal campaign against cattlemen who trespassed on Indian lands, once turning back 2,200 steers that were being illegally shipped into the Cherokee Strip; he then created outrage in Kansas when, as reported in the *Barber County Index*, "Chapman shot and killed two cowboys in a quarrel over trespassing cattle." Amos Chapman himself became something of a rancher when he retired from government service, worked a spread near Seiling, Oklahoma, and raised a family with Mary Long Neck Chapman, a family that walked in both the white and the Cheyenne world. Amos died the week my father was born in July 1925. He too keeps the secrets of war and its memories, and when the conflict was over he also enforced the law. I look at the Buffalo Wallow Fight monument again, and then look at myself. If you stay here long enough you become part of the landscape, I thought. I was covered in dirt and from the road I could have been lost and not seen, a faded apparition in dust to dirt to earth now redeemable. Colonel Miles said Amos was "one of the bravest of the brave men I have ever known." Others said he never had a biographer but they were wrong, you can find Amos in any of Johnny Cash's songs and as I walk away from the buffalo wallow I sing one, and then offer him and the Kiowa and Llano Estacado a Cheyenne honor song.

Buffalo Bill Cody in Paris. Rocky Bear is at Cody's right, and Red Shirt to his left.

"William F. Cody and Amos Chapman were the best-known bordermen of later days," wrote Randall Parrish in *The Great Plains*. William F. Cody and Amos Chapman were products of the age, but after that they go their separate ways. Amos was defined by the land, by the people, and by blood. Whoever Buffalo Bill Cody was, he too undoubtedly knew the West, it was just that the parts he did not care for he subsequently reinvented, so in a sense the man became a fragment of the greater myth and to the enigma of Buffalo Bill was sacrificed the identity of William F. Cody. There is a photograph of Cody in Paris, where in stance and air he has the appearance of an eccentric archaeologist holding court beneath the canopy of his field headquarters at the conclusion of a successful expedition. On display are his specimens, relics from the American West, but these Lakota chiefs are very much alive and Rocky Bear and Red Shirt look appropriately circumspect. William F. Cody understood that the American West was too big for onlookers, the curious, and spectators, and so he crammed it into an arena, after which it fit the movie screen and conscience more easily. Some of the first Westerns were made in France, the men in white and black hats settling scores on swathes of moor and marsh and steppe in the Camargue. The Marquis Folco de Baroncelli de Javon convinced Joe Hamman to shoot in the Camargue, as to Folco de Baroncelli the Camargue was the Wild West, complete with wild Indians, wild horses and lumbering bison. In spirit it was close, and maybe that is what matters most. Folco de Baroncelli wanted to know how close it really was; the horses were wild, but the bison were actually bulls, though the question that intrigued him the most was whether his Indians, the Gypsies, were really Indians at all. For his answer he turned to William F. Cody, and on October 27, 1905, when Buffalo Bill's Wild West Show returned to Marseille, Folco de Baroncelli hosted a reception for his hero and appealed for his expertise. After the show went dark for winter on November 10, Cody and his entourage left the city and obliged de Baroncelli by visiting the Gypsies of the Camargue. The Lakota gave Folco de Baroncelli the name Zintkála Wasté, Good Bird, which he interpreted as Faithful Swallow, for in addition to the respect he showed them, the Lakota appreciated the horses of the Gypsies, and in them they recognized a culture that knew the power of the Horse Nation.

The terms *Gypsy* and *Indian* are alien to the people they describe; they are names from the Columbus brain. *Gypsy* is a corruption of *Egyptian*, but the people described were no more from Egypt than the Lakota were from India. Many of the *Gypsies* Buffalo Bill Cody met were Kalderas, the tribe of my mother's ancestors, and one of the six major Romany speaking 'Gypsy' tribes. Whether the ethnographic conclusions were drawn by the hardened frontiersman William F. Cody or the showman Buffalo Bill, the Marquis Folco de Baroncelli welcomed them. Cody declared that there were "striking resemblances in color, type, customs and vocabulary" between the Gypsies and the Indians, particularly the Kalderas and the Plains Indians, and it would appear that the similarities in equestrian skills and care convinced him that the two peoples were directly related, supporting de Baroncelli's "hypothesis of a dark skinned race of nomads who followed the setting sun." A tangible relationship may be found in what is present, what is evident, and what does not have to be supposed: that both are present in an indigenous reality of diverse tribal cultures that dress in memory and are defined by story. The journey is taken through language and why would a storyteller tell a stranger without any accounting for what the stranger might do with that telling? The Romany language is rooted in the east with a resonance as ancient as the birth of man. To hear that language spoken is to pass through time and constellations, it is a river of human experience that has cut through wall upon wall of civilizations and in each layer of the canyon the river has carved is exposed a different age, a different cruelty, a different beauty, each an inflection on those primeval tongues spoken by tribes and heard by deities. The deities chipped and painted and suspended in stone watch as impassive guides to the extraordinary passage of ordinary existence from the farthest points east and west. What was seen was told and what was told was remembered.

My grandfather spoke Romany fluently, whereas I can count the words I know on one hand. One of those is *gadzo*, which is more a concept than a noun, as *vé'ho'e* is in Cheyenne; *gadzo* means "not one of us," and *vé'ho'e* is Cheyenne for "spider" or "white man." Satank, a Kiowa chief and the most esteemed Koiet-senko warrior, gave a succinct summation of the tribal experience when speaking for his people at the Medicine Lodge Treaty Council in 1867: "In the far-distant past there was no suspicion among us. The world seemed large enough for both," he told the white men. What Cody may actually have recognized in the Gypsies was the way they regarded the world, for when the world became smaller, reticence and silence became allies and the suspicion of strangers kept tribal people alive. A good deal of what can be seen in the world has passed the way of the Gypsies and Indians, or they have passed through it, and as they went along they traded bits of themselves for bits of others, and they bent so they would not break – and so the bits of others could be made theirs – and they would not become the others. That road is long and so we keep traveling. Whenever I look at that photograph of Buffalo Bill flanked by Rocky Bear and Red Shirt in Paris I see a friend who is a descendant of Chief Red Shirt, and the thought that some of his grandfathers and mine met seven generations before he and I reminds me of the journey, of mortality, of going on. I first heard my daughter's heartbeat in the town that Buffalo Bill Cody made.

The past is always present in the future because we carry the memories of our ancestors within us. We are their journey, just as they are ours. This book is about journeys. This was a part of mine. It is not just history. I am alive.

There is nothing easy about leaving, I thought. And then we come back.

AUTHOR'S NOTE: *The terms 'emigrant' and 'immigrant' appear throughout* PROMISE. *Immigrant is used when a piece is presented from an indigenous perspective, and emigrant when the presentation is from a pioneer or Euro-American frame of reference.*

SERLE L. CHAPMAN

FOREWORD

Promise: Bozeman's Trail to Destiny is an all-inclusive book that recounts the history and consequences of the Bozeman Trail from three perspectives: through the eyes of the emigrant, the soldier, and the Native American. The motivating factor behind the establishment of the Bozeman Trail was gold. In 1862, gold was discovered on Alder Gulch in Montana territory, and in the proceeding years scores of miners flocked to that area via the existing circuitous routes. Soon there was a clamor for a more direct route, and both Jim Bridger and John Bozeman seized the moment and opportunity to charter new trails to those goldfields around Virginia City. Bridger knew that the Native Americans were determined to protect their sacred lands east of the Bighorn Mountains from white encroachment, and so he led his party up the west side of the mountains. Bozeman made no such allowances and took his wagons east of the Bighorns, straight through the hunting grounds of the Sioux, Cheyenne and Arapaho. Bozeman's was by far the easiest route to travel, but the reality of the journey is told in the following pages.

In the spring of 1866, Colonel Henry B. Carrington was ordered to lead the Second Battalion, Eighteenth U.S. Infantry, up the Bozeman Trail to build three forts and garrison the area. Lieutenant George Templeton was one of only two officers who served on the Bozeman Trail for the entirety of that military operation, and through extracts of his diary, Templeton brings an officer's perspective to this book. Templeton describes the trail to his new post in Montana territory, Fort C.F. Smith, and the circumstances that culminated in the Fetterman disaster.

The book's emigrant perspective is provided by noted historical author Serle Chapman, in the form of a letter from a woman who is traveling on the Bozeman Trail in 1866. The letter describes the landscape, the wildlife, the hardships encountered on the trail and her wagon train's brush with the Lakota and Cheyenne. Serle utilized actual emigrant diaries from the Bozeman and the Oregon Trails in his research, and the piece features an introduction by respected Bozeman Trail scholar Dr. Susan Badger Doyle.

The Native American perspective is another meticulously researched, well-written feature by Serle Chapman, which follows the life of a young Cheyenne warrior from Sand Creek to the Fetterman Fight. The description of the Fetterman Fight is a virtual blow-by-blow Cheyenne account of the battle, detailing which Cheyennes and Lakotas did what, where and when – ten years' research that documents numerous pieces of information that have rarely been shared outside the Cheyenne community.

The final section of the book contains in-depth interviews with many noteworthy and knowledgeable people, including a truly amazing group of Native Americans – the descendants of Red Cloud, Sitting Bull, Holy Bull, Little Wolf, Sharp Nose, Red Shirt, Tall Bull and Medicine Crow – many of whom share information that has never been published before. These people are tribal historians, and the keepers of stories and songs.

There has never been a book like this on the Bozeman Trail. *Promise: Bozeman's Trail to Destiny* gives all sides a voice, and I am sure that you will enjoy it.

by Rick Ingoldsby

PRESIDENT • FORT PHIL KEARNY/
BOZEMAN TRAIL ASSOCIATION

1908 reunion at Fort Phil Kearny and Fetterman Battlefield monument dedication. Left to right: Lieutenant Wheeler with Fort Phil Kearny veterans William Murphy, William Daley, Colonel Henry B. Carrington, Sam Gibson, Frances Grummond Carrington, J. Strawn, S.S. Peters, and Jack Owen.

by George Magpie

WOLF CHIEF • BOWSTRINGS SOCIETY
CHEYENNE NATION

Our people touch the earth and they make the magic. I'm proud of our people. I'm proud of the way many still try hard to respect Cheyenne culture and to do good things. To somebody from outside of our culture, that statement might not sound like anything out of the ordinary, but when you stop to consider what happened to the Cheyenne people from the 1800s to the present, it is actually quite extraordinary that we have any of our culture left. One of our great problems is what we have lost culturally, or rather, what was taken from us.

The Cheyenne military societies dwindled to virtually nothing. Thirty years ago there were just a few descendants left, those of us who wanted to keep the societies alive. I was in the Crazy Dogs then, and we decided to try and bring that society back, and so we worked to lift the Crazy Dogs to a level that the society had formerly held. Because so much had been lost, it took a lot of time, effort and debate; it was common for somebody to say that something was supposed to be done a certain way, and then have somebody else disagree. That was a consequence of what was lost – who was right? It was hard to know, but we succeeded. The Crazy Dogs, the Kit Foxes, the Elk Horn Scrapers, and the Bowstrings military societies didn't just come back together, they grew back, and culturally what we have today grew from what we had left.

I'm not some big medicine man, I'm just a man who has learned some things. One of the things I know is Cheyenne history, and so I can say that Serle Chapman knows a lot of Cheyenne history. I want our people to know our history, to know what really happened on the Bozeman Trail, and to appreciate what the consequences of it were, and I think *Promise: Bozeman's Trail to Destiny* communicates that as well as any book ever could. Just from the Cheyenne perspective, it's very complicated, and Serle touched it. When Serle wrote the Hundred-Soldiers-Killed-Fight piece about the Fetterman battle, he wrote it with an Indian's thoughts and from an Indian point of view, and I like the way he did it. From what I understand of that period of our history, he has really grasped it and presented it accurately. There are aspects that are different from what is already out there, and some issues that will challenge people. Serle had to scrap for all of the pieces of the story from a lot of people, and many sources, and if I had been writing and researching it, I wouldn't have done it much differently.

Our old storytellers from the Fetterman and Custer eras weren't trying to make a book, and so the manner in which the stories were told and preserved reflected that. Back then, the people didn't want to talk about the battles they fought against the bluecoats because they feared retribution; they were scared to tell the story of the Little Bighorn battle for years. When people started to say something, those stories were only told in the dark. The circumstances our people found themselves in forced a lot of that knowledge underground and, like so many other things, some of it became lost.

In bringing back the Cheyenne military societies we were contributing, and continue to contribute, to the preservation of our culture. I know Serle is doing his best to do the same with this book.

Washita Battlefield Commemoration, 1930. Left to right: John Otterby (interpreter), Chief Magpie, Little Beaver, and Left Hand. *xvii*

INTRODUCTION

The beloved older ones teach that in the beginning Ma'heo'o, the Creator, the "Great One," planted Tsetsehese-stahase, "The People," in this sacred red Earth to walk the Road of Life. Then one day, a great holy man came to them and taught them their strong spiritual ways. He predicted a time when the humble, ordinary red Earth children could share the land with their relatives who would come from the east, and eventually with their yellow and black relations. He instructed them to call those from the east Ve'hó'e, "Spider" white people, and it saddened Him to describe the difficulties they would encounter on the road that lay ahead of them.

Just as He said, the "Spider" white people came to this country, bringing their own laws and ways of life. In this coming together, many of the Ve'ho'e cultural practices conflicted with those of the natural, ordinary people of this land. The greatest source of conflict was over land, and the Vé'ho'e justified his land hunger under the "Doctrine of Manifest Destiny."

The newly established United States government took the land by treaty, by setting aside reservations, and then through allotment. Subsequently, other means were devised to appropriate land. In the early 1860s, the citizens of Colorado Territory called for extinguishing Cheyenne and Arapaho title to territorial lands.

Governor Evans of Colorado sent out a circular calling in the "friendlies" to the nearest military fort. Black Kettle, the most peaceable of all Cheyenne peace chiefs, took his band into Fort Lyon, and was told to set up camp along Sand Creek. Believing they were at peace, Black Kettle's people settled into a relaxed atmosphere. Left Hand with ten lodges of Arapahos eventually joined them in the encampment situated in the big bend of Sand Creek. They never anticipated a military attack.

Methodist minister become military officer, John Milton Chivington, led his troops in an unprovoked dawn attack upon the peaceful, sleeping camp on November 29, 1864. Despite the fact that Black Kettle tied an American flag with a small white flag of peace on a lodgepole visible to the troops, the firing continued. The majority of those killed were women and children, reflecting Chivington's sentiment that "nits make lice." The butchery and mutilation committed by the troops was barbaric. Fetuses were severed from the wombs of their mothers, small children were used for target practice, others had their heads bashed against boulders, and men and women's genitals were cut and used as hat bands, tobacco pouches, and saddle horn covers. Chivington and his men paraded into Denver displaying over one hundred scalps.

Black Kettle wanted peace with the Ve'ho'e, and he obviously did not understand their insatiable greed for the land. At the time, the "Spider" white people wanted Colorado Territory, but when gold was discovered in Montana, they had to have a passage to those goldfields. This road cut across the prime hunting territory of the northern group of Cheyennes and their allies, the Oglala Lakota. It crossed Powder River country, a shortcut to the gold, the yellow metal that Ma'heo'o put in many places on earth. That road became known as the Bozeman Trail.

by Dr. Henrietta Mann

Until her retirement Dr. Mann (Southern Cheyenne) served as the Endowed Chair in Native American Studies at Montana State University. Rolling Stone magazine heralded Dr. Mann as one of the ten foremost professors in the United States, and the National Women's History Project named her among the elite "five 20th Century women educators." Dr. Mann was the highest ranking American Indian woman in the administration of U.S. President Ronald Reagan.

Southern Cheyenne and Arapaho chiefs and headsmen following the Camp Weld council, September 28, 1864. Standing, left to right: Bosse, Notane, Heap-of-Buffalo. Seated, left to right: Neva, Black Kettle, Bull Bear, White Antelope.

Emigrant

A Letter Home

by Serle L. Chapman

The following is Serle Chapman's imagined account of a woman's journey over the Bozeman Trail in August 1866, written in the form of a letter to her sister. She is traveling from Atlanta, and her bitter memories of the recent destruction of Atlanta run throughout her narrative. That awful event reverberates in Bozeman Trail history as Captain William J. Fetterman's last Civil War action was the Battle of Jonesboro, which resulted in the fall of Atlanta. Her letter begins at Fort Laramie and continues along the trail, weaving an eloquent narrative. Although this unnamed woman's account is fictional, it is based on actual people, events and realities of the trail experience during the momentous summer of 1866.

DR. SUSAN BADGER DOYLE

Fort Laramie, Dacota Territory, August 1866.

My Dear Sister,

Here I stand on the threshold of bounty or decay, my fate entrusted to the Almighty, for we are upon the eve of our departure from this, Fort Laramie. It is not what one might expect, in appearance being more town than fort. The settlements we have passed thus far, the tiny drops of hope and optimism engulfed by the plains, lack any notion of permanence, and in standing, do not exceed those the frontiersfolk refer to as rag towns.[1] There are no cobbles to line the streets or buildings constructed of granite to welcome, but rows of false fronted stores made of rough hewn timber or adobe with a patchwork of boards upon which to walk. Be that as it may, there is a security here I am loathed to leave, be it truth or the pretense of civilization, one or the other resides. I have to confess, dear sister, I shed a tear yesterday for there is one grand building here, tall and white with a fine balcony and cultured porch,[2] which enkindled a memory of home. How different it may have been had we not been dealt such a cruel blow as to stand helpless as the flames of war devoured our home and that which had become so familiar. Oh, to be in Atlanta as it was before.[3] Benjamin says little of his return. I have not asked him, nor has he volunteered to tell, for he says nothing of the war until he sleeps, and then I hear it all. When asked, we tell how our past was lost to the flames, but only dead men keep secrets and Benjamin, thank the Lord, is still alive, though sister, not the man you might recognize. Praise be, it was a miracle that we were reunited.

It is hard for us here, surrounded as we are by Yankees, each one of them a reminder that it would be best if we were to take our leave. A soldier came forth from the fort as we were setting up camp and in manner did decree that our journey would end were we not to follow his order, that being the appointment of a captain for our train. Benjamin did not take his intrusion kindly, but he was not alone and so no harm was done. We have the twenty wagons required, and passed two boys off to swell our complement to thirty-four armed men.[4] A Mr. Jacob Tisdale, a man the others are convinced is familiar with this territory, and of whom it is said has a wife waiting in Fort Hall,[5] was elected captain. Benjamin and I then accompanied a Mr. O'Hanrahan to the fort as it was necessary to file a paper with the provost marshal, stating that all agreed, and that we were in compliance.

I wished to see the fort, blue bellies[6] or no, and Benjamin wanted to take stock of would-be provisions, but the ride was farther than I expected. Benjamin joshed that here he was on this vast frontier with only two Celts for company, but Mr. O'Hanrahan either did not appreciate or understand the joke. I asked him about Ireland but he said that he had never seen Ireland, only his father who was Irish, and whom he described in an unbecoming manner. I do however believe that Mr. O'Hanrahan is a man of his word – either that or he possesses an Irish brogue hitherto unheard. He quickly apologized for his indecorum, and Benjamin, much to my relief, did not react and said he was not to worry, for the Scots do not possess such a delicate disposition, particularly one such as I who is so well versed with our bard.[7] Mr. O'Hanrahan just nodded and then shared his stories of Bannack,[8] saying how he missed the throng and so knew not what to do but to return to that country and try his hand in Virginia City. He talked of this road we are to take to Montana, Mr. Bozeman's trail, and what peril we might face.

Mr. O'Hanrahan asked Benjamin if he had heard the old booshway[9] talk about Indians, this being a mullato who visited our camp the night before last. Benjamin said he would pay no heed to a negro, particularly a negro dressed half-way Indian. Mr. O'Hanrahan said the mullato was acquainted with Mr. Bridger and had family among the Crow Indians, and therefore it was prudent to hear him out, but Benjamin said he paid that little mind as he had heard that Mr. Bridger was just another squaw man[10] of tales even taller than his stature. The manner in which Mr. O'Hanrahan spat and then laughed caused me some confusion. He nodded towards the sutler's store and said that was where Bridger held court. It appears that Mr. Bridger positions himself upon a bench outside the sutler's store and weaves fantastic yarns, Mr. O'Hanrahan having once been the beneficiary of such, when Mr. Bridger had pointed to a mountain distant and stated that the peak had been a hole in the ground when he first frequented this country! Mr. O'Hanrahan may well share Mr. Bridger's talent, claiming that a tame antelope makes the fort its home,[11] but where it was upon our arrival he did not know and suggested that the Indians might have "plum got tired of boiling up cats and dogs," and so the poor thing might have met its end in a kettle. You would so enjoy his colorful diction, albeit privately. Benjamin joined in the jocularity, warning Mr. O'Hanrahan that I too had Indian blood, which left the poor man totally bemused and stepping over his tongue to explain that he had never seen a red-haired

Indian. I quelled his unease and told him that our savage strain was many moons ago, fearing any attempt to explain the joke, or the ancestry that we may or may not share with Mr. Ross, would serve only to complicate matters. I fear Benjamin does forget that Mr. Stand Watie, whom he still so admires, was also an Indian.[12]

Upon thither bank sit so many tipis, it being 'Squaw Town,'[13] according to Mr. O'Hanrahan. Here but a few weeks past, a treaty[14] was proposed to the Indians, but Mr. O'Hanrahan heard that all did not go well. The Indians wish for us to travel by an alternative route to that which we have resolved to follow to Montana, hence the army has departed to secure future safe passage.[15] They are belligerent and bold, says Mr. O'Hanrahan of the Sioux and Cheyenne who prowl the road, but in appearance the Indians here are far from that. They are bedraggled to the threshold of wretched, with little suggestion of the brooding ferocity we saw in the countenance of the Pawnee. They are Sioux and, dear sister, the sight would cause you disquiet. There stood a girl, neigh, a waif, with a bairn drawing life at her breast, a child once innocent cradling one that is. The bairn is fair of complexion, so I wonder if the soldiers here know the way to this river a little too well. Aye, that was many moons ago, the bairn might say, as I, in years to come. The pock marks dappled on their skin may yet be the lesser of their scars. These are not the Sioux of Red Cloud,

Red-tailed Hawk

Mule Deer

Rattlesnake

Yucca

the name so oft-repeated it would have one believe he was the only chief our companions did know, Red Cloud being the chief who led his tribesmen from the council here.

Cholera it seems is Mr. O'Hanrahan's great fear. He said that in years gone by, the road from Independence to Fort Laramie was a graveyard, and it concerns him that he might carry it with him from here or somewhere near.[16] We observed burial scaffolds of Indians aplenty in that country, but those who took this course before us choose to conceal the graves of their loved ones as best they could, said Mr. O'Hanrahan, save the wolves or Indians got them, for he believes it is the Indians' habit of taking clothes from the dead that spreads disease amongst them.[17] He said one poor man who lost his wife retraced his steps for some two hundred miles to secure for her a fitting headstone, and then returned to where she lay on foot, pushing the headstone along in a barrow.[18] In the cemetery at the fort there is a burial scaffold adorned with all manner of fixings. Mr. O'Hanrahan said closer inspection would reveal parts of wild animals and ponies' heads nailed to the scaffold, and this for him was testament to the Indians' primitive nature. But a beautiful tale he told, that the scaffold was of the daughter of a chief who had fallen in love with a soldier here, but their love unrequited and the hardships of this country took her last breath.[19] What is love, I wondered, if not our most primitive need?

It is with some chagrin that I must tell you that Benjamin improved our provisions for the journey not one bit. Though a smile it brought to his face, his purchasing a new Henry rifle ill accorded with my feelings, and I could not hold my tongue when he described this gun as the beacon that would lead us to salvation. I asked the Lord to forgive him, for at times he is lost in his own wilderness, a like wilderness to which I regret he may be leading me, for what is it I see in this gathering of strangers? Are we not corralled in this darkness, leaving what we are, to find who we once were, and to escape that which we have become? This pretty grove of trees aglow with our home fires may beckon some with its appeal but lo, wait until dawn, and see the hives mosquitoes leave upon the skin. Of this truth, of these marks of penance, not one of us will be spared. Mr. Tisdale offered reassurance tonight that when we reach the Platte River there are sure to be others who would welcome our company for the journey forth. This news did not please some, but Benjamin said he cared little. It pains me to confess that he is a mystery not only to our new found companions.

I have made the acquaintance of two pleasant ladies, Mrs. Gretchen Frantz and Mrs. Lodisa Porter. Mrs. Frantz is traveling with her son and daughter. Her son is a strapping young man who speaks not two words of English but bears their burden without complaint, if complain he could. Her daughter I fear may prove to be the cause of some consternation. She's bonnie all right, but her resistance to wearing a bonnet to conceal a measure of her flaxen locks, in addition to her fondness for bloomers, has not escaped the attention of many a man in this train nor the soldiers who were a little too insistent that we required their escort. I understand that it is a goodly distance to Montana, and for Mrs. Frantz it may seem further. She misses her kin in Prussia and is lonesome for her husband, a watchsmith by trade, who awaits her in Montana. Mrs. Porter is accompanied by her husband, a man of a somewhat nervous disposition who is in the habit of warbling 'Oh Susanna,' then smiling and bidding one and all good day, be it morning, noon, or night. Mrs. Porter volunteered to tell of her husband's misfortune, his having been a doctor by profession until his regular patients became addicted to laudanum, his cure-all and elixir of choice. We inquire not as to their circumstances as so much of us must go unsaid in the name of regeneration. Mrs. Porter has heard that the Platte River was one thousand miles long and six inches deep. Of that, I said, we would soon see.

Oh, dear sister, what bedlam it seemed we had come upon. Wagons corralled, wagons in line, oxen bellowing, mules braying, raucous men in song and anger, and the aroma of all and sundry wending its way downwind. Mr. Tisdale instructed us to inspect our goods and make ready for the crossing while he himself made provision for us to unite with another train. If one had been of a suspicious nature it would not have been unreasonable to assume that Mr. Tisdale had planned this rendezvous, for the teamsters of the corralled freight wagons welcomed him like the prodigal. If mutineers are amongst our number we shall soon see. Mr. Tisdale may have the gait of an officer, but beneath the spit and polish a scoundrel may reside. Mr. Porter rejoiced that there was no need to worry about snakebites

Powder River Pass

now. Benjamin shook his head until Mr. O'Hanrahan explained that somewhere in those wagons was whiskey enough to cure each and every one of us should we get bitten.[20] For sure they had all manner of goods, but what was earmarked for the forts and what was destined for Alder Gulch I did not care to know.

My, how we were plagued by mosquitoes, so much so that taking Mr. Bridger's ferry across the river was close to blessed relief.[21] It is a river of some beauty but I imagine little sympathy, for from where I looked it was not six inches deep. A beautiful sonnet, the song of a meadowlark, greeted us as we reassembled and rolled away. We were detained a while but that mattered little, and I gave thanks that our outfit was none the worse for wear, our mules being as stubborn as they ever were, our two milk cows plodding along with heavy bows and sighs, and the colts Benjamin bought for this journey prancing when he so wants them to amble along. There is no such thing as routine out here, but Mr. Tisdale has set in motion the semblance to get us through. We are to be ready to move out by five o'clock each morn, then prepare to noon when the sun is at its most unforgiving. Somewhere towards five o'clock in the evening, dependent upon water and feed, the wagons are to be corralled and camp set within that perimeter. While our men take care of the stock, we must prepare to take care of our men.

Whatever else befalls us, I do not think we shall starve on this trail, less we are robbed or imperiled by hell or high water. Our grub box alone, that being the end board of our wagon supported by two barrels, can at any given sitting be laden with a combination of dried apples, peaches (canned, of course), beans, bacon, ham, potatoes, codfish, coffee, sugar and molasses. Mrs. Frantz does churn so we have fresh butter, and Mrs. Porter uses her Dutch oven to fine effect. Both of us are getting a good deal of practice baking bread and suckeyes,[22] although it is rather unpleasant when the dough turns black due to the unwanted ingredient of mosquitoes. We have set smudges every evening since we camped at Fort Laramie, but little seems to deter these pests. Benjamin procured a stash of hardtack, crackers and several sacks of flour before our departure, and he fashioned platforms on each side of our wagon upon which he has secured barrels of water. When he is more like his old self, he takes pleasure in reminding me that it was his bart that got us this rather fine six-griddle cast-iron stove. Between our three families, we muster our chairs and some feed boxes so that those who care to join us can partake. For being out in the wilderness, so far we have made out some very comfortable meals.

Mr. O'Hanrahan is in the habit of joining us for supper, and each evening he is accompanied by an alternate troupe of freighters. I am convinced that our cooking is the attraction for Mr. O'Hanrahan, but I fancy Mrs. Frantz's daughter, Heidi, is the draw for the other boys. Tonight one of their number, a fellow by the name of Fairweather, came calling on Mr. O'Hanrahan but proceeded to regale us all with anecdotes he has collected. Mr. Porter was the audience he desired, the

Cottonwood

poor man becoming paler by the sentence as Fairweather recited how a man from a train such as ours, but destined for California, did resolve to shoot the first Indian he saw, and how that Indian turned out to be a squaw. Fairweather said the squaw was "no trifling loss" to the Indians, and so they confronted the teamsters and demanded that they turn over the man who killed her, which they did, and that the Indians promptly skinned him alive. Mr. O'Hanrahan corroborated the tale and said it occurred a day or two's ride east of our camp.[23] To the relief of us ladies, Mr. Tisdale took coffee with us and commandeered the conversation. He hopes that tomorrow we will make camp on Sage Creek and the following morn take Bozeman's cut-off. We will have to be diligent, he said, for the signs are that Indians may try to molest us or run off our stock. Mr. O'Hanrahan said the Sioux were the worst horse thieves in Christendom, and that when they weren't stealing they were begging, and when they weren't begging they were trying to take your hair. Benjamin asked him, if so approached should we feed the Indians or shoot them?

Mr. Tisdale was somewhat aggravated by Benjamin's inquiry, presuming his tone to be sardonic. He made his displeasure plain by detailing recent incidents in which pilgrims such as ourselves had been killed and grotesquely mutilated by Indians, offering to take Benjamin to a tree near Bozeman's road in which they found a man's scalp dangling.[24] With all the verve of the author of a penny dreadful, Mr. Tisdale said Benjamin should pray that the Cheyennes don't get the opportunity to take me captive as they did a Mrs. Eubanks, a woman he claims he saw after she had been returned to Fort Laramie.[25] There was but one solution, he said, that being the extermination of the wild Indian, although he had doubts as to the army's ability to do so. Most in our company agreed, Mr. O'Hanrahan suggesting that bounties on the scalps of Indians would encourage territorial militias to do what the army couldn't, and bring civilization to the wilderness.[26] Benjamin calmly addressed them both, saying that he did not wish for them to be so concerned, for General Sherman had made Georgia howl as he had promised to do, and that he had little doubt that the Indians would face his reckoning too. As for civilization, Benjamin said, he saw the Bloody Angle, and with that he bade them good night.[27]

For a good few moments I feared that they might stretch Benjamin up to the nearest tree, but as you and I know, dear sister, we fell so utterly to the wrath of that general's hell hounds that whatever demons Red Cloud holds merely cavort about the flames of the unknown. Benjamin was right, and though he may not be the man he was, a man of conviction he is. To calm the troubled waters I asked Mr. Tisdale if I might propose to the families in our number that we attempt to school the children in the good book on the Sabbath, being that many are averse to traveling on the Sabbath. He said he thought it a fine idea if I was prepared to teach and organize the schoolroom, which of course I am. I do so miss teaching the children back home. If a wagon or a grove of trees is to be the schoolroom so be it, for school it will be!

Oh, how harsh is this country since we commenced upon Mr. Bozeman's road. Be it only a few days ago, the sweeping grasslands and river bottoms lined with timber are a distant memory, replaced by the monotony of sagebrush and soap weed.[28] This is a land in which you can see the horizon of tomorrow, where in places along this road there is scarcely a rock or tree. How grateful we ladies are for one another's company and each other's wrappers[29] when relief is needed. Neither that necessity, the curse, or this land have respect for modesty, so we accept with willingness our full-skirts becoming begrimed, as when one extends theirs for the other, they provide a curtain for our dignity. Although feeling rather indisposed, it is as well I joined the others and took advantage of our previous surroundings, for if I had not, a week or more may have passed before I could have attended to our wash. It is quite a sight, all set to suds, lining the river bank with baskets, kettles, washtubs, and piles of linen. Mrs. Porter noted the presence of a black-eyed girl who she thinks is with child, who washed her clothes and wore them as they dried. We presume that she is with the freighters and is likely Indian or Mexican. It is troublesome to record that she may be the object of some unwanted attention, but this I cannot verify as the train is near half a mile long and the freighters we believe she is traveling with are some way toward the rear.

Prickly Pear Cactus

We are being washed and baked with some frequency now. Our skin is dry and burnt, lashed for good measure with sand in this interminable wind. Mr. Porter has taken to sleeping under their wagon, believing that laying in a shallow trench barricaded by sacks of flour will increase his chances of survival should we be stampeded by buffalo or attacked by Indians in the night. Everyday he raises the alarm, insisting that he can hear hoof beats, and we have now resigned ourselves to telling him that it is only the wind. The worst storm to date hit us last night. I slept in the wagon so wasn't inconvenienced too much, but Benjamin was sodden when he finally gave up on our tent and took shelter under this faithful old oilcloth cover. This straw bed is none too uncomfortable, but the swaying of the wagon in the storm reminded me much of our great ocean crossing when we were but seven and nine years old. It is an apt description that the plains are a sea of grass, but nothing came so close as last night, the lightning plummeting to earth in vast unholy sheets, the

Pronghorn

features of wagons and mounds or incipient bluffs rising stark through the glowing canvas of our humble bushel, with the rain and hail pounding what shadows dared to turn and face until they were nothing but withered spines of braggarts. The battering did however offer its rewards, the dawn being flushed with flamboyant strokes of light ablaze, the beginning of the horizon and the end of the sky settling on the plain with the sun rising up out of nothing.

As we nooned I watched a hawk circling, the fan of its tail aglow like that glorious dawn. For all we are consumed by this country, at times there is nothing to see but distance. If this wilderness blooms with roads and ribbons of steel maybe we will see an empire, but presently what awaits this fractured nation are the scattered materials from which empires are made. Fortune beckons those who march towards this horizon, so we inhale the bitter smell of livestock, whether calm or fanned by wind, and rest our hopes on straining wheels and creaking axles one mile, one meal, one day at a time. There are days when it occurs to me that Mr. Frémont[30] did exaggerate a little, as when our wagon wheels begin to shrink and the clatter of spokes and tires is the toll of a bell without chime but warning. The freight teamsters buried a man today. Fairweather shot himself while hunting antelope. Mr. O'Hanrahan said they were gutting the animal when Fairweather reached for his gun and it discharged, he seemingly having forgotten that he had left it cocked, and so he dropped to rise no more.[31] What comfort could be found was in knowing that at least others may bid him a passing thought, as Mr. O'Hanrahan suggested his final resting place should be within sight of this camp on the Stinking Water, from where hymns and scripture rang out into this empty space to carry him home.

Mr. Tisdale nooned with us today. Benjamin and he conducted themselves cordially, even after Mr. Tisdale informed me that after further consideration he did not feel able to commit to my idea of schooling the children on the Sabbath, for he is of the opinion that with the imminent change of season, and the mood of the Indians, we cannot lay idle for an entire day. Mr. Porter began to sob upon hearing the news, leaving us in a quandary as to what to do. It was strange indeed, for within a matter of minutes his composure had returned and he strode off to where their mules were hobbled near the springs, then saddled one, and rode off in a westerly direction, using his whip to some purpose. Mr. Tisdale said he was sure that he would catch up to us, if in fact he didn't go around us. I drove with Mrs. Porter until we made camp at what the men called Dry Fork.[32] Her husband did not return. Mr. O'Hanrahan set out with three men at first light but returned within the hour without any good news. There was no sign of Mr. Porter, but ample signs of Indians. Mr. Porter had seen the elephant, said Mr. O'Hanrahan.[33] I shed a tear for Mrs. Porter, as what else can be done for the heartsick? It was only at the dawn of this very day that I scaled the hithermost bluff on this desolate plain and from that arc of sculpted earth did look into a crowded heaven. We rolled on, the road deteriorating into random patches of dry and wet sand, so I fear our days of making twenty miles or more are at an end.

Such a beautiful animal, I thought, as I watched antelope skittering in distant clouds of their own making, never considering who or what had made then take fright. So entranced was I that had the men in front not in near unison suddenly taken up their arms, I might not have noticed the Indians until they were upon us. If they were of a mind to molest us I could not tell, though it surely would have been a forlorn endeavor being as hopelessly outgunned as they were. Emboldened by whatever fables bewitch their souls, they sat astride their mounts like highwaymen bedecked in masks of nightmares. A lull descended, challenged only by their garb which was alive with contorted human and animal forms, the hair of both and strips of hide and bone and feathers shillyshallying in the breeze. Mr. Tisdale stepped forth and began to mime afore them as if the five were painted minstrels from a stage in Gehenna. One sat his horse in front of the others and began a muddle of gestures and speech. His jaw was set and his expression stern, with streaks of yellow and red smeared on his face from hands that may have pleaded but received no mercy. His hair fell onto his chest, tethered only by a thin plait that hung down his back, and what appeared to be a small stick tied into a forelock. Two feathers daubed with red twitched when the wind caught his hair, and sunlight flickered on the gold epaulets and buttons of a blue army blouse that preserved him from being near naked.[34] Without moving his hands from a musket resting across his lap, he summoned one of the others to come forward. This one was younger. He sidled up to Mrs. Frantz's wagon and stopped. His hair was loose and a xylophone of bones covered his badly scarred breast. The rangy piebald he rode was lathered, the red and yellow symbols scrawled upon it glistened as did the paint sullying his own face.[35] With a hatchet firmly in his clutches, he looked inside Mrs. Frantz's wagon and then nonchalantly trotted back to he whom I presumed to be their leader. Thereafter Mr. Tisdale became agitated and started shaking his head. The Indian in the army blouse motioned repeatedly towards Mrs. Frantz's wagon. Mr. O'Hanrahan walked up the train, quietly instructing the men not to shoot and for all to stay calm, and then he joined the ensemble. He too shook his head, said something in their language, and waved at our wagon. Benjamin walked forward. He spoke no Indian, but said the one in the army blouse kept repeating 'swap' in English. Mr. O'Hanrahan informed him that they wanted to 'swap' for Heidi and were prepared to trade a number of horses, including a big black gelding one of them was riding, which for all the world looked like an army horse. Benjamin came back to the wagon, and with Mrs. Frantz's son unloaded a good stack of the bacon, some coffee, and a box of hardtack. The Indian in the army blouse was unmoved. Nobody stirred. Then he called out and the other four charged forward, snatched the provisions, and all bolted away screeching.[36]

A rumor started that one of the Indians was wearing Mr. Porter's shirt, and an ugly mood fell across many of the men in our train, although the freighters appeared not to share their unrest. As there were only five Indians, many of the men had desired to kill them and were somewhat demanding in wanting to know why they hadn't been given the opportunity to do

Coyote

so. Mr. O'Hanrahan and Mr. Tisdale attempted to explain that these had been some of Red Cloud's Sioux, and that had the men known anything about these Indians, they would have noted from their appearance that they were prepared for war, not trade. Mr. O'Hanrahan said that "those five were in no aching hurry" to attack a train as large as ours, but they were in the business of trying to incite a posse to take up the challenge and chase, for there had quite probably been many others lurking nearby for just such an eventuality. Mr. Tisdale inquired of Benjamin if he had noticed the prior owner's blood on the army blouse and the tresses of human hair they paraded, and if now he would attest to the savage intent of this horde from hell. Benjamin replied that he fought aside a man at Spotsylvania[37] whose attire he found to be curious, so one day he had asked him why he wore a necklace of dried prunes, only to discover that it was a necklace of human ears. Mr. Tisdale retorted that if Benjamin encountered those Indians again that they would as soon take his hair as his bacon, to which Benjamin said that giving them bacon to cross this country they claimed was a more appealing trade than forfeiting his hair. Benjamin advised Mr. Tisdale that if he wanted to know how much more irascible a man gets when he's hungry he should go and ask the Yankees from Andersonville or the Southern boys who were kept in Fort Delaware.[38] Were Mr. Tisdale not hesitant as to the character of some of the men in the train should we be attacked, it is my belief that Benjamin would have no saving grace. He said there exists all manner of men with whom he has cause to quarrel, but as yet these Indians out here are not amongst them. Sister, I have yet to see there be room enough for two roosters in the same hen house, even in the wilderness.

I could not count the eyes feasting upon us from each clump of sagebrush or in the dirt laced with chinks of sand, each sun-polished grain winking as the spokes of the nearmost wheels threw up spume from this ancient sea. This land once flesh is now bone, each coulee a rib, silent and concealed, where a horseman awaits with head bowed but not sleeping, mounted on a pale stallion that leaves no tracks. I saw a grave that seemed neither old nor freshly dug.[39] If it was her husband, Mrs. Porter didn't see him, this man struck mute with agony still gurgling in his mouth, a loner now beholden to the ruts of this road and these dry creek beds. The train halted. Riders were approaching from the north. Mr. Tisdale had posted outriders but no signal came, only the phantom cavaliers shifting in pale light. They galloped on with little rapport between any horse or rider, for the sun was sucking their shadows from their bodies until the brittle-legged horses lurched from the convulsing figures being hung by the courtiers of Venus aside the road and on the plain, their thin bodies clinging desperately to the saddle, material and immaterial now starkly in view. "Indians!" the Yankee commander shouted at Mr. Tisdale, demanding to know where on the horizon the Sioux had evaporated. However brief his reply, it was enough to curtail their pursuit.

The commander of the troupe did, I think, have the rank of lieutenant, and though harried he was not without composure. Mr. Tisdale described to him our encounter with the Sioux, referring to the table-top hills that had loomed at our backs as Pumpkin Buttes, and suggesting that the bluebellies might find the red men there. The officer doubted that they were the Indians he was after, the raiders he sought having just made off with a string of mules and horses from the fort.[40] Still flanked by his detachment, we crossed the Powder River with minor travail, it being a dingy stream that in color is a work of Titian, but in prepossession is akin to a muddy bootlace. Emerging from dense stands of cottonwoods where who knows what might lurk, I never imagined being so pleased to see a barren waste such as that which is overlooked by this fort they call Reno.[41] There is small agreement between the little regiment of flagging buildings, in appearance suggesting both a state of simultaneous disrepair and construction. Why some and not others among the indecorous sheds were given the benefit of a stockade I did not ask, for one bull pit[42] is much like another, and even after a day such as this there exists nothing to recommend a protracted stay. We swelled an already embittered throng, camping within a stone's throw of the fort in the company of a train of freighters bound for Virginia City with several yokes of oxen and

The site of Fort Reno with the Pumpkin Buttes in the background

a cluster of mules. A group in similar employ but itching to get to the new fort on the Bighorn River with their wares transported by mule teams,[43] and a coterie of emigrants demanding to be anywhere but here, completed the disgruntled caravan. None, it seemed, wished to proceed with the other, due to competition on the part of the freighters, and the expectation of a rank slow pace with either on the part of the emigrants.

A melee ensued when the officer who had been in pursuit of the Indians came forth to conduct a census pertinent to our wagon train, our progress thereafter being either helped or hindered by his adjudication. A gentleman I presumed to be the captain of the suspended emigrant train confronted the officer, accusing the men at the post of stealing cattle from teams on his train, and calling both the officer and the post commander petty tyrants and blowhards. The officer threatened him, with what I do not know, leaving the man to hop up and down as he stomped away bellowing, "Here's your mule, Pumpkin Rinds! Here's your mule!"[44] I wondered what influence whiskey was having on idle hands here, or whether he was just addled by the wind and sun, though Mr. Tisdale had sympathy with his fellow captain's predicament. The officer was satisfied with our train and advised Mr. Tisdale to attend the sutler's store, wherein he would note the military regulations governing the movement of civilian wagon trains on the Virginia City road, and thereupon he was to secure in writing permission to proceed to Fort Phil Kearny. Mr. Tisdale informed us to take nothing for granted, albeit that our census was satisfactory. He said the other train captain was fit to be tied because the army, or rather the cousin of the officer who conducted our census, had changed the regulations as to how many armed men constituted a viable train, and from being five over he was now, accordingly, twenty or more under.[45] He said even with some of the freighters choosing to delay at this post, we still met the requirements and that he was going to see if he couldn't alleviate the misery of the other pilgrims by inviting them to join our wagon train. The officer's cousin is apparently post commander at Fort Phil Kearny from where he dictates what happens at all of the forts they are building on Mr. Bozeman's road.

I was not sorry to learn that some of the freighters were taking their leave. We heard them inquiring of the officer as to what had happened to the 'Gray Backs,' and asking if the 'Johnnys' ran off.[46] I didn't care to hear those terms either one, and it did so aggravate Benjamin. Mr. O'Hanrahan told us that they left some Southern boys here for a year with some Indian scouts, and with these scouts he was much impressed, which explained why he cuffed one of the tomcats who continued to insult both our boys and those Indians.[47] I expect they had to break them all until they succumbed to wearing blue. I saw the black-eyed girl for the first and most probably the last time as they took her into one of the buildings. Sister, you and I witnessed the lustful appetites of General Sherman's hell hounds in Atlanta when they took our maids and I regret a similar fate awaits this girl. The sutler appraised Mr. Tisdale and Mr. O'Hanrahan of the Indian trouble that has plagued this vicinity of late and a somber mood descended to dampen the earlier protestations that had less to do with a will to kill Indians than the failings of bravado. It appears that they suffered a bloody July with a train of freighters attacked at a place called Clarks Springs between here and Fort Phil Kearny. At Crazy Woman Creek, where Mr. O'Hanrahan says we will likely have to make our next camp, the Sioux attacked a small train with an army escort; and not more than two or three miles south of Buffalo Springs, a spot we passed today, some emigrants driving stock were attacked.[48] These attacks, the sutler reported, occurred within four days, between July 20 and July 24. Mercifully, the grave we passed near the fort was not that of Mr. Porter, but the victim of the latter incident. Lo, here is the anguish of mortality. Hopes wrecked, love torn asunder. See not the woman sorrowing for she resides within you and me. How everything we were warned of comes to pass. The Sioux raided a train nearby the previous Sabbath and by the following Tuesday two more fell victim a stone's throw from the fort. Oh, for somebody's darling.[49]

The sutler did go into considerable detail, said Mr. O'Hanrahan, as to the mutilations the Indians inflicted upon the officer killed in the fight at Crazy Woman Creek.[50] The Indians took not only his life but his dignity, and I wonder if we did not see his bloodied hand-me-downs earlier today. Guilt will not let me be, but I am ashamed to admit that my compassion deserts me. Should we fall foul of them, we have but anecdote as to what cruelties the Sioux will inflict upon us, whereas I have seen with my own eyes what those who don the Yankee blue will do. What horror was brought to the officer on that creek? What horror was brought to us that terrible November? The flames shadowing Sherman's rabid breed, his bummers let loose to rape, pillage, and set ablaze, with both black and white reduced to our knees. With our men away and us helpless, was it not Sherman's bummers, my dear sister, who threw our beloved onto the front lines or into cattle carts, and let the train take on their righteous cause so that when it reached the Ohio River there was not a one who was not enslaved? They marched to Savannah, they marched to the sea, may they all now march to hell. Their kind it seems are building these forts. Anything to preserve the Union, Mr. Grant.[51]

I wish to stay here not a moment longer than we are all forced to. Alas, Mr. Tisdale says that will be a good two days as the wagons underwent inspection and require maintenance. If nothing else, the Powder River offers a ready source of timber. For the first time in days we have burned wood and not buffalo chips, but why their dung is so plentiful yet the beasts themselves so elusive, I have not fathomed. I have heard it said that north of here they still roam in some numbers, hence the Indians' chagrin, and I hope it is true as I do so wish to see them before both us and them are gone. The water here comes with an awful white scum,[52] and so much dirt boils up from the land that it crosses my mind that I might never take another mouthful that isn't laced with grit or first sampled by flies.

We made the acquaintance of a new traveling companion this morn. Mr. O'Hanrahan cheerfully introduced him as our new chief cook and bottle washer, which evidently found favor with the man and his smile. He doffed a very fine gentleman's tricorn that showed some accord with his frock coat and boots, but little or nothing with what remained of his wardrobe. "The name's Moses Clark, but you folks can call me Squanto," beamed this carpetbagger who had fallen on hard times, or this raggedyman of a rich man's son. When asked where he was headed, he said anywhere that he damned well pleased, and when asked why, he said because he could. The fancy Dan's duds were a gift from a dead man whose team he had driven half-

way to California before the man, a doctor, died near South Pass, Wyoming.[53] Evidently he wasn't much of a doctor. Mr. O'Hanrahan was curious as to why he wished to be called Squanto and he explained that he had much in common with Squanto for, like himself, Squanto had been a man in bondage, but when freed he did resolve to aid the pilgrims, just as he was doing now.[54] Mr. O'Hanrahan was still none the wiser, save that the negro was uppity. Like a carny barker to a gallery he played, professing to all that Indians were now not to be feared as his presence would guarantee our safety, him having ridden into battle for the Union with Chief Opothle Yahola in '61.[55] That Chief Opothle Yahola is a Creek and these here are Sioux and Cheyenne ought not be of concern because, he said, the important thing was that they are all Indians. With that he went to work with any team in need. A wheelwright and blacksmith both, in a haze of smoldering charcoal[56] the labor on his body evoked the quarters of the stolen horse the Indian had wanted to trade. Labor he did, as was his word, for the pilgrims and their wagons, but ourselves feeling rather restive, did decline the invitation. Mr. O'Hanrahan said he knew he was a working-son-of-a-gun, and that we can not deny.

Until near the moment of our pulling out, there was much discussion as to what might be done for Mrs. Porter. The men deemed it proper not to take her council and as they talked about her she took matters into her own hands and was ready to leave before a consensus had been reached. I do believe she had nothing to go back for, and nothing to wait on at this miserable government workhouse,[57] and thus felt whatever trials might await us to be more agreeable. Benjamin committed his word to Mr. Tisdale that he would take a measure of responsibility for Mrs. Porter's well-being and thenceforth there was no dissent, our little team remained intact and our three wagons rolled out as before, still positioned in the first half of the cavalcade. I would estimate that nigh on half the freighters did take advantage of trade at the fort, the balance staying with us, and our number reinforced by the disgruntled civilians and their high skipping leader. Mr. Tisdale captains the front of the train and their man, Wishburn, now oversees the rear. What a dry stretch this has become; were it not for our barrels we would have had no water at noon, and Moses Clark, after initiating a consultation with Mr. Tisdale, trudged up and down the train atop his mule advising not to waste water on wetting the wheels.[58] In the event it was good advice, for when we arrived at Crazy Woman Creek there was but a smattering of ochre tinged sludge.

For all we are parched and weary, for all we are fretful, we take hope and comfort in the Lord and the blessings he bestows upon us. Behold our camp nestled in a crib scythed from arid desolation, and how cottonwood sentinels do beseech this starblown darkness with outstretched limbs, one sentry from amongst them now arched over me with stars hanging in its branches and hanging in the dreams untold that fade and die in the ether of night and heart and mind. Coyotes yammer without release for the cries of the wild and the cries of the Indian do appease the

Buffalo Bull

Bald Eagle

Bighorn Mountains

nocturnal, save in native chorus restitution. Restlessness be quieted for move we shall in His care if it is what He decrees. Tis light, we are already on the move today.

As the ribbons of cloud straggling across the sky blushed at the sun's insistence, forms were born from the dawn, emerging without sound or struggle, black and paralyzed and distant. Indians lined up and waited in our minds. "I believe them to be buffalo," said Moses Clark. And they were. Fearless, stubborn, or slow in mind and body, they trundled off the bluff in a dark, seething flow with no heed to our approach. Sister, they walk like fat ladies squeezed into ill fitting shoes that lace up tight to bloomers which are fur trimmed pantaloons. Giddy calves skip aside their hulking elders who bob their huge shaggy heads in feigned greeting with every step, glancing left and right to acknowledge their companions and to grumble about the trouble their young might make. They fall without complaint and death comes to them with little panic. Mr. O'Hanrahan and a gaggle of men gutted close to ten where they dropped and hacked away with axes and bowie knives until they could fill three wagons with the ragged torsos and floppy limbs, the plain stained with thick and standing pools of blood. Slathered in gore, the butchers remounted still grinning like imbeciles. It is good meat, so they say, but I regret that Mrs. Frantz's son will not be partaking. He was somewhat indisposed yesterday and not four hours into our trek today he has weakened to the verge of collapse. Now prostrate in their wagon with his face wan and brow scorching, we fear the bloody flux has got him.[59] I doubt that he will be aided by administering either the quinine favored by his mother or a concoction of Mr. O'Hanrahan's that by its scent is rich in whiskey. I have suggested a dose of opium and if it becomes possible, a treatment of hydropathy. Hereafter until his recovery, our three wagons have the labor of just one man, a predicament that did not escape the attention of Moses Clark. His offer of assistance did at first fall on deaf ears, then, without any spectacle, he addressed Benjamin thus: "We may not be running from the same trouble, but we are all running. So let us get to where we are running to and then be disagreeably inclined." He then hitched his mule to Mrs. Frantz's wagon and took his turn at driving.

Afore noon we came upon a different country. Gone are the spiteful squalls choked with sand and dust that crack land and lips and skin, and here now is the balm of crisp air and sweet relief fanning us with a cool breeze. That range which blistered the horizon on our approach to Fort Reno, and swelled ever more with each passing day, now suspends heaven for us to pass under. To the eyes of men, this cluster of mountains did at conception resist any notion of separation, and standing defiant these great chunks of slate dropped from on high wait for eternity in paupers rags of snow and pine.[60] We are given to believe that the Crow Indians named them after the mountain sheep, those nimble warriors of the crags with heads encased in helmets of tangled horns the Indians do so admire. Oh, what handsome land this is! How verdant the steppes that are suddenly veined and wrinkled by streams and their stragglers, the water followed and its secrets shared by crescents to-and-fro of brush and timber. Where in miles past we only saw their nests, now we are observing eagles gliding atop the wind until their great wings become kites that cleave through this watercolor blue. Lo, we have a shadow that is not our own, some sixteen horsemen on a ridge not too far distant. A burst of gunfire showered lead in their direction but the horsemen were unperturbed, sliding along the skyline to whom and whatever they cared.

We drove without much pause well into the afternoon until our outriders reported that the Indians had disappeared. Mr. O'Hanrahan and our reeking buffalo hunters took their leave and rode directly into the stream,[61] but the entire train had not arrived, let alone corralled, by the time they rejoined us. Mr. O'Hanrahan was more wet than clean as he took coffee with us as we waited. Directly upon Wishburn's wagons finally pulling in and the entire train forming a defensive corral, Mr. Tisdale began to berate Wishburn. It was, he said, near criminal to demonstrate such poor judgment and conduct when the lives of others were threatened by such, "Namely shooting at the Indians and then not keeping them wagons together."[62] Without a by your leave, Wishburn struck Mr. Tisdale and a bout of fisticuffs ensued which, with his ever willing smile, Moses Clark attempted to calm with Mr. O'Hanrahan one step behind. Struggling from Mr. O'Hanrahan's grasp, Wishburn took the Lord's name in vain and said he wouldn't be told what to do by a nigra.[63] Then he spat, pulled a big navy pistol, and called for a rope, telling Moses Clark it was his lucky day because he was going to let him pick out his own tree. Benjamin was the first to respond to his request. He handed a rope to Wishburn and stood at his side until he ushered Moses Clark towards the nearest cottonwood. Not a moment later, Benjamin was bent over Wishburn beating his head with a mallet as a blacksmith might fashion a horseshoe on an anvil. "You'll not kill that man or any other man without cause," Benjamin repeated over and over as Mr. Tisdale restrained him and ordered three men traveling with Wishburn's train to carry their captain away. Benjamin patted Moses Clark on the arm as he walked by him without any further acknowledgment. Hope as we might, it is a fact we oft try to hide that harmony does not follow strangers to self and each other, and amongst this crowd of searchers there is none who truly recognize their own cherished congregation on these wheels.[64]

My dear sister, it may surprise you to learn that few, if any, of those in the Wishburn party were affronted by today's drama. They care little for Wishburn, having tired of his disrespect in most every regard. They desire only to reach Alder Gulch, but have doubts that they will do so, encumbered as they are with this objectionable fellow whom they

Clear Creek

Rock Creek

claim is unrecognizable from the man they elected. Mr. Tisdale told them that in our train we had a fine collection of people with as many different dispositions and characters as there were backgrounds among us, and that whoever we were, and wherever we were from, we recognized the one thing that would carry us through: a respect for mutual dependency; one man and one woman, bound together with the next man and woman, by that single aim of reaching our destiny. He said he wasn't of a mind to tell them what to do for it was their choice to make, but they needed to appreciate that we could well continue without them, and while we welcomed their numbers we did not need the trouble, and to that end, if they wished to continue as a part of this wagon train, they ought to give consideration to electing Mr. O'Hanrahan as their new captain. Lastly, he said he did not care to abandon Wishburn to the wolves and so we would leave him at the fort, but that none amongst them, or us, were to comment upon his infirmity should any military personnel inquire. He estimated that it would be days before Wishburn recovered his faculties, by which time we could be in Bozeman or beyond. Save for Mr. O'Hanrahan, who objected to being elected captain of a train, there was no dissent and much accord. Throughout, Mrs. Porter had sat silently at my side, her hands clasped on her knees as she rocked back and forth. As a moment of silence fell, her frail voice struggled to find 'Nearer, My God to Thee.' Thoughts of her husband being at the mercy of whatever wolves bay must haunt her. It was a touching and impressive chorus when all around participated, each word and breath and sigh smoking in the chill of the night amidst the clement light of campfires.

Winter must come early to these parts with what now lies between dusk and dawn a whisper of portent. The flow aside the banks is already claimed, the ice knitted thin and pure and brittle as a veil to this virgin stream. We ate heartily last night, the buffalo making a fine, succulent roast with little gristle. Such approval did it meet that we enjoyed a second helping for breakfast. Mr. Tisdale shared coffee with us, which I think was due to him feeling obliged to fathom what mood or torment Benjamin was under. These men, it seems, know each other through violence, and from violence trust is dredged and friendship made, and to that insatiable overseer they do relate the covenant of truth and law and life and death. I asked Benjamin if he might ask Moses Clark to drive Mrs. Porter's team today and the suggestion found favor with all. I could hear Moses Clark's voice and laughter for most all of the day and it was as well that he took the reins, the terrain being broken with one rather intimidating descent. We rested in proximity to Father DeSmet's lake, whereupon Mrs. Frantz wished to collect some water to aid her ailing son, believing that it likely held some blessed medicinal quality. Having learned of the lake's repute, Moses Clark did attempt to dissuade her but to no avail; only when she tasted it for herself did she abandon the notion, the water being quite brackish. Mrs. Porter reassured her that this mountain air would work wonders for the boy and he would be as fit as a fiddle before the week's end.[65]

It wasn't long before the train shuddered to a halt again. At our appearance in whatever dream or nightmare he was having, a lookout perched atop a hill began a sequence of staccato signals with a flag.[66] Leaving him marooned in his crow's nest, a cabal in blue apprehended us, being duty bound to inform us that we could not camp within three miles of Fort Phil Kearny because Colonel Carrington wished to preserve feed for the army's stock, and neither could we proceed along Mr. Bozeman's road until the post commander had granted us permission to do so. There were some who felt aggrieved at having to corral so far from the fort, considering it unmindful on the part of this Colonel Carrington to have us so removed when, if the mood of his troops was any indication, Indian molestation could occur at any time of night or day. I myself found the arrangement to be quite satisfactory. Upon learning that some of the officers here had their wives in attendance,[67] I had thought how pleasant it would be to visit the fort to see what refinements these ladies had brought to the wilderness and what, if any, diversions could be found by way of apparel. However, I shall resist, believing that my need for such comforts is not so great as to require my entering another post named in honor of a Yankee general.[68] We struck out on this trail of a Georgia gentleman[69] to free ourselves from the Yankee stranglehold, and to rebuild our lives in a land far from their gaze or reach, yet

Lake DeSmet

Pilot Knob overlooking the Bozeman Trail on the approach to Fort Phil Kearny

hereabouts we are still at their beck and call. Mr. Tisdale estimated that our layover could be at least two or three days, what with Indian troubles and the colonel's regulations to account for.

The night was punctuated with the unholy wailing of wolves, their howls a mournful chorus that chills the soul and surrenders only to dawn.[70] Mr. Tisdale and Mr. O'Hanrahan started recruiting the teams directly after breakfast and, at around eight o'clock, an officer from the fort who I believe held the rank of captain arrived and undertook the census with tepid enthusiasm and an economy of conversation. We were to know what he wanted us to know, and that was our ration. He confirmed that which hitherto had been rumor about Indian depredations here, warning that the first indication of trouble could be a scalp being lifted or our stock stampeding with a party of Sioux in pursuit. That, he cautioned, was how sly they could be as they creep around in wolf skins, and whether we were to resume tomorrow, the next day, or next week, depended upon if we could present at least sixty armed and able men with adequate guns and ordinance. Mr. O'Hanrahan confirmed that we could, and that he and Mr. Tisdale were in the throws of compiling a new report to submit at the fort, due to some of the freighters wanting to stay and try their luck on robber's row,[71] their intent being to wait on their comrades who were trading at Fort Reno. The captain inspected the list that had been endorsed at Fort Reno, instructed Mr. Tisdale and Mr. O'Hanrahan to continue, and then proceeded with the routine. Disappointments were slung across this man's face and in his eyes ran every dog he ever booted or wanted to, a pack snapping at his heels that through the bottom of a bottle no longer ran but wobbled like distorted carnival freaks chasing the mongrel that had snatched his ambition. A survivor of the war but not want, had he died with glory on some bloody eastern field this fort may have carried his name, but as it is he is left with life and ghosts and 'Oh, Be Joyful.'[72] I don't know him, but I do. I am married to a man of ghosts. He called Mr. O'Hanrahan over and asked him what had happened to Wishburn. We all have our misfortunes, Mr. O'Hanrahan answered, requesting to take him to the fort. The captain stroked his chin whiskers and moved on.

Benjamin asked Mr. Tisdale if he could accompany him and Mr. O'Hanrahan to the fort.

Fancying that Wishburn was his responsibility, he didn't care for them to be inconvenienced. Moses Clark chimed in, saying that as he had been the one Wishburn wanted to hang, he felt obliged to go too, just so he could be assured that Fort Phil Kearny was where Wishburn would stay. They laughed, gathered up Wishburn in a buggy, and left to get the new list endorsed. How I appreciated the solitude of the day, taking the opportunity to read the Bible, reflect, and give thanks for our blessings. My dear sister, this country here does remind me of the Highlands of our childhood, and in it I can almost see the glens folding about the majesty of each ben.[73] With this nip in the air it could just be, or it could if there were a wee mist. The men returned from the fort without incident but loaded with tittle-tattle. Between the snap of sparks careering skyward, the lurid prattle about a negress at the fort crackled around the campfires. This woman, a laundress, is of questionable repute and her popularity is the cause of some disagreement between the colonel, who they branded a pompous bugger, and the officer who inspected our train today.[74] Or that is what the men are claiming. What servants there are at the fort are, of course, negroes, and it is ironic indeed that having supposedly fought to free them, these fine Yankee officers are still in the habit of keeping them. It being the Sabbath tomorrow, Mrs. Porter desires to attend service at the fort and Mr. Tisdale announced that we would depart thereafter, in order that all who wish to can join whatever congregation exists. I cannot deny the Lord or turn from a friend in need and so I shall swallow my pride and go to their fort.

At our backs the sun struggled through reefs of cloud laying along the eastern rim of the world, the shards of light unfolding around the valley like lace to a grand parlor window.

Black Bear

The fort sits there, perched on the plateau to rope the wind, besieged by bluffs and hills on a brocade trimmed by the shelving mountains looking down upon the tamers penned inside their stockade. Little is complete save their burly stockade;[75] rows of tents are pitched where, presumably, buildings are planned, some of which seem to be in various stages of construction. From its appearance I would venture to guess that the next structure to be completed will be the colonel's house, which isn't to say that others won't quickly follow as this is a hive of activity with quite a contingent of civilian contractors engaged at the post and the nearby sawmills, all hauling timber, cutting shingles and the like. There was no chapel, but so niggardly was the flock that it didn't much detract, though we were amply compensated by the regimental band's stirring renditions of hymns that graced the morn.[76] Benjamin declined to set foot within the fort again, and his making me aware that the chaplain had participated in the ruin of Atlanta was a severe test of faith.[77] With Mr. Tisdale and a few others from our advance train, Benjamin chose to accept the hospitality of a young couple who have made their home and business aside Mr. Bozeman's road, just outside the stockade.[78]

It was to them that my mind raced when a terrible commotion was loosed as we readied to rejoin the train. It was all a blur. Iron rang and clanked and leather flapped between the drumming of hooves. A buckboard reeled into the post. Men looked and then ran to aid or avenge. Men with mouths agape scuttled out of the way. A young private ran over to the buckboard, checked, and vomited. We turned our heads as we stepped back, but we were already captives to the cargo's putrid aroma. It was havoc, a primitive chant we could not resist. 'Look,' it called, and so we did. There sprawled in the back he lay, his bloating, naked body feathered with arrows and hacked into shanks of meat. With a skull marbled by drying, bloody membrane, this soldier or harvester was now a friar, mendicant and maimed, forced in death to wear a grotesque leer with bulging eyes as white as eggs staring vainly toward heaven. No warning of attack had come from the hill, this man had been missing and now was found.[79] We were allowed to move on. Mr. Tisdale and Mr. O'Hanrahan rode up and down the train exhorting every team to keep together and stay together. Reluctant he may have been, but wagon master could just be Mr. O'Hanrahan's calling. I doubt that we made more than five or six miles thereafter, anxiety and the rugged terrain conspiring to bring forth the silent inquisition of dream, desire and cause. Hereupon, what price are we prepared to pay? That collected by the waiting horseman from those whose ribs are now but branches sprouting in disarray from the pit where they were hastily planted? We passed this dead man's rickety bazaar as we started on this trail, and now he has a new home by the side of the same road.[80]

How gray it has become, snow spitting in our faces and plumes of dirt lifting the wagon covers so they flap with mock applause for the rip unraveling this mortal coil. Benjamin didn't return until breakfast, having been on picket duty guarding the herd. There were no alarms, just darkness, and we rolled out into the remains of the night with azure seeping down the edge of the world and pooling at the foot of the mountains to reveal petrified fingers groping at the plains, the places where the hands of this blind seeker had once gouged coulees and draws as they stumbled around in this immense tract that bleeds into beauty, foreboding and infinity. We twisted up the creek, the wagon tracks in the dusting of snow shifting in the wind so as we nooned the trace of our passing was more from the belly of a gigantic serpent than an armada on wheels. Mrs. Frantz's son collapsed after the days exertion, and I regret to say that I think he has taken a turn for the worse due to struggling to work when sick.

The men continually bemoan that this land about lay idle in the hands of Indians when it would undoubtedly offer up a productive yield for cattle or crop. We long to see fences, and we long for freedom, but shall it be us, our minds or the mountains that are first hemmed in? I cannot imagine a time when these mountains we look toward today will not inspire fear and awe, for we are yet unfound, yearning for the civilization within us, but having to acknowledge that restoration is in the wilderness that surrounds us. Will those who follow us live within the bosom of what we tend and cultivate, but yearn for the wilderness that beckons within? Pray, what shall be the dreams of the dreamers? Shall time be their abstraction?

Goose Creek is not wanting for the pristine. My dear sister, I heard a song last eve that put to shame each and every balladeer I have yet heard. It is a scream of passion that rings with all the joy and pain and desperation of a heart that can't live alone. It rises and pleads, and when the gut is hit and the heart drops hollow and hurt, the vibrato pleads to the night and the mountains, such are the operatics of the bull elk. They strut as our stags do, but their call to arms for love is pure poetry aside our red deer's bellow. I believe that with each hour that passes we see more and more buffalo, but although surprising, to our relief no Indians. Mr. Tisdale and Mr. O'Hanrahan impressed upon us once more the need for vigilance and order in keeping the wagons together, and they did recount how it was in this vicinity that a Mr. Sawyers was ambushed by Arapaho Indians a year ago. It is my understanding that we shall be taking a cut-off blazed by Mr. Sawyers but a few weeks ago when we reach Montana.[81] The weather has improved some but it has reinvigorated the mosquitoes which around water are again as thick as smoke. Mr. Tisdale has decided that we shall leave later tomorrow, wishing to take advantage of the opportunity to harvest fresh meat and fish, this river seemingly teeming with trout. There was tranquillity this night, the moon a thumbprint sat emaciated and distant in the cape it jealously guarded from the embers that throbbed black and orange and pulsed with the fiddles and songs of the men when the flames had lapped up what they could of the night, but then the music ended and morn did come.

From atop the ridge overlooking the camp, Moses Clark began twirling a white shirt above his head and then hurtled down the hillside, his back nigh on flat to that of the mule's, as if he were breaking a wild mustang. "Indians!" he yelled, coming to a halt in a heap of mule flesh, brays, and white shirt. "Indians riding in!" Women grabbed their children and each other, and the men grabbed their guns, several running to support those guarding the stock. Mr. Tisdale drilled the men as Mr. O'Hanrahan cantered toward the ridge. He was barely out of camp when four Indians appeared above us. They paused, conferred, and then one descended sedately. He stopped at the bottom of the slope, and the gray he was on stamped and nickered. Nobody moved. He lifted his right hand with his fist clenched, save for his index and middle fingers which were extended, and in his left hand he held out a piece of paper. Mr. O'Hanrahan made a sign we could not see, the camp being to his back, at which the Indian folded the piece of paper, closed his left hand around it, and then extended the index finger of that hand and made a sawing motion across it with the index finger of his right hand.[82] The Indian held out the piece of paper again, flicking it at Mr. O'Hanrahan, and they set their horses forward and met halfway. Mr. O'Hanrahan took the piece of paper, called Mr. Tisdale forward, and handed it down to him. Mr. Tisdale studied it and then read out loud, "When any Indian is seen who holds up this paper he must be treated kindly. Well I'll be darned." The addendum was Mr. Tisdale's, the note having been written at the direction of Colonel Carrington, a testimonial of sorts to foster goodwill and prevent hostilities breaking out between these Indians and any train they waylaid.[83] Mr. O'Hanrahan and Mr. Tisdale pointed toward a flat, downriver from the camp, and meandered back. The Indian gesticulated at the others on the ridge and they disappeared while he trotted after Mr. O'Hanrahan. They were Cheyennes, they were friendly, and they wanted to 'swap' with anyone who wanted to 'swap' with them.[84]

Tiger Swallowtail

Grizzly Bear

Women held onto their children as they peeked around the wagons at the Indian. He paid them no mind, and both horse and rider preened as if this was a well-rehearsed performance. The old hand's skin was the color of pennies, and in his blue-black hair dollars and dimes swung on a thin plait and pieces of the sun flowered in each where the coins had been forged with precise blows. Two feathers flopped in his hair in rhythm to the prancing gray, and fur-wrapped braids framed what I took to be a charm, a small bundle secured behind an agate arrowhead with weasel tails and beaded strings of white, red, yellow and black[85] trickling onto a shirt that resembled a long poncho with hair-fringed sleeves. Slats of dyed porcupine quills patterned the shirt, with wads of beaded chevrons and diamonds and crosses between which Thomas Jefferson[86] rested his head, the presidential gong being a finishing touch that even the mountain sheep or antelope or deer whose hide it had been would surely have envied. On his legs he wore garments akin to a cowboy's chaps, save they were buckskin, fringed, painted yellow, and between the calf and foot boasted a scrap fashioned like a pennant that was embroidered with bits and pieces of hooves[87] that flapped about his beaded moccasins and wafted the hair from a buffalo's beard that straggled behind the heels. A long strip of blanket hung from his waist to below his knees,[88] and unlike the Sioux we encountered, he made use of a saddle; two pieces of flat wood covered in hide with the pommel and cantle shaped from wood and deer horn. His paraphernalia was completed by beaded bags with trailing fringes, painted rawhide containers,[89] and a Hudson's Bay blanket.

His three companions were waiting downriver with a pack of their kin, the women busily pressing the merits of their wares, with children and dogs yapping and scampering between the women, their wares, and their would-be merchants. The men looked on from here, but were wishing they were there, as is the way of all men when their women are so engaged. Of those still mounted, one held a lance that resembled a great fur-covered shepherd's crook, and another had a red shield with the feathers of eagles, hawks and sandhill cranes cascading from its center, pinned at the side of which were grizzly bear claws clinging to the tips of a black crescent moon.[90] The one with the shield had crow feathers poking out from the back of his head and a lock with beads hanging over his left eye.[91] They both wore long braids and brass arm bands, and had hoops in their ears, but for all the similarities in adornment there were also marked differences I found intriguing. One of them bound his braids in red cloth while the other used hide,[92] and the one with the shield had a camp blanket draped around his waist, as opposed to the other who had acquired a floral patterned cotton shirt. The women displayed a certain uniformity, their smocks being of buckskin with sleeves styled like wings, and upon these capes were symmetrical beaded motifs garnished with the teeth of elk. These dresses fell below the knee, and in so doing obscured the trappings they wore on their legs,[93] though a beaded tassel was attached to them at the knees and dangled to their moccasins.

An old woman shuffled toward me out of the throng. Stooped and chuntering in breathy, lilting phrases, she was separated from the others by not only age but appearance. She wore a dress of hide that had a fold like a bib that drooped over her breasts, the red paint in which it was covered flaking where it was bunched at the left shoulder and pulled together at the sides by drawstrings.[94] A strip of skin passed around her scrawny shoulder where the garment was gathered, and the boney contours of her weather-beaten face became increasingly animated as she rattled on. I recognized not one word, but I understood her meaning; she fears the day when it will only be upon the wind that the shrieks of their dogs and offspring muddle with the scraping of their travois'[95] in that strange panting that signals their approach. Their painted ponies will be suffocated then, and their chants of blood and war delivered from the depths of time will be silenced by providence. Thus their stone age chorus will fade into twilight's memory, and they will be but one more ghost story, for our Lord created this country, and only for a time did He see fit to people it with red men. He set buffalo upon these plains to give the red man reason for being, but as the buffalo disappear so will the Indian, receding as a parched lake in high summer before the advance of civilization. Neither their prayers nor treaties will halt the railroad which is carrying them to their destiny, for that is the story of all history, the Lord giveth and the Lord taketh away. Such is the fate of all men. The old woman begged for life, but I gave her what she asked for, a box of matches.[96] Bacon, tobacco, sugar, gingham and vestiges of formal wear from socialites who had lost hope of need or invitation were exchanged for buffalo robes, moccasins and brightly painted rawhide satchels.[97] Some of their men intervened when the robes were up for grabs, trying to elicit barts for lead and ball, but they rode away in a rookery, thrashing and squawking in top hats and tails.

I wonder if in assemblage and custom they are not like our fathers' clans, that long ago pride we carry forth in our hearts; do their hearts beat so for their tribe? They remind me not a little of gypsies, those wayfarers of the stars and lanes who came with goods and chattels and blessings and curses on tongues immersed in the primordial.[98] Now, alas, what are we? For have we too not become travelers on that same road, we nomads to the night

Bull Elk

and covetous desire? Gold, I wonder, will you suckle these infants mild, or are we to have the fate of outcasts too, becoming beggars and thieves to others. How dear, how dreadful they are to behold, and grateful I am to have seen them before they vanish. How dear, how dreadful are we? Our faces swollen and bitten by mosquitoes, and our grubby clothes and sour odor unmasking our rank intent to bring forward their judgment day. Curiosity met by curiosity, we promised today but death cheats and what of tomorrow?

Heidi was jiggling a doll she had traded for, and with its smoky smell and beads it was indeed representative of its maker, even having nits or the appearance thereof, which discouraged further inspection. In minutes she was nursing the doll as she sobbed, standing over her brother who was slumped by the rear of their wagon. Mrs. Frantz had insisted on the boy being set beside the wagon to get the benefit of the sun while most everybody else trooped off to gawk at the Indians or trade with them, and it would seem that in their haste to do so nobody had checked under the wagon where a rattlesnake must have been taking the shade. The boy had been bitten on the left arm, and with his mind dulled by illness, he either didn't hear or couldn't react to that fearful buzz. Mr. O'Hanrahan applied a tourniquet, for what good it might do, and made hopeful noises about being able to reach a doctor at the fort on the Bighorn River, but his arm already had the appearance of a bulbous club and his breath was short and shallow. I had expected that he might expire before the debate as to whether to give him hartshorn[99] or whiskey subsided.

Mercifully the road was kind and the river crossing not exceptionally problematic, the Indians having drawn Mr. O'Hanrahan's attention to a ford they use. Had it been any other way I think the jolts would have likely hastened the demise of Mrs. Frantz's son. By noon he was more dead than alive, and Mr. Tisdale advised amputating the boy's arm for he would surely die if the cankerous black lump was left to poison the remainder his body. Volunteers to perform the surgery were few in number, Mr. Porter having been the only doctor to speak of. A short, chubby, balding man with spectacles nipping the end of his nose came forward from Mr. O'Hanrahan's train. His name was Theodore Tippetts and he said he had seen such operations performed many times during the war, he himself having tended to patients as a hospital volunteer. Benjamin asked if anybody had a better handsaw than the one he was holding, and when nobody did he invited Mr. Tippetts to assist. A tent and table were hastily put up, and I collected some fresh water from the creek. Mrs. Porter consoled Mrs. Frantz and Heidi, but from outside the tent you could clearly hear the bone bark as the blade grated against it. Fonts of blood spewed then slowed to a pitter-patter around the ruined limb, and Benjamin looked at Mr. Tippetts, shook his head, and the boy was gone. Mrs. Frantz was uncannily calm, asking if we could carry her son over the next creek, for then he would at least have made it to Montana. On the way we passed another who's journey had ended, his shallow grave a wreck of decomposing flesh, ripped cloth, and excavated bones, the wolves being more conscientious grave diggers than his comrades.[100]

Moses Clark fashioned a coffin for the boy out of supply boxes,[101] while Benjamin insisted on digging. He was the only son I had, Mrs. Frantz explained through her broken heart. His sister cradled the doll with nits, and her mother rocked her baby. So we leave yet another beneath slabs of rock to watch over those who travel this road.

We sallied away into the rumpled plains, the immense folds of sod harboring cruelty with grace, as on the eye there is clemency but in the soul there is reflected this expanse of loneliness that is becoming a wasteland to possibilities and dreams. So gradual the fade from grace, to the savage haunt, to nothing at all. The road heaved at the land's whim, and dust from our wheels shifted to where we were now bound to follow, searching for the reclusive orchard keeper's meticulously arranged trees aside the next creek, the next river, the next ideal. The stench of carrion drifted by from time to time, and then we'd come upon a magpies' ball hosted by a buffalo or elk our predecessors had left as a mark of their passing, for why else would they leave an animal to rot that hadn't been butchered?[102] The Cheyennes did apparently

Bozeman Trail Crossing near Fort C.F. Smith

Rocky Mountain Bighorn

Bighorn Canyon

Watching over George Pease's grave on Twin Creek

impress upon Mr. O'Hanrahan how they were constantly on their guard between here and the Yellowstone for attacks not only by white men, but by the Crow Indians who they deem to be near as treacherous as the white men, it appearing that they have thrown in with the soldiers at the fort on the Bighorn River. To their treachery I cannot vouch, but the Crow do cut imposing figures, wearing a pompadour of sorts that scales their flowing locks and neat braids. We met a small band of them without distress, their leader being the negro Mr. O'Hanrahan had brought to our attention near Fort Laramie.[103] In contrast to the Crows who present a panoply of dentalium shells, ermine tails and pastel colored beads, the negro is a ratty, wall-eyed old timer with the features of a Moor. Mr. Tisdale asked him how far on the army were with the fort, and he said not very, but they had the ferry running. With that, he gave a warning about the Sioux massing to strike the forts, and then rode on with his exotic escort.

There was trepidation as we approached the Bighorn River, with dire tales of everything from pilgrims drowning at the crossing, to caulked wagons sailing away, to attacks by ferocious bears, being told inside our heads. The valley spread before us, undefiled save for the rupture forced by the road, and we rumbled on without thought for any consequences but singularly on our cause. A mob of mule deers burst from a coulee onto the trail and across many a frayed nerve; indignant at our intrusion, the haughty young bucks in velvet suits sprang away with their noses in the air and their heels flicking contemptuously at the stems of wild oats that leant this way and that and then resumed waltzing with the wind. Rank swathes of dung billowed from the river bottom with forlorn bellows and moans and bullwhackers' hollers and the cracks of their whips on the flesh of beeves, the infernal babel rising against the bloodred sun boiling amidst shoals of bloodstained cloud clinging to the western horizon. Mr. O'Hanrahan returned from Abaddon with word that the teamsters were swimming the oxen across while ferrying their dismantled wagons and goods over. It was taking a good ten minutes for each wagon, and there were forty or more backed up, so we laid over three miles up from the commotion.

It turned cold in the night. A party of Crows emerged out of the murk lounging upon the morning, and they trotted by our camp on their way to the river. The chill did not encourage them to wait for the ferry, they simply stripped off and tied their garments into a bundle which they fastened to the bridles of their ponies, and then plunged into the river, sliding off the backs of the ponies and holding onto the tails in the depths as their mounts pulled them across. We watched with a mix of envy and disdain, the latter diminishing as we saw the ferry at close quarters and were told the fee. For the sum of five dollars per wagon we got to ride this pitiful raft that far from being finished was so poorly constructed that a true boatwright would have been hard pressed to convince anybody that they had made anything but a start. Upon the rough-hewn planks one wagon at a time was loaded with most all of the provisions and wheels removed, the four oars that are little more than felled lodgepoles then being taken up by the passengers. Moses Clark and Benjamin did a fair stint before they undertook the rounds repairing axles, this at least being an excellent location for such, given the amount of available timber. A fine cooperative spirit prevailed which overcame any notion of ill temper, the freighters setting the example, for they put aside their eagerness to unload their goods at the fort and set their mules to drawing the raft ashore while the teamsters took up ropes for landing. A good number of the freighters' mules appear somewhat played-out so it is as well that they have reached their destination, though I fear they may be disappointed in this fort they have named C.F. Smith,[104] being as it is presently just a collection of neatly arranged tents with signs of foundations. We had an enlightening conversation with some prospectors who were on their way back to Virginia City. It was their opinion that the soldiers at this fort were more concerned with chasing after buffalo and any other game that happened along[105] than protecting emigrants, an attitude to which they felt a measure of resentment. I would however add that at least these soldiers have not seen fit to disregard all for the sake of a stockade, which gives the traveler some confidence as it suggests that they feel able to repel the hostile Indians, whether they can or cannot, and they do appear to be going about the business of building this fort methodically. Benjamin inquired about Adobe Town, saying he wished a piece of the $350,000 pulled out from the streams thereabouts two years ago, but the prospectors advised him to stake his claim in Nevada City, so, my dear sister, we shall see.

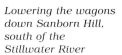

Lowering the wagons down Sanborn Hill, south of the Stillwater River

So close are we now to the edge of the earth. Hereabouts the world has been prized apart, and the guts of the world torn from its belly in a frenzy or firestorm at a time unknown with a ferocity unknown, those scars from the ravages of colossal beserkers or their masters lacing the chasm through which the river does chase.[106] The land is marbled by scorched earth, the orange veins entwined with cactus leading the lost and found to a serrated maze of unholy spires that rise and fall from a caked and burned-out floor, until all there is are the shapes of ruined cities through plumes of dust and haze, the smashed pillars of palaces littering the ravines aside the road over which mountain sheep reign. How hard it would be to scrape a living here, how hard it is to cross these Badlands with the

The Thomas/Schultz grave near the Yellowstone River

THE BOZEMAN TRAIL

The Bozeman Trail crossed the divide from Red Lodge Creek and descended a steep hillside to the Rosebud Valley one-half mile southeast of here. Jim Bridger opened the route through this area in June 1864, and three weeks later John Bozeman followed his route as he led the first train over the Bozeman Trail. Diarists often noted the steep descent to Rosebud Valley. Abram Voorhees wrote on July 24, 1864: "in afternoon we went down a long crooked & sideling hill, it was steep and rocky & the worst one to go down we have found." George W. Fox called it "the big hill" on August 27, 1866.

From the base of the hill, the Bozeman Trail went down the east side of the valley to the Rosebud Creek crossing just below the confluence of Butcher and East and West Rosebud Creeks. The trail crossed at present Smith Bridge, two miles north of here, and then went northwest over hills to the Stillwater River crossing. In August 1866 Bridger led a large train down the east side of Rosebud Creek to a new crossing above its junction with the Stillwater River. This new route then went up the south side of the Stillwater to the earlier crossing, avoiding the hills.

snow on the peaks at our backs a windsong lest we forget.[107] As we nooned at a spring near Pryor Gap,[108] Mrs. Frantz picked up a rock, held it close, and then scratched upon it a eulogy to her son. She asked Moses Clark if he would set it atop a high place and he did consent and removed his hat as he read, "Hush now my sleeping babe for even the toll of eternal silence will not quiet my song for thee." Mrs. Porter cried, and Heidi wrapped her arms about her Indian doll. Moses Clark was gone fifteen minutes or more. This road gets harder.

We trudged away from these tortuous Badlands and the terrain crumpled before us as if in remorse for the arid trial we were forced to endure. At the Clark's Fork River winter let forth and spattered the wagons with rime, and the breath from our toil with all the lows and neighs bellied about the wagon train in misty clouds like a presage to the wilderness of the railroad and the approaching age. The landscape stretched to the horizon anew, great rolls of earth swept up against the gray sky in every direction. Mr. Tisdale retrieved a note that was scuttling down a creek among some fallen leaves.[109] It gave a warning about Indians, but nothing about from whom, to who, and when and where, and so we lumbered on and climbed barren slopes where the road took the high ground and the element away from any surprise. I think the mountains are following us, rising from the south like the vertebrae of some long-dead gigantic beast with its flesh but a shadow now owned by the sun.[110] The train stuttered to halt as we came upon the edge of a bluff that tumbled down into a valley. Mr. O'Hanrahan was pacing up and down muttering about there being a better way to traverse this region that, in his words, "don't require all manner of acrobatics," impressing upon those who walked his way that all anybody needed to do was follow what he called the Rosebud out to the valley of the Stillwater. Benjamin nodded sagely and then asked Moses Clark if he was ready. For all that there may have been a better way, we were going this way, which was down the side of the hill.[111]

Women and children and the odd dreamer milled around like lost sheep as the stock was funneled left and right and the teamsters took over the donkey work. They lashed ropes to the rear of the wagons, two hands taking the strain at the wheels, and as many as they could muster hauling back from the snubbing post. It looked quite peculiar, the wagons with their wheels double locked dangling from a post, with men grappling with the wheels, and at the tongues fighting to restrain the wagons, as one by one they made a somewhat precarious descent. As tempers frayed, Moses Clark span yarns about how he had done this many times almost single-handed by felling trees, then stripping them of all but a few branches, and tying them to the front of wagons and under rear axles, claiming the branches were a more reliable brake than a mess of impatient miners.[112] I do believe that

31

Grizzly Bear

Bull Moose

Looking west to Yellowstone Ford

man could say anything followed with that laugh of his, and others would take up the joke. When all was said and done we took it as a good omen that among our number we only collected two broken bones in the descent.

The nights are chilly and the moon is but a child's boat that is doomed to sink within days into the all-knowing black austere sea, thus leaving we seekers at the mercy of Orion, having to decide whether or not to follow the giant's sparkling footprints through this wall of stars. There are days when it feels as if even hope is lost, for though I know our navigation has not gone astray, were it not for the solace of the scriptures I would succumb to such failings. We passed the mass grave today of men and a boy who I do expect believed that they too were on the right road. I wondered if anybody was missing them, and so I recorded their names in a notebook, for if they look down upon us they will at least know that their passing has not gone unnoticed: Rev. W.K. Thomas, age 36 years. Chas K. Thomas, age 8 years. James Schultz, age 35 years. C.K. Wright. All killed and scalped by Indians.[113] How scant a memorial, a stranger's hand in a faded notebook. We are on watch for bears as well as Indians now as two were sighted today. One, a grizzly, was minding his own business, rooting through the berry bushes that line these creeks, when we came upon him. He pushed his big flat face into the breeze, raised up, and then shambled off with a volley of lead in pursuit, the balls causing the dirt to sputter about him as, with a start, he bounded up the creek with hunks of flab slapping against his hump. He was not hit, and thus far has not returned. Alas, sleep may be a reluctant caller below this clique of mountains that are huddled together in the manner of drunk old men.[114]

With the kiss of first light on their white pates, the aged crags regained their majesty and offered us shelter from a brutal wind as we wound along the Yellowstone. Mr. O'Hanrahan left camp before dawn with five pickets he had commandeered from the herd to reconnoiter the ferry and the ford, and the messengers pale between shadows soon returned, bobbing up and down in the saddle as the horses cantered through the crisp morning air with a country yet unclaimed by any but darkness stretched out behind them. The ford was Mr. Bridger's and the ferry Mr. Bozeman's, and he said he doubted that he would have a great deal of sentiment for either after they had served their usefulness.[115] The current was strong and there were among us concerns for the stock, though after learning the toll for the ferry, some favored chaining the wagons together to ford the river, and hence taking our chances with the stock. The ferry was an improvement on the last, but not greatly so, it being a rickety contraption with ropes that droop pulley to pulley, and rendered idle by the wind. Mr. Bozeman did step from the shack out of which he operates this enterprise, and proceeded with an oratory that, every sentence or two, returned to the subject of the ferry and the small matter of the $10-per-wagon fee. Realizing that his audience wasn't entirely captive, he said that on account of the delay caused by the wind he would reduce the charge to $6 per wagon with horses and mules at fifty cents even. If one can be a tatty aristocrat, that would describe Mr. Bozeman. He is, I fear, a man to whom there is no elixir that would defy his selling, a trait not becoming of a Georgia gentleman.

Mr. O'Hanrahan was quite correct, the layover was miserable and the entire experience did little to engender favorable sentiment. What will live longest in the memory are the messages fellow travelers had scrawled upon the trees there, the bark having been stripped away so that the bared

The site of Fort Ellis below Mount Ellis

trunks could carry their themes.[116] One boast read, "Chicago train of one wagon, one man and one yoke of dead beasts. All well." If it be true, there will be many back east who would like to make the acquaintance of such a man, though I doubt the undesirables who came calling this evening would be so celebrated in dime novel, myth, or legend. The rain was beating down and Mr. Tisdale called a halt to the drive with another river laying afore us. On the back of the rain, mist rose in silence from the river until distant tiptoes became the slop of hooves in mud. Four silhouettes gently steamed in the firelight. One called out as Benjamin and Mr. O'Hanrahan headed towards them, appealing to our Christian nature for food and hot coffee. They dismounted and plodded toward our fire, the sludge sucking at the pieces of animal skin holding their shabby boots together until their footsteps were akin to the slapping of dead or dying fish. They squatted like stray dogs begging for scraps, their expressions whittled by a hunger a feast could not satisfy, and their eyes hollow and fixed and glazed. What teeth they had were random and had no doubt been rearranged, and spittle drooled from their mouths as they slobbered over deer meat and questions. They claimed to be miners and that their stock had been run off by Indians. They had narrowly escaped with their lives, and this, they explained, was why they were riding unshod Indian ponies, for they had managed to track the red horse thieves to their camp, and there took these nags as part payment.

There were no stars, and the fire hissed every time a drop of rain dripped from their rancid clothes into the flames. The only one who spoke cuffed his nose with his sleeve, snorted like a hog, tossed his plate aside, and then reached into his pocket and delicately lit a cigarillo, regarding all who sat about him with the poise of a madam surveying clientele from the balcony of a saloon. He asked how we got along with the Sioux, and informed us that the Sioux were civilized compared to the Blackfeet, and that it was the Blackfeet we would now have to reckon with, jabbing his finger back up the trail in the direction of what he called some Blackfeet handiwork, referring to the Thomas party's mass grave. Then he gloried in a tale about a trader the Blackfeet had once taken, and how they had trussed him up to a tree and skinned him one leg at a time. As he and his friends had fallen on hard times, they had, he said, been forced into another line of work. "Our own handiwork," spat

Virginia City

one of the others, and there began a fit of whinnies and wheezes and guffaws. He reckoned it was handiwork for which we should show gratitude, and he pulled out a tobacco pouch that he described as "an old squaw's teat,"[117] and lamented how aces and eights[118] "did rob me of the squaw skin belt I done made to go along with it."

Moses Clark said he didn't care for his tone or manner, particularly in front of the ladies. The drifter wiped what grease was left on his fingers in the back of his hair, fingered the brim of his sweat-stained hat, and asked how much we wanted for "the boy." Mr. Tisdale stood and was about to speak when the drifter continued, saying there was some worth in keeping blacks alive because no man wanted to do the work of oxen or mules, but that redskins[119] only had value when dead. "Specimens and the like," he said they called them, explaining how he had fancy gentlemen in New York City and Washington, D.C. who collected Indian scalps and skulls and bones, recounting how once he'd had a heck of a time satisfying the demand for mummified papooses, and babies they pickled and set on shelves in jars.[120] Mr. O'Hanrahan and Benjamin had never returned to the fire, but now they did with triggers cocked and nine more guns. The drifter said this wasn't gratitude, and Mr. O'Hanrahan clubbed him across the jaw with the butt of his rifle and he toppled into the fire and Moses Clark booted him from the flames. Mr. O'Hanrahan told the other three idiots to take him, and they stumbled out of the shadows and dragged him to his pony where hung wigs black and dull, large and small, save they were not weaved nor the hair given willingly. As a trapper might present a

Aside Alder Gulch

pelt, these were the remains of some Indian family, and the matted crusts of the scalps clapped softly with each other as these drifters or road agents[121] or simple barbarians tramped away to infest this land and others with a plague that was their very being. Oh my dear sister, what depravity stalks the souls of men.

There were none who objected to an early start, and we drove on just as sunlight started to splinter the wagons and the gloom that was hanging over the divide. An angular form, as black as the water standing part way up its legs, observed our passing while munching on some foliage. Water dribbled from its distended muzzle, and its antlers flared in the pose of hands open in supplication, but before anybody took a shot, the moose lolloped away on its long, skinny shanks to the safety of the timber. On another day somebody might have ridden after it, but not today. Today we were getting close, and after so much nobody wanted to take the chance of meeting a grisly fate away from the train, last night having rid us of any complacency. The road was broken and overhung by cumbersome earthen dunes that the wind had carefully sculpted into drifts then abandoned to grasses that yellowed with the season. Where on the flat there had been rain, upon the pass[122] it had fallen as snow, and the huge black mountainous blades that sliced through the sky around the Gallatin Valley had pines with boughs shingled in ice. We lost one of the colts as we clattered into a canyon;[123] its leg ricked in a hole, the wagon bumped on, the leg snapped, and there was nothing that could be done and a cheer went up with the shot. The horse's death was instantly of little consequence, though no cause for celebration. It was fences. There were fences in the valley, and more cheers. Then cultivated fields, and more cheers. Then a house, the first in my estimation since Fort Laramie, and I cheered. The train rolled by a two-headed peak[124] that bubbled from the plain, and men without guns welcomed us to Bozeman City and pointed out where we would find a blacksmith's shop and a flour mill.[125] After all of these miles and all of this wilderness we could probably have found them among the five or six buildings that were standing, but it was good to just stop and listen without fear of being shot or scalped or robbed. We nooned at Tom Cover's mill, and Benjamin scratched his head for most of the afternoon, trying to conclude why the man had exchanged gold dust for flour.

Moses Clark gave consideration to setting up in Bozeman City, either with or in competition to the farrier, but I think his fondness for Mrs. Porter did influence his decision to continue with us, though I must stress that there is no indication of impropriety. He is indeed a gentleman we have grown to respect, and I do believe Benjamin would have missed his company if he had chosen to stay. How the Lord does work in mysterious ways. They say that over yonder hills is Virginia City and that from the heights we must scale the view of the Madison Valley is close to heaven. If that is true, my dear sister, I shall be ever nearer to you, nearer than at any moment since that day they took you in Atlanta. Oh, how I shall follow this longing in my heart until it guides me home to you, my dear sister, home together safely in the arms of the Lord.

Brigadier-General
Patrick E. Connor

THEY MUST BE HUNTED LIKE WOLVE[S]

Colonel Chivington: Can we ge[t] a fight out of the Indians this winter? I think from the tempe[r] of the men that you have and a[ll] I can learn that you will give these Indians a most terrible threshing if you catch them, an[d] if it was in the mountains and you had them in a canyon, with your troops at one end of it an[d] the Bear River at the other, as [I] had the Pi-Utes [*sic*], you could catch them; I repeat, if you catch them . . . you will give them a good dressing down.

Connor's communications with Chivington of October and November, 1864 – prior to the Sand Creek Massacre – from: Rebellion Records, Series I, Vol. XLI. Part IV, 259. Colonel John Chivington writing in the Denver Republican, May 18, 1890.

They (the Cheyennes) are tryin[g] to induce the Sioux in that country to join them in a war against the whites. They must be hunted like wolves. You (Colonel Nelson Cole) will not receive overtures of peace or submission from Indians, but will attack and kill every male Indian over twelve years of age.

Extracts from Connor's 1865 Powder River Expedition communications from O. R., I, Vol. 48. Connor to Major General Grenville M. Dodge, April 14, 1865. Connor to Colonel Nelson Cole, July 4, 1865.

Military

Extracts from the Diary of
George M. Templeton

First Lieutenant George M. Templeton's military service began on August 22, 1862, when he enlisted as a private in the 149th Pennsylvania Volunteers. Within a matter of weeks he was Corporal Templeton, and by July 1863 Templeton and the 149th were on the field at Gettysburg. Discharged from the Volunteers in February 1864, Templeton entered the ranks of the regular Union Army and was promoted to captain, serving with the Thirty-second Regiment of United States Colored Troops. Established under the Bureau of Colored Troops, the Thirty-second Regiment was organized at Camp William Penn, Pennsylvania, between February 7 and March 7, 1864. In common with the other regiments of U.S. Colored Troops, the Thirty-second was commanded by white officers, the rank and file comprised of freedmen, veterans of the Underground Railroad, and ex-slaves from states that had seceded from the Union. Ironically for officers such as Templeton who would later go west to pacify Indians, the 'Colored Troop' regiments were not exclusively African-American; among the enlisted men were some of the 20,000 American Indians who fought on both sides in the Civil War. The Thirty-second saw action in South Carolina, the theatre where, at Honey Hill on November 30, 1864, Templeton's right leg was strafed by Confederate fire, an injury that aggravated him for the rest of his life.

Following his service in the Civil War, a sojourn as a student was but a temporary hiatus in his military career, and in December 1865 Templeton applied for an officer's appointment in the U.S. Army. On May 13, 1866, a month after the Civil Rights Act granted full citizenship and rights to all persons born on U.S. soil with the exception of American Indians, Templeton headed to the Western Frontier. When he left Fort Leavenworth, Kansas for the lands of the Lakota, Northern Cheyenne and Arapaho, Congress was proposing an amendment to the Civil Rights Act that would be preserved under the Fourteenth Amendment, that no person born in the U.S. could be deprived "life, liberty or property without due process of law."

In his diary for 1866, Templeton does more than take the reader on a journey to garrison the Bozeman Trail, he provides an insight into the prevailing attitudes of his military peers and the hopes, fears and prejudices that enabled Manifest Destiny and Reconstruction to juxtapose in the struggle for the soul of the nation. Emancipated they may have been, but as Templeton went West, Black Codes ensured that Reconstruction did little more for African-Americans than substitute the term 'freedman' for 'slave,' while in the Powder River country the lieutenant's brothers-in-arms in the Eighteenth Infantry cataloged Lakotas and Cheyennes as "wild game." Templeton's detachment was on the Bozeman Trail by July 1866, and on Crazy Woman Creek he discovered a people who weren't prepared to be deprived of "life, liberty or property without due process of law." Surviving the engagement at Crazy Woman Creek, Templeton reached Fort C.F. Smith on August 10, 1866, and was one of only two officers to be stationed on the Bozeman Trail throughout the U.S. military's attempted occupation. Ultimately, with the war lost by the army but soon to be won by the railroad, Lieutenant George Templeton marched away from Fort C.F. Smith on July 30, 1868, arriving at Fort Reno on August 1, from where, on August 18, he left as that fort's last commanding officer.

The following extracts from Templeton's diary are reproduced with his handwritten grammatical errors.

Lieutenant George Templeton's original diary is held in the Everett Graff Collection of the Newberry Library, Chicago, Illinois. The portion of the diary reproduced here is done so with the assistance of the Sheridan Public Library – Wyoming Room collections and archives, and Elmer 'Sonny' Reisch.

Fort Laramie

"It will be valuable some time, provided the country is ever settled, which I think doubtful."

THE TRAIL

July 6th-

We came on the Platte 18 miles from where we camped last night. In the afternoon visited Chimney Rock, which I think is a greater curiosity than C.H.R. (Court House Rock). There is a conical hill raises out of the plain about 200 feet and from this there is a perpendicular pillar rises 150 feet. It is about 50 feet in diametre. At the distance of a few miles it looks quite insignificant.

July 7th-

Marched to Fort Mitchell 27 miles; are either in or very near Dacota. Passed through Scott's Bluff, a very wild rocky pass. At Mitchell met a hunter who had two squaw wives and a number of children. After going into camp 8 indians came into camp, one of whom was a squaw. They are Sioux and are camped nearby, on their way to the South Platt. They have an exceedingly airy suit, consisting of one shirt and a breech clout each. Their long black hair hangs down over their shoulders in elegant confusion except the scalp lock which is braided. The place where the hair is parted is painted with vermillion also spots on the face. We gave them a few hard tack each, and they left. I am disgusted with the noble Indian of the plains. They are a disgusting dirty set, so far as I could judge and I have reason to think that those that were in camp today are a fair specimen.

Chimney Rock

Major General
William Tecumseh Sherman

I HOPE THE PRESIDENT WILL CONTINUE TO BEFRIEND THESE ROADS

All I ask is comparative quiet this year (1866) for by next year we can have the new cavalry enlisted, equipped, and mounted, ready to go and visit these Indians where they live.

It is our duty, and it shall be my study, to make the progress of construction of the great Pacific railways . . . as safe as possible.

I hope the President and Secretary of War will continue, as hitherto, to befriend these roads as far as the law allows.

The Indians seem to oppose the opening of the new road [Bozeman Trail], but that must stimulate us to its prosecution, and you may rest assured that you will be supported all that is possible.

We must try and distinguish friendly from hostile and kill the latter, but if you or any other commanding officer strike a blow I will approve, for it seems impossible to tell the true from the false.

Sherman to Grant's chief of staff, August 21, 1866. U.S. Congress. 39th. 2nd sess., House Executive Document, No. 23, p. 6.
Annual Report, November 5, 1866, pp. 21-22.
Sherman to Grant, May 14, 1866. U.S. Congress. 39th. 2nd sess., House Executive Document, No. 23, p. 2.
Sherman to Carrington, September, 1866. U.S. Congress. 50th. 1st sess., Senate Executive Document 33, p. 30.

Bridger's Ferry

July 8th-

Marched 16 miles, camping on Horse Creek. Found about 25 lodges of Sioux Indians in camp there. The chief's name is "Standing Elk." They are very well dressed most of them having blankets and hats and many having a considerable number of ornaments. One young warrior was stalking around with a sword, seeming to think a great deal of it. Some had cavalry hats and other articles of soldier's clothing. Most wore leggings. I noticed one young boy who had a string of tin ornaments 4 feet long dangling from his hair. I saw many things that I have read of, such as the squaws doing all the work, their carrying their pappooses slung in a blanket on their backs. The chief put on a great deal of dignity and didn't want to talk any. He smoked the pipe with the other Indians present at the time and passed it to Mr. Wands but did not pass it to Mr. Marr who was present: This I think was a token of disrespect to white men. We are now in Dacota, Scott's Bluffs which we crossed yesterday being the dividing line.

July 9th-

Marched 24 miles camping 10 miles from Laramie near Bordeaux' Ranch. Passed in sight of about 50 lodges of Indians, camped near Horse Creek. The country passed through today is truly a waste. The ranchmen say that they can raise nothing on the land.

July 10th-

Arrived at the Fort about 8 A.M. Reported to Major Van Voast and Mr. Wands . . . Laramie is built on the west side of the Laramie River and about a half mile from the junction with the Platt. Laramie Peak is said to be 60 miles west.

July 11th-

Took dinner with the officers of the post upon invitation. I examined the grave of the wife of "Big Ribs" an Sioux Chief, who died at the post while the treaty was going on. The body together with all her personal effects were put in a square pine box 8 feet long, 4 wide and 3 deep. This was elevated on four posts some 8 or 10 feet from the ground, and a red blanket was nailed on it. They had killed her two ponies and nailed their heads to the eastern posts and their tails to the western. Although I could not see into the box I am told that the top is uncovered to enable the spirit to wing its way to the hunting grounds, where there is no dearth of game.

July 13th-

Marched 22 miles camping on the Bitter-Cottonwood Creek.

July 14th-

Marched some 28 miles camping on the Platt, a few miles from Bridger's Ferry. Near here is a gap in the hills where the river runs through. It is a very picturesque, and I would like to go through in a boat. Bring a Chaplain for the 2nd Batt. from Fort Laramie, and a queer genius by the name of Glover, who was sent out to take stereoscopic views of the scenes at the treaty. He wants to go to Col. Carrington's Head Quarters.

July 15th-

Marched 23 miles, camping near the mouth of Sage Cr. Crossed the Platt by means of a rope ferry at a place called Bridger's Ferry, about 4 miles from where we camped last night. While at supper last evening Lieut. Bradley killed a rattlesnake under his chair. At the ferry spoken of they charge $4.00 per load, and only can take one wagon at a time. Day before yesterday they made some $600. They do not charge for U.S. troops or wagons.

July 16th-

After leaving camp crossed some high rugged hills, some of which seemed to contain iron ore. Twelve miles up the Platt we turned up the valley of Sage Creek, marching 16 mls. The country is very barren, grass enough for the mules being procured with difficulty, and the only water being in a few holes in the bed of the Creek.

July 17th-

Marched at 4.40, the earliest yet, and camped at Humprey's camp at 1 P.M. This camp is on a gulch, which most of the time is dry, but owing to the heavy rains that have been in this locality there are many holes full of water. In the bank of the creek 3/4 of a mile N.E. of the crossing there is a vein of coal 12 feet thick. It will be valuble some time, provided the country is ever settled, which I think doubtful.

July 18th-

There were two roads leading from this place. Did not know which was the right one. Mr. Kirkendal's train took the left hand one and rather than follow behind his wagons I took the other. Saw the Big Horn mountains dead ahead covered with snow. They are said to be 9000 ft above the sea level. The Pumpkin Buttes are on the right. They are pretty high and have flat tops. Made a very long march of 33 miles camping some where, none of us knew where. Some thought, at Cactus Springs, others at Dry Creek.

July 19th-

A march of 18 miles brought us to Old Fort Reno on the Powder River, a small stream 20 yds. wide. Found Co. "B." 2d Batt in charge of stores at the Post. Capt. Procter extended the courtesies of the place to us. The fort has a stockade and two long barracks for men and officers' quarters for about two companies. The Indians have been troublesome, having run off some 40 head of stock lately, coming right up to the fort for them.

July 20th-

Marched 20 miles camping on Crazy Woman's Fork. This is a day long to be remembered as the one on which I had my first Indian fight. As soon as I arrived at the creek Lieut. Daniels and myself rode down the creek about a mile having been told that we would find good grass there. Just as we turned to leave, not

Colonel
Henry B. Carrington

A SATISFACTORY TREATY?

On June 16, while encamped four miles east of Laramie, I was visited by Standing Elk, chief of the Brulés (a band of the Sioux). He was thoroughly friendly – was entertained in my tent, and asked "Where was I going?" I told him; he answered me as follows: "There is a treaty being made at Laramie with the Sioux that are in the country where you are going. The fighting men in that country have not come to Laramie, and you will have to fight them. They will not give you the road unless you whip them."

The Indian commissioners before they adjourned passed a resolution which they sent me by the courier who brought my mail, advising me that a treaty had been signed by them and left at Laramie, with certain presents for Arapahos and Cheyennes, requesting me to inform such tribes within my command of the fact that they might go and sign and receive their presents. Having received no copy of that treaty and no names of chiefs who have already signed it, I do not see how I can give to the Indians (if they wish peace) any indication of what they are to sign or receive. The commissioners announce "a satisfactory treaty" with the "Ogallallas" [*sic*] and Brulé "bands," and yet some of those Sioux are in my command, hostile.

The commissioners did all they could, but as when I left I wrote you so, since my impressions derived from closest scrutiny of the Indians I saw are confirmed that I shall have to whip the Indians, and they have given me every provocation.

Henry Carrington
Colonel 18th U.S. Inf.

U.S. Congress. 50th. 1st sess., Senate Executive Document 33, p. 5.
Carrington to General H. G. Litchfield, AAAG, Dept. of the Platte, July 30, 1866.

43

Crazy Woman Creek

having been able to find a good place, Lieut. (Daniels) remarked "look there" and spured his horse up, going away ahead. I looked over my right shoulder, but could see nothing, but upon looking over my left, I saw between 50 & 60 indians mounted and in full chase, about 150 yds in the rear. I spured up old Pegasus, punched him with my gun and did everything to increase speed, but the horse seemed to me to be moving very slowly. After Mr. Daniels had gone 200 yds. he was shot with an arrow through the back and fell off his horse, the saddle turning. I could do nothing to help him and did not expect to get away myself, so continued on. The Indians had almost surrounded me again. I arrived at the Ford of the Creek and were within 20 feet of me, – i.e. those behind were. I plunged my horse down an almost perpendicular bank into the creek and as I was half way over the Indian closest fired a carbine at me, but fortunately missed. Previously they had fired a few arrows, but seemed to want to capture me. Found the ambulances on the other bank of the creek: got them back and soon had them and the wagons in corral on a little mound, but as there were ravines all around it was not a good place to remain, so after getting some water by sending out an armed party we moved about 3/4 of a mile up the creek to a high bluff. While doing this we had quite a skirmish all the way. The indians being all around us and taking advantage of every inequality of the ground. But they are great cowards, for if you point a gun at them they will drop down and not raise their head as long as you keep it so pointed. After getting on the top of the hill corraled and dug rifle pits. The Indians tried to get into camp by creeping up the ravines and running for high ground, but a shot from one of the men sickened one and soon after most of them withdrew. This was near sundown, but they only went a short way and held a council, and leaving a few pickets the majority went into the woods on the other side of where we first saw them. About dusk I saw a dust rising on the road to New Fort Reno, and at first thought it was more Indians, but upon looking with the glass discovered that it was a train. In advance of it saw one soldier on foot. As soon as the Indians on post saw the dust they left and while going towards their main party discovered this soldier. I fired my revolver to warn him, and he ran about 100 yds and they holding up their guns (a sign of peace) he stoped and walked right up to them, when they killed him. Captain Marr and I rode over to communicate with the train and found it to be one from Reno under charge of Capt Burrows, going to old Reno after supplies. Found the murdered man, who proved to be a Corp. and Lance Sergt. of the Capt's. Comp. who had been out hunting buffaloes. Our going across the plain didn't give the Indians time to scalp him but they took his coat and trousers. The Capt. crossed his train and camped with us. We then felt pretty safe. I have no doubt but they would have attacked us had no relief come. While I was away the Chaplain and one man started for the Old Fort for some assistance. Had I been there they would not have gone, as I considered ourselves safe, but intended to send them after dark had the train not come up. I was never in my life so glad to see a train of wagons. I, in common with most of the others, had narrow escapes from balls. One man had his gun struck by an arrow, and another had his trouser waistband cut by a bullet. Some of the Indians were armed with guns and some with bows and arrows & spears. A few had rawhide sheilds. Most of them were naked, except the breech clout, which is their custom when going into action. Nothing but a remarkable interposition of Providence saved me, especially in the chase. I never before thought death so near. Anyone who does not believe in God must reason against reason and revelation. I couldn't bring myself to disbelieve in his existence, if for nothing else, from the fact he is the answerer of prayer. He gives me everything that I ask for that he considers good for me. From my heart I thank him for his gracious preservation of my life. The funeral of the corporal was a solemn scene. By moonlight, followed by 5 or 6 officers, the body was carried in perfect silence to a grave formed by one of our rifle pits, and all uncovering, it was committed to its last resting place.

July 21st-

Capt. Burrows thought it unsafe for me to continue; in fact he would not allow me to proceed, even after the escort of 20 men came from the fort, at 5 A.M. Went out with a party and recovered Lieut. Daniels' body which was terribly mutilated, having been tomahocked and scalped, and had 22 arrows shot into it. They cut off one finger to procure a ring that was on it.

July 22nd-

Marched back towards Old Reno and met a large train about half way out. The Capt ordered it back, and intend starting all together on Monday. Burried Lieut D. in the grave yard at this place. Had command of the funeral escort, consisting of half of Co. B. The chaplain made some remarks at the grave. My opinion in reference to the noble Indian has changed lately; annihilation is now the word. Five Indians came in among our herd and tryed to stampede the mules but they would not stampede. It was a very bold act, but did not succeed. They did not attempt to shoot any of the herders. Wrote to Mrs. Daniels in reference to the death of her son.

July 23rd-

Marched to Crazy Woman's Fork in company with the two large gov. trains, overtaking Kirkendal's train which had started last evening. Camped on the west side of the creek near where Lieut Daniels was killed.

July 24th-

Marched to Clear Fork which is a magnificent mountain stream of the purest cold water. While nearing the stream Indians were seen and skirmishers thrown out. They proved to be Cheyennes and friendly, all had been up at Fort Reno (Fort

Assistant Guide and Interpreter, Eighteenth U.S. Infantry

James P. Beckwourth

HOW TO SWINDLE AND KILL THE CHEYENNES

In two hundren [*Arch.*] gallons there are one thousand six hundrend pints,* for each one of which the trader gets a buffalo robe worth five dollars! The Indian women toil many long weeks to dress these one thousand six hundrend robes. The trader gets them all for worse than nothing, for the poor Indian mother hides herself and her children in the forests until the effect of the poison passes away from the husbands, fathers, and brothers, who love them when they have no whiskey, and abuse and kill them when they have.

*A pint of Beckwourth's whiskey cost approximately six cents and, as he boasts in his autobiography, it was not uncommon for him to arrive in a Cheyenne camp with four kegs of whiskey and leave with over one thousand buffalo robes.

Bonner, *The Life and Adventures of James P. Beckwourth – Mountaineer, Scout, and Pioneer, and Chief of the Crow Nation of Indians.*

*Phil Kearny) and the chiefs had papers from Col. Carrington. Some of the chiefs
with the following euphonious names, "Pretty Bear," "Dull Knife," "Black Horse,"
&c, &c. After going into camp these men came into camp and in a short time
their squaws & youngsters came also. All begging, and having buffaloe robes
and dressed skins for sale & "swap." There were several hundred of them. They
were well dressed and I think they are better looking than the Sioux. Took a
smoke with them, all sitting in a circle. Capt Burrows gave them some flour and
sugar & coffee. Three of them rode back toward Kirkendal's train and soon came
back, with a note from the ox train saying that Kirkendal had been and was then
being attacked, and that they needed assistance. Capt. Marr and 4 or 5 men
rode to Fort Reno for aid. In the evening a few men rode up from the two trains
for an ambulance to bring up their wagon master who had been wounded. They
had killed one or two Indians, one of whom was the man with the red breches
that took such an active part in our fight. They said they saw my hat that I lost
in the chase the other day.*

July 25th-

*Arrived at Fort Reno (Fort Phil Kearny) about noon and met Col. C & Lt Dilsay
about a mile out. Met Capts Haymond & Ten Eyck & Bvt Capts Phisterer,
Brown & Adair. Col Kinney came out and met us before we started from camp
with about 70 men and a howitzer. I am to be assigned to his company. They
have a very fine place for a fort here. Nature sames to have made the place on
purpose. An elevated plateau about 600 ft by 800 ft overlooking both forks of
the Piney which are clear and pretty well wooded with cottonwood. Fine pine 3
miles distant, which they are hauling for the purpose of building a stockade.
They seem to have given up the idea of sending the troops out to the
Yellowstone for this winter.*

July 26th-

*Met Bvt Capt Bisbee & lady. Recd. order to report to comdg officer of Co. D. 2d
Batt. As a 1st Lieut. Met "Old Jim Bridger" one of the very few relics of the
mountaineers of former days. He is an old grey haired man and cant last long.
I had expected to see a blustering proud person, and was much surprised to
find him very unostentacious, poorly dressed & one of the cautious sort. He
says the Sioux would give 1500 ponies for his scalp. He has no confidence in
any of the Indians unless perhaps the Crows, who have never been known to
kill a white man. He has been in this country over 30 years & says "Long Hair"
a Crow Chief, gave him permission to hunt all through this country more than
20 yrs ago.*

July 30th-

*Had an alarum last night on the picket line, caused by a cow coming in without
giving the countersign.*

July 31st-

*Am informed that I will be Q.M. and Commissary at Fort Ransom (Fort C.F.
Smith). The post on the Yellowstone will not be established this year.*

Aug. 2nd-

*Am receiving Q.M. and Com. Stores. Packed 17 wagons for "Fort C.F. Smith"
Which is to be the name of the new fort on the Big Horn.*

Aug. 4th-

*Marched early, with a post train of 2 ambulances and 9 wagons, and a supply
train of 25 wagons. In addition to the two companies there is a detachment of 30
mounted men of the garrison who are to bring the train back. Camped near
where "French Pete" was killed and the garrison had a fight. The road was very
rough. The country is improving in appearance, the little swails having at least
brush growing in them. Saw no Indians.*

Lake DeSmet

Aug. 5th-

Marched early, and camped on Goose Creek. We are beginning to come into the country talked of so long – "the finest country in the world" – it would be better if there were more timber, but the grass is very fine. Saw a number of buffalo at a distance. Marr rode out and killed one. Sent out a cart and some men and brought in the hind quarters. I saw some very fine scenery. After going into camp a rain storm passed over the mountains. I cant describe the magnificence of it.

Aug. 6th-

Marched at 5 1/2 A.M. and camped on Tongue River, crossed one fork 2 miles before coming to camp. The water is very clear. The men caught quite a number of the finest fish, some of them trout, that would weigh two or three lbs. Marr Killed another buffalo. Had plenty of fresh meat for the men. The country is improving every day. This is a fine valley & the the scenery is magnificent.

Aug 7th-

Camped on Little Horn River. We saw any number of buffaloes today, and when we came over into the Little Horn Valley we found it covered with them. I went up on a butte and could see at least 10000 of them at one time. They were scattered over the country like herds of cattle, not in the compact manner that descriptions had led me to believe. Hurrah I am a Nimrod – I have killed my first buffalo. We wounded three or four. One of them attempted to make a charge but was too badly wounded.

Aug. 8th-

Camped on "Mud Cr." I think it is some 10 miles from Big Horn.

Aug. 9th-

Marched some 10 mls and camped on Rotten-grass Cr. We are still some 5 miles from Big Horn River. Day before yesterday passed the grave of George Pease from Chambersburg, who had been killed by Indians on Tongue River.

Captain
William J. Fetterman

A COMPANY OF REGULARS COULD WHIP A THOUSAND AND A REGIMENT COULD WHIP THE WHOLE ARRAY OF HOSTILE TRIBES

I, with three other officers, while riding out to view the country a few days since, fell into an ambuscade of Indians who fired a volley at us. Our escape was a very narrow one. Returning with a few Infantrymen who happened to be near gurading some wood choppers, we scoured the woods but the Indians had decamped. We are afflicted with an incompetent commanding offcier viz. Carrington, but shall be relieved of him in the reorganization, he going to the 18th and we becoming the 27th Infantry. We have four companies of Infantry and one of Cavalry at this post and we are favored with the presence of four ladies.

The locality of the post is pleasant being about 7000 feet above the sea. The atmosphere is very dry and is almost oppresively so to a new comer. The climate so far as we have experienced it is delightful. Today we have Spring like weather. The country is rough but abounds in game of every kind. Enroute from Laramie being mounted I had a very exciting buffalo chase, and wounded three, but they are very tenacious of life and would not die. Our table though scarcely supplied with Eastern delicacies is always provided with game of some description. While chasing the Indians the other day we passed buffalo, elk, antelope, wolves and a large bear, but were too intent after the nobler game to pay them any attention.

Extracts from Fetterman's letter to Dr. Charles Terry, dated November 26, 1866. Everett D. Graff Collection, The Newberry Library, Chicago, Illinois.

Guide, Eighteenth U.S. Infantry

Jim Bridger

DAMNED PAPER-COLLARED SOLDIERS

Colonel (Carrington), your men who fought down South are crazy! They don't know anything about fighting Indians.

James X Bridger his mark

Vestal. *Jim Bridger, Mountain Man.*

Aug. 10th-

Marched to the river and camped about 4 miles from the ford. The Colonel rode forward and selected a site for the fort. I think the river has an average width of about 80 yds. & is muddy and full of islands. The timber is mostly small, being (Bridger says) a second groth. The Col. Reports a good deal of pine near where the fort is to be. The valley on this side at this place is 2 1/2 miles wide. On the other it is more elevated and seems to be more broken.

Aug. 23rd-

Was on as officer of the day, but everything passed of lovely. Had a lovely moonlight night with the addition of a fine exhibition of the Aurora Borealis. Am quite busy making out vouchers for Q.M. Returns. Have some men burning charcoal for blacksmithing puposes.

Aug. 24th-

Rode down to the hay field and called on Capt. Marr's party. Thought I saw an Indian, but it turned out to be a small cottonwood bush swaying in the wind. When I came back found the camp excited by reports of Indians seen by Col. Kinny & others while out about 5 miles from camp.

Aug. 27th-

About 6 A.M. saw 7 horsemen approaching on the other side of the river. Informed the Colonel and then went down to the fording. They proved to be Indians and upon my calling over "How" the head man answered "How" and added Saronka. I knew from what I had read in "Astoria" that that was "Crow." I signified that that was all right and took the boat over for them. In the mean time others had been coming in and soon there were about 60 warriors and squaws on the bank. Brought over three warriors and their squaws and taking them up to the Colonel and there we tried to hold a confab with them but could not understand each other very well. However we learned that they belonged to a large party of Crows that were camped a short way down the river: That they were friendly and wanted papers &c. They were well dressed and the finest looking indians that I have ever seen. They all swam over the river and came up to camp. It was truly amusing to see them crossing the river. They stripped and tying their clothes either on their heads or in packs enclosed in a robe, they would swim over and bring them out dry. The packs were fastened by a lariat to the horse's neck and being very light floated nicely. They would start into the river on the horse's backs and after they had got them well started they would slide off and catch their horses by their tails and in that way, whooping and yelling, they came to the shore. They conducted themselves very peaceably and after we had given them some rations they departed.

Aug. 28th-

Ten buffaloes in sight at Reveille, two of them on the other side of the river. My horse broke his picket rope last night and as soon as I could catch him I rode down to the river intending to intercept them when they should cross over. Laid in wait about an hour when they moved up a few hundred yards above where I was and crossed to an island. While I was getting into position, a couple of men ran down from the camp and fired at them one of the balls striking one of them. Of course they returned to the other side of the river and as they were going up the opposite bank they recd. several more shots, one breaking the hind leg of one of

Fort Phil Kearny

51

Fort C.F. Smith

them. Another shot from my gun hit one in the back, dropping him for good. Just then Indians were reported approaching from the direction in which they had come yesterday. Ceased firing and in a short time they came up & seeing the wounded bull, with three legs starting away, gave chase. It was a fine scene and one spoken of by everyone who writes of Indians. The Indians are certainly bold riders and hard on horseflesh. In this case they ran up close and fired some arrows and then fired two guns which dropped him. I was somewhat provoked at their interfering in my hunting as we could easily have killed both of the buffaloes. Sent the cart over for our buff. (the Indians had appropriated the one they killed) and at the same time went over to bring over some of the Indians. They came up along the bank of the river singing one of their songs and I could not but remember the songs I heard in an Indian show in boyhood. They proved to be another body of Crows. We gave them papers & some rations and they came up and entered into trade with the sutler, exchanging robes for beads blankets &c. They say there is a village of 1500 Sioux on Tongue River, who have banded to put a stop to all travel on this road. They say these and the Arrapahoes have been at their camp trying to get them to enter into a treaty with them to carry out the same object. The Colonel held a long talk with them, telling them not to make peace with the Sioux until they should make peace with the whites, and promising that we would be good friends and would all live together in peace and intimating that we would back them up against the Sioux. They all jumped up saying "How," "How" and shaking hands all around. In the evening a train came up from the States. They think it doubtful whether we will receive a train with Q.M. Stores for some time, as they seem to be nearly frightened to death at the Fort.

Sept. 1st-

In the evening were somewhat surprised to see a mulatto ride into camp. He proved to be the redoubtable "Jim Beckwith" formerly chief of the Crows. He came to announce the approach of Genl Hazen Asst. Inspt. Genl. Dept. of the Platt. The Genl. arrived soon after, accompanied by a Lieut. formerly of his staff and who had recd. his appointment in the Regular Army while at Phil Kearney. The Genl. took dinner with us. Capt. Paxson Com Sub. Vols. was also with him on a kind of inspecting tour.

Lieutenant George W. Grummond

WE ARE SURROUNDED! A WARNING UNHEEDED

I moved rapidly forward on the Big Horn road [Bozeman Trail] accompanied by Lieutenant H. S. Bingham, 2nd U.S. Cav. and followed by Sergeant G. R. Bowers and two men of my command and one Sergeant of the 2nd U.S. Cav. About forty Indians were in our front and retreating rapidly before us. About two miles from where I left the Colonel commanding we overtook one Indian; Lieut. Bingham with his revolver wounded his horse; the Indian then jumped off, turned to the right towards some high bluffs about two miles off running very fast. Lieut. Bingham firing his last shot at him (and I having no weapon but my sword) we drew our swords and gave chase. We came up to him after a run of about one and a half miles and tried to cut him down but he was so active dodging our blows and running under our horses it was no easy matter. While thus engaged Lieut. Bingham raised his head and looked around and cried out to me: "We are surrounded." Looking up I saw as near as I could calculate about seventy Indians in our rear charging directly for us. We immediately wheeled our horses and putting spurs to them dashed towards a large bluff in our front, the only place where I could see an opening. I passed through this opening clearing the Indians about half a length of a horse . . .

The Indians now came pouring in from all directions and surrounded the hill, I judge from one hundred and fifty to two hundred. Part of them dismounted from their ponies and closed up all around us firing their arrows rapidly at us. The chances were now very desperate for us. I dismounted the three men and undertook to fight them until help should reach us; we fought in this manner about eight minutes; two of the men were now badly wounded and one horse and it was evident to my mind that five minutes more would finish us. The Indians were now within three rods of us and swarming all around us in every direction.

G. W. Grummond
Lieut. 18th U.S. Infantry
comdg Mounted Detachment.

From Grummond's December 9, 1866 report:
Engagement with Indians near Fort Philip Kearney [sic], D. T.
December 6th, 1866.

53

Mitch Boyer

WHY THE INDIANS KILLED THESE SOLDIERS

On my way to Fort C.F. Smith last Spring, a Sioux Indian came into my camp on the Little Horn River, remained with me that day and night and the next day, and told me all about the massacre (Fetterman Fight) . . . He stated that there were eight Indians killed on the battle ground, and about fifty wounded, and twenty-two of the wounded afterwards died. He also said that the soldiers fought bravely but huddling together it gave the Indians a better opportunity to kill them, than if they had scattered about. He said that the soldiers' ammunition did not give out, but they fired to the last. He said the Indians took all the ammunition the soldiers had left but some soldiers had no ammunition left . . . The great majority of Indians were Sioux. There were about 150 warriors of Cheyennes. There were about 60 Arrapahoes [*sic*]. I asked him why the Indians killed these soldiers. He said that the principal reason was that the whites were building forts in this country and traveling this road driving off their game, and if they allowed it to go on, in two years they would not have anything for their children to eat. Another reason was the principal Chief of the Missouri Sioux had died just before the massacre, and the bands had gotten together and determined to avenge his death. The chief's name was White Swan who died a natural death on the Powder River. He stated that there were 1800 [Indians] on the ground but only half of them engaged in the fight. That the fight did not last very long, about one hour. That some of the soldiers were a mile in advance of others, and when the Indians rose up from the ravines the advance soldiers were killed in retreating to the main body and that the main body huddling together were killed as before stated.

Testimony of Mitch Boyer, Records of the Special Commission to Investigate the Fetterman Massacre and the State of Indian Affairs, 1867. Exhibit F, pp. 3-4.

"Beckwith says there is something bad going to happen ."

THE DISASTER

Sept. 9th-

Beckwith and the four men came back. They left Genl. Hazen on the other side of the Yellowstone, all well.

Sept. 13th-

About 20 indians came down off the hills on the other side of the river and a few of them came down the road to the fording. I didn't like their looks at any time but the officers and Beckwith said they were Crows &c. Beckwith & myself went down to the ferry and he talked with one that came down to the bank, but when he saw the guard taking arms (I being officer of the day,) he ran away from the bank. Beckwith said they were Crows and wanted to go over to them. I saw that this would be the quickest way of finding out who they were, and got the canoe out and went over with him taking the precaution of taking 4 armed men with me. As soon as Beckwith had a few words of conversation with one of them he whispered to me that they were Sioux. I am free to confess that from that moment I didn't feel safe, and urged Beckwith to recross the river. He felt quite safe and wanted to talk. I stood it about 10 minutes until I saw some coming around on the right and left and then told "Jim" that "he must cut his talk short." During this time three or four others had come up and had said "how" and shaken hands. I wanted a couple of them to come over to camp, but they said the whites didn't love the Sioux and would not consent. They said they had been over to the Crows & had made a treaty with them & wanted to make peace with the whites through them, and that there was a Crow chief then with them going down to Tongue River to their village, where there were 1200 lodges. All this means that they had been over to get the Crows to make a treaty with them to clean out all white people from this road. Well I told them to send this Crow chief up and they said they would. We had not much more than got into our canoe, before they rode off about 200 yds from where we had talked and killed a miner that was coming down from the mountains with two horses loaded with game.

Sept. 14th-

Was roused out about 6 A.M. after I had been up & gone to bed again, by an alarm of Indians firing on the wood-detail down in the woods. Ordered "fall in" and in 4 seconds was on the way with 25 men. Again when we got down we learned that about 15 indians had chased one of Marr's men, and had come so near getting him that he had to leave his horse and take to the bushes, the Indians getting the horse, of course. He was slightly wounded by an arrow.

Sept. 18th-

Beckwith says there is something bad going to happen as his medicine did not act right last night. He has some of the Indian ideas of premonition and dreams, and a good deal more of cunning. He has undoubtedly imposed greatly on the Crows with whom he lived. The day passed without our knowing anything of anything bad having taken place. It is very cold unpleasant weather, snowing & raining all the time.

Sept. 21st-

Immediately after Reveille 25 men went out to the spot pointed out by Whalen, and found the bodies of the missing soldiers. They had evidently been waylaid and fired on while passing a large rock. From appearances the Corpl had been killed, by the first shot, but Fitzpatrick had run about a hundred yards and there been killed and horribly mutilated, having his skull crushed in and a number of arrows shot into him. The Corpl also had several arrows in him, in addition to two bullet wounds. Buried them in the afternoon, with military honors.

Oct. 20th-

Lt. B. met a few Crows, who told him that there were two white men in their village from this Post. I presume they are Beckwith and Thompson. I am glad to hear that there is any sign of their being alive. I had about given them up as dead.

Oct. 30th-

The Crows to the number of about 50 or 60 came in, in the evening. "Shane" the interpreter and Thompson who went with Beckwith came with them. We misunderstood the Indian who came in, in reference to Beckwith; they wished to tell us that he was dead, as we found much to our sorrow to be the case. Thompson says that he complained of being sick on the same evening that he left here, and soon after commenced bleeding at the nose. On his arrival at the village he and Thompson were taken into the lodge of "The Iron Bull" and were his guests while they remained. There Beckwith died and was burried by his hosts.

Oct. 31st-

Held a council with the principal Indians. They had a great deal to say, and from all I can see I am of the impression that if the government does not take decided measures very soon in regard to the Sioux, that the Crows will enter a league and for the first time wage war with the whites. If the proper number of troops could be sent out next spring, the Crows would be glad of an opportunity to pitch into the Sioux and give them a good whipping. But as it is now they are so few in number in comparison with the Sioux that they are afraid to make war, but would rather submit to a disgraceful peace.

Nov. 4th-

There are still a few Indians in camp and a few came in this morning. About the middle of the forenoon we saw wagons coming down the hill about 6 miles south of this and concluded at once that it was the Colonel. But as no one came in we were of the opinion that they were surrounded by Indians. This opinion was strengthened by seeing puffs of smoke that resembled smoke from guns. A small party went out and learned that it was a train from below bringing Q.M. Stores and a large emigrant train, all under charge of Lieut. Counselman, who is assigned to D. Co. as 2nd Lieut. They had come through without any trouble and the puffs of smoke seen were from cook fires. The Cheyennes and Arapahoes had come around them on the way up and said "good Cheyenne" &c but they wouldn't allow them to come in.

Nov. 19th-

Jim Leighton and a few Indians came in from the village. They say the village is some 20 miles distant. I forgot to say that two Arapahoes came in the other day with the Crows. They have left the Sioux and want to live friendly with the whites. There were some Cheyennes at the Crow village too but they were afraid to come. The Arapahoes to the number of 76 lodges joined the Crows yesterday and are going to trade with Smith. They (Cheyennes) are very angry because the Crows wont let them trade. The latter say that as soon as they (the Cheyennes) come to the fort and get permission from the Col to trade, they can do so and not before. The Colonel told me that Genl. Hazen reported in his written report to HdQrs that I was the best Quartermaster in the Department.

Dec. 5th-

Smith the Crow Trader sent the Colonel a letter, stating that the Crows who had been over at the Sioux village, had returned and brought news that large war parties of the Sioux were then returning, bringing large numbers of horses mules & cattle and great quantities of groceries, dry goods &c. They report the capture of Fort Reno and Bridger's Ferry, and say that they are going to attack Fort Phil. Kearney with 2000 warriors and then are coming here, and advise the Crows to move away immediately. Smith says many of the Crows spoke out and said they

Area where Fetterman and Brown were found

56

Colonel
Henry B. Carrington

THE DETAILS OF "FETTERMAN'S MASSACRE"

On the morning of the 21st utimo, at about 11 o'clock a. m., my picket on Pilot Hill reported the wood train corralled and threatened by Indians on Sullivant Hills, about a mile and a half from the fort . . . Upon tendering to Brevet Major Powell the command of Company C, United States Cavalry, then without an officer, but which he had been drilling, Brevet Lieutenant-Colonel Fetterman claimed by rank to go out. I acquiesced, giving him the men of his own company that were for duty and a portion of Company C, Second Battalion, Eighteenth United States Infantry. Lieutenant G. W. Grummond, who had commanded the mounted infantry, requested to take out the cavalry. He did so . . . I knew the ambition of each to win honor . . . Hence my instructions to Brevet Lieutenant-Colonel Fetterman, viz: "Support the wood train, relieve it, and report to me. Do not engage or pursue Indians at its expense. Under no circumstances pursue over the ridge," viz, Lodge Trail Ridge. To Lieutenant Grummond I gave orders to "report to Brevet Lieutenant-Colonel Fetterman, implicitly obey orders, and not leave him." Before the command left I instructed Lieutenant A. H. Wands, my regimental quartermaster and acting adjutant, to repeat these orders. He did so. Fearing still that the spirit of ambition might override prudence, as my refusal to permit 60 mounted men and 40 citizens to go for several days down Tongue River Valley after villages had been unfavorably regarded by Brevet Lieutenant-Colonel Fetterman and Captain Brown, I crossed the parade, and from a sentry platform halted the cavalry and again repeated my precise orders . . .

In half an hour the picket reported that the wood train had broken corral and moved onto the Pinery. No report came from the detachment. It was composed of 81 officers and men, including two citizens, all well armed, the cavalry having the new carbine, while the detachment of infantry was of choice men, the pride of their companies. At 12 o'clock firing was heard towards Peno Creek, beyond Lodge Trail Ridge. A few shots were followed by constant shots, not to be counted. Captain Ten Eyck was immediately dispatched . . . and just as the supporting party reached the hill overlooking the scene of action, all firing ceased. Captain Ten Eyck sent a mounted orderly back with a report that he could see or hear nothing of Fetterman, but that a body of Indians on the road below were challenging him to come down . . . He rescued from the spot where the enemy had been nearest 49 bodies, including those of Brevet Lieutenant-Colonel Fetterman and Captain F. H. Brown.

The scene of action told its own story. The road on the little ridge where the final stand took place was strewn with arrows, arrow heads, scalp-poles, and broken shafts of spears. The arrows that were spent harmlessly from all directions show that the command was suddenly overwhelmed, surrounded, and cut off while in retreat. Not an officer or man survived. A few bodies were found at the north end of the divide over which the road runs just beyond Lodge Trail Ridge. Nearly all were heaped near four rocks at the point nearest the fort, these rocks enclosing a space of about 6 feet square, having been the last refuge for defense . . . Fetterman and Brown had each a revolver shot in the left temple. As Brown always declared that he would reserve a shot for himself as a last resort, so I am convinced that these two brave men fell by each other's hand . . . Lieutenant Grummond's body was on the road between the two extremes, with a few others.

I give some of the facts as to my men . . . Mutilations: Eyes torn out and laid on the rocks; noses cut off; ears cut off; chins hewn off; teeth chopped out; joints of fingers cut off; brains taken out and placed on rocks, with members of the body; entrails taken out and exposed; hands cut off; feet cut off; arms taken out from sockets; private parts severed and indecently placed on the person; eyes, ears, mouth, and arms penetrated with spear-heads, sticks and arrows; ribs slashed to separation with knives; skulls severed in every form from chin to crown; muscles of calves, thighs, stomach, breast, back, arms, and check taken out; punctures upon every sensitive part of the body, even to the soles of the feet and palms of the hands . . .

It is the opinion of Dr. S. M. Horton, post surgeon, that not more than six were killed by balls . . . I have said enough; it is a hard but absolute duty.

I am Very Respectfully Your Obedt Servant
Henry Carrington
Colonel 18th U.S. Inf.
Comdg Post.

Henry B. Carrington. Official Report of the Philip Kearny Massacre, January 3, 1867 – Letters Received, Department of the Platte, Records of the United States Army Commands, Record Group 393, National Archives.

57

Lieutenant General
William Tecumseh Sherman

DESTROY ALL OF THE SAME BREED

Of course, this massacre should be treated as an act of war and should be punished with vindictive earnestness, until at least ten Indians are killed for each white life lost. You should prohibit all leaves of absence and put whom you please in command of the sub-districts. But, at once, there should be organized a strong force under your best commander and sent into the Indian country to avenge with terrible severity this and past acts of the Sioux. You must be fully prepared now, but if you need more men, let me know. If Indians can act in Winter, so can our troops and so they will if properly led. You should not allow the troops to settle down on the defensive, but carry the war to the Indian camps, where the women and children are, and should inflict such punishment that even Indians would discover they can be beaten at their own game. Of course, it is useless to find fault with officers there, but the truth should be ascertained and reported, but this should not delay the punishment of the Indians as a people. It is not necessary to find the very men who committed the acts, but destroy all of the same breed.

Sherman to General Philip St. George Cooke, December 28, 1866, Letters Received, Department of the Platte, Record Group 98, National Archives and Records Service.

58

"We must act with vindictive earnestness against the Sioux, even to their extermination, men, women and children. Nothing less will reach the root of the case."

LIEUTENANT GENERAL
WILLIAM TECUMSEH SHERMAN

From Sherman's telegram to General Ulysses S. Grant, directly after Fetterman's defeat.
Senate Executive Documents, 40th Congress, 1st session, No. 13, p. 27.

were on the side of the whites and would help them if the Sioux came. I was on as officer of the day and with the fatigue party piled logs all around the front and left of camp on the inside of the stockade, making quite a good place to shoot from.

Dec. 28th-

A Crow came in from the Sioux village and brought the news that the latter had attacked Fort Philip Kearney about 12 days ago. They sent a few men to dash up to the fort and then fall back. Over a hundred men followed them out and fell into ambush and were all killed. The Sioux say there were 113 in all. They had 1500 warriors. They say that after the fight some spies remained behind to watch what the white people would do. They saw them send a large party of horsemen out from the fort in the direction of a pine ridge, and soon after a large number of wagons went in the same direction, from which they argue that the fort has been abandoned, and they said they were gong to plunder it soon. They also say that a party went to Fort Reno and found the fort abandoned and saw the marks of where a great many trains had gone towards Fort Laramie.

Dec. 29th-

The Crows are still talking about the fight at Phil. Kearney. I think they are trying to intimidate us to see if we wont abandon this fort. The Crows made what they call "Dog Soldiers" yesterday. They are a kind of club, and have a good deal to say in the government. They say when the camp shall be moved and where they will go. They also prevent the young men from leaving camp to hunt and run away the buffalo before they can make a surround. They sent up a delegation to drive the squaws away from the fort. As soon as the squaws heard the "Dog Soldiers" song they hurried away as fast as they could.

Dec. 30th-

Two other Crows came back from the Sioux village. They reduce the number of the killed at Phil. Kearney to 97. The Sioux told them that they cut off that many noses, and carried them away in a buffalo robe, and counted them after they had gone away. The Sioux also told them that they had 12 warriors killed there and that 3 died on the road and 1 in the village. They said they left those 12 along side of the white men to see what the white people would do with them. This is a very unusual thing for Indians to do, and I am of the opinion that they were so hard pressed that they could not carry their dead off the field.

Dec. 31st-

The Sioux told the Crows to move away from here, as they were coming to fight this fort and they didn't want to fight them. They say they will come next moon, and think they will have no difficulty in killing us all.

Postscript-

Two Sergts of the 18th came in from Phil. Kearney on foot, carrying dispatches. They confirm the loss of Capts Fetterman & Brown & Lieuts. Grummond and Bingham, and some 90 men. There are 11 cos (companies) at Phil. Kearney, troops having been sent from Laramie. Carrington has gone to Fort Casper. Genl. Wessells is in command of the Mountain District, which has been reorganized. They have been giving us up as dead and I suppose we are so reported in the states. They had made repeated efforts to communicate with us but had failed.

Geo W Templeton

60

Fetterman Battlefield monument

February 7th, 1867

General of the Armies of the United States

Ulysses S. Grant

PREPARE AT ONCE FOR THE ABANDONMENT OF THE POSTS

I think it will be well to prepare at once for the abandonment of the posts Phil Kearny, Reno, and Fetterman* and to make all the capital with the Indians that can be made out of the change. In making this removal, it may be necessary to establish a new line of posts to protect travel from the railroad north from some point west of Cheyenne; your knowledge of the country will enable you to fix this to the best advantage; I would advise that but little confidence be placed in the suggestions of citizens who have made their homes in the territories, in selecting points to be occupied by troops. My experience is, and no doubt it is borne out by your own, that these people act entirely from selfish and interested motives . . . I recommend this early movement in the abandonment of the posts referred to because by delay the Indians may commence hostilities and make it impossible for us to give them up.

*On March 3, 1868, the day after he issued this recommendation, Grant added Fort C.F. Smith to the posts that were to be abandoned. Grant did not intend to abandon Fort Fetterman, and listed it by error.

Grant to Lieutenant General Sherman, March 2, 1868. Letters Received, Department of the Platte, Record Group 98, National Archives and Records Service.

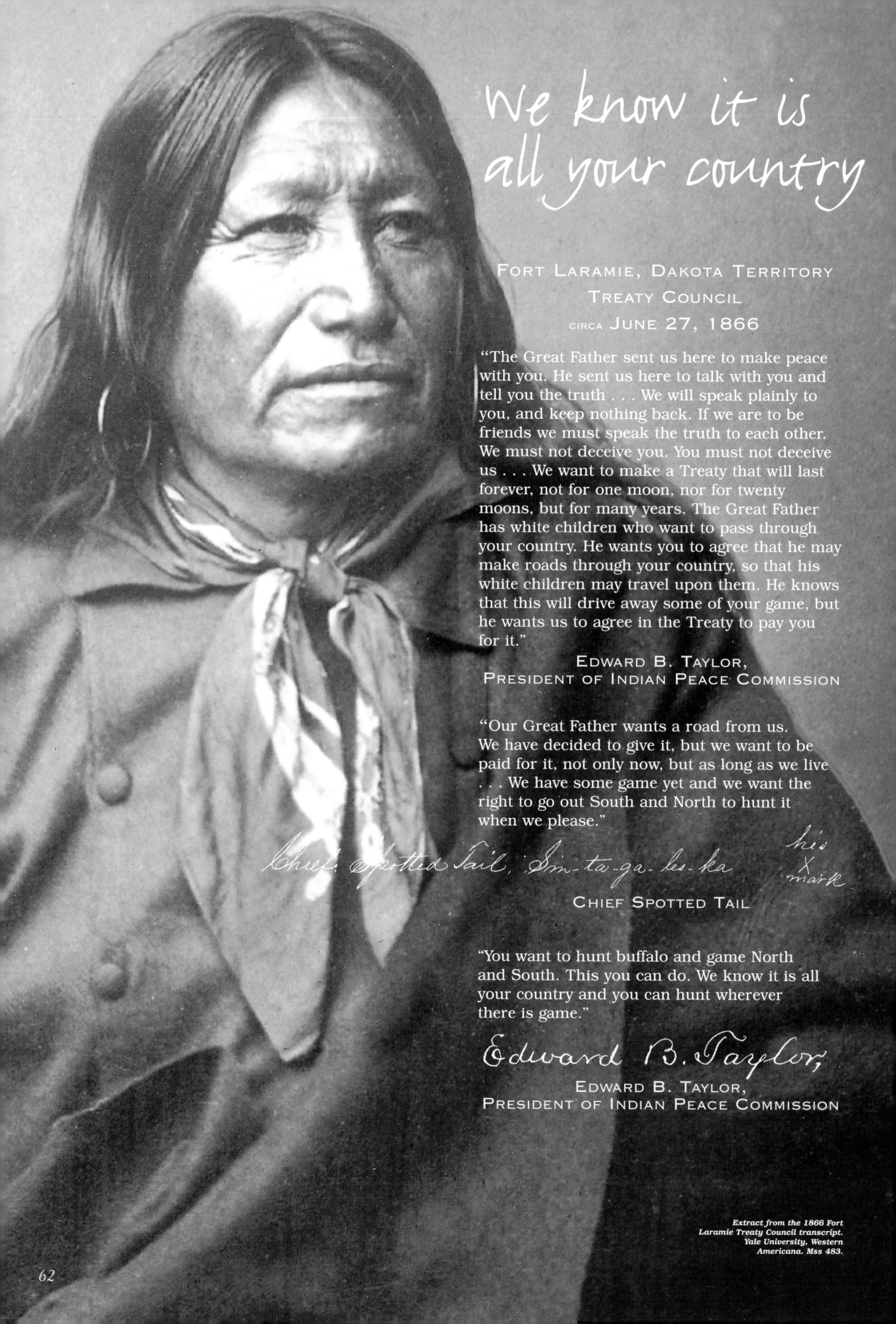

We know it is all your country

FORT LARAMIE, DAKOTA TERRITORY
TREATY COUNCIL
CIRCA JUNE 27, 1866

"The Great Father sent us here to make peace with you. He sent us here to talk with you and tell you the truth . . . We will speak plainly to you, and keep nothing back. If we are to be friends we must speak the truth to each other. We must not deceive you. You must not deceive us . . . We want to make a Treaty that will last forever, not for one moon, nor for twenty moons, but for many years. The Great Father has white children who want to pass through your country. He wants you to agree that he may make roads through your country, so that his white children may travel upon them. He knows that this will drive away some of your game, but he wants us to agree in the Treaty to pay you for it."

EDWARD B. TAYLOR,
PRESIDENT OF INDIAN PEACE COMMISSION

"Our Great Father wants a road from us. We have decided to give it, but we want to be paid for it, not only now, but as long as we live . . . We have some game yet and we want the right to go out South and North to hunt it when we please."

Chief Spotted Tail, Sin-ta-ga-les-ka his X mark

CHIEF SPOTTED TAIL

"You want to hunt buffalo and game North and South. This you can do. We know it is all your country and you can hunt wherever there is game."

Edward B. Taylor,

EDWARD B. TAYLOR,
PRESIDENT OF INDIAN PEACE COMMISSION

Extract from the 1866 Fort Laramie Treaty Council transcript. Yale University, Western Americana. Mss 483.

Native American

Register of Claims Filed and Allowed and Warrants Drawn on Treasurer,

Claim No.	NAME OF CLAIMANT	DATE OF FILING			AMOUNT OF CLAIM	NATURE OF CLAIM	DATE ALLOWED			No. of Warrant	AMOUNT ALLOWED
		MONTH	DAY	YEAR			MONTH	DAY	YEAR		
11107	Lemons, J. Y.	July	8	1912	8 30	Road Work	19 Aug	22	1912	614	
11149	Larsen, Jr.	"	16	"	4 00	Bridge Work # 27	"	22	"	995	
11150	Leetch, Will	June	29	"	25 92		"	22	"	996	25
11184	Lanham, G. W.	May	27	"	63 00				1912	707	63
11311	Letcher, B.	Aug	31	"	4 00				1912	673	
11243	Lawrence, James	Sep	5	1912	4		18 Oct	1	1912	754	
11244	Lichte,	"	5	1912	4 00	do	Oct	1	"	755	
11233				1912	1 60	Mdse	Oct	1	"	745	
					5	Appraising Road	Nov				
11289	Lexington	Nov		"	5 00	Auto Livery	"	"			
11310	Larson	Nov	12	"	2 00	Grading	"	16	"		2
11311	Letcher, B.	Aug	31	"	4 00	do	"	27	"		
11312	Lange - Adolph	Oct	25	"	17 00	Roadwork	"	16	"	6	
11341	Lecher - Pete	Nov	9	"	16 00	Bridge work	"	16	"	40	
11371	Lindeman	Oct	28	1912	190 30	Fuel delinquent	Dec	9	"	805	
11372	do	Nov	2	"	80	Printing Ballots					
11373	Lechers M	"	14	"	21 00	Three past term					21
11374	Lexington	"	26	"	10 40	Grading				806	10
11420	Lingel	"	6	"	4 00	Election					
11421		"	6	"	6 00					84	
11422		"	6	"	9 20						
11494	Lexington	Nov	11	"	16 00	Appraising	"	203	"		16
11495	Lecher - Casper	Dec	7	"	24 00	Roadwork # 27	"	9	"		24
11496	Lester W	"	9	"	4 00	Appraising Road					
11497	Lecher - Mishie	Oct	26	"	4	Work	"	11	"		4
11498	Lichte - Fred	Nov	9	"	14 00						14
11499	Landmark John	Dec	1	"	21 00					7	21
11549	Lichte, Hugo				3 20					61	
11574	Lacin that					Mdse				882	
11645	Lowry, J	Jan			8 00	Shed for team	Jan 14		1913	614	
11658	Lexington,				48		Feb		1913	958	
11681								21	"	938	
11733	Lexington						June	16	"	840	
11734	Lockler,										
11745	Lingel	June	16	"		Road work Napier	"	16	"		
11894	Linderman Co	Apr	7	"		Printing	Aug	13	1913		
11897	do	Feb	4	"	6 47	do	Aug	13	1913		
11898	do	May	3	"	3 40	do	"	13	1913		
11905	Lowry Geo. W.	"	7	"	8 00	Bailiff	"	13	"	1031	
11904	do	Feb	1	"	14 00	do	Aug	13	1912		14
11896	Lang, D. L.	"	28	"	8 00	Election Service	Aug	13	1912	1029	
11902	Loewenthal Bros	Mar	25	"	10 88	Supplies	"	13	"	1034	10
11900	Linderman Con	Jan	24	"	20 15	Printing	Aug	13	1913	1030	20

Hundred soldiers killed Fight

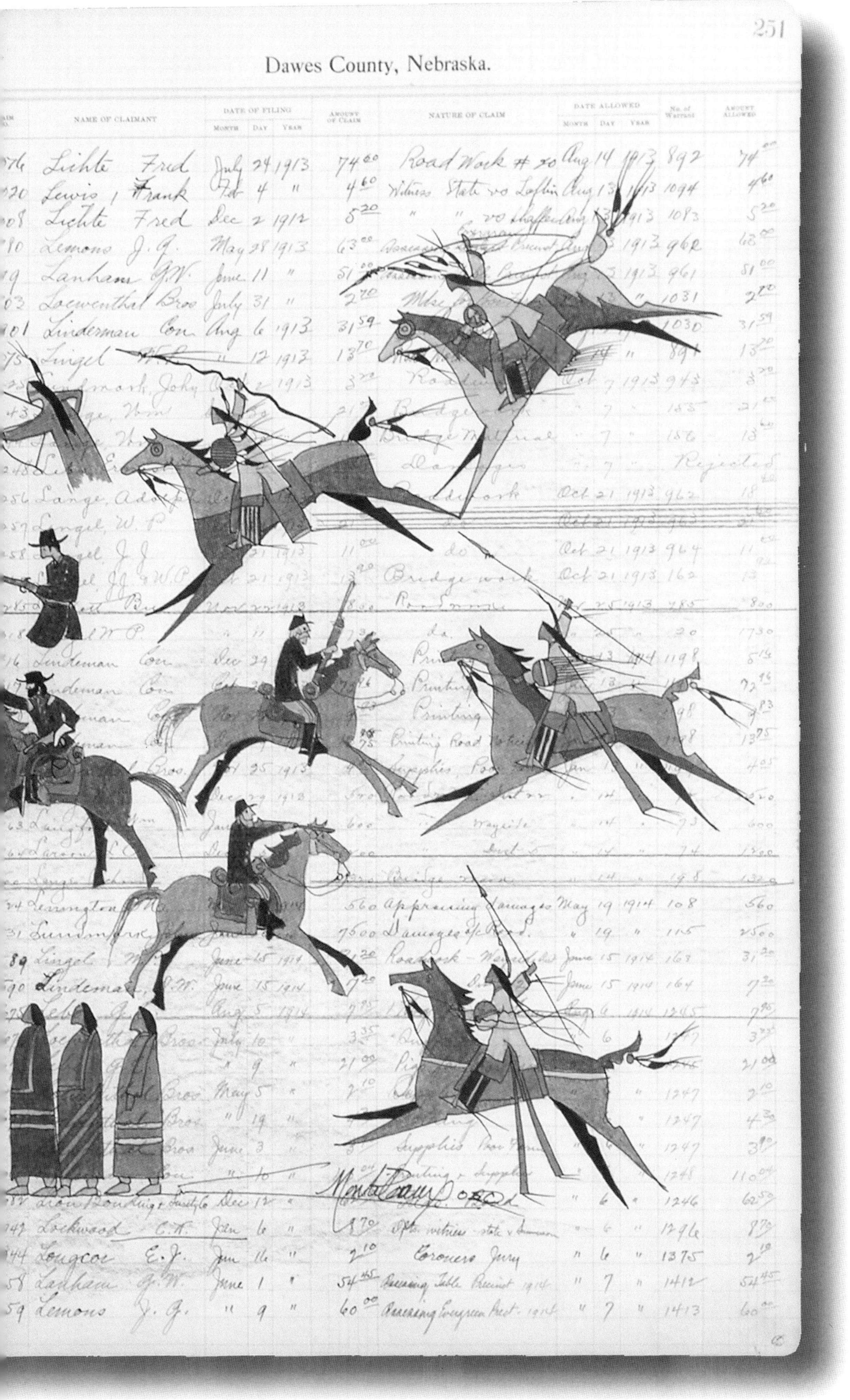

ETTERMAN FIGHT *by Donald F. Montileaux*

I counted my first coup that day.[1] One walking soldier had a dog face, more than the others I saw laying around him, and when I slapped his face with my lance it left no mark because of the hair that covered his skin. I stopped and looked down at him. His eyes were as those of a fish, like mist on water, and I saw that there was life in them. I looked into those eyes, the eyes of a man, not a fish. He was staring up at the sky when I counted coup on him but as I sat above him my pony shied and so for him I had replaced the sky. He watched me now, knowing that I had seen that he was alive. The ve'hó'e[2] always looked sick to me, but this one's skin looked more dead than usual, the cold was making it the color of a jay's wings. He had two arrows in his body, one in his ribs on the side of his shiny round-things,[3] and the other in the soft part at the top of his leg, below a black bag with shining metal on it. Laying on his back between two big rocks, I thought maybe he could be floating away from here. I do not know if he was crying or if his eyes were always of water, and then I saw a story in his eyes that my grandmother would tell about how before the buffalo some of our people had lived near lots of water and eaten fish.[4]

     I'll remember that day by the sounds. When we first charged, one of my pony's hoofs punched through some ice on the creek and at that moment I feared that he might break a leg. It was the same sound the walking soldier's head made when a Little Star[5] (Oglala Lakota) hit it with a club. I was not the walking soldier's sky anymore. His eyes went away. "Nephew, answer him!" my uncle said. "He wants to know why you did not bring a knife." The Little Star took the kill, but in our way my uncle claimed the second coup, which he did as the Little Star called out to me. I could not make their talk, but my uncle could. The Little Star pulled up what he could of the walking soldier's head and took his scalp. I had not thought of taking it. I just thought how much the walking soldier reminded me of a starving coyote I had once seen die as she gave birth. I don't know if the Little Star kept the

Hundred-soldi

scalp, I think he may have left it on a rock, such was the feeling that day. It did not seem so easy to me to kill a man when you were looking into him and him into you, although that is what many of our men had to do. Our great prophets, Erect Horns and Sweet Medicine, who brought to us Ésevone and the Maahótse,[6] our Sacred Bundles and ways that were given to us by the Great One, had told of the coming of these times and now they were upon us. The ve'hó'e first came in the Time of the Dogs but they did not stay.[7] Now we knew what they wanted, and for them to have it we had to lose life itself – the ways of

The original location of Julesburg, Colorado

our people given by the Great One – and it was our sacred duty to protect them.

I had not been in a fight such as this before, but I had been to war. I had not seen more than fourteen winters when we were in the south country, in the winter camp on the Bunch of Timber River (Smoky Hill River). It was there in the Big-Hard Face-Moon (December) that they came, wounded, cold, hungry and terrified, those who had escaped from Dry Creek (Sand Creek).[8] These were my grandmother's people and it hurt my eyes to see them, and it still hurts my ears to hear of it for the wailing of all in mourning still comes back to me. They had done nothing and their young men were out hunting when the soldiers came and for two days shot them down and butchered them like antelope in a pit. Most of them were women and children and old ones. The soldiers injured many and chopped them all up, so the survivors could not even recognize their dead relatives. A grandmother was scalped and left to stumble among the dead and dying with the skin of her forehead hanging down over her eyes.[9] They cut babies out of women's bellies and cut out the under parts of women and wore them on their hats and hung them from their horses. This is not all they did but I do not want to say anymore. In council it was decided that a pipe should be taken to the Inviters (Lakota Sioux),[10] the Sage Men (Northern Arapahos) and Cloud Men (Southern Arapahos),[11] and so it was done. Our men rode to Turkey Creek (Solomon River) with the pipe and the Sioux, the Northern and Southern Arapaho, all smoked it. We were at war with the ve'hó'e.

We came together in a great camp on Cherry Creek and it was here that the Little Star, Pawnee Killer, said that he wished to attack the ve'hó'e town (Julesburg) on Tallow River (South Platte River). Tall Bull and White Horse, the Dog Soldier chiefs, were with him and soon it was agreed. We were strong then, so strong that not even the coldest moons would stop us, and I do not remember that we ever went to war in the winter before this.

Dawson South Bend, Sand Creek

The Sioux had smoked our pipe first and so their wise ones were given the honor of leading the rest of us. As we moved all of the people were shielded by the brave ones of our military societies, the Kit Foxes, Elk Horn Scrapers and Bowstrings rode at the head and both sides of us, and the Dog Men protected our backs. Near White Butte Creek (Summit Springs) the chiefs consulted with the war leaders and there decided how we would fight. The soldier fort (Camp Rankin) was nearer the mouth of Lodgepole Creek than the town and so our men were asked to attack the soldiers first and then to plunder the town. This is why young boys and women were permitted to go along, for we were to take ponies for the plunder and carry it back for the poor people in camp. The soldier fort was inside a great dam of mud and logs and so our men had to fool the ve'hó'e into attacking them. Many said they would do it but Big Crow was chosen

s–Killed–Fight

BY SERLE L. CHAPMAN

for this work, work which was not going to be easy for the land there was flat and open with little cover. Big Crow was an Elk man and he now carried one of the crooked lances that only the bravest men of the Elk Horn Scrapers military society held. Standing-in-the-Water had carried that crooked lance before the soldiers butchered him at Sand Creek. Standing-in-the-Water and White Antelope died close together. White Antelope was also an Elk man and they told us that he tried to stop the soldiers at Sand Creek even though he had no weapons; he stood before them with his arms folded singing his medicine song as they charged. I don't think I ever saw him but he must have been a brave man. Both my father and uncle were Elk Horn Scrapers and I too became one.

Big Crow chose nine men to ride with him against the soldier fort while the rest were to hide and wait for his party to lead the soldiers into the sand hills where they would be surrounded and rubbed out. Our scouts, who we called wolves, watched everything from a hill that had grown higher than the others to the south of the fort. Big Crow, Starving Elk, Old Crow and the others rode down the big ravine below the wolves, and with the sun they charged a handful of soldiers who were outside the fort. Even from a great distance I could tell it was Big Crow leading on his bay. The sun was only waking but became a flame in the white-metal shining on his horse's bridle[12] and he was fond of a white man's red shirt which he would wear with red cloth in his hair. All was well, for as these soldiers ran into the fort, a lot of pony soldiers rode out of it after Big Crow's men. Closer and closer they came, riding straight for the hills, but then some young men lost patience and galloped out from where we were hiding. Our leaders were not happy with them but nothing could be done, it was time to fight. The pony soldiers turned back to their fort and got mixed up with some of our men. I still do not know why some of these soldiers got off their horses to fight on foot but whatever it was, it caused them to be killed.[13] Over half of the soldiers got away but it was

A Dash for the Fort, *Big Crow's ledger drawing depicting his pursuit of William M. Hudnut between Julesburg Station and Camp Rankin.*

not all bad as many of our men had seen this and were already riding on the town. Some attacked a string of wagons on the white man's road which seemed to confuse the pony soldier chief (Captain Nicholas J. O'Brien), then another party sent up a cry and charged at a stage coach. Here I saw some white men run faster than any I have seen since. They ran from their town of cedar logs to the fort, beating the soldiers who had come back out to fight over the wagons, but they were soon running away. Big Crow nearly caught one of the ve'hó'e; he had long hair on his face and he was riding a buckskin horse. This dog-faced man[14] had charged out of the stage station, and when we got there we found some of our people eating hot food! It was funny to see these fighting men who were all prepared for battle sitting around a long table enjoying the white men's breakfast. The ve'hó'e had left their stage station, a coach, their singing wires and piles of plunder, and so we packed all we could onto our ponies while the men cut the wires.

The whites became scared and so the soldiers set fire to the prairie to try and stop us, but it was us who burnt them along the Tallow and Moon Shell (North Platte) Rivers.

You could ride for two days and still look upon night as dawn, such were the flames in the valley. So many raids were made on ranches, wagons and telegraph lines that soon the soldiers could not use the talking wires, and so to taunt them we went back to their town on Tallow River and then camped on their wagon road to Denver.[15] It was during these raids that Little Bear and Man-Riding-on-a-Cloud found nine white men who had cut up our relatives at Sand Creek; they had been soldiers and carried the scalps of Little Coyote and White Leaf. We knew this because Little Coyote wore a strange shell in his hair and White Leaf was a light-haired one. These ve'hó'e were left to stare at the ground they had bloodied as Little Bear and Man-Riding-on-a-Cloud wiped the tears of Little Coyote's and White Leaf's relatives. The chiefs said enough had been done here and decided to move north to the Black Hills and our strong hunting grounds near the Black Dust River (Powder River). We made our way across the Moon Shell and Surprise (Niobrara) Rivers, and the men cut down the talking wires wherever they were found. The soldiers tried but could not stop us, and so we went all the way to Bear Lodge River (Belle Fourche River). Spotted Tail's Inviters untied their ponies' tails here and went to make meat, but others joined us, including my uncle who had come from our people on the Black Dust River. After the soldiers' town was attacked, the chiefs had sent runners out from our camp on the Red Shield Society River (Republican River) to find our people, the Notamé-ohméseheestse,[16] and the Little Star people, who were the Sioux we knew best, and now the criers told of their return.

It was good to see my uncle; he was dressed as we were and his hair was all coiled up like a horn.[17] These southerners wore some white-man clothes but we did not, and their talk sounded queer to us, though my grandmother being a southerner could understand it all. I was happy that we would soon be back in the heart of our own country. The runners had told them some of what happened at Sand Creek but there was much more to tell. Even those of us who were there on the Bunch of Timber River when the survivors came did not hear it all and it was not until we crossed to the Black Dust River and the River of Tongues (Tongue River) in the Leaf Moon (May) that more was told. The Sage People who had been with us had joined their relatives here after we left the Black Hills and they had with them a very strange person, a white man with no fingers who became one of their strong fighting men.[18] He said that after Sand Creek the soldier chief had taken all of the scalps and the parts his soldiers had butchered from our relatives' bodies and shown them to many white people in a big house in Denver who all made a loud cheering and were happy.[19] It made our blood hot and though we were ready to fight our ponies were not, they were weak from crossing so many rivers, and so we waited for them to make fat again.

The Cheyennes all came together here, we northerners, the Notamé-ohméseheestse, and our southern relatives, the Heévaha-taneo'o.[20] It was a great camp and my father told us boys to watch and learn. He said that twenty-two winters had passed since all of us Cheyennes, the Tsetsehésestahase, had gathered like this in the north country, when our people went against the Sósoné'eo'o (Shoshone). In my eyes our lodges made a powerful crescent moon with the opening facing the Holy Mountain – Bear Butte – the ten bands of our nation each clustered in their ancient places, the places the Four Sacred Persons had guided our people to.[21] We were on the north side of the entrance, and in the belly of the crescent moon, in the south, stood the two sacred lodges – to the west the lodge of the Sacred Buffalo Hat, and to the east the lodge of the Sacred Arrows. Many of the people here had been in the presence of the two Sacred Covenants when the Chiefs were renewed on Turkey Creek, and Little Wolf was made the Sweet Medicine Chief, in the summer before the massacre on Sand Creek. Here in this land of health and happiness we lived as many generations had lived before us, with ceremony and feasting and dances. Some Óoetaneo'o (Crows) came in the night to steal horses but they did not choose well. Among Bull Bear's herd were many wild ponies, and one of the Crows was tricked by a young black stallion who was their leader. The Crow wanted him, but the black stallion did not wish to be a Crow pony and so he bucked the Crow off and started screaming. Gentle Horse, Black Kettle's younger brother, took a few men and soon came back with Crow scalps. This is how things had always been, without fear of the white men because it was as if they did not exist. Of course, we knew that the white men would come here one day. Our men had already fought with some of them who wanted to make a road (the Bozeman Trail) through the buffalo by the Black Dust River,[22] and so our chiefs and war leaders decided that we should fight them before they came back to kill our women and children.

Wolves were sent back to the Black Dust River, while one of our military societies, the Crazy Dogs, guided everybody down the River of Tongues where camp was made beneath the Big Sheep Mountains (Bighorn Mountains). The Crazy Dogs soldiered the buffalo hunt there and when enough meat had been made for the next moon the chiefs told them to move the camp to Lodgepole River (Clear Creek). The Little Star people had some of their best men in this camp and I think The-Man-Whose-Enemies-Are-Even-Afraid-to-

Red Cloud

I WANT THE GREAT FATHER TO MAKE NO ROADS

Look at me. I was a warrior on this land where the sun rises, now I come from where the sun sets. Whose voice was first sounded on this land – the red people with bows and arrows. The Great Father says he is good and kind to us. I can't see it. I am good to his white people. What has been done in my country, I do not want, do not ask for it. White people going through my country. The white children have surrounded me and have left me nothing but an island. When we first had this land we were strong, now we are melting like snow on the hillside while you are growing like spring grass. I have two mountains in that country I want the Great Father to make no roads through, the Black Hills and Bighorn Mountains. I was born at the forks of the Platte and I was told that the land belonged to me. The Oglalas are the last who come here but I came here to hear and listen to the Great Father's words. They have promised me traders, but we have none. When you send goods to me they would steal all along the road so when it reaches me it was only a handful. They hold a paper for me to sign and that is all I get for my goods. I know now the people you sent out there are all liars. Look at me, I am poor and naked.

Mahpiya Luta

Compiled from the Transcript of Interviews with Red Cloud in Washington, June 3 – 7, 1870, National Archives and Record Service, Record Group 75, Letters Received, Upper Platte Agency.

See-His-Horses was their leader. They also had Red Cloud, one of their band leaders, who had been a big fighting man among them when he was young. I remember that at this camp somebody made a present to Red Cloud of some long-glasses that they had captured on Tallow River and he was much pleased with them. Red Cloud did not seem to be a fighting man anymore as the Little Stars had other, younger men, who had been given that work. I knew two of these because they became Elk Horn Scrapers; one was their light-haired one, Crazy Horse, and the other was the son of The-Man-Whose-Enemies-Are-Even-Afraid-to-See-His-Horses, and it was he who led them in the fights that were to come on the Moon Shell River. I admired them but did not think them stronger than Little Wolf, Roman Nose, Wild Hog, High-Back-Wolf or many of our own brave men who were chosen to make the slim-horned moon in the Shield Dance our military societies held on Lodgepole River. Our men had journeyed back and forth from our camps to the Moon Shell River, showing the ve'hó'e that they did not fear them, and now they were being honored in the Shield Dance, the bravest standing closest to the fire, the others formed like a bow behind them.

Near the soldier town with the walking-across-logs (Platte Bridge Station), Yellow Wolf Chief's party took two hundred and fifty mules from the ve'hó'e, and Bear's Tail and Woman's Heart brought soldier scalps for the people to dance. There was little honor in taking the short-hair of the ve'hó'e and we did not do it often. All of the parties who had been sent to watch the white man's road (the Oregon-California Trail) had returned with horses, mules, strange food wrapped in metal, and white-man cloth that the women made into fine shirts. Most agreed that the best place to strike the ve'hó'e was the soldier town with the walking-across-logs on the Moon Shell River.[23] The chiefs held council during the Shield Dance; they were for attacking the soldier town with the walking-across-logs, and so they placed the final decision in the hands of the military societies who said it would be so. Crazy Mule, one of our holy men, advised moving camp to Foolish Woman River (Crazy Woman Creek) and this was done. The day before we left to fight was one I shall never forget. All of our military societies prepared for war and made a strong heart parade around the camp. The Crazy Dogs rode first and the eagle feather trails of their antelope horn bonnets floated like smoke across their ponies' backs, the sacred rattles on which the sun's paths flowed above the moon and stars rubbing against their long, red lances. Behind them, Little Wolf and Roman Nose held the Crooked Lances of the Elk Horn Scrapers, and Tall Bull's and White Horse's Dog Soldiers followed the rest, the bravest southerners and northerners together. We left with the next sun and with its passing went that vision of our military societies, for only in memory did I see such a parade again.

It took three sleeps to reach the fort. The Crazy Dogs soldiered all of the Cheyennes and Sage Men on the march but it was the Elk Horn Scrapers who were to lead the charge. The Little Stars and the other Sioux had more men but the Heévaha-taneo'o had better weapons, they had been around the white men more and so had some guns. Our leaders thought that these soldiers here could be tricked like the others and so, again, a small party of maybe ten men were sent to fool the soldiers and bring them over the walking-across-logs to their deaths. Many Cheyenne women had traveled with the men, two hundred or more, and some followed to watch from the hills. I was with them but wishing to be in the fight. It was peculiar to see our men not riding to battle; the Crazy Dogs had made them all dismount and walk their horses into position as so many riders would have brought a big cloud of dust the soldiers would have seen. It was not good; the soldiers would not come out and they fired a thunder wagon toward us.[24] On this day we lost High-Back-Wolf. One of our priests, White Bull, a powerful man with mysterious medicine, had advised all to keep metal away from their mouths for if they did not they would be killed by white man arrows, the soldiers' bullets. As a young man White Bull had been a Crazy Dog but now he was an Elk Horn Scraper. He wore two eagle feathers and dragonflies flew up and down his leggings between the sun of the day and the sun of the night. I was a little afraid of him. It is said that High-Back-Wolf was sent to bring our men back from the walking-across-logs, but New Dog told him that he would rather die than run from the ve'hó'e and so they stayed to fight. High-Back-Wolf forgot White Bull's warning and when he charged the soldiers a Sósoné'e shot him.[25] He did not die right away and so New Dog tried to hide him in the brush until morning because it was difficult to take him across the river in the dark. Some soldiers found him and had started to cut him up, but Crazy Head was able to get his body before they had finished.

Crazy Head brought High-Back-Wolf back to his father that morning and we did not attack that day, only the wolves stayed to watch and taunt the soldiers. Our leaders said we would try again the next day, which we did. The young men were told not to break cover before the soldiers had been tricked into chasing the scouts, and that if they did they would be quirted and their ponies might be taken or killed. Some of the hills surrounding the fort were all broken up and the Elk Horn Scrapers hid in those canyons to the north with some

*Above: Platte Bridge. Right: Platte Bridge
Station, later renamed Fort Caspar.
Ledger:* The Bravest Coup, *Tomahawk's
depiction of the Cheyenne attack on
Sergeant Custard's wagon party.*

of the Little Stars, the rest of them waiting in a dry creek bed to the east of the walking-across-logs. The Dog Soldiers covered themselves in the tall grasses along the river west of the fort and the Sage Men went along the creek. Red Cloud watched from the hills with his long-glasses, and with him were Morning Star,[26] The-Man-Whose-Enemies-Are-Even-Afraid-to-See-His-Horses, Box Elder and some of the older leaders. The ten scouts were to bring the soldiers along the road to our men, then they would charge and the soldiers would be caught in the trap by the others and cut off from the walking-across-logs. All were ready soon after the sun but the soldiers would not come out and chase our scouts, and two soldiers stood on the other side of the walking-across-logs waving High-Back-Wolf's scalp on a long stick. Then, with the sun not halfway above, pony soldiers on gray horses trotted onto the walking-across-logs and turned toward the Dog Soldiers.[27] It is good, they are riding, they won't go back, I sang to myself. Little Wolf and Lame White Man signalled the attack from the hills, and Little Horse led the Elk Horn Scrapers' charge out of the canyons behind them. The Dog Soldiers attacked first, and the pony soldier chief (Lieutenant Caspar W. Collins) whipped his American horse, a big gray that was crazy, to face them. Then the Little Stars put up their war cry and rode down on them, and the pony soldiers made two lines and galloped back towards the walking-across-logs, but they became lost in the whirlwind of our men, their cries, and the calls of so many eagles, the war songs from the Dog Soldiers' eagle bone whistles. Some were knocked off but some kept riding, then the soldiers in the fort brought the thunder wagon to the river. I could not see what was happening until the pony soldier chief broke free and then rode back into the fighting, and it was as if his horse wanted more fighting and he could not stop it. The next time I saw him he had an arrow sticking out of his forehead, and when he fell Slow Bull took his horse.[28] The soldiers were getting away and so our southern relatives started shooting down at them, the bullets flying very fast and our men sending arrows with them. Maybe two handfuls of soldiers were killed before the rest crossed the river, the walking soldiers at the fort joining in with guns that shot faster than any I had seen before this, and we let it go.[29]

There was some bad feeling as the men came together in the hills. Many southerners were angry and said the Little Stars stopped fighting and let the soldiers get away. A lot of our men agreed, but the Little Stars said they were not women and that they quit because they were being hit by Cheyenne bullets and arrows. One man said that some of the Little Stars were friends with the pony soldier chief who we shot in the head, and later I found that was true, but I do not know if this was why they let them get away.[30] It was here that some Cheyennes vowed never to fight alongside the Sioux again. Some never forgot this, but others said it was foolishness and that it was making their ears hurt. Roman Nose did not need to talk to be heard and those who saw him became quiet. The wolves had signalled from the hills that soldiers and wagons (Sergeant Amos Custard's wagon train) were coming from the north and he was going to stop them. Roman Nose had run his white war horse and it was eager, pacing on its second wind with blue lightning streaking down its legs and an enemy scalp dancing below its jaw. His war bonnet trailed down both flanks of the horse, and on the heart side the eagle feathers were white with dark spots and on the other side they were red and black. A single buffalo horn curled from the center of the brow-band and a kingfisher flew there, with a hawk tied to the east, a swallow to the south, and a bat at the northeast.[31] Each of these brought Roman Nose powers: the bat gave him eyes in the dark and swiftness; the swallow flies close to the ground and darts fast to confuse the enemy so when they shoot at the swallow he is no longer there; and the kingfisher hits the water in such a way that when he leaves the water it heals, so the kingfisher brings the gift to heal bullet wounds like the water. White Bull made this war bonnet for Roman Nose and it is said that Thunder came to White Bull in a dream, and with him was a hawk carrying a soldier's long knife and a gun. Thunder gave White Bull this knowledge – how the bonnet was to be made without any white-man things, and the paint that must be worn, and the ceremony that went with it. The bottom half of Roman Nose's face was painted black with charcoal from a tree that had been struck by lightning, and across his forehead was paint from yellow earth, and over his nose was the red of buffalo fat mixed with earth from the Red Paint River (Cheyenne River). Roman Nose's body was spotted with yellow hail paint, for now he wore Thunder's war bonnet.

When they saw Roman Nose, the hearts of the enemy became weak but ours became strong. He, too, was an Elk Horn Scraper, and how I wished to be one. Today I was ready to be a man and my father knew this. He called me to him and I rode to the wagons behind him and my uncle, Roman Nose leading all of us Cheyennes. We came upon them quickly but they were ready, shooting their fast guns from behind the wagons and piles of boxes and sacks they had made. Left Hand, Roman Nose's brother, had started this fight before we got there. He had chased some soldiers into the river but there were too many for him to kill and they shot him. I do not think Roman Nose knew this when he called for those with guns to move closer to the soldiers and for the rest to stay back. There was much shooting and waiting, and then Roman Nose rode forward and said that he was going to empty the soldiers' guns, and after that we should all charge. This is when I think he knew his brother had been killed. He galloped in front of the soldiers and rode four times around the wagons but none could hit him or Wolf Tongue or Twins who were following. On Roman Nose's signal the soldiers were rubbed out by the Cheyennes.[32] There was so much anger that this was done before I had even kicked my pony forward.

Many thought this was enough and untied their ponies' tails, but others were angry about their relatives the soldiers had killed at the wagons, and so those men said they would stay and wipe their tears.[33] The rest of us moved back to the Foolish Woman River and all talked about the fighting as we rode. Of course, we did not see it all the same way. The Little Stars and their relatives held their Sun Dance to the north of us, and some of our people prayed with them but did not dance, and it was the same when we held our Medicine Lodge.[34] Half Bear and Stone Forehead, the Keepers of our Sacred Covenants, were in this camp. Stone Forehead,[35] the Keeper of the Sacred Arrows, held the Arrow Renewal Ceremony before the Medicine Lodge. Our great holy man, Box Elder, had seen trouble coming. The wolves had brought him the power to see into the future and there were few with stronger medicine than Box Elder, one of our wisest chiefs, the protector of Oxohtsemo, the sacred Wheel Lance, and the man in the center of the Spirit Lodge. When others heard of what Box Elder had seen they

Morning Star (Dull Knife)

73

He Dog

CRAZY HORSE

I and Crazy Horse were both born in the same year and at the same season of the year. We grew up together in the same band, played together, courted the girls together, and fought together. When we were young men, the Oglala band divided into two parts, one led by Red Cloud and one by The-Man-Whose-Enemies-Are-Even-Afraid-to-See-His-Horses, the elder. Later this half subdivided again into two parts. I stayed with the more northern half, of which I and Big Road, and later Holy Bald Eagle and Red Cloud, were appointed Shirt Wearers. Crazy Horse remained with the southern quarter of the tribe. The council of this division awarded shirts to Crazy Horse, American Horse, The-Young-Man-Whose-Enemies-Are-Even-Afraid-to-See-His-Horses, and Sword. It was many years after our first battle before we were made shirt-wearers, about 1865 by the white man's calendar.

Crazy Horse always led his men himself when they went into battle, and he kept well in front of them. He headed many charges and was many times wounded in battle, but never seriously. Crazy Horse always stuck close to his rifle. He always tried to kill as many as possible of the enemy without losing his own men. High-Back-Bone and Crazy Horse were sworn friends and went on nearly all of their war expeditions together, and one was as great a war leader as the other. All the time I was in fights with Crazy Horse, in critical moments of the fight Crazy Horse would always jump off his horse to fire. He is the only Indian I ever knew who did that often. He wanted to be sure that he hit what he aimed at. That is the kind of fighter he was. He didn't like to start a battle unless he had it all planned out in his head and knew he was going to win.

Sunka Bloka

He Dog was 92 years-old in 1930 when Eleanor Hinman conducted the interview from which this extract is taken.

remembered the words of the great prophet, Sweet Medicine: *If the people have trouble or sickness, one chief must renew the Arrows*. And so it was Black Shin, a So'taaeo'o Council Chief respected by both the Notamé-ohméseheestse and Heévaha-taneo'o, who took the pipe to Stone Forehead. With our lodges now set as the new moon, Black Shin's body and buffalo robe were painted red, the color of life, before he carried the pipe to each band and spoke of his vow to the Great One – Ma'heo'o – and the Four Sacred Persons, and told that the Arrows were to be renewed. Box Elder was right, for with the Breeding Moon (August) came word of more soldiers and wagons in our country. Last Bull[36] and some other Kit Foxes had seen them near the Gourd Butte (Pumpkin Buttes) and said that it might not take the soldiers more than one or two sleeps to reach our camp, and so we moved fast. We boys brought in the pony herd while Bull Bear rode through the camp telling everybody to prepare.

The chiefs called for only the Dog Soldiers and Elk Horn Scrapers to go for they wished the other military societies to stay and defend the helpless ones in camp. It was not long before Red Cloud brought the Little Stars and we set out to meet the soldiers. Tall Bull carried a red flag on this day as he had been given the honor of signaling the attack. The ve'hó'e had not moved far from the Gourd Butte, the walking soldiers in two lines with a long string of wagons between them, with about as many pony soldiers as we had fought in the battle at the walking-across-logs.[37] The soldiers had two thunder wagons and some of our men thought that they knew how far these guns could fire, and so we waited along two ridges where they might not hit us. We were ready, and from above we stung them like the wasp. They made a circle with their wagons and put their white-man buffalo in it and fired at us from there, but I think the white-man buffalo were more scared of the thunder wagons than we were as they danced a strange dance every time they thundered. We did not have much of a fight[38] because our leaders wanted to know what the ve'hó'e were doing in our country and where they were going, more than they wanted to rub them out. Two sons of the Little White Man (William Bent)[39] could speak their language and so Morning Star and Bull Bear sent them to talk to the soldiers. I think these two boys must have made the soldiers feel queer for one was wearing a soldier coat and the other was blowing a soldier horn that they had found when we attacked the stage station on Tallow River. They came back and said the soldier chiefs (Colonel James A. Sawyers and Captain Williford) wished to talk and that they wanted to cross our country. Beaver (George Bent)[40] had told them that if they agreed to hang Chivington we would let them through. They did not agree, and so Red Cloud, Morning Star and Bull Bear went to see what they wanted with us. They were not happy when they returned. The whites said they did not want to fight but wanted to go to the Big Sheep River (Bighorn River) where they wished to build a fort and make a road

A Stand at the Village, Red Lance's depiction of General Patrick E. Connor's attack on Black Bear's Arapaho village

to it. Morning Star told them they would not have to fight if they left our country and that no roads could be made here. Red Cloud told them to leave the country between the Black Dust River and the River of Tongues and to go where the sun disappears until they passed the Big Sheep Mountains and then walk to the Big Sheep River. Both Morning Star and Red Cloud said they did not care if the soldiers wanted to live with the Óoetaneo'o[41] but that they would make no roads or forts here. It was then that the soldier chiefs said a fort was already being built between Gourd Butte and Foolish Woman River on the Black Dust River.[42] I do not know if Red Cloud and Morning Star thought we should fight when they heard this, but it is said that Tall Bull wanted to. Red Cloud warned them not to come back and let them go when they gave him a wagonload of presents to share with us. This was bad trouble and the southerners said we must be ready, for other ve'hó'e would now come to take our country, just as they had taken theirs.

My father went to look at this soldier fort with my uncle, and they were attacked by some Wolf Men who were with the soldiers but they did not catch them.[43] We did not know what to do: here were soldiers in the heart of our country with Wolf Men and they had built their fort above our crossing on the Black Dust River. It did not get better; Little Horse carried news that the Sage Men had been attacked by the soldiers and Wolf Men on the River of Tongues and many women and children had been killed and the village burned.[44] White Bull had been in that village the day before the soldiers came, and Roman Nose went to him to seek council. Soon Roman Nose was preparing in a sacred way to protect our people, and throughout our camp the sound of so many voices rolled around as hooves on the prairie. We did not have to look for the soldiers; they had been found. Some Little Stars came and said their relatives from the north were camped on the Antelope Pit River (Little Missouri River)[45] when they had seen soldiers (the commands of Colonel Nelson Cole and Lieutenant Colonel Samuel Walker) coming this way. These northern Sioux[46] of Sitting Bull, Black Moon, Jumping Bull and Four Horns were strangers to most of us then, but we came to know them; they were great men. They said these soldiers were weak but that they all had fast-shooting rifles and thunder wagons, and we found this to be true.[47] Heap-of-Birds and Woman's Heart were the first to ride against these soldiers. When we came upon them they were near our camp, but these soldiers looked lost and probably did not even know they were on the Little Black Dust River. The Sioux had whipped a party of them and had they not had so many guns, and we so few, I think we would have rubbed them all out. I asked my uncle what kind of pony soldiers were these who could not even keep their own horses alive?[48]

Vicinity of Connor's attack on Black Bear's village along the Tongue River

Their trail was easy to follow; everywhere they went they left dead and dying horses, and I had never seen that before. It was only the Cool Moon (September) but a bad wind had come, and I thought that we would not have to kill them because the winter would do it, so poor did they look. "Roman Nose is coming! Roman Nose is coming!" It did not matter if the soldiers heard for soon they would see all of us. Some pony soldiers tried to run away but their horses were too thin, and when our men chased them back they jumped off their horses and ran back to hide behind the shield of wagons they had made in a bend of the river. Roman Nose trotted his fine white pony forward and the rest of us rode out of the hills. "I shall empty the soldiers' guns! Then, will you charge?" He did not order, he asked, and then galloped to where the soldiers could hit him. Four times he rode in front of the soldiers and each time they fired with their fast-shooting guns, but no bullet could kill him that day as Thunder's power was strong and he had prepared as White Bull instructed. As he turned we were ready and we charged, and it was then that a bullet struck Roman Nose's pony and it fell beneath him. We could not ride over the soldiers, their guns were too many, and then they fired the thunder wagons and so we rode back to the top of the hills. Our hearts were not good, and I think this is what Box Elder saw: that we could be strong and brave but it might not matter because bows and lances and clubs could not fight guns. This was Roman Nose's Fight[49] and it was the last time I saw him empty the soldiers' guns. A white man pecking-thing caused Roman Nose's death,[50] and after that it was Crazy Horse who emptied the soldiers' guns.

Some of the Little Stars and their relatives kept fighting these soldiers, but our leaders said we would put it in the bag, and so we did and went to the Black Hills. On the way there was a lot of talk about Roman Nose and Wolf Man. It was mysterious and what he did I do not know, but in Roman Nose's Fight Wolf Man was shot twice but had no wounds. I had heard of this before but seeing it was different, and he left the name Wolf Man on the way to the Black Hills and was given a new one, Bullet Proof. On the Antelope Pit River our chiefs called for a buffalo hunt, and the wolves soon brought news of the herd that knew us, Ésevone, the Sacred Buffalo Hat, being head chief of the buffalo. The buffalo were good to us but, in the middle of the hunt, our men came close to fighting with some Sioux. They were not Little Stars, but we recognized some of them because they were of the same band as Crazy Horse's uncle, from the Greasy Foam River (Missouri River).[51] They rode fast into the herd and scattered the buffalo as we were hunting and started calling out that these buffalo were not ours to take, but the Crazy Dogs did not agree, and as was their way they would not stand aside. It looked bad until our chiefs asked our men to look about them, to see the Holy Mountain and to think how it would be to bloody the ground near Bear Butte. Much was said about this later but we left it and went back to the Antelope Pit River. Roman Nose stayed there with Black Shin's southern So'taaeo'o. Black Shin's son-in-law, Gray Beard, was like a brother to Roman Nose and where one was, the other would not be far away, and so they waited for winter to come and go on the Antelope Pit River. Most of the Southerners were homesick for their own country and so they went south from the Black Hills and crossed the Moon Shell River in the Dirt-in-the-Face Moon (October). When the Dog Soldiers reached Turkey Creek, we Northerners were back on the Black Dust River with Little Wolf. White Bull had not had enough of fighting, and so he led a party to the fort at Gourd Butte for the soldiers to see that we would not run from our own country. They did not come out, and so White Bull went north to raid the Mo'ohta-vahatá-taneo'o (Blackfeet), but fought some Kahkoe-stséa-taneo'o (Flatheads) instead.

We knew that the ve'hó'e were coming and that soon we might be strangled in the web of these spiders. The Kit Foxes were often given the work of watching the soldiers' fort

A Surprise Encounter, *Brave Wolf's depiction of a skirmish with Connor's troops near the Powder River in September 1865*

near Gourd Butte, and throughout the winter Sage Men came to help them when their ponies were strong enough to ride in the deep snow. They said that these soldiers did not look as if they wanted to fight, but our leaders warned that others would come with the new grass who would want to fight and that something had to be done. Morning Star, White Head, He-Jumps-Like-the-Rabbit, Little Moon and Black Horse were among our chiefs who had heavy hearts. They wondered if it might not be wise to try and make a talk with the ve'hó'e. How, they asked our brave men, could we whip the soldiers when no matter how many soldiers we killed more came? Yet when our men were on the ground there were no more to take their places. It was said that even counting young boys, here in our own country we Cheyennes did not have more than four hundred fighting men. One man had more fingers than we had guns between us, but the soldiers on the Tallow, Moon Shell and Black Dust rivers all had guns, some that shot fast, and they made even weak men like those at Roman Nose's Fight hard to kill. The Little Stars had more fighting men but did not have many more guns.[52] Some still had the bad feeling from the fight at the walking-across-logs, while others said they did not wish to fight alongside the Sioux that chased away the buffalo when we were hunting. "When the spiders come into our country they will bring their sickness," the chiefs always cautioned, telling of how we were once many until half of our people had been taken by the white man's cramps.[53] All listened, but just as some

said they would find a soldier chief in the spring and talk, others said it was better to die young than grow old and helpless, and so if they found a soldier chief in the spring they would fight to protect our country and way of life.

It was a terrible winter. We starved and we froze. We had not made enough meat because of fighting the soldiers, and being at war with them had stopped us from collecting the presents the Great Father had promised to us many moons ago after the Big Issue on the Horse River in the Long Meadows.[54] We lost many mothers and babies, and more than once I watched as old ones walked out of a lodge and into a blizzard as they would not take food that might fill the belly of an infant. The cold went away for a few days in the Hoop Moon (February), and it was then that The-Young-Man-Whose-Enemies-Are-Even-Afraid-to-See-His-Horses came to our camp and told us that the ve'hó'e had sent tobacco to his father and that he had gone to talk to them at the white man's trading-place the soldiers took near the Horse River (Fort Laramie).[55] He said that they too had been eating their ponies, and his father went because they had no food. Red Cloud would also be there soon, he said. His father wanted to know what we thought of it and if we would tell the Sage Men, but the Sage Men were now on the Elk River (Yellowstone River), and a runner might die if a blizzard came up before he got to them. Of course, The-Young-Man-Whose-Enemies-Are-Even-Afraid-to-See-His-Horses was welcomed; he was an Elk Horn Scraper and the society listened to him in council, but few said they would go to the soldiers' town. In the end it was Bob Tail who said he would go and listen. By the next moon others among our people decided that they would also go: Morning Star had received a message from Red Cloud, and as they had been the ones who had warned the soldiers at Gourd Butte not to make a road through our country, he agreed to talk to the ve'hó'e. I remember that when Roman Nose went south with Black Shin's people in the Muddy Face Moon (April), Morning Star, Black Horse, Pretty Bear, Wolf Lying Down, Spotted Elk, Red Arm Panther, Turkey Leg and an old man chief of the Sage Men, Cut Nose, had already gone to make the talk with the ve'hó'e on their singing wires.[56] Turkey Leg was always curious about the whites; he lived in the south as much as he did with us and only once did he speak of fighting them, but that was after this.[57]

When Roman Nose left it seemed as if he had taken some of our courage with him, for when all learned that he had gone a sadness came upon us, a feeling that spoke to us and told us that now we could not beat the soldiers if they came. Some acted as if they had heard it and followed it, saying that they hoped Morning Star would touch the pen for them, but most of the Elk Horn Scrapers did not. Roman Nose was one of our brave men, but we had others, and we would watch and wait and pray that Ésevone would bring the buffalo to us and that once more we would be sleek and fat. But what we saw were ve'hó'e swarming across our country as ants on a hill, their guns and wagons and white-man buffalo scaring away the buffalo and elk.[58] My uncle said that the ve'hó'e were dirty and did not smell good and he was right, but I did not know it then as I had not been that close to any of them.

They would shoot the buffalo and leave them to rot, and their horses and white-man buffalo left the land bare along the road they had made and where they camped. They were all crazy for the chief-metal[59] and I did not know how Morning Star or any of the other chiefs could understand these crazy people enough to be able to make a treaty with them. I heard that some of the young men among the Little Stars had already tried to make war on them but that Red Cloud, The-Man-Whose-Enemies-Are-Even-Afraid-to-See-His-Horses and Buffalo Tongue had shot their ponies and torn their lodges to stop them. Soon those fine men changed their minds.[60]

It was at the end of the Planting Moon (June) that some Little Stars came and told us what had happened at the big talk. They said The-Young-Man-Whose-Enemies-Are-Even-Afraid-to-See-His-Horses and his uncle, Yellow Eagle, told them that Red Cloud would send a pipe soon because there was going to be war, but that Red Leaf and The-Man-Whose-Enemies-Are-Even-Afraid-to-See-His-Horses were still talking about what to do. The ve'hó'e at the soldiers' town had lied to them and they were sending many soldiers to build more forts on the Black Dust and Big Sheep Rivers that would make the spiders' road holy.[61] They said they did not know if Morning Star or any of our chiefs who went to make the talk knew of this, or if they had touched the pen. Most of the Little Stars had left when they saw the soldiers' dust to the south, and in that dust was all the white man talk they wanted to hear. The-Young-Man-Whose-Enemies-Are-Even-Afraid-to-See-His-Horses had told the ve'hó'e that if the soldiers came they would not have a horse to run away on after two moons, and

that all of their big fighting men were gathering on the River of Tongues. These Little Stars asked if we would send a scout to the Long Knives with a message telling them not to pass the fort near Gourd Butte because if they did it meant war. Last Bull reminded them that the Kit Foxes were the first among us to fight the ve'hó'e on the road and that they had set the prairie on fire to stop them from finding our villages.[62] Our leaders said they would wait for those who had gone to touch the pen for they wanted to hear what they had to say, but that they would give them the message to take to the soldiers.

The women wished to move into the Black Hills to avoid any trouble, but we waited on the Bear Lodge River for Morning Star and the others. Morning Star said he had not touched the pen but had told the ve'hó'e that he might be ready to do so when the leaves fall. The ve'hó'e said that all they wanted was to pass over as much of our country as fit between the wheels of one of their wagons. They said that they would not stay and would not make war upon us if we did not make war upon them, and for that we would get presents and would not starve again. After Cut Nose's people put their marks on the treaty, Morning Star said he left and did not see the soldiers The-Young-Man-Whose-Enemies-Are-Even-Afraid-to-See-His-Horses spoke of, but that some Little Stars had told him about them on his way back. White Bull was angry and did not believe the white chiefs wanted only enough land for a wagon to take between its wheels. Even if they did, that meant we had to give them the road and we did not want them to have a road through our country because of what that would bring. "What are the soldiers coming here for? To measure out how much land fits between the wheels of a wagon?" he asked. Morning Star and Black Horse said they did not know but that they would go and see the soldier chief and ask him when he came into our country. Many said that was good for they did not want to hear this kind of talk from great chiefs, and so they should go, which they did, taking their people to the River of Tongues. Lame White Man said he would take the Little Stars' message to the soldiers but that he did not care to have anything else to do with the ve'hó'e. Lame White Man came north to avenge Sand Creek and never went back. The wolves[63] soon brought news to our camp that the soldiers were near the Big Lake (Lake DeSmet), moving toward Buffalo Creek (Piney Creek), far north of the fort near Gourd Butte. We knew then that Black Horse and Morning Star would soon find out if the soldiers were for peace or war.

A storm of grasshoppers fell from the sky in the Mid-Summer Moon (July) when Black Horse and Morning Star found the soldiers.[64] The soldiers had with them a black-

Two Moons

HUNDRED-SOLDIERS-KILLED-FIGHT

A small party, of which I was one, was sent out to spy on the fort (Fort Phil Kearny) and see if it could be taken without much loss. We saw it was too strong to take and so reported. Then the leaders decided to follow the usual plan of drawing the soldiers out by a small decoy force and then kill them all when out of reach of the fort. One morning a strong body of white men came out with wagons to get timber for the fort. When they were about halfway to the Pine Woods, a small party of Indians were sent to attack them. The wagons drew up in a circle and, as planned by our leaders, another force was sent out from the fort to help those with the wagon train.

Now a select party of warriors, mounted on the best and swiftest ponies, were sent over to the crossing of Lodgepole Creek. These men, not many in number, were ordered to draw the soldiers into the hills where the big body of Indians were hiding. The Indians attacking the wagon train rode off as the soldiers from the fort drew near, and these now turned to the right, crossing the creek, in pursuit of the Indians at Lodgepole Creek. These Indians did their work well and fell back slowly toward the Lodgepole Hills. The soldiers followed and were well into the hills before the big body of Indians attacked them. The soldiers now turned back for the fort but were surrounded and had to dismount. Then they turned loose their horses and fought on foot. The fight was soon over and every soldier killed. The Cheyennes had two men killed in this fight.

Ése'heo'o-nésese

This passage is taken from Two Moons' account of the Fetterman Fight. Two Moons shared this information with George Bent in Colony, Oklahoma, while visiting his southern relatives. At the time, Two Moons was living on the Northern Cheyennes' newly designated Tongue River Indian Reservation. In Life of George Bent, George Hyde presents Two Moons' recollections of the fight in full.

white man some of our people called Buffalo Cow Teat, and so Black Horse sent Bob Tail with word for him and the soldiers.[65] I was not there and so do not know it all, but Black Horse, Morning Star, Little Moon, Wolf Lying Down and He-Jumps-Like-the-Rabbit were the chiefs that smoked with the one they called the Little White Chief.[66] I was pleased that our oldest living chief, White Head, sent Pretty Bear, Man-That-Stands-Alone and Brave Soldier to do his talking with the ve'hó'e, for that work was below such a great chief. The black-white man made the ve'hó'e-talk and said the Little White Chief was not going away, he was going to build forts and make the road holy as The-Young-Man-Whose-Enemies-Are-Even-Afraid-to-See-His-Horses had said. Black Horse and Lame White Man told the Little White Chief that if he did not take his soldiers back to Gourd Butte he would have to fight the Little Stars, but the Little White Chief did not care and fired his thunder wagon to show that he was not scared. He said he wanted peace with us and so gave the chiefs a talking paper and some tobacco, sweet-water, meat from the sharp-nose-dog, and pounded-fine-powder.[67] They said there were many horses, white-man buffalo and strange hatchets they had not seen before for digging the earth,[68] and that as the sun went over more and more soldiers came. Some of these were walking soldiers, some were pony soldiers, and some were blowing horns of yellow-metal that made a horrible sound like a sky full of geese crying all at once.[69] I have heard this myself and it is a horrible sound. It is said that Black Horse wanted to trade some of the Little White Chief's presents with the white man who talks with the bird's singing tongue, and so they stopped at his camp, which was north of Buffalo Creek on Crow Standing Off Creek (Prairie Dog/Peno Creek).[70] A lot of our leaders did not want this trader here for he gave whiskey to the young men and it made them crazy. Others like him had done this to our relatives in the south and we did not want it.[71]

Red Cloud had sent scouts to watch our men with the Little White Chief and they followed them to the trader's camp. The-Young-Man-Whose-Enemies-Are-Even-Afraid-to-See-His-Horses, Black Twin, No Water, Big Road and Little Hawk were with Red Cloud, along with some Little Stars the Cheyennes did not recognize. They wanted to know if they had given the Little White Chief their message to turn back to Gourd Butte and what his answer was, but they did not like his answer or that Black Horse advised making peace with the soldiers because he thought we could not beat them in war. Red Cloud's blood became hot and he asked Black Horse if he had forgotten that the whites could not be trusted and that they had always lied to us and stolen from us, just as they had stolen from our fathers. Red Cloud said if Black Horse needed reminding he would do it, and then some of the men with him took out their bows and struck Black Horse and Morning Star many times before letting the other Cheyenne chiefs have it. I do not know if Red Cloud or The-Young-Man-Whose-Enemies-Are-Even-Afraid-to-See-His-Horses also did this, but they did not stop it. When they were done with them, Red Cloud told Black Horse and Morning Star not to forget what he was about to say: if the white man wanted it all he would have to fight for it, and the Little Stars were not afraid to die in their own country as their fathers before them had. Black Horse asked the trader if he would take his family and men to the Little White Chief with Red Cloud's words, warning him that the Little Stars might come back for them. Had the trader's ears been better he might not have died near his camp. The Little Stars did come back and rubbed them all out, giving life only to the trader's wife and children who were their relatives.[72]

It is true that nothing lives long, only the earth and mountains, and this is what White Antelope had sung as

Chivington's Long Knives butchered him on Sand Creek. We were not afraid of becoming grass on the hills as those who had gone before us, and many were with Red Cloud, but his talk had been blackened by this shameful act. Black Horse's words may not have sounded good to the Little Stars but he was a chief, a man who had seen many winters pass, and our people had lived and died with the Little Stars for generations before this, and to us it was not right to beat our chiefs in the way the ve'hó'e beat their white-man buffalo. We were still on the Bear Lodge River when we heard of this. Morning Star was not only a chief, he was a relative of Red Cloud's, and it was the Little Stars who gave him a new name among them, Dull Knife. We did not think it right that he had been insulted in this way either. The Little Stars had counted coup on these chiefs, yet coup is counted on an enemy, so were we to believe that we were now enemies of the Little Stars? Morning Star and those other chiefs took their people into the Big Sheep Mountains and then went on our cloud trail to the Moon Shell River. Few held onto bad feelings for them; we knew that they did not want the soldiers here or to give the ve'hó'e the road, and that they had only gone to talk because they did not know what else to do – the soldiers' guns and hunger would be strong enemies in the cold moons. Our leaders did not want trouble with the Little Stars either, and we were not ready to fight a war with the soldiers. The ponies that had survived the winter were not yet fat enough and neither were we. The chiefs asked the headsmen what would happen if we fought now and reminded all that we could not lose any more of our people to hunger when the hard-face moons came. War stopped us from making meat, and if we left the buffalo too long the buffalo might forget us, they said. We did not want to be trapped between the Little Stars and the soldiers if they were at war, for we knew that the soldiers would kill us in our lodges if they found us and then say that they thought we were Little Stars. Criers carried the news around our camps that the Sweet Medicine Chief wished his people to be in their stronghold – we were to move over to the Roseberry River (Rosebud Creek). My father said that was good, as from there the wolves could see everything and the people would be able to go whichever way they needed to, in peace or war. We did not follow right away; my uncle wished us to see the buffalo on the Red Shield Society River because he said the buffalo were leaving us and that soon we might not see their great herds in that country.

There were some good times on the Red Shield Society River but we did not get fat. We camped for a while with Old Spotted Wolf's and Turkey Leg's people who were with the Little Stars of Pawnee Killer, but the buffalo did not come as they used to, and all knew it was because the ve'hó'e were making an iron road.[73] Before this, I had never heard my father say that we were like snow when the sun comes in spring and that if something was not done, we would soon melt into the great pool of ordinary-people who already flooded the soldiers' town near Horse River.[74] My father never spoke badly of these people as some did; he talked of Spotted Tail as being a big fighting man until too many of his family drowned in the flood that might yet take us all. "If this happens we will no longer be the People Alike," he said. I knew then that he was hearing the great prophet, Motsé'eove, inside his head: *The buffalo will disappear. When the buffalo are gone, the next animal you eat will be spotted. Soon you will find among you a people with hair all over their faces. Their skin will be white. When that time comes, they will control you. The white people will be all over the land and at last, you will disappear.* This is what Sweet Medicine told. At the end of the Breeding Moon (August) we went home to the Roseberry River. All the way north we kept hearing of the Little Stars' war with the Little White Chief's soldiers and when found our peoples' lodges we also found that some had already joined this war.

Old Bear was the first Ohméseheestse chief to go against the soldiers on the spiders' road (the Bozeman Trail). Old Bear was one of our four Old Man Chiefs when we whipped Hae'esta'ehe (Lieutenant Colonel George A. Custer), but at this time he had only been a Council Chief for two winters. He was the only Ohméseheestse chief who was for war and he said that he would not walk in his own country like a blind man, for his eyes could see the soldiers making a town on the Big Sheep River (Fort C.F. Smith). Old Bear, Pipe Woman and Wrapped Braids took many mules from the soldiers there and they said those ve'hó'e must have been scared of water because they were slow crossing the river to chase them. When the elk started calling, some Óoetaneo'o brought tobacco to our village. These Crow chiefs came in peace and so they were feasted before our chiefs heard

Lorence Bjorklund's artistic impression of Crazy Horse

The shield purportedly carried by Crazy Horse

Golden Eagle

what they wished to say. The soldier chief (Captain Nathaniel Kinney) at the fort on the Big Sheep River had sent them because he wanted to smoke with Little Wolf; he did not want to be at war. Little Wolf, Box Elder and Old Bear told the Óoetaneo'o that they had heard and soon the soldier chief would know if they had listened. Council was held and the chiefs and headsmen decided to go to the Big Sheep River to hear what this white man had to say to us in our own country. It was good that we did not have to go far because we had no ears to hear what the soldiers wanted. They asked if we would go with them and the Óoetaneo'o against the Little Stars. Our chiefs said nothing, and in the silence was their answer.

Morning Star and those who were for peace were back with us now. Their horses were thin and they looked very poor, and so Morning Star said he was going to the soldiers' town to touch the pen. We did not see him or his people again until the Dust-in-the-Face Moon (October) was eaten.[75] White Bull was the one who said what most were thinking, that he did not like it, but none tried to stop Morning Star or the others as this was how they thought it had to be to keep their people alive. We moved to the River of Tongues and it was there, when we were camped near Buffalo Tongue's village, that we heard the Little Stars and their relatives from the Greasy Foam River were going to attack the soldiers' town on Buffalo Creek (Fort Phil Kearny) when the leaves had fallen and the buffalo hunt was over. Two Sage Men, Sorrel Horse and the white man without fingers called North, told how many horses and mules both they and the Little Stars had taken from the soldiers' town and that those soldiers were foolish and only knew how to fight in lines. The Kit Foxes were for war but, other than Old Bear, our chiefs would not go along with it until more had been said. The Kit Foxes believed there was going to be another Sand Creek and that we would be cut up by the soldiers from the Buffalo Creek fort if we did not rub them out. We had seen that the soldiers at the fort on the Big Sheep River were like old women and so we did not think about them. Two Moons, who was then not such a big man among the Kit Foxes, said he would go with Wrapped Braids and some other Kit Foxes to fight the Little White Chief's soldiers.

The Kit Fox men cannot have crossed more than one river before wolves came with word from the Buffalo Creek fort. Chiefs Little Moon, Wolf Lying Down and He-Jumps-Like-the-Rabbit – who had all made the ve'hó'e-talk with the Little White Chief – had been surrounded by a hundred of his soldiers who were going to kill them all until the Little White Chief stopped them.[76] They had only gone to the soldiers' fort to ask the Little White Chief if they could hunt in the valley of the River of Tongues without being shot by the soldiers, as they feared the soldiers would think that they were Sioux. The three chiefs had only a woman, a boy and three men with them because Black Horse and White Head had

White Bull

ONE-HUNDRED-WHITE-MEN-KILLED

The ridge on which the bluecoats had flung themselves down was high and narrow, only about forty feet wide, just where the monument stands now. On every side but the south the ridge fell away very steeply into the bottoms far below. That was no place for horsemanship, more especially as the slopes were covered with snow and ice, and the weather had now become so cold that blood froze as it flowed from a wound. The chiefs called out, ordering the Indians to leave their horses in the ravines and to fight on foot.

When the Indians were already crowded close up to the top of the ridge on both sides, Long Fox, leader of the Mniconju on the west side, stood up and yelled, "Let's go!" Then all the Indians jumped up and rushed forward. Flying Hawk (White Bull's uncle) fell dead there, shot through the right breast. The other Indians rushed on – right in among the rocks. They fought hand-to-hand with the troopers, stabbing and scuffling there in the smoke and dust. It was a dreadful mix-up, the kind of fight we call 'Stirring Gravy.' That charge ended the battle.

Pte San Hunka

During the summer months of 1930 and 1932 Stanley Vestal a.k.a Walter S. Campbell conducted several interviews with White Bull, portions of which appeared in Sitting Bull, Champion of the Sioux; Warpath: The True Story of the Fighting Sioux Told in a Biography of Chief White Bull; *and* Warpath and Council Fire. *This extract is taken from the interviews that became* Warpath: The True Story of the Fighting Sioux Told in a Biography of Chief White Bull and Warpath and Council Fire.

kept their people near the Big Lake. The Little White Chief said they could go and hunt, and then gave them some food and let them camp near his cut-open-house,[77] but the soldiers came for them in the night. Others had seen the Little White Chief with two bad, old scouts: one was Medicine Calf (Jim Beckwourth),[78] the black-white man with whiskey who led Chivington to Sand Creek, and the other was Big Throat (Jim Bridger),[79] the vé'hó'e married to a Sage Woman who had taken the soldiers to kill her people on the River of Tongues in last year's Breeding Moon. The Little White Chief made promises to these chiefs but had now thrown them away. He would not even speak to White Head when he went to ask about this. Old Bear was truly not blind; we would have to join with the Little Stars and the Greasy Foam River Sioux, or wait for the soldiers to come and kill our helpless ones. We only wanted to be left alone in our own country, but we knew this would not be so if the soldiers stayed. When Morning Star came back and told what had happened after they had touched the pen, we knew it would be war. Turkey Leg had seen Chivington at the soldiers' town while Morning Star's ears were being filled with the double-speak of the vé'hó'e.[80] He had already told this to Red Leaf, who was going there to touch the pen but was now for war. Now our hearts were finally made black.

The fingers of the River of Tongues gave a good many places to set up camp. Our lodges were near the Sage Men on Muddy Creek, and the Little Stars and their relatives were downstream from us, though it did not take that long to ride there. With the end of the buffalo hunts came more talk of war. There were not many more of us that could have joined, but I remember seeing Pawnee Killer and his people in the Hard Face Moon (November), and then more and more Sioux of the Greasy Foam River band came and covered up the land between us and them. We had seen them on the Black Dust River and we heard that their old man chief had died there. I found out that they called this chief White Swan and that in his life the vé'hó'e had done him much harm, and because of that he had always been for war with them. Before taking his spirit journey he had asked his people to remember his words and to make war on the vé'hó'e whenever they could, and so this is what they had come to do – to go with the Little Stars and fight the soldiers. Crazy Horse's uncle, High-Back-Bone, was a big man among them, and we did not know many of them other than him. Crazy Horse was taught much by his uncle, and we thought of Crazy Horse as one of us, which is how we knew High-Back-Bone. I think Crazy Horse liked to be with us. Little Wolf, White Bull and Roman Nose had taken him into the Elk Horn Scrapers and given him powerful medicine. Some of the Little Stars made too much big talk but Crazy Horse did not; he was a very humble man. Of course, Crazy Horse's mother had come from

the Sioux of the Greasy Foam River, and her name was Rattle Blanket Woman. I have heard it said many times that a sister of Spotted Tail was his mother but I do not believe that is so. This sister of Spotted Tail became his mother after Rattle Blanket Woman passed on, and this happened when Crazy Horse was an infant. The man he called his father was a Little Star who was also related to High-Back-Bone, and this man carried the name Crazy Horse before giving it to him.

As a boy I did not ever think that I would see the bravest men of the Little Stars and the other Sioux pass near lodges of Crow-people as if they were not enemies, but I saw this here in the hard-face moons, although I did not ever see it again. In the years that have passed since then, the white men's split tongues have made much about this in their talking papers, claiming that Red Cloud took presents to the Óoetaneo'o chiefs and called for peace between them so that the Little Stars could fight the soldiers and save the buffalo from the whites and any iron road. If Red Cloud did this thing nobody ever talked about it. I do not remember it and I do not know any Crows who remember it. The Crow-people helped the soldiers at the fort on the Big Sheep River (Fort C.F. Smith); without the Óoetaneo'o those soldiers would have either starved or been rubbed out. Other than that, I think the Crow-people wanted to stay out of the way, as we had tried to. There were some Crow-people among the Sage Men, but they were relatives. The Sage Men had a chief who had been a Crow but this caused

Little Wolf

HOW A BRAVE CHEYENNE CAN DIE

The ponies of the ten men chosen to be decoys were brought into the center of our camp for all to see, and my white horse was among them. I looked at the ponies and said, "I shall send my brother in my place. My horse is not very fast, so I will send my brother who has a very fast horse." I went to my brother's lodge and found him sat at his fire with Bull Hump. "Brother, I have been called to go and attack the fort; take my horse and you go." My brother told me to take back this horse as he did not want it. My brother had a very fast horse. Bull Hump then made us well again. "My friend," he said to my brother. "You have seen that these are my finest moccasins. Will you then take them? I want you to take them. I have heard that you are going to give your body to the enemy and so I give you these moccasins to lie in." My brother took Bull Hump's moccasins and he rode to the fort on his fast horse, the black one.

When the soldiers were trapped, I dismounted from my white war pony that I had ridden in so many battles. I gave my brother this horse as the one he had ridden to the fort was exhausted and could not move. My brother was wearing my war shirt and I offered him my war bonnet, and gave him the lance I had carried in many famous fights. "With all these warriors looking on, it is a good time to show how a brave Cheyenne can die," I said to him. He was the first to ride against the dismounted pony soldiers and he was shot fighting among them. The white war horse was also killed. The main body of Indians charged into the pony soldiers after my brother and like a mighty wave, flowed over them. I buried my brother with all the things he wore in the battle. "Lift my head up the hill and place me where I can breathe the fresh air," was all he said.

O'kohome-xáaketa

This passage is compiled from one primary source and two secondary sources. The primary source is George Bent, to whom, in 1877, Little Wolf gave the details of his brother's death. The secondary sources are the works of George Grinnell and Father Peter Powell. The first quote in this passage appeared in Father Powell's People of the Sacred Mountain, and the last was told to George Grinnell by White Elk and is included in The Fighting Cheyennes. Cheyenne historians and educators have reviewed the presentation of Little Wolf's role in the Hundred-Soldiers-Killed-Fight account and believe it to be accurate, the body of the additional information having been contributed by them, as well as confirmation and clarification of previously published sources.

Area of the great winter camp along the Tongue River

trouble. The Crow-people had fought a good battle against us and the Sioux on Arrow Creek (Pryor Creek, Montana) five winters before, and this Crow chief of the Arapaho warned his Óoetaneo'o relatives that our men were coming to rub them out. The Crow-people had strong medicine that day and we did not whip them.[81] The Sage Men did not care so much, they were always good at trade and the Crow-people had many fine horses, some that they got from the Pierced Nose people[82] who would come from where the sun goes. My uncle said that we only ever fought the Crow-people because they would not stay in just one half of the country between the Big Sheep Mountains and the Black Dust River, but I do not know if that was so. Anyway, our leaders had not yet called for this war with the soldiers, but Thunder comes when he pleases. That was our feeling; we knew war was coming.

A big party of Little Stars and Greasy Foam River Sioux went to make war on the soldiers at the fort on Buffalo Creek in the beginning of the Big Hard Face Moon (December). A handful of Sage Men went, led by the white man without fingers, but we did not go. I think the Greasy Foam River Sioux would have gone by themselves. Like us, they had fought soldiers like these around the time of Roman Nose's Fight and they thought they could whip them. White Swan had told them the same thing, and I think they wanted to honor their chief in this way. I wanted to go, and my father saw this and told me not to worry because plenty of fighting was coming. In the days that followed this I became an Elk man. I remember the morning when the crier announced that the Elk Horn Scrapers would gather that night and called out the names of the men who would dance. When the sun was at the center, the Elks went to the lodge of the one who was to offer the dance, and there a feast was given. This was when the older men in the society, the ones who were too old for war but held the Elks' songs, honored the eight bravest Elk men by telling them that they were to ride, which meant that they would be the leaders of the dance. My uncle dressed me for the dance, and when the songs began my father and mother walked with me to the lodge where the feast had been given and to where the Elk men returned, having prepared in their sacred manner. Little Wolf was the head chief of the Elk Horn Scrapers, and, with my father at her side, my mother offered the reins of three horses to Little Wolf, which he took and then gave away to the family of Bobtail Horse and Hollow Wood who had lost a sister.[83] Two of our strongest men, Wild Hog and Lame White Man, were chosen to take the front and back, and I then stood amongst the dancers between them, the eight men on horseback riding one after another, four on each side of the line of dancers, the four young Elk women following the dancers, and behind them the drummers. From the feast giver's lodge all went

Spotted Wolf

to the entrance of our camp circle and danced south, stopping at different lodges to honor that family, until we came to the end where the Crazy Dogs were.

The Elk Horn Scrapers are a very old military society, one of the four that came with Sweet Medicine. When I was a boy the people looked to the Kit Foxes to protect the Four Sacred Arrows, and the Elk Horn Scrapers to protect Ésevone, but how it will be when I am gone, I cannot say. Maybe it will change. There is a story that is told as to how the Elk Horn Scrapers were given this name, and if you think about it you will see that it is true. There was once a girl of great beauty, and many men wished to court her but she would not look at them. The Dog Soldiers and Kit Foxes had danced for her but she did not notice them, which left those that would become the Elk men in a fog, as they did not believe that she would see them. A man of great power then spoke to them and said that if they brought him the spike horn of a yearling bull elk and the shank bone of an antelope he would create medicine that would make the girl fall in love with one of them. They did as he asked and he carved the elk horn into a snake from the sun, a blue racer, and painted it yellow underneath and blue above and then made many cuts in it. He called the young men to him and showed them the blue racer he had carved, and then they watched as he scraped the antelope bone against it. "Do this when you dance and she will become yours," he said, and that is what happened. Of course, there are rivalries between military societies, particularly between the Elks and the Kit Foxes, and this is why for many moons the Elk Horn Scrapers were teased by the others, who called us 'Blue Soldiers.' It was not so long ago that our people were camped on Where They Strike the Drum Creek (Brown Creek, Wyoming) and a trader came to them with gunpowder. Some Elk men invited the trader into a lodge and he went, taking his gunpowder with him, but when he sat and smoked he made a spark fly from the pipe to the gunpowder, and the Elk men in the lodge got blue burns on their bodies. The Elk Horn Scrapers did not want this name 'Blue Soldiers,' but then came the Hundred-Soldiers-Killed-Fight, where we took it and made it our own.

Some of our young men began the rituals of war. If we were not going against the soldiers we should fight their allies, they said, and so all of the talk was about the Sósoné'eo'o; the Sósoné'eo'o were with the ve'hó'e, and it was a Sósoné'e who had killed High-Back-Wolf. A few set out here and there but it did not seem to mean much to our leaders until four men came back and said that soldiers from the fort on Buffalo Creek had attacked them. A council was called and this was discussed. Some thought that the soldiers might have chased off the Sioux, then followed them to their villages, and now might be marching on us. The wolves had not yet brought such news and we soon learned that it was not so from four Little Stars. The-Young-Man-Whose-Enemies-Are-Even-Afraid-to-See-His-Horses had brought the pipe to our leaders, and if they smoked it we were at war. One of those with him was the younger brother of Crazy Horse. This boy, Little Hawk, rode a very fast horse that his brother was soon to ride at the Hundred-Soldiers-Killed-Fight.[84] They said that they had attacked the soldiers and might have rubbed them out but for some of their young men wanting to fight all at once, which had made the soldiers go back inside the fort.[85] Now their leaders wished our brave men to join them as they were going back to attack the fort and believed the soldiers could be rubbed out. Little Wolf spoke and asked them to tell their leaders that it would be decided in council and a wolf would bring the answer, and those

Tanager

Bull Elk

who were for war would soon follow and smoke the pipe. The Little Stars left, saying that their people were waiting at the Big Springs but would not wait long. What was good and bad was spoken, and most felt as Little Wolf, Box Elder and Old Bear did, that if we did not go to meet the soldiers now, more soldiers might come to these forts and then they would all come together and kill us in our homes. This is how it looked through our eyes. It was decided that half of our men who could fight would go, and half would stay to protect the helpless ones as we could not lose all of our young men to the guns of the ve'hó'e. The Bowstrings were given the honor of guarding our camp and the Elk Horn Scrapers were given the responsibility of leading our other brave men against the soldiers. The Crazy Dogs were also to stay in camp, but then Crazy Mule gave them strong medicine that they could not turn away from. Crazy Mule had power and he blessed the Crazy Dogs with it. I saw this with my own eyes, there on Muddy Creek; how he called to the Crazy Dogs to shoot at him, which they did, but nothing could make him bleed. He told the Crazy Dogs that the soldiers' guns would not hurt them and so they must go and fight them. It reminded me of Bullet Proof after Roman Nose's Fight. This was all our own country and we did not want war, but the ve'hó'e were here, the soldiers were here, and maybe an iron road would soon be made here. If we were to die, we would die with the buffalo as the People Alike.

I remember that I nearly tripped over a dog on my way back to our lodge. Suddenly all the dogs of the camp were everywhere, scampering around in little bunches as if each was chasing the other's tail, tumbling and snapping in mock fights as if they knew that we were going to war. In the old days some of them would have been taken to carry packs, but I think that those who came now just followed in the excitement. My mother was not there when I got to our lodge, my father said she had gone to bring me the swiftest horse from our herd. He called me to him and told me what I knew he had to, that his son was now the fighting man of this lodge, and so his time as a warrior had passed and he would now stay behind so that I might gain honors. I was supposed to be a man but I could feel that my eyes had started to make tears anyway. Like the dogs, I was excited but also a little afraid, and I felt some sorrow for my father who was not yet old. "Old men for council, young men for war!" my grandmother chanted over and over. "Do not fear the enemy, be afraid of the old man's teeth and the song of your sweetheart's mother if you turn back," she said. I did not have a sweetheart, but our women had many songs to shame a man who did not show courage, and it was said that it was worse to hear those songs than to face the enemy. "Grandson, nobody will remember your name if you grow old enough to sit on the cold side of the lodge. Take courage!" She patted my arm and then set up a song for me that went like this: "Grandson, only the rocks stay on the earth forever. Use your best ability."

Before leaving, my mother had collected much of what I must take, and there I saw some of my father's finest things: his bow made from the horn of the mountain sheep, his quiver, his war rope and his war shirt. The arrows in the quiver were made by Blue Feather,[86] arrow maker of the Elk Horn Scrapers, and my father held the quiver aloft and told me that these arrows must be as the kingfisher, that they must fly straight, fast, and like the kingfisher, never miss. I knew what it meant to be offered these things and to take them – that I must not bring shame to them or my father, and that I must show courage, for if I took these things and dishonored them I would be talked about. He wished for me to take them and so I did. When my mother returned she said nothing, but handed me a bag full of pemmican and some new moccasins. I wished to say something to her but the words got stuck in my throat and I did not. I did not even look at her; it was too hard and it was not right for her to show any fear for me. My uncle was waiting, mounted on a strong roan and holding his best war pony. Tethered outside our lodge was a heavy American horse we had captured at the walking-across-logs and a brown and white spotted pony I would lead until it was time. My father tied an antelope horn around the spotted pony's neck[87] and would not allow me to leave until he had checked that I had all I needed and that it was all packed onto the American horse in the right way. It was good. My uncle began a Wolf Song and soon they could be heard all around the camp as groups of men stopped outside different lodges to sing, and then received presents before leaving. This is what my uncle sang: "Call them together until we go away and we will dance until morning."

I will not forget how it was that night. The moon was full, the camp was alive with many voices and clouds of breath as the songs sat on the cold air. Little Wolf was to lead us all, and the white war pony he was leading seemed to be shining beneath the moon. We gathered together in a line behind him and circled our camp, each man mounted on a strong horse and leading his best war pony, and most singing: "I am going to search for a man. If I find him, there will be fighting. Perhaps he will kill me."

Some Sage Men joined with us, maybe fifty or so, and their chiefs rode with ours at the front. From where I rode with my uncle I could see the men who carried the pipes: Little Wolf, Box Elder, Crazy Mule, Black Moccasin, Old Bear and Painted Thunder, with the Sage Men leaders Medicine Man and Black Bear. Medicine Man was one of our people but became a Sage Man when he married one of their women and then became a great leader amongst them. Black Bear was part Sioux, and it was his people who had been attacked on the River of Tongues. Behind them came more of our leaders: Lame White Man, Crazy Head, Wild Hog, Big Nose and White Bull, with the Sage Men, Black Coal, Little Chief and Eagle Head. Little Horse was a good man in a fight and he would have ridden with these brave men, but he was a Contrary and so had to ride alone. When it had been decided that we would ride against the soldiers, Little Horse had gone to Ésevone's lodge to ask Half Bear if he could wear Ésevone, the Sacred Buffalo Hat, in the fighting against the soldiers. There was ceremony to this and it was done. Half Bear sent a good man to carry Ésevone and to watch over Her. Little Horse did not see Ésevone until this man placed Her upon his head before the fight. The next morning, when the sun was halfway, the wolves met us and told us that the Little Stars and their relatives were still there on the Big Springs, so we made ready and charged upon them, which was our way of saying, "Friends, we are here to fight beside you!" I think they were surprised at how soon we had come. Little Horse was not with us but we knew he would be here. If the whole village had moved with us, Half Bear and his wife would have carried Ésevone, but the Keeper has responsibilities to all of the people and so he must stay with the helpless ones. This is what he did, keeping Nimhoyo'o (the Turner)* close to the village.

After we made camp close to the river, our leaders called a council. They wanted to hear what was in the hearts of the Little Stars and the Greasy Foam River Sioux, and then they would bring that news to us, but before that they wished us to show the Sioux that we had strong hearts, and so we dressed in our finest clothes and rode our swift ponies around the Sioux camp. The Sioux were hot for a fight and wished to move right away, but our leaders wanted to talk a while and asked them how they thought this fighting should be. As it was, we left without knowing. Some spoke for sending a handful of men to trick the soldiers into coming out of the fort on Buffalo Creek and then rubbing them out with many, just as we had tried before at the soldiers' town on Tallow River and at the fight by the walking-across-logs.[88] Red Cloud described how he had watched the Little White Chief's soldiers in the fight at the beginning of this moon, and he said they were fools who would chase a few into many and death. So Red Cloud was for this way, but others made big talk for attacking the fort and burning it. Our leaders did not think going against the fort was good and reminded those who did that you could not count ten good guns between all of the men here and that these soldiers all had good guns. A foolish man with a weak heart and a gun can kill many men with strong hearts but no guns. The Greasy Foam River Sioux

*See Reflections – Douglas Spotted Eagle.

American Horse

THEY KILLED ONE HUNDRED MEN AT FORT PHIL KEARNY

The mounted soldiers were riding in advance in columns of fours. The dismounted men followed closely. After firing at the troops American Horse and his party slowly retreated into rough ground over ridge where two long lines of warriors were lying in ambush; and troops walked into the trap set and were completely surrounded. . . . Two men jumped into a pile of rocks and did a lot of shooting before they were killed. The soldiers, when they discovered that they were trapped by hundreds of Indians . . . were badly demoralized and did poor shooting. The Indians had only seven killed and eight wounded. . . . One of the Indians killed, having a very brave heart, succeeded in riding into the midst of the soldiers shooting right and left.

Wasicun Tasunka

Eli S. Ricker stated that American Horse visited him in August 1906, at which time he commenced interviewing the Oglala chief. Ricker subsequently presented an account of the Fetterman Fight that is attributed to American Horse, from which this extract is taken (see note 118).

Fort Phil Kearny

had the most guns, but they were still not many, maybe thirty or so. They were old, long-nosed guns from white-man traders. A few had short-nose guns but these looked like those the Se'senovetsé-taneo'o (Comanches) took from the Hairy Nostril White Men (Mexicans) when they had iron bellies.[89]

The wolves rode ahead with the next sun and waited at Crow Standing Off Creek, and here, just above the big forks, we made camp. The young boys, myself included, had much work to do now for we had to make the war lodges. In raids and war we camped this way, trying to find cover in the creek bottoms and the brush, and where we might also find cottonwood bark to feed our ponies. These lodges were not big and were not easy for the enemy to see in the winter when they became covered with snow. We tried to collect young willows, which we planted in a circle and then bent over so the shape was something like the beaver's lodge and, as the beaver does, we covered them with what we could find: branches, bark, leaves; some men would use their saddle blankets for this. You could make a small fire in these lodges and when it was cold, like it was then, use your blanket and buffalo robe to sleep under. This camp on Crow Standing Off Creek was arranged as the main camp, so we had our circle with the Sage Men nearby, and the Sioux had theirs. We young boys had to take food and water to our leaders but we could not offer them certain parts of the buffalo out of respect to Ésevone. If a leader ate any meat from the head, hump, back or loin of the buffalo before facing the enemy it could bring a curse upon us, but after the fighting they could eat what they wished. I do not remember that any man liked to eat food off the white man's metal, and so we used sharpened sticks. As I told you before, when Roman Nose ate food that had been touched by a white man's fork it brought him death. Serving water also required ritual and training, and it was not something that anybody could do, the one who carried the water dipper being the Owner of the Heart Bladder.

In those days it did not mean much to me, but it was at this camp that I first noticed the women who had come with their men. When I look back at it, I did not understand that those women, who were mostly Little Stars, had not just gone to help their men prepare but were actually there to fight the soldiers. The white men say four Crow-people came with us and that one of them was a woman. If that was so I do not remember seeing them. The Sage Men held their own council this night before coming together for the main council. They were pleased to have Sorrel Horse and the white man, North, back with them. I think it was these two who did most of their talking as they had seen most of the fighting with the Little

White Chief's soldiers. Not everybody saw things the same way in the main council. Red Cloud was still for sending a small party against the fort to trick the soldiers into coming out and following, and he was joined in this by Red Leaf, Buffalo Tongue, Little Wolf and our leaders, and Medicine Man and Black Bear. The white man without fingers, North, spoke for the war leaders of the Sage Men and they were with the Greasy Foam River Sioux who did not think such a thing would work as it had never worked right before. High-Back-Bone said that few of the men gathered had shown that they had good enough ears for this because whatever was asked of them, some always charged too soon and could not wait. Of course, he spoke truly, but the only other thing left to do was to attack the soldier fort, and we did not want to because it meant leaving too many hearts on the ground. After much talk, High-Back-Bone spoke again and all agreed with him that the soldiers fought in a foolish way and lined up to be killed, but that they also did something good – the soldiers did as their chiefs asked in a fight – and although this was not our way, if we were to trick them it would have to be our way, for we had come to wipe them out and not just to count coups. It was agreed that we would try this again – that we would trick the soldiers into a trap like catching antelope.[90] Every man knew that the soldiers did not fight for honor or to count coup, they fought for the pieces of white-metal[91] that made them lie and steal. We were here for honor, to protect our helpless ones and the good ways of our people. It was different.

Little Wolf went away from our circle to find the lodge of Little Horse, who, as a Contrary, could not ride or camp amongst us. Little Horse had seen Thunder riding on a white horse and it had made him weak and much afraid; this is why he had to take the road of a Contrary, which is not an easy road to take. He carried a sacred Contrary Bow, and from this he gained much power, and it protected him from Thunder's voice. In my life I have not seen many Contraries, but those I have appeared to be like Little Horse, who was always covered in sacred red paint and who carried a bundle of white 'male' sage to purify the earth where he stepped and to wipe off any who might touch the Contrary Bow, as in this way they would be purified and saved from the lightning. Little Wolf asked him what he would think if this was to be his last time to walk on earth, which was a way of asking a Contrary if he would accept the honor of leading us into battle. Everybody believed that Little Horse was going to lead us, but Little Wolf did what had to be done by asking. Talking to a Contrary is a sensitive matter for they talk backwards; to a Contrary 'yes' means 'no' and that is how it went. Little Horse already had strong medicine from his Contrary Bow, but now he would also have Ésevone and Her power would guide and protect us while confusing the enemy. Little Horse showed no fear in battle and many spoke well of him. He had led the Elk Horn Scrapers' charge at the walking-across-logs, and in his queer way he told Little Wolf that he would lead us again.

We were ready to move again before the sun and we rode down the right fork of Crow Standing Off Creek, staying in the coulees so that we might not be seen so easily. The wolves

Decoys as seen from the fort

had gone before us and would signal danger. The wolves watched over the ridges and buttes, and if the elk, buffalo or deer told them something, they would tell us with mirrors, blankets or by the way they rode their ponies. On this day there was nothing. The sun was not halfway to the center when we reached the little forks of Crow Standing Off Creek, where the prairie is flat. The Greasy Foam River Sioux had been out front since the Big Springs and it was their criers who called for us to halt. They sent out in a loud voice, "Take courage, death is not the enemy, the enemy we will find! Are you ready to find that man?" Our leaders told us to go no further. The Sage Men also stopped, and then we all moved to the side. I do not know all that happened but I think that some of the talk must have got mixed up, because the Greasy Foam River Sioux and some of the Little Stars wanted to go right away and trick the soldiers out of the fort and rub them out. Maybe one of their mysterious people had dreamed something; I do not know. Whatever it was, they wanted to end it. Once more, we did not go along with this. Some of the Sioux looked at us in a black way but our leaders said we could not do this as we had not yet been able to prepare in a sacred manner. The Sioux and the Little Stars understood but said they would go anyway, and most of them did, although some of their younger boys stayed behind to make their camp. I think their holy men had prepared them before their first fight of this moon and while they were waiting for us on the Big Springs. I

Lame White Man

do not know this, but I think it must have been so. Like us, just before a fight, each man would then make medicine as he had been taught by those who protected and guided him.

We boys did not have much to say; it was not our place and we knew that if our hands did not speak for us through the work of making camp we might feel a bow across our backs, or worse, be shamed and left behind. The men made much talk and I heard some say that we should leave this and go to raid the Sósoné'eo'o. Some bad feelings were in their words; those who had been in the fight at the walking-across-logs had not forgotten what had happened with the Little Stars there, or that not far from this camp some of their big men had counted coup on Cheyenne chiefs. Those who still wished to go along with the Greasy Foam River Sioux were asked if they could not remember how we were insulted by them when they chased the buffalo away from us in the Black Hills. My uncle spoke about these things for a while and then said that when two men quarrel it should stay between themselves and not come between all of their people and what is best for those yet to be born. "We can all see that Morning Star is not here," he said. "But this is because he is a man of honor. Morning Star touched the pen and so cannot fight. Today his son is with us, so Morning Star should not fight. And what of Morning Star's son?" he asked. "He is here to fight for the helpless ones, not for the Greasy Foam River Sioux or the Little Stars. I believe my brother cares more about the good of all of our people

than the bow the Little Stars put to his father's back. It is good that the Sioux are fighting with us," he said, "as we have been friends for many winters. Should they rub out the soldiers today, that too is good, for then you men who wish to take horses from the Sósoné'eo'o can do so before there are more soldiers to fight. Have you forgotten that there are plenty of soldiers where the sun rises?" With that he said no more.

With the bitten moon showing in the last part of the day as a stone in a shallow stream, the wolves called and then brought their news into camp: the Sioux had not rubbed out the soldiers as the soldiers would not be fooled.[92] We had done our talking for the day and so did not join their council, but some Sage Men who had gone with them knew their tongue, and they came and told us that many amongst the Little Stars and Greasy Foam River Sioux thought that we would have to attack the fort as they did not believe the soldiers could be tricked. Of course, this is what they had said before and maybe they were right, but I still did not think that we would attack the fort. From this hill of old age, when I look back across this land that was my life, I often see this next day as one of the strangest. I remember that it was quite warm but ice still held pieces of ground and the edges of water. The criers called all of the leaders and brave men to council, and from what I could hear in the shadows it did not seem that we would continue with this because we could not agree. Again, we were not for attacking the fort on Buffalo Creek but many of the Sioux were. We could see it through each others' eyes and so there was no bad feeling. My uncle told me that a chief of the Greasy Foam River Sioux, Black Shield, said that they had one amongst them who could see beyond what a man could see because this one had the power from two sets of eyes so, if it could be agreed, we might send this one out to find the enemy and then talk some more when we knew what this one had seen.

I did not know it then, but this one that Black Shield spoke of was called His Crazy Mule[93] and they respected his power. I was with a good many of our own people, and at first we did not know what was happening and so we stayed back until we were told, and then we followed. Most of us were mounted but we did not go far from the camp. The leaders of the Greasy Foam River Sioux and Little Stars put their ponies together at the bottom of a ridge to the west of Crow Standing Off Creek. It looked to me that the Sioux knew what was going to happen, for they were all crowding together and their voices were quiet. A sorrel

horse came through them and they moved aside like long grass before a deer. It was a very good-looking horse, so good that I did not notice its rider until all of the Sioux had moved away. A hé'e-ma'haeso[94] was on this horse, and if you have ever watched a snake move across the ground, that is how this hé'e-ma'haeso rode. It was peculiar to see, but later I found out that he was blind. A hé'e-ma'haeso is a man who lives as woman. Pipe Woman was that way. This one the Sioux called His Crazy Mule was wearing a dress made from red trader's cloth with elk teeth falling down it as rain on a man's face. I have often wondered how this hé'e-ma'haeso collected those elk teeth, and I think maybe from a relative or through trade, for I have seen many women of the Sage Men wear such dresses. I never saw the hé'e-ma'haeso's face for a black cloth covered his head, but beneath it he was blowing an eagle bone whistle. He went away for a while, and then came back over the ridge to where the Sioux leaders were and spoke to Black Shield, then went away again. He did this three times and Black Shield sent him away three times, and his riding was very poor. The hé'e-ma'haeso then stayed away longer, so long my uncle said that we should go closer so that he might hear what was being said. We heard the hé'e-ma'haeso before we saw him again; the sun had fallen behind the mountains and where the cold pushes out the warmth you could hear the sorrel horse's hooves beating upon the earth and the whistle that was now coming and going just as the cry of an eagle. The

Black Coal

sorrel horse galloped over the ridge towards the Sioux leaders; the hé'e-ma'haeso had let go of the reins and he was holding his arms as if he had something in each hand. When the horse came close to the chiefs it slowed, then shied, and the hé'e-ma'haeso fell off. The hé'e-ma'haeso was still holding his hands in that strange way as he crawled nearer to Black Shield. "Answer me fast, I hold a hundred of the enemy in my hands. Do you want them?" he asked.[95] All of the Sioux sent up a cry and some of their men pushed forward to count coup around the hands of the hé'e-ma'haeso. The hé'e-ma'haeso had found the enemy and a hundred would die if we went to fight them tomorrow.

All now knew that whatever was decided in council, we would rub the soldiers out. Little Wolf was for trying to fool the soldiers again and talked of bringing the soldiers away from their fort and down the part of the white man's road (the Bozeman Trail) that is on the land shaped like the blade of a knife, below the Lodgepole Hills (Lodge Trail Ridge). Some of the Sioux said they had done this before and it did not work. Little Wolf then spoke before the council. "Friends, you have heard it said of me that when I see something that I have been looking for, I want to get it. I do not want to see it and then leave it. When I was young I was once asked a question and so now I ask you young men here that same question: if your family is hungry and you only have one arrow, where will you wait? Of course, you will wait at a water hole. Now I ask you, if you are hidden near that water hole will you have the patience to hold onto that one arrow and wait until you know that you cannot miss what you aim for? Or will you shoot your one arrow at the first antelope or deer that comes by? Friends, that ridge upon which the whites take their wagons is your water hole and your family is hungry, so will you waste that arrow and leave their bellies empty?" Little Wolf was different from many war leaders; he did not want the Elk Horn Scrapers to go into a fight without knowing what he expected of them and how he wanted them to fight. It was as if he could see a battle before it happened and in this way he would decide how it should be fought. My uncle said that he had seen Little Wolf quirt men who spoke against his way or before he had finished making ready. High-Back-Bone knew of this and said the Sioux must listen and fight this way tomorrow. I remember that then the only ones making the talk were High-Back-Bone, Black Shield, Crazy Horse, American Horse, He Dog, Sword, The-Young-Man-Whose-Enemies-Are-Even-Afraid-to-See-His-Horses, Red Cloud, Black Twin, Little Wolf, Wild Hog, Crazy Head, Lame White Man, Old Bear, Black Coal and North. These men knew about war; they had been honored for their deeds by being made Shirt Wearers, war chiefs and headsmen of military societies.

It was not too long before these men were joined by other chiefs: White Hollow Horn, Big Road, Red Leaf, Bear's Rib,[96] Red Dog, Medicine Man, Black Bear, Black Moccasin and our holy men, Box Elder, Crazy Mule and White Bull. Those are the ones I remember. Soon after, criers were calling that a decision had been made. Wrapped Braids was asked if he would take three good men and go to the fort on Buffalo Creek before the sun. This he said he would do, and Two Moons was one he chose to go with him. This was asked of Two Moons because he knew much about the Buffalo Creek fort. Two Moons would see if we could rub the soldiers out in the fort without leaving too many hearts on the ground. All of the other fighting men were to leave camp with the sun and move down the right fork of Crow Standing Off Creek to the ridge Little Wolf and High-Back-Bone spoke

of, and there we would wait for Two Moons' word. The leaders of the Greasy Foam River Sioux and the Little Stars said that every day, before the sun was halfway above, the Little White Chief sent men from the fort to his cut-open-house and that if the fort could not be taken High-Back-Bone would lead a party of men to attack them. They said the soldiers always came out to fight when this happened, and so tomorrow, when the soldiers came, they would leave those who were going to the cut-open-house and ride away. As they were about to do this, ten men with strong hearts who were sheltering near Lodgepole Creek (Big Piney Creek) would show themselves to the soldiers who were still inside the fort, and then make those who were already outside of the fort angry so that they would chase them. These ten men were to fool these soldiers into following them away from the fort and over the Lodgepole Hills and onto the white man's road (the Bozeman Trail). All around there, we would wait some more, and then we would have them. We would come out of the earth and charge upon them, becoming fast water in a river flowing around the soldiers, who would choke beneath us.

It is said that both Little Wolf and High-Back-Bone were to be among those ten men sent to fool the soldiers but, in the end, they gave the honor to others which, when I think of it now, was wise for they were

needed more by the rest of us. High-Back-Bone asked Crazy Horse to lead these ten men, and we were all happy about that, not just because he was an Elk Horn Scraper but because most of us believed that he was the bravest fighting man we knew among all of the Sioux. I think High-Back-Bone also gave Crazy Horse the honor of riding for him so that the big bands of Sioux who were there would each have two men in this party, so Crazy Horse rode for his mother's people, who were also those of High-Back-Bone. I do not know if this is true but if you think about it you might see that it is so. The Sioux from the north were very few here, and so they did not have a man chosen for this work. Crazy Horse was joined by young White Swan, American Horse, The-Young-Man-Whose-Enemies-Are-Even-Afraid-to-See-His-Horses, Lone Bear and He Dog; from our people, Little Wolf's brother, Big Nose and Wolf Left Hand went; then Black Coal and Eagle Head of the Sage Men. I remember well how Little Wolf gave this honor to his brother. The ponies of the ten men chosen were brought into the center of our camp for all to see, and Little Wolf's white horse was among them. Little Wolf and his brother had quarreled, about what I do not know. I was only a boy then and nobody felt that they needed to tell me. Whatever it was about, Little Wolf looked at the ponies and said, "I shall send my brother in my place. My horse is not very fast, so I will send my brother who has a very fast horse." He could have taken the honor himself – his white war pony was swifter than any big American horse – but instead he walked the pony to his brother's lodge. There he found Big Nose talking with Bull Hump, the son of Morning Star. Little Wolf showed the reins of the pony to his brother and asked him if he would not take the honor of being among the ten men who must lead the soldiers to us. I heard that Big Nose did not even look up from the fire when he told Little Wolf to take back his horse as he did not want it. Little Wolf said that was good as Big Nose had a faster horse. Bull Hump then made them well again. "My friend," he said to Big Nose. "You have seen that these are my finest moccasins. Have you been looking for them? I think you have. Will you then take them? I want you to take them. I have heard that you are going to give your body to the enemy and so I give you these moccasins to lie in. It is an honor for me to give them to you. You have found them." Big Nose took Bull Hump's finest moccasins, and then Little Wolf gave his brother his best war shirt, the one fringed with many scalps. Big Nose knew that he must bring honor to them and their owners and that such honor came with death in battle. Little Wolf hobbled his own pony outside his brother's lodge and then had a boy bring his brother's best pony and tied them side-by-side. It was this one, the black horse brought by the boy, that Big Nose rode in the Hundred-Soldiers-Killed-Fight.

The bitten moon was white-metal in both the darkness and on Two Moons' breast, or so it seemed in that place between sleep and waking where I could not tell if the shining light was the moon or Two Moons' necklace. It was still night when the four Kit Foxes left camp. Their ponies' tails were not tied up and they were not painted, but Two Moons' hair was tied with red cloth and over his saddle hung a Kit Fox skin. We knew that these things might not be seen by the Little White Chief's eyes, but that he would see the long-nosed gun[97] he had. It was good for us that Big Throat was on the Big Sheep River and that Medicine Calf was dead, for their eyes could not now see for the Little White Chief either. The sun had not yet chased in the morning when the Sioux honored their men who had been chosen to trick the soldiers. The Sioux all gathered in long lines, and High-Back-Bone and Red Cloud went up and down, leading out each man until they made their own small line. We just watched, and when they had finished, Big Nose, Wolf Left Hand and the two Sage Men joined them. We did not see them again for a little while. The other party went next, and the white man without fingers was to make the charge on the wagons going to the cut-open-house, but High-Back-Bone was still to be the leader, and he went to see that all of the talk was not lost. High-Back-Bone would call when to let it go and signal when the ten men should take courage and face the soldiers. Back then I thought North, the white man without fingers, was crazy because he could never get enough fighting. It is said that he was sent because he always shouted many bad things at the soldiers in their own tongue and that this made them hot to fight. Some good men stayed at the camp to watch over the herd of carrying horses, but the rest of us rode like this: the Greasy Foam River Sioux were in front, then we were beside the Little Stars, and then came the rest of our people with the Sage Men. The sky was the color of stone when we reached the place where Crow Standing Off Creek is broken in two by the hill where the ve'hó'e put their road, and the cold was eating the feeling from our fingers. Our party was four times that of the Sage Men, and the Little Stars and Greasy Foam River Sioux were three times as many as us.[98] Here we waited for Two Moons' word.

A wind started to come off the Big Sheep Mountains, and I remember how, after looking up into the mountains, all of the inside of my nose felt like ice. I was looking up at the mountains thinking about High-Back-Wolf, for it was there that his brother and Crazy Head laid his body after the fight at the walking-across-logs. He was a fine man, and I was thinking how good it would have been to have him with us today, but then my uncle brought me back. One of our wolves was coming with two of the Kit Foxes who had gone to the fort, and my uncle told me to be ready. They said that Two Moons had gone into the fort alone and pretended that he needed some white man arrows[99] for his gun so that he could hunt. When he came out he said that we could not rub the soldiers out in the fort without leaving many hearts on the ground. Two Moons and Wrapped Braids had gone to tell this to High-Back-Bone and so we must make ready, the earth must hide us from the soldiers as we wait for the ten men to do their work. Right away the Sioux military societies started to soldier their men, reminding them of what must be done. Lame Deer, a chief of the Greasy Foam River Sioux, came to us and said that we Sahíyelas and Blue Clouds, for that is what they called us and the Sage Men, must make up our minds now, for the fight was coming and we had to decide where we were going to attack the Long Knives from. Many of the Little Stars were already making medicine and preparing to charge the soldiers on foot from Crow Standing Off Creek, while some of the Greasy Foam River Sioux had begun riding to the east side of the hill. Little Wolf went to Crazy Head, Lame White Man and Wild Hog, and then sent a boy on a fast pony back to Little Horse. When he came back, Little Wolf sent word to Black Shield and Black Twin that we would wait on the west side of the hill, beyond the creek, with the mountains at our backs. We would ride from where Thunder came. The Sage Men came with us and I think that this was the best place to hide, but it was not the best place to charge from because it was quite far from the ve'hó'e road and the Sioux would be in the fight before us. Our leaders told us not to worry, saying that this fight would not really start until we got there and that when we did, this little distance would have given our ponies their second wind. It was good, although some of our men did not think much of what Lame Deer said to us. They remembered what he said and I think that made it easier for them to fight him[100] after we whipped Hae'esta'ehe (Lieutenant Colonel George A. Custer).

I started to feel afraid as I looked about me there. Here were all of these brave men putting their strong heart songs on the wind without voices, listening to our holy men and preparing in a sacred manner, and here was I, just a boy. I had no shield or war bonnet to offer to the four Sacred Persons or the Powers, for I had not earned honors in war or yet been blessed in dreams. I watched Little Wolf paint his pony in the way of the Elks; his pony was white and so upon it he put red lightning, many coups and enemies killed. The Elk men with black ponies painted them with white and yellow, and some, like my uncle, tied a scalp to the bridle. My legs started to feel queer and I think my uncle could see that I was not feeling good. My legs were hollow and a sickness had come into my belly. It was very cold

Black Elk

HOW MY FATHER GOT A BLACK LEG

I was three years old when my father's right leg was broken in the Battle of the Hundred Slain (Fetterman Fight).* From that wound he limped until the day he died. . . . I can remember that Winter of the Hundred Slain as a man may remember some bad dream he dreamed when he was little, but I cannot tell just how much I heard when I was bigger and how much I understood when I was little. It is like some fearful thing in a fog, for it was a time when everything seemed troubled and afraid.

I had never seen a wasicu (white man) then, and did not know what one looked like; but everyone was saying that the wasicus were coming and that they were going to take our country and rub us all out and that we should all have to die fighting. It was the wasicus who got rubbed out in that battle, and all the people were talking about it for a long while; but a hundred wasicus was not much if there were others, and others without number where those came from. . . . When I was older, I learned what the fighting was about that winter and the next summer. Up on the Madison Fork the wasicus had found much of the yellow metal that they worship and that makes them crazy, and they wanted to have a road up through our country to the place where the yellow metal was; but my people did not want the road. It would scare the buffalo and make them go away, and also it would let the other wasicus come in like a river. And so when the soldiers came and built themselves a town of logs (Fort Phil Kearny) there on the Piney Fork of the Powder, my people knew they meant to have their road and take our country, and maybe kill us all when they were strong enough.

It was about when the bitten moon was delayed in the Time of the Popping Trees (December) when the hundred were rubbed out. . . . I am quite sure that I remember the time when my father came home with a broken leg that he got from killing so many wasicus, and it seems that I can remember all about the battle too, but I think I could not. It must be the fear that I remember most. All this time I was not allowed to play very far away from our tipi, and my mother would say, "If you are not good the wasicus will get you."

We must have broken camp at the mouth of the Peno soon after the battle, for I can remember my father lying on a pony drag with buffalo robes all around him like a baby, and my mother riding the pony. The snow was deep and it was very cold, and I remember sitting in another pony drag beside my father and mother, all wrapped up in fur. We were going away from where the soldiers were, and I do not know where we went, but it was west. It was a hungry winter.

*Black Elk's father also bore the name Black Elk, but in subsequent military reports and accounts of the Fetterman Fight he is identified as 'Black Leg,' primarily due to the injury he suffered that participants, and then secondary sources, made reference to when recounting the battle. See note 113 and Johnson Holy Rock's interview in *Reflections*.

Black Elk quoted in Neihardt, Black Elk Speaks, and DeMallie, The Sixth Grandfather, the latter from Neihardt's complete transcripts of his interviews with Black Elk as translated by his son, Ben Black Elk.

Heháka Sapa

where we were, but I felt all dried out as if I had been walking in the sun. I had done nothing to earn my paint, but my uncle covered my face in white paint so that the soldiers would have a hard time seeing me and to give me courage. I remembered how good it had been to see my uncle after the butchering had happened on Sand Creek, and then I could hear the stories the survivors told, and then I saw that grandmother the soldiers scalped and how she was blinded by her own skin that had fallen down over her eyes. I saw this, only now I could see that it was my own grandmother. I did not feel so sick anymore, I felt mad. I felt ready.

When I looked about me I was no longer so small. Little Wolf and Old Bear were here and to me these men were like the sun.[101] Little Wolf's face was painted yellow, our Sun's holy color, and up and down his war bonnet flew sacred birds, a blue swift hawk leading these messengers of the Ma'heono. I seem to remember that he was wearing a white man's spotted shirt that was mostly blue, and over that, resting by his heart, was the Chiefs' Bundle. This long parfleche held within it the medicine that was the rope that tied the Sweet Medicine Chief to the great prophet, Sweet Medicine himself. Little Wolf was proud of a soldier's long knife he had captured. One side of it was painted blue and the other red, and from where I stood I could see the blue side. The ve'hó'e got to see both sides in the battle.[102] Wild Hog, Lame White Man and Crazy Head were among our bravest war leaders and they were waiting by Little Wolf. We had White Bull's and Crazy Mule's powers with us, and when I think of this now it seems to me that the mysterious ways of these men killed more soldiers than our arrows. Crazy Mule had the power to make men foolish, he would stare at them until they became crazy, and he did that to the soldiers on this day. Crazy Mule came to the fighting with us but I did not see him shoot any arrows or guns; he just sat on his pony and stared at the soldiers. I'm sure their bullets hit him many times, but he had the bulletproof power and so they could not hurt him. But more than anything else, Ésevone was with us. She was with Little Horse now and he was waiting where we could all see him, as he was to call the charge. Ésevone was upon his head and She would lead us to victory, Her horns standing holy with sacred red paint giving strength to those who were shown upon them. Though it was not sunny, the night and day of the beads on Ésevone's brow band, and Her hair that was as flame, brought us light there in the wrinkled timber of that ravine.

From where we waited I could not see any of the Little Stars by Crow Standing Off Creek, and the Greasy Foam River Sioux were on the winter side of the ridge. The earth had truly swallowed us up. The wind breathed hard on us once, and in that breath we heard some firing from over near the Pine Woods,[103] but it was not much. It was quick and went when the wind stopped breathing, and men started looking at each other to see if others had heard it, and that it had not just been a pony stepping on some sticks. But it was not a pony, it was shooting, and it was the thunder wagon that told us this. The big voice of the thunder wagon was not thunder today; from so far away it was no more than the moan of a sick man, but that moan still called some of our men to jump upon their ponies.[104] Some of these ponies had been in battle before, and they knew why we were waiting and started to pace and shake and throw their heads. The wolf who had come with the Kit Fox was sent amongst us, calling softly that none must let these ponies tell the soldiers' horses that we were here. Most got off again and stood and held their ponies, and they stopped nickering, and there was nothing else but the breathing of the wind which came and went. It got colder with the waiting, and I can remember thinking that my fingers might not work and I would not be able to shoot my bow. My uncle had his hands beneath a blanket which he wore like a long, vé'ho'e robe,[105] but most were wrapped in buffalo robes or had calfskin capes over their war shirts, and we all wore leggings.

The sun must have been going to the center when the shooting came back. It was nearer now, like gophers talking, but then it was gone again. I thought I could see horsemen coming over the ridge, riding good but then pulling up and acting crazy. They looked like the hé'e-ma'haeso when they did this. The hé'e-ma'haeso had become a picture from an old dream and these men came from there too. They were here but maybe they were not. They were the dreamers or the dream. Big Nose's black war pony was part of the dream and then it was not a dream, or at least I do not think that it was a dream. It was not easy to see from where we were, and the riders went in and out as they came down the slope towards the white man's road. There were no soldiers, or none that we could see, until Crazy Horse brought them. I could not see Crazy Horse but I could see a red-yellow pony with a white face and a man leading it on foot.[106] The soldiers came up in a cloud behind this man and fanned along the edge of the Lodgepole Hills as feathers in a bustle.[107] Bullets fell around him, the hail from that blue cloud, but he was not hit, although I thought the pony must have been shot in the leg when the man began looking at it that way. Yes, this was Little Hawk's swift pony, and so the man had to be Crazy Horse. As far away as we were, you could see his long hair like the color of that pony, hanging loose and falling over a red blanket which he had tied over his war shirt and blue leggings. It did not seem that the soldiers wanted to follow Crazy Horse, and they stood looking down at him, walking soldiers in the middle of some pony soldiers. I could not see very much of the others until Big Nose came back, riding very fast towards Crazy Horse, who had limped slow away from the soldiers on the hill. Big Nose rode back and forth between the soldiers and Crazy Horse, and then below these two we could again see Black Coal, The-Young-Man-Whose-Enemies-Are-Even-Afraid-to-See-His-Horses and He Dog, each twisting about as if scared to stay and help but scared to go away and be talked about.[108]

The soldiers fired at Big Nose and Crazy Horse but it was only a few plumes of smoke. A pony soldier on a white horse (Lieutenant George W. Grummond) trotted down the hill and others in lines followed. He stopped, and then the walking soldiers and the other pony soldiers lined up again with him. Big Nose went beside Crazy Horse and reached down to pull him up onto the back of the black horse, but Crazy Horse waved his arm at him, as if telling him to go. They looked to be quarreling. Big Nose turned the black horse and rode back towards the others who were waving and shouting. Crazy Horse got back on the red-yellow pony, tied his war rope, and then put the pony to walking. It was moving very badly for such a fine horse. The soldiers started again, slowly, and then we looked up and saw that Big Nose was among them, riding in and out of them on a dragonfly's wings. And then he was gone. The black horse was now thunder on the white man's road and all but Crazy Horse had come together in a pack. Crazy Horse was closer to the soldiers than he was to our other nine men, the red-yellow pony with the bald face limping as if on many rocks. The pony soldier on the white horse moved forward, faster than before, and then he was galloping, holding out his long knife.[109] Crazy Horse still moved slow. Other pony soldiers were coming, the one with the long knife now so close to Crazy Horse that I thought he must cut him. But it was good that Little Hawk's pony was so swift, for it carried Crazy Horse away from the pony soldier's big white horse, and now the rest of the soldiers were on their way towards the road, not as a river but like the last melting snow of winter, trickling over and down the side of the Lodgepole Hills. Little Wolf gave word for us to mount, and we did, and then leaned along the necks of our ponies to cover their eyes and hold their muzzles to stop their talk.

We Cheyennes could all now see the soldiers; they were on the ve'hó'e wagon road (the Bozeman Trail) walking by the little hill that sits at the beginning of the land shaped like the blade of a knife.[110] They were together there, horses and men, moving in that odd way they have, but then the pony soldier on the white horse rode ahead and other pony soldiers went with him. Our men who had fooled them were still on the road, but closer to the end that splits Crow Standing Off Creek. The pony soldier on the white horse was riding faster now, and all but a handful of the pony soldiers had left the walking soldiers and were doing very poor shooting. Those who stayed with them had another pony soldier with a long knife (Captain William J. Fetterman) who seemed to be telling them what to do. These walking soldiers had big coats on, and I decided that one of them was mine and that I would take it.[111] They looked very good to wear in the cold, and the walking soldiers stepped along the road like sandhill cranes with the wings of their long coats flapping. Of course, I hoped that they would not fight like sandhill cranes. The pony soldiers with them had long guns and were riding in two lines, but the other pony soldiers following the one on the big white horse had shorter guns.[112] These with the one on the white horse did not keep together and move slowly like the others; they were as buffalo running toward a cliff. In the Time of the Dogs we used to hunt buffalo that way, tricking them into running off a cliff, and that is how it was this day with these pony soldiers. Crazy Horse, Big Nose and the others were at Crow Standing Off Creek when the pony soldier on the white horse was riding where the road falls to the water. Then this soldier went west, off the road, as if to reach the creek and our men faster.

Sandhill Crane

Crazy Head

Low Dog

American Horse crossed the creek first and kept riding, our other men following fast with Crazy Horse at the back. The soldier on the white horse also kept riding, but his pony soldiers were now further behind him and had stopped shooting. Some of the walking soldiers were not much more than halfway to where the road goes down to the creek. Most of us did not know it then, but our leaders had made a sign for the ten men to make when we were all to charge upon the soldiers. The only ones who were told this were the chargers: Sorrel Horse of the Sage Men, Black Twin for the Little Stars on ponies, Yellow Eagle for the Little Stars who were to fight on foot, Black Shield of the Greasy Foam River Sioux, and Little Horse, who would lead us. They did not tell us all because they knew some among us would see it too soon, or think that they had seen it, and then show themselves to the soldiers who would again get away. When they crossed the creek Crazy Horse took four men and American Horse took the other four, and then these two small parties rode across each other to make one star, and then rode across each other again to make another star, and this was the sign to charge. At one star, Little Horse held his Contrary Bow in his left hand and a tanager swayed gently on the lance with every twitch his pony made. He stood alone, between us and the Sage Men, where we could all see him and he could see over to the creek. When the men turned to make the second star he put his ash wood whistle to his mouth, passed the Contrary Bow from his left hand, behind his neck, and into his right hand. With the making of the second star he blew his whistle, we rose up, and he gave the cry of the burrowing owl. Now Little Horse could not turn back and we followed, Ésevone guiding us into battle and our voices those of sandhill cranes, calling to the enemy that we were here and today they would die.

My pony stumbled and I thought that I might fall before even getting across the part of the creek that was bent in front of us, but it was just ice and I pulled him away. My back felt as though there were ants all over it, and my heart was so full that at first it was hard to breathe. The Little Stars were as fire on the prairie surrounding the pony soldiers, and had they not been on foot I think they would have rubbed many of the soldiers out as they ran away from Crow Standing Off Creek. We came as one arrow from the west, the Little Stars of Black Twin were another, and the Sage Men were the first. From our side of the hill, I think Sorrel Horse was the first man on horseback to get into the fight with the pony soldiers. I could not see the Greasy Foam River Sioux, but I could hear them and I could tell by the way the walking soldiers on the road above us were moving that they were being attacked. The pony soldier on the white horse was fighting hard. He had got to Crow Standing Off Creek before the Little Stars charged. I thought he must be a chief among the soldiers for he fought more than the others and was a shield to them. It was hard for the

Short Bull

pony soldiers to get their big horses to take them back up the hill. It was not too bad on the road, but everywhere else the ground was hard and their horses could not go fast on the ice. We found this trouble too. Little Wolf was calling to us to stop the pony soldiers from climbing the hill, he wanted us to cut them off from the walking soldiers, but we could not do it. We had been too far away and the pony soldiers were already scattered on the side of the hill like a handful of dirt.

It was now that some of the soldiers got off their horses and tried to hide behind them as they went up the hill, shooting and standing, then scrambling and shooting some more, but their horses did not like it and would jump and pull to get away. Those still on horses were whipping them, and it was odd to see these men moving so fast and their horses moving so slow. One of them fell off and seemed to pull his horse on top of him. I saw three arrows in this horse, and as it lay on the soldier it looked like it was hitting its head on the ground whenever it tried to get up. Some Little Stars counted coup on the soldier but were pushed away from him by much shooting. Then the shooting stopped, and the soldier's arms started to claw at the ground but his legs would not work. Maybe the horse had broken his back. I do not know. Wherever he is now, he is crawling still, for the women of the Little Stars finished him. The pony soldier on the white horse was still among the Little Stars, and I was much closer now, so close that I could hear the iron hooves of the soldiers' horses on the hard ground and the noise the pony soldier chief's long knife made when he cut the head off a young boy who tried to shoot him but snapped his bowstring.[113] It was like air being pushed out of a wet buffalo bladder. Their big horses were screaming and it hurt my ears. Here, we Cheyennes became three parties: Crazy Head rode through the Little Stars with many of us following, and went up the road, chasing some of the pony soldiers. Wild Hog stayed to fight the other pony soldiers with Little Wolf, and Lame White Man took at least two handfuls of men to the south, going along the flat ground in the valley as if riding towards the fort. I did not see Lame White Man again for a while.

Some of the walking soldiers had hidden in some big rocks on the hill, near where the road falls to the creek. The pony soldiers we were after were trying to get to them. We fought alongside the Little Stars here and I saw Low Dog, one of our relatives who lived with them. He was a young man then but still looked very fierce, and he was on foot, darting between our men and horses, trying to get the soldiers in the rocks to stand and shoot him. They did not, but soon they killed a Greasy Foam River Sioux who rode right into the rocks.[114] Two of these ve'hó'e had the fastest-shooting guns I had ever heard and they used them well.[115] Their shooting was too fast for me to count the Sioux they were hitting. We stopped firing arrows at them from horses and stayed a little below, where we were harder

Site of the Hundred-Soldiers-Killed-Fight, or Fetterman Battlefield

to hit. Here we let many arrows go, more and more until their shooting became slower. Our arrows were so many that they looked like grasshoppers filling the sky. It got crazy. When you moved it was as if you were in the woods walking on sticks, that is how many arrows were on the ground. For a while it was not good because our own people were hitting each other, but then some of our men crept closer and soon they were among these soldiers. Many followed Crazy Horse into the fighting here, the Little Stars and some Greasy Foam River Sioux getting all mixed up with the soldiers. We did not think that it would take them long as this was how they liked to fight, close and by hand, counting many coups and rubbing the soldiers out. Crazy Horse had a young man who followed him in this and other battles; his name was Good Weasel, and if the people could not see Crazy Horse they could see him, and it gave them great heart. As always, these two fought well here, but I heard that Crazy Head and Low Dog killed more soldiers in those rocks than any other men.

I did not know it then but this would become as three different fights in one. The fighting in those rocks was done, and so Crazy Head charged south along the road towards the other pony soldiers. A few soldiers were killed here who did not fight so good. It was like shooting arrows into rabbits, as they did not seem to know where they were running. It was not that far down, and we could see that the pony soldier on the white horse was still alive, but he did not live much longer. There was a lot of smoke from the walking soldiers' long guns and when they fired they were lost in it. The pony soldiers and the rest of the walking soldiers were all bunched there, where the hill that held the road slid into a crooked basin that did not end until the bottom of the valley. This was very hard to climb up as it was all icy. The pony soldiers made up-and-down lines along the top of this basin, shooting toward the west and north, and the walking soldiers were in up-and-down lines with their backs to the pony soldiers, shooting to the south and east. There was not a good way to get to the walking soldiers because the ground was flat on the top of the hill, and so, from over the road, the Greasy Foam River Sioux would wait until the soldiers had to reload and then try to get closer. It is true that the soldiers were not easy to get to, but they were surrounded. Some of the pony soldiers were not shooting, they were trying to hold onto their big horses. The smell of blood and smoke was all around, and even now when I see a herd of elk I can see these soldiers. Just as elk cows with their thin-legged calves will crowd together and turn one way and then another and then back again in fear, so did these soldiers. It seemed as if the two soldier chiefs were shouting at each other, but I do not know if they were, as everything was lost in the screams of dying horses and men, the snap of guns, our strong heart cries and the thunder of our ponies' hooves hunting the soldiers who broke away. We moved as swallows, cutting through the air with our arrows, our ponies on the wing taking us above the fighting where it all became quiet. But it was not, that is just a place you go to sometimes in a fight.

We were back with Wild Hog now, and Little Wolf was calling out and telling us what to do as he stalked back and forth, watching the soldiers. Until then I had not seen many of the ten men who had brought the soldiers to us, but I know that all of them who did not have bad wounds fought at this end of the ridge. I saw He Dog and his brother, Short Buffalo, fighting on foot near our men until the soldiers let their horses go. We had moved under the pony soldiers and were shooting more and more arrows at them when Big Nose came up the big basin. His horse was worn out and he said that all of the men who had tricked the soldiers needed new horses to fight because the ones they had were finished – this is why He Dog was on foot. When those words came out of his mouth the soldiers let all of their horses go. Many of our people rushed forward from all sides to claim the soldier horses, and when they did this the walking soldiers started running back down the road in the direction of the fort. Crazy Head went after them, trying to hunt them like buffalo, but we did not. We shot many arrows into them instead for they were in the open now. I do not know if He Dog and Short Buffalo caught any horses or if they just chased after the walking soldiers. Little Wolf told us to let it go as others were waiting for them. The pony soldiers, who now had no horses, began to shoot very fast in all directions, trying to stop us from wiping out the walking soldiers. I think the pony soldiers with the faster guns were meant to keep us fighting until the walking soldiers could be seen from the hill near the fort where the soldiers waved flags,[116] or until more soldiers came out of the fort.[117] The pony soldiers moved slowly in that peculiar way that makes soldiers easy to hit, with little steps, up and down, all knotted together. But then the one who had ridden the big white horse was killed and they became as elk cows again and did not seem to know where to go. One of the Little Stars killed the pony soldier chief. Some said it was American Horse and that it was good because the pony soldier chief had wanted to catch American Horse, Crazy Horse and the others, and now he had. I do not know, but whoever it was, they rode very fast at him and hit his head with a war club.[118] His soldiers were too far away and shooting too poorly to hit anybody who counted coup on him, and the last I saw of the pony soldier chief some women of the Little Stars were stripping him and putting fire to the insides of his legs.[119] With burnt thighs he would never ride on us again.

Area where Big Nose fell and was laid until the battle was won

Another pony soldier took their dead chief's place and he was very brave.[120] He looked crazy, pointing his gun at us, looking around, and shooting. He had a very good cry but I do not know what it was, maybe a bear. The other pony soldiers were not so brave but had got behind some big, flat rocks. The brave one did not get there. A Sioux wearing a red calfskin cape and blue and white leggings rode him down as you would a crippled bull and shot him through the heart with an arrow.[121] The others were shooting at us from behind the big rocks, and Little Wolf was angry as this is what he had wanted to stop. A storm was coming and might have been upon us before these soldiers were rubbed out. That would have been bad for us as wet snow on our bowstrings would make it hard to shoot. It was now that Little Horse let his pony go, and then others did the same, the ponies loping down the side of the hill where some young men were waiting to catch them. Little Horse crept around the side of the pony soldiers in the flat rocks, as if going behind them, but then I could not see him anymore. Our men started to creep closer but it was not easy, the bullets and the ice made it slow work. Big Nose was still mounted on the black horse when he was offered another. Little Wolf took the reins of his white pony and again held them out to Big Nose. "Brother," he said. "With all of these men watching here it would be good to show them how a brave Cheyenne gives his body to the enemy." Big Nose took the white pony.[122] He would ride at the pony soldiers in the rocks so when they shot at him, others among us might be able to kill some of them and get closer.

Then a strange thing happened. A soldier holding a yellow-metal horn went galloping down the wagon road on a gray horse, and behind him was a soldier with an upside-down head who was hanging on to him.[123] My uncle called to me and we rode after the two soldiers on the gray horse, but we could not get our ponies up the slope and onto the road fast enough; it was too slippery. As we tried this, Big Nose charged at the pony soldiers in the flat rocks, and their guns crackled like a big fire but he was not hit. Some soldier horses were still loose on the road, and we watched as Big Nose claimed two with his quirt and turned to ride back on the soldiers with Crazy Head, but then we heard a shot and we saw Big Nose crumple; his arms went loose, his head hung limp, and he was all shaky. Another bullet hit the white pony, and then another and another, and it jerked and screamed before its legs wobbled and gave in. It seemed that Little Wolf had been right; his pony was not fast enough. Both were killed, though Big Nose did not die really dead until two days after the fight. This made our men more angry. From the road I could see that Little Horse was now about the length of a lodge pole from the soldiers, and this is where he fought as the pony soldiers had no shelter at their backs.[124] We could hear firing to the south, quite near, and we knew that this must be where the walking soldiers were. For a while the firing kept going, over and over, but it sounded to me that the beating was not so strong and the guns were dying. From the road we could see a cloud of smoke, and so we went towards it. I told you earlier about counting my first coup, and I did this here, on the road between the pony soldiers and the walking soldiers. The walking soldier I counted coup on must have been hit by our arrows when the bluecoats were all running down the road. I did not think to take his scalp because we did not take the scalps of the ve'hó'e very often; we could see no honor in it and so we would not dance them.[125] That is why I did not take it and did not care that the Little Star took it.

The walking soldiers were in some more big rocks, near the wagon road on the little hill that sits at the beginning of this knife blade ridge.[126] We could see the wolves signalling from the Lodgepole Hills, and then from the west riders were coming. Many of the chiefs were watching from that slope above the creek, not far behind where we had waited for the soldiers. Red Cloud looked at the fight with his long-glasses, and Big Road, Red Dog, Bear's Rib, Medicine Man, Black Bear, Red Leaf, Painted Thunder, Black Moccasin and Box Elder were there with him. None of those chiefs came to the fighting, but High-Back-Bone did. After the small party had attacked the wagons near the Pine Woods, High-Back-Bone had

*White Horse kills
the ve'hó'e*

come back and watched some of the fighting with the chiefs. We were not close enough to hear what he said, for he rode around the bottom of the hill and then up to where the men were waiting to rub the walking soldiers out, but we had already seen what he would say – more soldiers were coming and so this must be ended. You could not count the arrows that were falling on the soldiers, but when we got closer we could see that there were still many soldiers alive. Their shooting had become slower and so our men made ready. This is where we saw Lame White Man again; he had taken those men to wait at this end of the road. That is how Lame White Man was: in a fight he could see where the enemy would go. He did that in the fight with Hae'esta'ehe (Custer), and then, as on this day, he was one of the bravest men who fought.[127]

There were many Greasy Foam River Sioux around these rocks and some Little Stars, but very few had ponies, most were on foot. You could not ride a pony into the big rocks where the walking soldiers were, and it was too icy to ride fast up the hill because it fell away on all sides, other than where the road came. Our men waited, the walking soldiers fired their long guns again, and then our men charged, running very fast. Some slipped and others just ran over them, trying to get among the rocks before the soldiers could shoot their guns again. Some did shoot again and we thought these must be pony soldiers who had gone with the walking soldiers. Their guns were better but their shots were not many as our men and the Sioux were among them. It was a terrible noise. It was no longer horses but soldiers who were screaming, their screams joining with the cries of our men, all mixed up like their bodies and arms and legs. The soldiers were hit with clubs and hatchets where they stood, and many were not all dead when they fell, but they soon were. Some tried to hide under the rocks, but the rocks would not move, and these walking soldiers were cut and slashed as they lay crying. They were heaped like buffalo at the bottom of a cliff and they were butchered the same way. It was like a bad dream. Later I saw the chief of the walking soldiers laying here, close to the man with the upside-down head who we had chased. The smoke hung in long clouds there, but then it went thin like mist and you could see into it. When I looked into it I thought I saw a soldier use a short-gun to kill another one.[128] I had not seen such a thing before and so I remembered it. Wolf Tooth, White Elk and Little Sun said that they saw the last four soldiers among these rocks shoot each other. I knew that this was Crazy Mule's work; he had made these soldiers crazy enough to shoot each other. The last soldier I saw die here was the one who had ridden the gray horse. He had no gun, only a soldier horn, and it took two men to kill him. When it was done, this one and the brave pony soldier I told you about were given buffalo calfskin capes for their journey.[129]

These were not the last soldiers to die. The men with Wild Hog had rubbed out most of the pony soldiers who were in the flat rocks, but some were running away. Their arms were spinning but their legs were not really moving. They looked like spiders, but those of us who were still on ponies hunted them like buffalo and it ended. I think Black Bear killed the last one.[130] We thought this soldier was dead, but he jumped back up and tried to run on calf's legs, but a calf that is just born cannot run faster than a wolf, and this pony soldier could not run fast without his horse. Black Bear took his gun and blue coat. I can remember the yellow lines on that coat because they weren't really yellow, they were nearly all black with the soldier's blood that had frozen on them. A dog ran from where the pony soldiers had been killed in the flat rocks. It looked sick, its tongue was hanging out and it was going in circles, yapping at those who were stripping the soldiers. It started to run up the road to where the walking soldiers were wiped out, but Big Rascal did not want even the soldiers' dog to live and so it was stopped with arrows.

We knew more soldiers were coming but we did not care; we wanted them to see this. We wished them to look upon the scene until their eyes were blinded by grief and their hearts weak. Here lie their friends, men who they believed to be strong, and look what had been done to them! Their bodies had been left to bloat or freeze, laying like young birds broken from a fall, their skin bare, waiting for the coyotes and wolves to chase the magpies away. They were all rubbed out. They were left helpless to stumble in the dark as blind old men. They were all sent away without strength or sight or fists to ever make war upon us. We cut them so that they would never be able to ride against us again, or march to our lodges to kill our helpless ones as they slept. We made sure that they would go hungry in the next life just as they had made us sick with hunger in this life by slaughtering the buffalo and driving away the game. A man without teeth cannot chew and a man without guts cannot eat.[131] They were reduced to this shame by a powerful foe. Who would challenge such an enemy as this? Who would make war on an enemy such as this when they too could be left on the ground in this way? Soldiers look upon your men, gather your things and run like frightened women back to the Black Dust River. We did not know their names, we knew only that they had come to starve us and to kill us in our lodges. We knew that they called peace, war, and war, peace. They came looking for it and we gave it to them.

The Elk Horn Scrapers killed many men that day, and most of us took their soldier coats and put them on. The sun was not much past the center, and when we were finished we got on our ponies and rode all around the battlefield shouting like this: "You have called us Blue Soldiers, now do you see these blue coats? Now we take that name! Do you see?" Then we made two lines on our horses like the pony soldiers did and trotted away. After the Hundred-Soldiers-Killed-Fight we would often ride that way. I was with the Elk Horn Scrapers when the fort on Buffalo Creek was burnt, but that did not happen until nearly two more winters had passed. We fought two more big battles against the soldiers before they went away, the one Crazy Mule led near the Big Sheep River fort, and the other when White Bull took some young men to Buffalo Creek and the soldiers hid behind the wagons.[132] The soldiers left our country under the Breeding Moon (August) in the year that some touched the pen.[133] Little Wolf was one of those and it was he that left the fort in flames. Morning Star, Big Wolf and Short Hair were with Little Wolf when he went to touch the pen. The old man soldier chief with a white dog-face (General William S. Harney) told Little Wolf that the north country would always be ours, that his soldiers knew it and so they would leave, and that the Buffalo Creek fort would be where the ve'hó'e would give us our presents. He lied. Little Wolf thought he had kept the north country for us, but the other chiefs did not. They did not believe the dog-face and did not think it right that Little Wolf touched the pen without the issue going through the Chiefs' Council.

We saw into the lives of our unborn generations on that day inside the empty fort. Many of our women had come to see the square ve'hó'e houses, and when they got there they became foolish, running around and laughing as if they had whiskey in their bellies. Anybody watching would have thought the soldiers' town of logs was a good thing. Little Wolf did not care to see this or to be reminded of the lies he had been told, and so the fort was burned. "We would starve if we stayed in one place like the ve'hó'e," he told the women. "And inside these towns of logs you would forget about the buffalo, and then our children would forget about the buffalo, and soon we would not know them. We must follow the buffalo to live!" Of course, he was right. It was just as Erect Horns had told us it would be: *When you have driven the buffalo away, you will live on spotted animals. You will not be healthy as you are now, but disease will come often. All the medicine power of Ésevone may be lost. You will marry early and people will have their hair turn gray when still young. Sweet Medicine will tell you a great deal more than I do. Always tell the others. Do not forget what I tell you. Do not forget what you have been told. I have spoken.*

It was only seven winters after the Hundred-Soldiers-Killed-Fight that Ésevone was hurt by one of our own people and the buffalo started to go away.[134] Erect Horns warned us that this would happen, and it did. Look what the ve'hó'e did to us then. This is what I saw that day in the fire that burnt the fort on Buffalo Creek. I have no more to say.

Without the help, advice, knowledge, interpretation and stories that the following people have shared with me over the years, I would not have been able to write the Hundred-Soldiers-Killed-Fight: Dr. Henrietta Mann, Douglas and Donna Spotted Eagle, Elva Stands-in-Timber, George and Rachel Magpie, Richard Tall Bull Jr., June Black, Stone Forehead (Father Peter J. Powell), Leona Buckman, Johnson Holy Rock, Oliver Red Cloud, Alfred Red Cloud, Wilmer Mesteth, Isaac Dog Eagle, Dr. Joe Medicine Crow, Ron Medicine Crow, and the late William Tall Bull and Ted Rising Sun. Ne-a'ese. Pilamaya. Ha-hoo! With respect to George Bent who preserved so much for future generations, and to George Bird Grinnell and George E. Hyde who were interested enough to ask.

I am glad you told us how big a country we have

FORT LARAMIE, DAKOTA TERRITORY
TREATY COUNCIL
CIRCA MAY 5, 1868

"I will tell you where your country is. Here is the Platte River. The north side of the river is the Northern Cheyenne and Northern Arapaho country. We will put a stake on the north side of the river, where the North and South Platte meet. Then we will put stakes at the other boundaries of your land: from that point west to Red Butte Canyon, on the north fork of the Platte, then from Red Butte Canyon north to the Bighorn Canyon; then east along the south banks of the Bighorn River, the Yellowstone River and the Missouri River, to a point straight north from the point at the fork of the Platte River. The eastern boundary shall be determined by the line extending straight north of the point at the fork of the Platte."

GENERAL WILLIAM S. HARNEY

"I am glad you told us how big a country we have."

CHIEF LITTLE WOLF

"Yes, that is your country but you must kill no more white men."

GENERAL WILLIAM S. HARNEY

"You spoke to me, General Harney, about killing no more white men. I understand you. But there is one thing I want to tell you. You told us where our land lies, but you have three forts on our land. Take them away and I will stop killing whites."

CHIEF LITTLE WOLF

"Chief Little Wolf, let these forts stay yet one more year and I will move them. The fort on the Little Piney (Fort Phil Kearny) will now turn into an agency, as the spot is very good for a permanent location. We will give you rations there, and also tools and implements to do your farming."

GENERAL WILLIAM S. HARNEY

Chief Little Wolf at the 1868 Fort Laramie Treaty Conference.

Jules Seminole was the U.S. government's Cheyenne interpreter at the 1868 Fort Laramie Treaty Conference, and this exchange is compiled from a statement made by Jules Seminole in 1920. Seminole's statement is from the John Stands-in-Timber papers, Father Peter J. Powell Collection, The Newberry Library. Father Powell included a fuller text of the Seminole statement in People of the Sacred Mountain, Volume II.

THREE CROW WARRIORS ON THEIR WAR PONIES

by

Kevin Red Star

Reflections

ELMER 'SONNY' REISCH

"I'm sure that when Carrington marched in to Fort Laramie it was as big a shock to Taylor as it was to the Lakotas, but I think Carrington probably got the biggest shock of all when he realized that Taylor had made no mention of the army's intention to build forts along the Bozeman Trail."

SONNY REISCH IS SITE SUPERINTENDENT AT FORT PHIL KEARNY STATE HISTORIC SITE, WITH JURISDICTION EXTENDING TO FORT FETTERMAN, FORT RENO, AND OTHER RELATED SITES ALONG THE BOZEMAN TRAIL

As the Civil War drew to a close, military officers like Patrick E. Connor, Richard I. Dodge, Philip St. George Cooke, John Pope and William Tecumseh Sherman were in tune with the idea that the gilded age was coming and that the nation was ready to explode in terms of westward expansion and economic development. These men were beyond military officers, they were the spearhead of the nation's industrial aspirations. Connor was a California entrepreneur turned soldier, and Dodge had been a railroad man before the war, but I think Sherman is the prime example of an officer who was hand in glove with the Industrial Revolution and who at war's end wanted to get back to the business of America. Both Sherman and Dodge identified the completion of the transcontinental railroad as critical to the course of empire, and Sherman's ambition was matched by influence as his brother was a U.S. senator with close ties to the Union Pacific. These men were charged with pushing the nation forward, with opening the way for railroads, for homesteading and for mining. Each aspect was crucial, especially mining, in the development of the various trails which rolled back the frontier, and as 1866 dawned you could not separate military conflict from economic design in the destiny of the nation.

When America looked westward to fulfill those aspirations the so-called Indian problem stared back. After the Civil War, Sherman became Commander of the Military Division of the Mississippi. Sherman and his peers were very much of the mind that when a problem arose there would be a solution, however brutal, and I think that the horrors of the Civil War somewhat calloused their emotions and shaped that attitude. When Sherman marched through Georgia, that action was his solution for that problem, and he was probably the most vocal advocate of extermination as a solution to the Indian problem. The elimination of the buffalo, and consequently of the Plains Indian culture, was a policy that found favor in high places. The political paralysis that developed with President Andrew Johnson's impeachment hearings and the rise of the radical Republicans handed greater influence to those who had won the Civil War, and Sherman and Phil Sheridan were preeminent amongst those. At the same time, there were other voices within the Republican party that had a clear sympathy for the Indians, but in many ways it was like the Vietnam policy a century later: there were people with ideals but no long-term solutions. The abolitionists had sympathy for the Native Americans; they might not have understood the problem or how to handle it, but they were opposing the idea of extermination, and then promoting an alternative: that converting the Indians to Christianity would be the solution to everything. In a country that was struggling to recover from the almighty division of North and South, the eastern Reconstructionists' opinions on the problem in the West was divided between extermination and assimilation, but I don't think that any of them could foresee, or had control over, the relentless rush of westward expansion. It took less than a man's lifetime to populate the West, not the centuries Jefferson had predicted.

The idea of garrisoning the Powder River country began with Grenville M. Dodge and Patrick E. Connor. They wanted to establish forts on the Powder and Yellowstone Rivers, the theory being that the military should march into the heart of the Sioux and Cheyenne hunting grounds to prosecute a punitive campaign and then build the forts. Connor launched that expedition in 1865 but it wasn't a well-thought-out policy and it was never clearly defined. When you review the military records you detect that there were ulterior motives, that a lot of things were going on behind the scenes that were unspoken. There is a school of thought that says a good portion of the policy for establishing the forts and garrisoning the Bozeman Trail was a conscious attempt by Sherman to divert the Indians' attention away from the railroad and to the posts on the Bozeman Trail. Of course, that remains speculative because it was unwritten and publicly unspoken, but it raises a significant ethical question: were these garrisons established as sacrificial tokens to achieve that greater, strategic objective?

You have to read between the lines of what Sherman was saying in the spring of 1866. He talks about wanting the president and secretary of war to "continue to befriend these roads" and then says "it is the army's duty to make the progress of the construction of the great Pacific railways as safe as possible." By mid-May he is encouraging the officers' wives in Carrington's command to keep diaries and is assuring Carrington that the territory he is about to enter is safe for the women and children, but then he writes to Grant's chief of staff and comments that all he wants is "quiet this year, for by next year we can have the new cavalry enlisted, equipped, and mounted, ready to go and visit these Indians where they live." The lack of foresight the military had on this amazes me, and I have trouble deciding how much was an active, conscious duplicity, and how much was just stupidity. I think Sherman was expecting that there would be opposition, but he did not give Carrington any offensive ability, particularly when compared with what Connor had at his disposal a year earlier and had failed with. I'm still not sure that Sherman fully anticipated the level of resistance that Carrington's men would encounter, and the other perspective would be that there was still a good portion of the army tied up with Reconstruction in the South, and at the same time troops were massing along the Texas border because of the possibility of war with France and Mexico.

The territory over which the Bozeman Trail ran and into which Sherman sent Carrington was not a 'no-man's land,' it was more of an 'every-man's land.' In a sense it was an intertribal area that became somewhat multicultural with the arrival of the fur traders. In terms of my own personal bias, I don't accept the idea that anyone had ownership of the land in the Powder River country, up to the Bighorn Mountains, and on to the Tongue and Bighorn Rivers – or that anyone had an irrefutable claim to it. There is no doubt that the Lakota, Cheyenne and Crow all have long and significant interests within the area that can be traced back a considerable amount of time, but there is also evidence that the Kiowa were once there and some Apache groups, and so that's why I question the concept of claims; in many ways, once you get into claims, you also get into the issue of having the strength to hold your claim. I think the tribes' best claim to this area is the spiritual interests they have in the land, like the Cheyennes' connection to the Medicine Wheel. It's not a single facet in any way, each tribe is a part of it and each tribe has their sacred places within it. There were multiple layers of people constantly moving through the area, and so I think the arbitrary setting of boundaries in the Fort Laramie Treaty of 1851 was totally invalid, and like most treaties it was written in language that is open-ended and open to misinterpretation.

At the 1866 Fort Laramie treaty conference, when the superintendent of Indian Affairs, Edward B. Taylor, the president of the treaty commission, responded to one of

Spotted Tail's demands by saying, "If you want to hunt buffalo north and south you can because we know this is all your country," I'm sure Spotted Tail must have thought that the Great White Father shared the Lakotas' perception of whose territory the Powder River country was. I would have definitely read it that way. Unbeknownst to the Lakotas was the political conflict in the different branches of the United States government where one hand didn't know what the other was doing. In Taylor and Spotted Tail you had a man that didn't have the authority to make promises, making promises to a man that didn't have the authority to say "build the road." Taylor definitely didn't have the support of the military on claims like that, and I'm sure that when Carrington marched in to Fort Laramie it was as big a shock to Taylor as it was to the Lakotas, but I think Carrington probably got the biggest shock of all when he realized that Taylor had made no mention of the army's intention to build forts along the Bozeman Trail. I don't think that Carrington was privy to a lot of what was going on at the upper command level, and I think he thought that the wheels of the operation were being well greased, and so he walked into something that he wasn't expecting, both in terms of Taylor's lack of disclosure and Red Cloud's vehement opposition. I have a tendency to think that most authors have embellished Carrington's meeting with Red Cloud and that it probably didn't happen; but if it did, I doubt that it was the dramatic confrontation that has been described with Carrington ready to draw his pistol and Red Cloud clutching his knife.

Carrington probably carried out his orders in spite of any doubts that he was developing, rather than because he really had a sense of what was going to take place. Carrington was a good administrator and his later career demonstrated that he was very capable. Was he competent in this situation on the Bozeman Trail? I'm not sure who would have been competent in the initial stages of Fort Phil Kearny with the Lakotas approaching the peak of their military power and the lack of direction or support he received. Sherman had supported Carrington's appointment to the position of Commander of the Mountain District, but Carrington lobbied for the command and he was not chosen on his merits, he was chosen because of his political connections – primarily his power within the Republican Party. Sherman had similar connections and ties, and so when Carrington became a full colonel in the regular army at a time when many others were being demoted, it was not an indication of his abilities as a soldier, but of his abilities as a politician. Carrington had served as a desk general during the Civil War, and not only did he have little combat experience, he had no experience of Plains Indian guerrilla warfare. He wasn't part of the West Point old boys network, and so there was some resentment towards him from other officers when he received what was a rare commission. I'm pretty sure that Major Van Voast was slighted by Carrington's presence. Van Voast was a career soldier, and here was Carrington, basically a political appointee, in charge of things. General William Hazen and Colonel Henry Maynadier hardly supported him either, and the indifference these officers felt towards him undermined Carrington's efforts.

Carrington was an academic, he was very well read, and he was considered to be a humanitarian in that era. I think he was a man of good intentions who believed in the ethical treatment of the Indians, even though he didn't have a real idea of Indian culture. When he went out into the Powder River Basin I don't think that he was considered to be any worse than many who had already served out West, and men such as John Pope and Philip St. George Cooke had been relegated to the frontier because of their failures in other areas. It would be easy to say that Carrington was incompetent and that was why the men didn't respect him, but his problems were borne out of this combination of factors and in many ways he was hung out to dry. At first Sherman instructed him to avoid war, but by mid-August General Hazen was proposing a "vigorous final campaign" against the Indians, and within a month Sherman was encouraging Carrington to "strike a blow." St. George Cooke also urged Carrington to strike, but rejected his appeals for more cavalry mounts. Carrington received the orders to strike but not the resources. It's almost unbelievable looking back on it, considering that Patrick E. Connor had commanded a prodigious expeditionary force just a year earlier and hadn't been able to strike at the same foe in the same country. To think that Carrington could strike with an inadequate force of infantry showed a total lack of understanding of what was transpiring at Fort Phil Kearny. Even if he could have put a thousand men into the field, those orders would have been impossible to carry out. Carrington is still a mystery to me, and how much he was a victim of circumstances and how much he was a victim of his own personal incompetence is a gray area. He was certainly a more complex man than people recognize.

When he left Fort Kearny and moved up the Bozeman Trail, Carrington thought he saw the mission very clearly, but he did not see the potential for imperilment, and if anybody else did they didn't express it to him. His command was not what I would call a first-line unit to send into the western theater. The Eighteenth U.S. Infantry had suffered

Above: Captain William J. Fetterman's grave in the Custer National Cemetery at the Little Bighorn Battlefield National Monument

tremendous losses during the Civil War, and so to just refit this shot-up unit with raw recruits and send it to the frontier on a mission that was ill-defined did not augur well. Most of the military personnel directly involved had never served on the frontier and they could not claim the title of 'Indian fighters.' Infantrymen obviously lacked the mobility to fight a formidable light cavalry like the Lakota and Cheyenne, and so they mounted twenty men out of each company of the Eighteenth with horses from volunteer cavalry units that were being mustered out. Many of the soldiers, particularly the officer corps, were experienced Civil War veterans, but with that combat experience came the mental and physical scars that must have affected their actions during this tour of duty. Captain Fred Brown, the regimental quartermaster, served through the Civil War, but at Fort Phil Kearny he became almost obsessed with this strange need to chase Indians. The "pursuit of nobler game" was how Fetterman explained it, and Brown would lead these mad dashes out of the fort to chase small groups of Lakotas for several miles. Brown was desperate to take Red Cloud's scalp, but that was pretty brave talk for a bald man. Lieutenant Adair, the adjutant, had a mini-ball lodged in the back of his neck that gave him continual headaches and probably contributed to him being committed to an asylum. Ten Eyck, whom Carrington relied quite heavily upon, had been in the Libby Prison, where his health had been broken, and so he was dependent on laudanum and alcohol for survival. Captain James Powell had so many balls lodged in his body that the lead poisoned his system. Powell was credited for avoiding on December 19, 1866, what befell Fetterman two days later. Powell was immortalized as the hero of the Wagon Box Fight but he was not a spectacular commander and he had some mental health problems that later resulted in him being declared mentally incompetent.

These were experienced soldiers, and in the Civil War they had all shown themselves to be combat leaders, but outside of courage and an ability to cope in battle they were empty-handed when they reached the Powder River as this was a learning experience for them, just as it was for the men that they led. They had Jim Bridger, Jim Beckwourth and Jack Stead along as guides and interpreters, and what fascinates me is the military's lack of sensitivity to the political fallout that could result from that. On the one hand these were experienced frontiersmen who came with high recommendations, but on the other hand each one of them was known and hated by the Lakota, Cheyenne and Arapaho. The ranks of the so-called Indian fighters had been decimated by the Civil War, and so the military had lost a good portion of what had been learned about Plains Indian warfare in the 1850s. Sherman himself was not a pre–Civil War Indian fighter. During the period from 1861 to 1865 there was a military breakdown on the frontier; regular troops were nonexistent and volunteers capable of atrocities like Sand Creek were wearing the blue of the United States frontier army. The political hierarchy of the United States had been so focused on the Civil War that they didn't realize that the situation in the West had changed. The tactics employed by Harney and St. George Cooke in the 1850s were obsolete by the

Private John Guthrie's graphic interpretation of the aftermath of the Fetterman Fight, showing the Second Cavalry mount, Dapple Dave, as the command's only survivor. Guthrie was a member of the expedition Colonel Carrington led to recover the bodies that remained on the field the day after the battle. Captain Ten Eyck's party had returned with over half of the dead the previous day.

1860s. Connor was considered to be a successful Indian fighter but when he reached the Powder River in 1865 he soon found out that massacring Paiutes in Nevada was entirely different than facing the military power of the Lakota and Cheyenne. Colonel Maynadier at Fort Laramie had experience of the area from the topographical survey he had taken in 1859, and so he was as close as the army came to someone who knew the territory, but he had been away from it for so many years that his ability to read things was dated, and I don't think he understood what was going on with the Indians. There was little thought, less communication, no sense of urgency, and a total lack of understanding on the part of the military as to what the situation was that Carrington would face. War was looming with France, Reconstruction had to be successful, and the nation's coffers had to be replenished – what was happening in a backwater like Dakota Territory didn't register very high on that list of priorities. Carrington's command had all of the tools to build forts but none of the experience to garrison them.

I don't feel that the Lakotas and Cheyennes had looked upon Fort Connor (Fort Reno) as much of a threat. The group of disheartened volunteers Connor left there can't have impressed them very much, but Carrington's column was definitely more threatening. I think Carrington became confused and perplexed by what was happening with the Indians because he did not understand the political or social dynamics within the tribes; one day he's meeting with a party of Cheyennes who aren't opposing him, and the next day a party of Indians who look like Cheyennes are raiding the post. There were very well-defined reasons why this was taking place and although intellectually he may have reached an understanding as to why it was happening, he was so totally immersed in the events of the moment that it was years before he could analyze it. During the same period, Colonel Maynadier and Commissioner Taylor gave Carrington positive information about the 1866 treaty negotiations, and even the president of the United States became lulled into the sense that the policy was succeeding. There was almost a denial that the Indians were upset and Taylor contributed to that greatly, but Bridger was giving Carrington a different perspective on his adversaries. There was a tendency to discount what Bridger had to say because he told so many tall tales, and there was also attitude, 'Who is this old geezer telling us what to do? We're soldiers!' I think Carrington was so focused on building the fort that he looked upon its completion as the solution to the problem. I don't think that there was a definite point at which he said to himself, 'I'm in trouble here,' but I think by November 1866 he had a growing sense of crisis; the pressure from the Lakotas hadn't abated, his memos weren't being answered, and the reinforcements he wanted weren't coming. In one of his reports Carrington was very dismissive of Red Cloud's ability to lay siege to the post, adding that he was prepared for the winter, the following spring and summer. If he had actually believed that, he would have been delusional, but that certainly wasn't the case.

I think there was a sense of demoralization at Fort Phil Kearny in November and December, a feeling that there was a lack of direction that probably affected everybody from Carrington on down to the lowliest private. Morale amongst the men was dropping; for one thing the civilian contractors were making $40 or $50 a month as opposed to the soldiers' $16. There were recruits who would just as soon take off for the goldfields, but there were also a lot of dedicated soldiers who are rarely mentioned. Alcohol and desertion became problems; officially there wasn't access to alcohol but I'm pretty sure that any supply train that pulled in had bootleg alcohol on it. The officers had access to it through the settlers, or a good doctor might help them out. In terms of the post, conditions were pretty good for existence, or survival; the barracks had been completed and there wasn't a problem with rations. The problems in that regard really started after the Fetterman Fight, when they rushed all of the reinforcements up from Fort Laramie without supplies, and consequently there was a three-month period at Fort Phil Kearny when it was terrible. But in November 1866, although there was probably a sense of demoralization, there was still a military command carrying on at the post. Fetterman's arrival at Fort Phil Kearny that month was probably a breath of fresh air to many – here was somebody with ideas who might provide them with some inspiration – but of course he was there for less than six weeks.

There was speculation as to how much red meat Fetterman had been fed before he got to Fort Phil Kearny. It seems that someone had given him some orders to "get up there and get things moving," and Carrington even made a statement to that effect, writing that Fetterman expected to take command. Fetterman was looked upon as a rising star, an opinion he shared. He fought in Sherman's March to the Sea and he had an impressive Civil War combat record, becoming the Second Battalion's temporary commander during the war. He was expected to make waves, he had probably been encouraged to make waves and to get things moving, and I'm pretty sure that he came ready to take over and fully expecting to. When Fetterman reestablished contact with officers that he had served with in the war – Brown, George Grummond, and to a lesser extent Powell – he became the leader of that

Tenodor Ten Eyck

119

faction, and I think he was well thought of by most people at the fort. Up until December 21, 1866, even Carrington seemed to respect him and would defer to him on combat issues. I wouldn't call Fetterman a stupid man, but he was a man that followed his instincts instead of his head.

Fetterman was a product of the age. His attitude towards Indians, describing them as "nobler game" as if these people were trophy animals, was considered the norm, not the exception. This was a time when Caucasians were looked upon as the 'superior race,' and men like Fetterman, Wishart and Templeton, all the way up to the likes of Dodge and particularly Sheridan and Sherman, all made statements that were representative of that. I suspect that if you had attended a meeting in a frontier town in the 1860s you could have heard the same hatred and fanaticism that was heard in meetings in Nuremburg in the 1930s. There were many things, not only statements from these officers, but many events that reflect the genocide that was an ugly part of our past. I think there were cases of planned genocide in some areas where a number of tribes were wiped out, but it was never a policy of the United States government. In many ways I think it was a tragic but unconscious result of Manifest Destiny, as opposed to the conscious, calculated and systematic genocide that was undertaken by the Nazis in Europe within half a century of Wounded Knee. The Holocaust will always be a horrible event and the destruction of the Native Americans will always be a horrible event, but I have trouble equating the two, which may just be my own sense of conscience.

Fetterman had no comprehension of the situation in the region, and he showed his ignorance on his second day at the post by trying to trap Indians using hobbled mules as bait. On the evidence of that, it would seem that what he knew about Indians probably came out of a dime novel or a James Fenimore Cooper story. The plan he hatched with Brown to take fifty civilian volunteers and fifty enlisted men to attack the Indian encampment on Tongue River shows just how little he and his supporters knew about the strength of the Indian forces ranged against the fort. It still amazes me that the reports about the warriors massing in the area were disregarded, or weren't believed because the sources they came from weren't considered credible, even if the information was true. Fetterman's boast about riding through the Sioux Nation was a statement that seems like total arrogance, but arrogance has never been a disqualification for being a good officer, and so I'm sure it was taken in that context. Like Carrington, Fetterman came into something that he was not expecting and the skills he brought to the game were not the skills to win the game, but they were the only skills he had.

I don't know how clear the order was that Carrington gave Fetterman on the morning of December 21, 1866. It seemed that Fetterman had some discretion and Carrington didn't appear to be upset when he saw the men on the south side of Lodge Trail Ridge, when he thought they were just moving down Big Piney Valley to intercept the Indians that were attacking the wood train. Did Fetterman directly disobey orders by crossing the ridge? I tend to believe that it was Grummond who led them over the ridge and that Fetterman followed him. Grummond was one of those brave combat officers who didn't have any idea what he was dealing with. His preferred weapon was a saber, which meant that he had to get very close to his enemy, and up until December the Indians had not shown any desire to engage in close-quarter combat. That changed on December 6 when he led a small party of men into a trap and only just escaped. On December 21 Grummond was leading the mounted troops, and I think the key to what happened over the ridge was that he and those mounted troops got too far in advance of the infantry, and Fetterman was probably with those foot soldiers. Whether Fetterman was marching to try and pull Grummond out of the trap, or whether everything just disintegrated rapidly once they were in the trap, we are left to speculate upon. If anyone is to be judged a fool, Grummond would be the one. We have a limited number of Indian accounts to work from, and we are getting some new archeological insights, but I doubt that anybody is ever going to have the definitive, final word on what happened over the ridge that day.

Years after the event, Eli Ricker conducted an interview with American Horse in which he described how he killed an officer in the battle, and that description seems to match what the post surgeon concluded were Fetterman's fatal wounds. There was a lot of room for error in the Ricker interview, and the only reason that I accept it as a possibility is because the claims attributed to American Horse in the Ricker interview do appear to correlate with the surgeon's report. I tend to accept the surgeon's analysis rather than Carrington's report about the bullet wounds in Fetterman's and Brown's temples and his theory that they shot each other. My opinion is that they didn't shoot each other. I don't know whether you could hold a black powder pistol steady under those circumstance and manage to count to three. It's quite possible that Brown shot himself, and it's true that the post surgeon's report didn't definitively state that Fetterman did not have a bullet wound in

Henry B. Carrington

the temple. The bullet hole might have been there, but when was it made? How Fetterman died and at what point he died remain mysteries of the battle, and maybe more Indian oral history accounts will come to light, along with new archeological evidence, that will provide an entire shift in the prevailing theories. I'm a documents-oriented person, and whether the American Horse story is true, or just an old man's or interpreter's embellishment, those of us who are documents-oriented have grabbed hold of it; even though it may not be legitimate, it's a document! I don't regard it as fact that American Horse killed Fetterman. In regard to what happened in this battle, outside of all the soldiers being killed and the Indians being victorious I wouldn't categorize anything as fact because we just don't know.

The 1908 Fetterman monument dedication. Standing, left to right: William Daley, General Freeman, Colonel Henry B. Carrington, John Owens, Mrs. Frances Grummond Carrington, Mrs. Freeman, Mrs. Strawn, J. Strawn, Dennis Driscoll. Seated, left to right: Jack Owen, William Murphy, J. Newcomer, Sam Gibson, and S.S. Peters.

Scalping was very much a part of the warfare on both sides at that time, and certainly the Indians hadn't cornered the market on that, or on mutilating bodies. I've never thought that the mutilation of the bodies of Fetterman's men after the battle was a barbaric atrocity; it was part of a religious belief system – if you believe you are going to have to deal with this same enemy in the future, then deal with him now. For those that aren't from that culture it looks horrifying, but there are plenty of examples of mutilation in the European tradition, going back to the Spanish Inquisition. Chivington's massacre at Sand Creek definitely set the tone as far as the ability of those who considered themselves to be civilized to stretch brutality and savagery to the limits. The Indians had a reason with religious connotations for the mutilations after the Fetterman Fight, but in Chivington's case it was a senseless atrocity. I don't know if there would have been another Sand Creek if Fetterman, Brown and Grummond had been presented with the forces and opportunity to attack the Lakota, Cheyenne and Arapaho villages on the Tongue River. I don't think that they would have run amuck like Chivington's men, but as Custer showed when he attacked Black Kettle's village on the Washita, there was the potential for tremendous collateral damage. Fetterman and Grummond were men who could survive in violent situations and they were willing to carry out violent warfare, but I'm not sure that they would have followed the Sherman maxim of 'kill every man, woman and child,' but we will never know.

Ten Eyck became the fall guy for the disaster, but I don't think that he could have done any more than what he did. He got there as fast as he could, and he didn't have a hope of any success offensively. I think he did the competent thing: he set up his defensive position, and that's all he could do, and so I don't think he deserves to have any blame ascribed to him. Both the special commission and military court inquiries into the Fetterman disaster provided a lot of information without any real conclusions. In my mind the inquiries brought forth more questions than answers. I think Carrington's testimony demonstrated his ability as a lawyer and neither inquest formally blamed him for the tragedy, nor completely exonerated him. The verdicts – or lack of verdicts – destroyed both Carrington's and Ten Eyck's military careers and didn't absolve Fetterman. I don't think that Carrington should be totally exonerated. They were looking for excuses when they tried to blame the defeat on the Indians' superior arms, and the evidence found at the Fetterman battle site shows that the Indians were relying upon their traditional weapons and that the few firearms they had were obsolete. At the Wagon Box Fight they had a few more-modern firearms, and that influx probably came from the Fetterman Fight. Even then the Indians had problems maintaining ammunition, a problem Carrington didn't have before the Fetterman Fight. There was plenty of blame to go around, from those involved at Fort Phil Kearny, to Sherman, to St. George Cooke, all the way through to the schizophrenic Indian policy of the United States government. I don't see any one individual as being the villain, I see them as people that didn't understand the circumstances. Ignorance was the biggest problem but ignorance is no excuse. The saga of Fort Phil Kearny is a unique story – a uniquely human story.

American Horse's so-called Fetterman Disaster Club

ALFRED RED CLOUD

"We had no books in those days, and everything that I'm sharing about my great-grandpa, Mahpíya Lúta, has been passed down to me through our language, so this is our family's oral history."

CHIEF ALFRED RED CLOUD IS A GREAT-GRANDSON OF CHIEF RED CLOUD, AND A NATIONALLY RESPECTED SPIRITUAL LEADER IN THE NATIVE AMERICAN CHURCH

They say "Wakan wicása hówasáka!" A man with powers and a strong voice! That was my great-grandpa, the great chief, Mahpíya Lúta, known to history as Red Cloud. He had a gift when he spoke, for when he talked people would always listen. When I was young, my father explained to me that it was the spirit within him that caught peoples' attention, and he conveyed how his father had revealed to him that it was an eagle's spirit that guided Chief Red Cloud. In photographs you often see the chief wearing just one feather, and that was a symbol of that eagle's spirit. Our people recognized that spirit in his words and so when he said something they were prepared to go with it. By the time the Bozeman Trail was being carved through the Powder River country, Chief Red Cloud's reputation was as strong as his voice: he had proved himself in battle, his courage recorded in story and song for all to hear, celebrating his deeds in some eighty engagements. In 1866 the chief displayed the wisdom from advancing years; the battlefield was for younger men and Red Cloud's place was in council where that eagle's spirit could influence the destiny of the people.

When my great-grandpa visited President Grant in June 1870, he told the Secretary of the Interior,[1] "I was born at the forks of the Platte and I was told that the land belonged to me." Over the years some authors who have written books about the chief have questioned that, along with a lot of other things he said, and so a lot of what exists in print about my great-grandpa owes more to their misrepresentations than the history of Red Cloud. When he said the forks of the Platte, the chief was talking about where Blue Water Creek flows into the North Platte, and that is where he was born. George Hyde speculated that Red Cloud was named after a meteorite that painted the sky red when he was born, but my grandpa told me that he was born in the evening when the sun was setting, so all around the clouds were red, and that's where he got his name. The chief's birth is recorded in Lakota winter counts for 1821-1822, and so that's our documentation. We had no books in those days, and everything that I'm sharing has been passed down to me through our language, so this is our family's oral history.

American Horse is one of our relatives, and many years ago he said that my great-grandpa's father had also carried the name Red Cloud and that he too was a chief. One of my great-uncles, He Dog, called him Lone Man, and people from outside of our culture consider that to be a discrepancy and they use it to try and diminish the authenticity of Lakota oral history. But there is no discrepancy; He Dog was calling Red Cloud's father by the name he was known by among the Brulés, because way back then the band system among the the Oglalas was still evolving, and the Wajaje band was associated with the Brulés at that time. My great-grandpa's mother was Walks-as-She-Thinks, a sister of the Oglala chief Smoke. One of the historical misnomers attached to Red Cloud involves Chiefs Smoke and Bull Bear, and contrary to popular belief my great-grandpa did not murder Bull Bear like these writers have claimed. Several versions of this incident exist, but two important factors need to be appreciated before it can be understood: first, that there had been rivalry between the Oglala bands lead by Bull Bear and Smoke that went back a generation; and second, the influence of alcohol. Bull Bear's death appears in American Horse's winter count for 1841-1842, and at that time the Oglalas were under a lot of pressure from the fur trading companies, Pratte, Cabanne & Company and the American Fur Company, who were involved in a trade war. As the demands from the fur companies increased so did intertribal warfare; as our bands vied with other tribes for control over more buffalo ranges, then pretty soon intratribal fighting started breaking out. More buffalo hides meant more whiskey, which meant addiction.

Chief Red Cloud

Bull Bear's and Smoke's people were at the center of this trade war, and in November 1841 they were both camped near Fort John, the post that became known as Fort Laramie. It was there, on Chugwater Creek, not too far from present-day Wheatland, Wyoming, that some American Fur Company traders brought kegs of whiskey into Bull Bear's camp. When he was an old man, Red Cloud told Charles Allen, then the postmaster at Pine Ridge, that one of the young men from Smoke's camp had taken a girl from Bull Bear's camp to be his wife, and the manner in which he had done this angered Bull Bear, and so, when the whiskey took effect, Bull Bear and some of his young men resolved to get her back. The popular story is that Bull Bear had taken one of Smoke's wives, but that's not what my great-grandpa said. Bull Bear was drunk when he arrived in Smoke's camp demanding that the girl be returned, and his young men were also under the influence of the traders' whiskey. Chief Smoke, who had been like a father to my great-grandpa, came out to answer Bull Bear and a brawl erupted between Bull Bear's and Smoke's hot-blooded young men. Red Cloud went to the defense of his uncle, Chief Smoke, and as the shots and blows were being exchanged my great-grandpa shot Bull Bear in the heat and confusion of that ruckus. It was not murder, it was self-defense. If Red Cloud had murdered Chief Bull Bear, a fellow Oglala, he would not have been worthy of touching the pipe for four generations. After the fifth generation the Red Cloud family would have been permitted to use the pipe, the sacred canúnpa, again. That is one of the great laws of the Lakota people and it was not invoked on this occasion, which tells everybody that Red Cloud was not guilty of murder.

The Oglalas became divided after this, with Bull Bear's people, the Kiyaksas, ranging further south, away from the Smoke people. The Smoke people covered three bands, the Itésica, the Oyukhpe and the Hunkpatila, who were lead by Chiefs Red Cloud, Red Dog, and Man-Afraid-of-His-Horses[2] respectively. These were the northern Oglala bands who claimed the Powder River country and who opposed the Bozeman Trail. The division between these bands and the Kiyaksas was not healed until the last days of what we call the Holy Road War, the war to close the Bozeman Trail. When the runners first came out with the news that the U.S. government wanted to make peace and a new treaty, Red Cloud took a pipe and 250 horses to Chief Little Wound, the son of Bull Bear. These two great chiefs sat down and discussed that incident back in 1841, and Red Cloud expressed not only his regret, but how he wanted to bring everybody back together again. Red Cloud asked Little Wound to join him in the treaty negotiations and to accompany him to Washington, D.C., if they were invited. Little Wound accepted Red Cloud's words and horses, and so with the signing of the 1868 Fort Laramie Treaty, the chiefs all started working together again.

A portrait of the chief at the Red Cloud Indian School.

Chief Red Cloud was in his mid-forties when the military crisis began in 1865 and the first troops and fort appeared along the Powder River. They didn't think much of Connor's or Sawyers' men, but the chiefs were angry about the fort they built. The Lakotas considered this area to be the territory of these northern Oglala bands, and so everybody looked to them for guidance, and any military action would be initiated upon their say-so. Red Cloud had been gaining status in the Itésica band since his teens; he first went out against the Pawnees and his record in war built until it was without compare among his contemporaries. Now people started to see his political skills and recognized that his strategy in matters of diplomacy adhered to that of a Lakota warrior on the battlefield – to take the offensive but be prepared to fight a rearguard to protect the helpless ones. Just as the Lakotas looked to these Oglala bands for guidance, many among those bands looked to Red Cloud for leadership. That winter of 1865-1866 was brutal, and by early spring the people were in poor shape, as defending the country against the wasícus invasion had drained their supplies and they had not been able to replenish their stores because of the war. Man-Afraid-of-His-Horses was the first to respond to peace overtures and took his people in to Fort Laramie so that they might survive the winter without starving. My great-grandpa didn't reply until later and arrived at Fort Laramie in March. That is when the arrangements were made for the 1866

treaty conference, and although Chief Red Cloud agreed to attend later that Spring, he made it clear that he was unhappy about the wagon trains and army invading the Powder River country along Bozeman's trail.

I was told that my great-grandpa never met Colonel Carrington. Red Cloud returned to Fort Laramie around mid-May and showed a good deal of patience in waiting for Commissioner Taylor to show up. My understanding is that the treaty council began on June 5 and my great-grandpa was gone by June 7. He didn't believe what Taylor was saying about only wanting to take as much land as fit between the wheels of a wagon, and that the 'Great Father' only wanted to make this road for his 'white children' to pass through our country. This song got old real quick as the chiefs had heard it so many times before. My great-grandpa knew that it wasn't a matter of just losing game where the road ran, it was a matter of losing our entire way of life. The Oregon and California Trail had taught him that. Red Cloud never agreed to reconvene with the commissioners; he only committed to sending scouts up to the White River, which he did, and then he called for a council on Lance Creek, about two days ride north of Fort Laramie. The northern Oglala chiefs were in the process of discussing whether they should lease the Bozeman Trail to the government, when two messengers arrived; one was Big Mouth, a headman from the Loafer band that camped at Fort Laramie, who Taylor had sent to call them back to the fort. The other was a scout who brought the news that Carrington and his men were on the way and that he had boldly stated they were going to build forts on the Bozeman Trail. This is what created anger amongst the people. Taylor had lied to them; he had made no mention of Carrington coming out or building forts when they met on June 5 or 6. The speech they say Red Cloud made to Carrington and Taylor was actually a message he sent back with Big Mouth: "The White Father sends his people out to ask if we'll sell the road and yet he sends his soldiers here to steal the road before we've said yes or no." In council he then said "I am for war," and Young-Man-Afraid-of-His-Horses, Red Dog, Sword, Crazy Horse, He Dog and American Horse were among the first to back him up. After this council the chief sent another messenger back to Fort Laramie. My great-grandpa was a man of his word, and if he said he'd do something he did it, and he wanted Carrington and the commissioners to understand that, and so Young-Man-Afraid-of-His-Horses delivered an unambiguous message: Do not come any further than the fort on the Powder River, for if you do, in two moons your soldiers will not have a hoof left. The commissioners and army could have averted the Holy Road War but they chose to ignore that warning.

Red Cloud knew how to lead the warriors, and the prospect of war created excitement among these young men. My great-grandpa didn't fight when the Great-Gun-That-Was-Fired-at-the-Camp happened in 1854. Like I said, he was a man of his word, and on that day when Lieutenant Grattan said to him, "Stay where you are and don't get involved in this," he said "okay" and watched them go to Conquering Bear's camp and get wiped out. And so the Long Knives were a relatively new adversary to him, the skirmishes of 1865 having provided most of the Oglalas' combat experience against them. When war was declared, the onus for leadership shifted to the Shirt Wearers and the military leaders; this is when Yellow Eagle, a brother of Man-Afraid-of-His-Horses, was chosen to lead the early raids, and Red Cloud concentrated on trying to build an alliance with other Lakota divisions and the Cheyennes and Arapahos. Intermarriages between the tribes helped him do that, but on one occasion also caused him some embarrassment. Chief Dull Knife, the great Northern Cheyenne leader, was considered to be a relative to the Red Cloud family through marriage. Dull Knife married a woman from the Itésica band,[3] so in the Lakota way he became part of that tiospaye, the extended family, and "Dull Knife" was his Itésica name.

Red Cloud's land – The Pine Ridge Indian Reservation

Dull Knife and my great-grandpa had been side by side when they stopped Sawyers' expedition in the Powder River country the year before, but one year on, Dull Knife was for peace with the soldiers. When Red Cloud asked him to join this war, he said he was going to go and talk to the soldiers, so the chief repeated the message he'd given Young-Man-Afraid-of-His-Horses and asked Dull Knife to pass it on to Carrington – to tell him to turn back and avoid war. I think my great-grandpa hoped that after Dull Knife had talked to the Long Knives he would change his mind and join him, but he didn't. Red Cloud was at the head of the group that confronted Dull Knife's party after they talked to Carrington. They didn't like what they heard, Dull Knife was for letting the soldiers take the road to avoid war. Because of their relationship and his ties to the Itésica, it was like Dull Knife had brought shame to Red Cloud and his band by siding with the Long Knives, so the men with my great-grandpa counted coup on Dull Knife and warned his party to keep out of the way and not to help the soldiers. Dull Knife was probably ten or fifteen years older than my great-grandpa and so he had to be in his late fifties at this time. In books they say Dull Knife fought against Fetterman, and some even claim that he was a decoy with Crazy Horse, but that's not how our history records it. Dull Knife was too old to fight but he had sons that did; it would have been strange for a man of such dignity to take that honor from his sons, and he didn't. Like Red Cloud, Dull Knife was a man of his word; he said he wasn't going to fight and he didn't. Like all of the chiefs, he did what he thought was the best for his people. That's what I heard.

It has become fashionable with some writers to undermine Red Cloud's role in this war effort. Many have printed that he wasn't even at the Fetterman Fight, but he was there. We call it the Battle-of-Kills-One-Hundred, and Chief Red Cloud was there with the other chiefs of his age and stature watching from a butte in the foothills to the west of the battlefield. The Cheyennes and some of the Oglalas were on that side, concealed below the chiefs. I think the chief had some long-glasses that he had been given after the raids in 1865 and he watched this battle with those, but one thing he didn't see was American Horse kill Fetterman because that never happened. American Horse did not do that. I am related to the American Horse family and I have some uncles on that side who I'm close with, and we talk about these things. One of my grandpas was talking about this, how they say American Horse killed Fetterman, and this is what he said happened: those two soldiers, Fetterman and Brown, turned on each other, but the Lakotas did not know if they shot each other, or if just one of them managed to get a shot off, which left the other one alive when they were overrun. Either way, it didn't involve American Horse because he was not in that part of the battle, he was at the north end. It was Mniconjus and some Cheyennes who finished Fetterman and his men in those rocks. All of the decoys – American Horse, Crazy Horse, all of them – fought at the opposite end to where Fetterman died. They had ridden their ponies hard and a long way, and then turned right back into this battle and fought their way up the hill after the cavalry. It was hard; they said it was all icy and difficult to ride up those slopes.

American Horse did kill an officer at that north end though: he hit him with his war club and then jumped off his pony and made sure with his knife; he cut his throat. I know that they claim that American Horse told Judge Ricker it was Fetterman, but it wasn't. None of our people knew who Fetterman was, and forty years after the fight, with the confusion from the heat of battle, neither he nor anybody else was going to remember how many stripes the soldiers had on their shoulders or sleeves when they killed them. What he did remember was that he killed a soldier chief, so if Ricker or the interpreter asked American Horse if he killed the chief of the soldiers, he would say yes because, in his mind, he did. The one leading the soldiers at the front of the charge was nearly always thought to be the soldier chief. In this battle, that was Grummond; he was out front leading the cavalry and he was the one who ran right into the Oglalas along the creek. He was the one that American Horse killed. In *Fifty Years on the Old Frontier* it says that my great-grandpa confirmed the 'American Horse killed Fetterman' story, but he did not. American Horse and Red Cloud were close, and my great-grandpa didn't say that, and wouldn't have said that. He most probably said nothing, which is our way of showing contempt. This is what I've heard through our family history. These writers and historians can get a story, interpret comments to fit their theories and then put it out as fact, but it doesn't matter how many times it is repeated, it doesn't make it true.

The Wagon Box Fight is another example of an event involving my great-grandpa that has been distorted. One of the most ridiculous versions is in *Indian Fights and Fighters*, particularly the assertion that 3,000 Lakotas took part in the battle and that 1,137 were killed. I was told that fewer than 350 Lakotas actually took part in what we call The-Attacking-of-the-Wagons, and that there were about sixty or seventy Cheyennes with us. From what I understand, we lost less than ten men on the battlefield and recovered about thirty wounded, some serious, some not. It looked worse than it was because of all the dead horses. I believe our Mniconju relatives have stories about a man who died there, Jiálepa,[4] whose deeds from Ti Ska Najiyapi are still remembered. My great-grandpa watched the fight from a hill to the east of the corral, and if you believe what is written, it left him either a broken man or, according to Judge Ricker, made so little impression on him that he couldn't even recall it. It's interesting that those who think we took mass casualties hold Red Cloud responsible for what they call a defeat, saying that he directed the operation, and these are mostly the same people who say he wasn't at the Fetterman Fight and so had no part in that victory!

The chief's role in the Fetterman and Wagon Box battles was the same; he was one of the strategists. The military leaders were on the field, those at the Wagon Box being High-Back-Bone, Crazy Horse, Sword, American Horse, He Dog and Young-Man-Afraid-of-His-Horses. The Wagon Box was never considered to be a defeat – one of the Long Knives' camps was hit, a herd of mules was captured, several wagons were destroyed, and enemies were killed. When we talk about these things among our relatives there is still disagreement about whether the attack was called off too soon because our warriors were regrouping and preparing for a final assault, which is when the other soldiers from the fort appeared with the cannon. They say that they came close to overrunning the wagons more than once. A lot has been said about the soldiers' rifles and how our people thought they were 'medicine guns.' They were! 'Medicine' is a rough translation for something of mystery, something that has a power attached to it, something out of the ordinary – those Springfield breechloaders were all of that in the context of that day. The gift of intelligence, the gift of knowledge, that's 'medicine,' and it took that gift to turn muzzle-loaders into breechloaders. The breechloader was not the big surprise – a few had been employed against us before; the surprise was the way the soldiers behind the wagons used them, and that each soldier had one. Usually only a few soldiers had breechloaders or repeaters, and the majority had muzzle-loaders, and so there would be a gap when they were reloading that could be exploited. With that gap, the Wagon Box corral would have been wiped out. I think my great-grandpa was satisfied that they had achieved their main objective, which was to keep the pressure up on the forts and the government, to let them know a state of war still existed. When we look back at it now, both Lakotas and white men, we can see that the honors were even at the Wagon Box, good men fought on both sides and took something from the battle.

After the Wagon Box it was just a matter of time until Red Cloud would agree to peace. I think that was when he made up his mind that he would listen to peace overtures because he looked at his people, stepped back, and analyzed the situation. However many Long Knives they killed, more came, and watching thirty or so soldiers stand off three hundred Lakotas gave him pause. The chief knew that the Lakotas could not keep a large fighting force in the field indefinitely like the U.S. Army could; that was contrary to our way of life. And he knew that we had a finite number of warriors, and that if they were killed in battle we could not go out and recruit others to replace them like the army could. Then there was the weapons issue: with every spring the army seemed to have a new gun or howitzer capable of killing more of our people faster, and yet we were mostly reliant on our traditional arms – bows and arrows, lances, and war clubs; most of the guns we had came from the Fetterman Fight. He knew that if he kept fighting his people would be wiped out. In November 1867 he agreed to a cease-fire and a provisional arrangement to discuss the treaty the following summer as long as the soldiers left the Powder River valley, "the only hunting ground left to our Nation," he said. It was agreed that Man-Afraid-of-His-Horses would go to the treaty council at Fort Laramie in May to reduce the risk of the army launching a campaign, while Red Cloud would stay out to give them more leverage in the negotiations. "We are on the mountains looking down on the soldiers and the forts. When I see the soldiers leaving and the forts empty, then I will come down and talk to you," was the message he sent. He kept the commissioners waiting but he kept his word. He did not trust the commissioners or the soldiers and so he could not rely upon them to keep their promises about feeding his people during the winter, and so he decided that they must hunt before going to Fort Laramie. On November 6, 1868, my

The hills from which many Lakota spectators watched the Wagon Box Fight

A trooper's view – looking out from the wagon box corral. The corral was composed of fourteen U.S. Army M-1861, 6-mule Quartermaster Wagon boxes

great-grandpa signed the treaty that we still fight for today, the treaty that said the sacred Black Hills would always be ours.

I look at where we are today, our Lakota people struggling to survive in this poverty they consigned us to, trying to hold on to our language, our culture, our traditional ways, and what land we have left, and I think of what my great-grandpa said: "They made us many promises, more than I can remember, but they kept only one. They promised to take our land, and they took it." Attorneys for the U.S. government try to make the case that Chief Red Cloud agreed to sell the Black Hills. They claim that he asked for $70 million when the government commissioners asked him how much he wanted for the Black Hills in 1875, but I never heard that he did. We had no concept of money back then, and it is my belief that the interpreters came up with that, not my great-grandpa. There was no term for 'millions' in our language. The chief showed the Allison Commission what he thought of the government's attempt to "lease" the Black Hills by visiting our Arapaho relatives instead of concluding that council. Because he was a man of his word, Red Cloud didn't encourage his band to go north from Camp Robinson to fight at the Little Bighorn, and how did the government reward him? By saying 'you will sell us the Black Hills or you will starve.' That was the basis of the Manypenny Commission's ultimatum to the chiefs at Red Cloud's and Spotted Tail's agencies. They told them to sign this amendment to the 1868 treaty because if they didn't their people would starve and the rest of the terms of the treaty would be null and void. At no time did my great-grandpa agree to sell the Black Hills; none of those chiefs did. "The Black Hills is worth to me seven generations, but you give me this word of six

Fetterman Battlefield monument

million dollars. It is just a little spit out of my mouth," he told them. What the government interpreters told the chiefs they were signing was vastly different to what was written in that document. Every one of them made a speech before they signed expressing their confusion and indicating that they did not know that they were agreeing to change the status of the Black Hills.

Years later, in 1889, General Crook tried to bribe my great-grandpa to sign the Sioux Act, a bill that took even more of our land and broke what was left of the 1868 Great Sioux Reservation into these parcels we live on today. He refused, and so they sought to replace him as chief with American Horse, just as they had tried to appoint Young-Man-Afraid-of-His-Horses chief when Red Cloud wouldn't go along with what the government wanted in 1880, just as Crook had attempted to do by making Spotted Tail chief of his and Red Cloud's agencies in 1876. It didn't work. "Red Cloud is our head chief, he is now and always will be," American Horse once told the president.[5] One of the provisions of the 1868 Treaty my great-grandpa insisted upon was that if any amendment to the treaty was to be made, three-fourths of the adult male Lakotas would have to sign off on it for it to be legally binding. The government never managed to get those signatures with the Manypenny Commission, or later on Crook's Sioux Act, so both are in contravention of Article 12 of the 1868 Fort Laramie Treaty – the treaty that came out of Red Cloud's War to close the Bozeman Trail. Before he went to the spirit world my great-grandpa said, "I was born a Lakota, and I have lived as a Lakota, and I shall die a Lakota." That is the true Mahpíya Lúta.

American Horse

1. Secretary of the Interior Jacob D. Cox.

2. "That name, Man-Afraid-of-His-Horses, wasn't translated very well by the interpreters. It actually means 'his enemies are even afraid to see this man's horses.'" *Alfred Red Cloud.*

3. Variously known as Short One, Short Woman or Slow Woman.

4. Jiálepa is one of the Lakota terms for meadowlark.

5. American Horse made this statement in 1880.

Site where the chief rests overlooking the Pine Ridge Indian Reservation

JOE MEDICINE CROW

"The Crows saved Fort C.F. Smith many times. Some non-Indian historians have taken the misrepresentations in the accounts of Colonel Bradley and Lieutenant Templeton and exaggerated them, so what is written about the Crows and Fort C.F. Smith is often distorted."

DR. MEDICINE CROW IS THE GRANDSON OF THE GREAT CROW CHIEFS MEDICINE CROW AND WHITE-MAN-RUNS-HIM, WHO FOUGHT ALONGSIDE GENERALS CROOK AND CUSTER IN 1876. HE BECAME THE ACKNOWLEDGED HISTORIAN OF THE CROW NATION IN 1948.

When I set my lodge, one pole rests at the western foothills of the Black Hills; one pole rests on the shores of Yellowstone Lake; one pole rests by the big falls[1] of the Missouri; and one pole rests at the junction of the Yellowstone and the Missouri. That is how Chief Sits-in-the-Middle-of-the-Land once defined the Crow country, and those were our traditional boundaries when the Bozeman Trail started hitting Crow country as it came north from the Platte, near present-day Casper, Wyoming. Practically all of the Bozeman Trail ran within Crow country, it was not just the stretch some call the final leg, west of the Bighorn River. As a matter of fact, Crow country extended clear to Bozeman, and the final leg of the trail was actually from Bozeman to the goldfields around Virginia City.

The Crow people have the reputation of being friendly with the non-Indians and they used to say that the Crows didn't know what the blood of a white man looked like as they had never killed one. It wasn't the Crows who turned John Bozeman's party back on Rock Creek in 1863, it was the Cheyenne and their allies, the Sioux. They were the ones that objected to the Bozeman Trail; the Crows never gave any resistance to it. When John Bozeman was eventually killed near Livingston, the *Montana Post* claimed that the Crows had killed him, but we didn't. Then they blamed the Piegans, but they weren't too involved in the Bozeman Trail. The Sioux would go clear to Livingston to steal Crow horses, and I heard an account that the Sioux killed him for bringing the white people through, but it's quite possible that his partner, Tom Cover, shot him to get him out of the way for some business or political reason, and then blamed it on the Indians. Neither the Sioux nor Piegans would have left Cover wounded and hiding in a bush, they wouldn't have passed up such an easy coup.

The Crows never tried to impede the white man because a long, long time ago, before the coming of the whites, a Crow medicine man prophesied their arrival. He said that they would come from across the big waters and that at first they would be weak, that there would just be a few of them and that we could wipe those out, but that they would keep coming, more

and more, like ants. Through his medicine he received guidance to work with these strangers, and so he advised the Crow people to take good care of them because eventually they would take good care of us. That was the philosophy of the Crow Indians towards the white man, and that concept has been passed along from Crow chief to Crow chief, right up until today. In the early days it was the trappers who found shelter with the Crows after being harassed by the Blackfeet and Cheyenne, and at the time of the Bozeman Trail it was the soldiers at Fort C.F. Smith who benefited from our protection.

The Crows saved Fort C.F. Smith many, many times. Some non-Indian historians have taken the misrepresentations in the accounts of Colonel Bradley and Lieutenant Templeton and exaggerated them, so what is written about the Crows and Fort C.F. Smith is often distorted. One Crow chief, White Mouth, is supposed to have welcomed the construction of Fort C.F. Smith because the Crows had no place to trade, and they would at the new fort – but the Crows never regarded Fort C.F. Smith as a trading post! Fort C.F. Smith was just a military post that had little or no effect on Crow trading activities. Unlike a trading post, they had very few supplies to trade there so, economically speaking, there was no impact on the Crows, and their ability to obtain

Medicine Crow

Iron Bull

food and equipment, gun powder and so forth was neither helped nor hindered. Trading posts first appeared in Crow country in the early 1800s, and several came and went at the junction of the Bighorn and Yellowstone Rivers. Fort Manuel Lisa was built there for Crow trade in 1807, and the Crows would also go clear up the Missouri to Fort Benton to trade. The Sioux, Piegan and Assiniboine were in that country but, notwithstanding the problems with the other tribes, somehow the Crows always managed to retain their trade opportunities before, during and after the Bozeman Trail. That continued to be their main trading area but they would also travel to Dakota to visit our sister tribe, the Hidatsa, to get fresh corn and beans.

There is also speculation that Fort C.F. Smith had the same negative social impact on the Crows as Fort Laramie did on some of the Sioux, but it did not. The Crows didn't go there, set up camp, and then drink and fool around, and Crow women didn't prostitute themselves there. At regular trading posts such as Fort Benton things like that could happen, but not at Fort C.F. Smith. Crow families didn't 'hang around' Fort C.F. Smith; it was far too dangerous. For a while Fort C.F. Smith was considered to be the most dangerous post on the frontier and only hardened Crow warriors, men like Iron Bull, would stay around there to help the soldiers. A couple of years before John Bozeman came through Crow country, the Crows had whipped the Sioux and Cheyenne in battle along Pryor Creek. This was the battle when Old Man Coyote, the Great Spirit's helper, appeared in the form of a mystic warrior and brought the buffalo and elk to help the Crow defeat our enemies. Some have claimed that the mystic warrior was Plenty Coups, but it wasn't. Plenty Coups was only a boy of twelve or thirteen then and my grandfather, Medicine Crow, was the same age. They were with a bunch of boys stationed on the north end of the battlefield, and they nearly killed some Sioux who tried to sneak up on them. This was a great victory for the Crows and so at the time of the Bozeman Trail the Sioux and Cheyenne knew that we could defeat them and that we would fight them again, and so the presence of our warriors at Fort C.F. Smith deterred them from attacking. If it hadn't been for the Crows that place would have been wiped out quickly, a fact Captain Kinney acknowledged in his reports through the winter of 1866-67.

A year later there was a return to exaggeration: Lieutenant Colonel Bradley implied that the Crows were near starvation, but that was not true; they were well able to take care of themselves. Bradley was just trying to build himself up when, as a matter of fact, it was the Crows who were supplying meat to the soldiers to keep them from starving. A lot of the confusion about the Crows trading at the fort came as a result of the buffalo hunts they undertook to feed the soldiers, a by-product of which was buffalo robes they offferred to the sutlers. It wasn't the poor Crows that needed help, it was Bradley and his men who were scared, half-starved, and in bad shape. Those reports wanted to indicate that the military at Fort C.F. Smith were helping the Crows and protecting them from the Sioux when it was just the opposite. You can't take these officers' accounts at face value, just like you have to watch these writers who promote the memoirs of old-timers like Jim Bridger. Jim Bridger liked to exaggerate, suggesting that there were Crows who wanted to join the Sioux in fighting the soldiers, but Jim Beckwourth was the best one. Jim Beckwourth gave himself about five Indian names, including Bloody Arm and Takes Five. I was always curious about this Bloody Arm, this half-black, half-white man who it was said had become a Crow chief, so many years ago I went to ask Plain Feather about him. Plain Feather was a great Crow historian with a remarkable memory for details, and he died in 1970 at the age of one hundred. We couldn't find any actual stories about this Bloody Arm that related to all of these great deeds he was supposed to have done from the 1830s onwards, but Plain Feather said that there was a man called Deer who came to his uncle's camp with some soldiers

Medicine Crow

from Fort Phil Kearny. Plain Feather's uncle was Iron Bull, and this old black-white man, Deer, returned to Iron Bull's camp west of Fort C. F. Smith, on his way back from the fort. It was then that this Deer claimed that he had been a Crow chief. Iron Bull let him stay in his lodge but after awhile he got sick and died there, so they buried him near present-day Columbus, Montana. I believe that was Jim Beckwourth. Our old Crow historians had no recollection of any of his alleged Crow deeds and I have never found any verification of them, only all kinds of fabrications. However, Thomas H. Laforge, the white Crow Indian of the book by Thomas B. Marquis, also made reference to burying Beckwourth near Columbus. I knew Thomas H. Laforge quite well.

Among the Crows, Iron Bull is also known as Itchua-chia, White Temple, and he regaled his nephew, Plain Feather, with many eyewitness accounts. Iron Bull was one of the few who was brave enough to carry mail for the military from Fort C.F. Smith to Fort Phil Kearny, earning $100 per month. Chief Red Bear considered Iron Bull to be his most trusted scout, and when Red Bear died and was succeeded by Chief Sits-in-the-Middle-of-the-Land, Iron Bull became his most reliable scout. Iron Bull attended the 1868 Fort Laramie Treaty negotiations with Sits-in-the-Middle-of-the-Land, and became chief when Sits-in-the-Middle-of-the-Land died of pneumonia near Meeteetsie, Wyoming. The whites called Sits-in-the-Middle-of-the-Land 'Blackfoot' but it had nothing to do with the Blackfeet Indians. The story goes that once, when returning from the warpath, he had to walk through an area that had been burnt by a prairie fire. During this trek he met some traders who noticed that his moccasins were all black, and so they nicknamed him Chief Blackfoot. Iron Bull made quite an impression on the whites too, and not just for his bravery – every morning, even if it was 20 below zero, he went down to the Bighorn River and took a quick dip. Taking a bath every morning was a ritual among Crow men no matter how cold it was, and my grandfather and I used to do that too.

Before they built the fort and operated a ferry, it was very difficult for the immigrants on the Bozeman Trail to cross the Bighorn River. The Crows showed them Spotted Rabbit Crossing. They guided them to a rock ledge aside the river and told them how to follow it to the crossing, but if they missed it they dropped like stones. In that area they also had to watch out for grizzly bears. The mountains here were loaded with grizzly bears at one time but they're gone now, just like the walls of the fort. When I was a boy we'd go there and the old adobe walls of Fort C.F. Smith were still standing. The troops collected limestone from a little stream coming off the

The Hayfield battle site near Fort C.F. Smith

133

SITE OF OLD CROW AGENCY 1875 — 1883

mountains called Lime Kiln Creek, and then heated it up to make the adobe for the fort's walls. They made glass there too. It has all gone now, except for a few shards of that glass.

Old Crow Agency, Absarokee, Montana

In 1851 the so-called Fort Laramie Treaty established the boundaries of 'Indian Country' for several tribes, including the Crows, Sioux and Cheyenne. The 1851 treaty commissioners outlined the tribes' designated areas that, effectively, were to be off-limits to non-Indians, but because the Bozeman Trail cut through that area they had to come back in 1866 to renegotiate for another right-of-way. The Crows weren't invited to participate in the 1866 treaty conference. It seems that the United States took the good nature of Crow people for granted, and had heard that the Crows didn't object to the immigrants passing through to the goldfields, so they concentrated on the actual protesters, mainly the Sioux. The Crows didn't want the immigrants to stay and, like the Sioux and Cheyenne, they didn't like it when the whites disturbed the buffalo, killed lots of game, and generally damaged the area. Even so, there was no attempt by the Crows to help the Sioux fight the white men, and Crow historians have no real accounts of the Sioux trying to enlist the aid of the Crows. The Sioux never gave up the idea that the Crows were their worst enemy, and the feeling was mutual. I think this idea that the Sioux and Crow might unite to close the Bozeman Trail started with Templeton and Bridger, who both misinterpreted what was happening. The stories about the Crows being camped near the Sioux on the Tongue River in the fall and winter of 1866 are made up. It makes a good story but it's just sensationalism. That would have been way too close for comfort!

When I was a boy I listened to my grandfathers, Medicine Crow, Yellowtail and White-Man-Runs-Him, talk about the old days, and from that time until now, I have never heard a Crow tribal historian mention that the Crows had been approached by the Sioux and had considered joining them in the fight to close Fort Phil Kearny and Fort C.F. Smith. I have read *What Half-Yellow Face Knows about the Fort Phil Kearny Massacre*, but I think there is some confusion there. At the time of the Fetterman Fight, Half-Yellow Face would only have been six or seven years old! Half-Yellow Face was one of Custer's Crow scouts at the Battle of the Little Bighorn, and in 1876 he was no more than seventeen years old. In 1866 he was a little boy, so I don't know how he could have given an account of the Fetterman issue; matter of fact, I don't know how he could have ridden for two days through the camps of the Sioux, as is claimed, with the Crows arrayed nearby. The non-Indians who documented this period in the late 1800s would put words in Indians' mouths and then attribute their theories to them. They'd make something up and put an Indian's name on it. Some so-called historians are still doing that!

White-Man-Runs-Him

At the Battle of the Little Bighorn, my grandfather, White-Man-Runs-Him, was only seventeen, Curley was sixteen, and the oldest man of that group was White Swan who was twenty-five. White Swan went along to look after these boys. Half-Yellow Face was with Major Reno, and he was the guy that kept Reno's and Benteen's men in water when they were besieged. Half-Yellow Face made a bunch of trips to the river and he had strong medicine so the Sioux couldn't see him. On one occasion he took a soldier with him and they brought water back, and afterwards that soldier got a Congressional Medal of Honor but Half-Yellow Face didn't get a damn thing. After the Little Bighorn he enlisted at Fort Custer.

When the army decided to abandoned the Bozeman Trail forts and the tribes were again called to Fort Laramie in 1867/68, it is alleged that Chief Sits-in-the-Middle-of-the-Land told the treaty commissioners that the quickest way to achieve peace was to give up the Bozeman Trail. That would have been a logical statement for him to make because if the forts and trail had been closed a lot of the Sioux may have left Crow country too, but I doubt that Chief Sits-in-the-Middle-of-the-Land made that statement because during that 1868 treaty council the chief didn't say much of anything at all – it was Pierre Chienne that made the treaty. Pierre Chienne was the son of French immigrants, and he was like one of those white men the old Crow prophet had told of years before. He was a trader and a mountain man who married two Crow women and had Crow children, and so he was really concerned about the treaty of 1868 and its impact on his family and the tribe. Pierre Chienne could speak the Crow language perfectly, and he told Sits-in-the-Middle-of-the-Land, "You leave this up to me. I know what they want and so I'll get the best deal possible." He practically wrote the provisions of that treaty that have served the tribe well to this day, one being that if the government wants more Crow land, the majority of Crow men must sign any such agreement. That is why we're more or less like a sovereign nation and don't fool around with the Bureau of Indian Affairs when we want to see the Great White Father in Washington, D.C. The assertion that the Crow position towards the Bozeman Trail at this treaty council was virtually identical to that of Red Cloud, or that the Crow had some empathy with the Sioux, isn't accurate at all and has been taken out of context.

Under the 1851 treaty, Crow country was set at 35,531,147 acres, but the 1868 treaty reduced Crow country to 8,000,400 acres. In 1868 you could have said that because of the Bozeman Trail the Crows lost more than the Sioux and Cheyenne, and yet we were the ones who had protected Fort C.F. Smith and hadn't objected to the trail. But that 8,000,400 acres was recognized as being good country and it's still a huge area. By 1868, the Crows realized that irrespective of the Bozeman Trail and the whites, intertribal warfare had restricted the tribe's ability to hold on to that 1851 area and so our land base was already dwindling. By agreeing to that reduction in the 1868 treaty, the Crows felt better able to protect that area and sought to use the U.S. Army to help with that. Occasionally we use the white man for our advantage, like at the Custer battle. That was an occasion where we used the U.S. military to fight our traditional enemies and to defend the Crow country. My grandfather, Medicine Crow, and his buddy Plenty Coups were selected to lead an army of 176 elite Crow warriors from present-day Livingston to Sheridan, Wyoming, to join General Crook in the 1876 summer campaign. The books call them 'scouts,' but they weren't scouts, they were elite fighting men. Chief Washakie brought one hundred Shoshones from Wind River, and at the Battle of the Rosebud it was the Crows and Shoshones against the Sioux and Cheyenne – the men who fought there used to say that Crook's soldiers were just in the way! Crook came up the Bozeman Trail from Fort Fetterman, and had a supply base near old Fort Reno, so the significance of the Bozeman Trail didn't end with the 1868 treaty. Non-Crows might think that we gave up a lot of land in that treaty and gained little by allying with the U.S., but when they placed the Sioux and Cheyenne on their reservations they were just like prisoners of war, but the U.S. government left us alone and we fared quite well compared to the Cheyenne and Sioux, who they punished.

Dr. Joe Medicine Crow

1. Great Falls, Montana.

JOHNSON HOLY ROCK

"My father was around Crazy Horse because they hung up north in the same area, so he could describe him. There are no photographs of him. I heard of him through my father and I have great admiration for the man."

JOHNSON HOLY ROCK'S FATHER WAS AN EYE-WITNESS AT THE BATTLE OF THE LITTLE BIGHORN, AND HIS GRANDFATHER, HOLY BULL, WAS A CONFIDANT OF CRAZY HORSE. JOHNSON HAS SERVED THE OGLALA NATION IN MANY CAPACITIES, INCLUDING A TENURE AS TRIBAL PRESIDENT.

My father figured he was somewhere between ten and twelve years old when he saw a line of horsemen coming along the ridge above the Little Bighorn River. He said one of them carried something that stuck up in the air with a piece of cloth waving from it in the breeze. These were Reno's horsemen in the moments before they attacked Sitting Bull's camp at the Greasy Grass, the start of the Battle of the Little Bighorn. Not too far north of Sitting Bull's camp were the lodges of my grandfathers, Holy Bald Eagle and Holy Bull, the twins referred to in historical pages as Black Twin and White Twin. Whenever twins are born into our family, one is always light and one is dark. Holy Bald Eagle was dark and so they called him the Black Twin. Holy Bull had a pallid complexion and so he was called the White Twin. The White Twin, Holy Bull, was my grandfather.

Historically, wherever Crazy Horse was camped you'd find Holy Bull's camp close by, so there's a connection there. Crazy Horse's group was called the Hunkpatilas, indicating the affiliation of that Oglala band with the 'Campers at the End,' the Hunkpapas. My grandfather's group was the Badger Band. Even after Crazy Horse ran off with the wife of Holy Bull's younger brother, an uncle of mine named No Water, there was still a sense of closeness between the bands of Crazy Horse and my grandfathers. My father said he was born along the Tongue River in the Moon of the Blossoming Rosebushes (June), and that is in the country where my grandfathers and Crazy Horse resided, north of the Black Hills into Montana and Wyoming. They were very independent, so much so that they rarely mingled with the southern Lakota bands, and became known to the military and U.S. government as the 'wild Indians,' particularly after they contested the laying of the Bozeman Trail.

Their opposition began before there was a Bozeman Trail, when the immigrants first started to cross Sioux country. The immigrants had to cross the Missouri River to start across the plains, and the Sioux bands occupied the territory along the river, and so were prone to coming into contact with them. The area the Sioux occupied stretched down to the north fork of the Smoky Hill River in Kansas, and so the military saw that they were going to have problems when the wagon trains began crossing, so in 1851 a treaty was proposed. The 1851 Fort Laramie Treaty was actually an agreement to a right-of-way, nothing more, for which the government offered the Indians $50,000 per year for fifty years to let the immigrants cross the plains. When the agreement was made it was understood that this was just a right-of-way for the Oregon Trail, not a right to cross all over the landscape. Unfortunately, after the commissioners went back to Washington, D.C., the Senate refused to ratify it, declaring that fifty years was too long and reducing it to ten years before they would approve it. The Indians were not notified until six years after the papers were signed, and they began to take issue with it, as it was not what they had agreed to. Soon after, they noticed an increase in military forces, and then forts started to be built along the way. "No. No, you can't do that," my grandfathers said. "We just said your people could cross on this trail, we didn't say you could build soldier forts," but they wouldn't listen until Fort Phil Kearny was surrounded. My grandfathers were among those who laid siege to the post; they had agreed to neither the construction of the forts nor the Bozeman Trail.

There was quite a force arrayed against the military there, although from time to time little tensions arose between the Lakotas and the Cheyennes. There was a residue of tension from the Platte Bridge fight a year earlier because neither group was satisfied with the way the other had performed there. Holy Bull had five wives and one of them was a Cheyenne woman, so I have Cheyenne relatives somewhere, although I've never met them. My father-in-law used to tell me about visiting the camp of Dull Knife when he and Little Wolf were trying to bring their people back home from Oklahoma. Dull Knife didn't know whether he should continue north, as he was afraid that if the military intercepted him, he was in no position to defend himself, so he stayed close to Pine Ridge, hoping that the prestige of Red Cloud would help them find safety. They went into Fort Robinson but they were incarcerated, starved and ready to freeze to death, and so they broke out of there and they scattered. Some of them stayed here on Pine Ridge; they filtered in and camped along little draws and waterways that eased into Red Cloud's area and settled on Cheyenne Creek. It was a little different in 1866 when Dull Knife was with the Cheyennes who went to talk to Colonel Carrington when he started building Fort Phil Kearny. Red Cloud didn't think Dull Knife and the others should be doing that, and he let them know it. One of my grandfathers, Holy Bald Eagle, along with No Water, Little Hawk and Young-Man-Afraid, were among those who confronted them near what became Fort Phil Kearny, but the alliance between the Lakotas and Cheyennes remained. After Sand Creek, when the survivors barely got away with the clothes on their backs, the Lakotas helped the Cheyennes, and it was the same after Custer attacked them at the Washita, and so these small disagreements came and went, but did not break them apart.

Holy Bald Eagle was active in the planning and execution of the maneuvers against Fort Phil Kearny. The Badger Band and Crazy Horse's group were real aggressive and they showed it at the Fetterman Fight. Holy Bald Eagle was among the Shirt Wearers for the northern group who, in 1866, were with Big Road's people. In the Fetterman Fight, Holy Bald Eagle led the mounted Oglalas. Holy Buffalo and No Water were also in that charge, but Holy Bald Eagle was the leader; he had the honor of being Chief of the Badger Band, and he was the senior ranking of the two because he had been the first twin born. Crazy Horse and Hump[1] were the Lakotas' overall commanders on the battlefield and they were going for broke; nobody was going into this fight just to count coups. In intertribal warfare, even with a rifle barrel sticking straight in your face, you'd lean over and whack your enemy on the head and ride on; that was the highest essence of bravery. But there were no questions that day, you didn't do foolish things against these soldiers. A Shirt Wearer knew that if he made any bad move he'd be looking death in the face. They were there to accomplish something, and whatever they had at hand is what they used, and only when it was over did they take stock of where they were in the fight.

In this battle, when the final charge was made, nobody was looking out for who was doing what, and so there are things that will never be totally verified by all sources. How Fetterman died is one controversy. The story about American Horse killing him is not reasonable – everything from the conditions, to how far American Horse had already run his war pony as one of the decoys, to the fact that he was fighting at the north end of the battlefield, not the south end where Fetterman died. It's just like Custer; over the years, some of our people claimed, "I'm the one that killed Long Hair," but my father was there. He said that after it was all over, one of his uncles came down and took him up to Last Stand Hill, and that all the soldiers looked the same, none of them had long hair. When the final rush was made that day and they enveloped them, no one knew who Custer was. After it was all over the warriors were intrigued because they'd heard so much about Long Hair and they wanted to see him, so they looked for a man with long hair but, like my father said, there was none. Custer had cut his hair, so they didn't recognize him, and they didn't recognize Fetterman either.

Another matter is whether or not Red Cloud was at the battle. Red Cloud was there, but more in the role of a general of the overall operation rather than a participant in combat. It was hard to control the warriors on the field because they were out there to gain prestige, so it was not like the army where the orders were passed down the line down to the ordinary dog-face who obeyed. The soldiers were trained that way; their commanders controlled them, other than on this occasion! According to historical pages, Fetterman was a very impulsive, rash person and he ignored his commander's strict instructions. He had a pretty good image of himself to think that with one hundred men he could ride through the winter camps of the Sioux and Cheyenne! In a sense, because of the nature of Lakota warfare, our leaders encountered similar problems. Each man was his own unless he had respect for a particular Shirt Wearer, like Crazy Horse. Men would follow Crazy Horse to hell and back just out of respect. When he told them the way it was going to be, there was a general understanding: "The weak ones go to the back, the brave ones come with me. It is a good day to die."

My father was around Crazy Horse because they hung up north in the same area, so he could describe him. There are no photographs of him. I heard of him through my father and I have great admiration for the man. Crazy Horse was the name of the uncle who raised him, and he gave him the name Crazy Horse publicly in a naming ceremony. Crazy Horse had light hair, was light skinned, and wasn't very tall or impressive physically. For some reason he had an undying hatred for white men, possibly because he may have learned what had happened to his mother, and he probably believed that he was a product of that. Being light skinned and light haired, the rest of the boys picked on him and so he kept to himself. He knew he was different, but he was also very smart, very talented, and he was not afraid to die. Crazy Horse had medicine made to protect him in battle, and that is how he became very skilled in mounted warfare. The thing that most of the other warriors noticed was that he never fired his rifle on a dead run from the back of a horse; if he was going to fire he'd jump off his horse, kneel and aim. Crazy Horse always hit what he aimed at. The other warriors said, "There's something strange about this guy, he don't fight like we do, he fights different." He wasn't very sociable, but he was a good strategist and tactician, and despite their own personal aspirations the warriors listened to him and did what he told them to do. If he had lived, things may have been different – maybe. Crazy Horse had a great mind for military matters, and if he had been born in a different time he'd probably have been a head war chief or five-star general.

Crazy Horse, Hump, Red Cloud, Black Shield and Black Leg are the names most often recorded in historical pages as the leaders in the Fetterman Fight. It is possible that there is some confusion over who Black Leg was. There is the suggestion that Black Leg was actually Black Twin, but I never heard anything reflecting that from my father, and at that time Holy Bald Eagle wasn't generally known as Black Twin. I think it is reasonable to assume that Black Leg was actually Black Elk's father. Black Elk Sr. fought in the Fetterman Fight and sustained a serious leg wound which crippled him thereafter, which would explain why the name Black Leg appeared in military reports. When they were dwelling on who did what in the battle, they were only hearing second- and third-hand reports from scouts who weren't there, but who may have talked to somebody who was, who mentioned the bravery of this man who was left with a black leg.

Of course, this information got through to me from my father, through my grandmother. Holy Bald Eagle died when the band fled after the Battle of the Little Bighorn. They were just south and west of the Little Bighorn, swinging around the Wolf Mountains and headed toward Canada when he took his long journey. They buried him there, in the foothills of the Rocky Mountains. Holy Bull then led the survivors of the Badger Band to the mother country, Canada, but they were on their way back within the year. This is when Crazy Horse was going to turn himself in because he was tired and weary, and his band was getting smaller and smaller by reason of constant harassment from the military. Holy Bull tried to dissuade him but Crazy Horse was insistent. Holy Bull wanted to stop off and visit the resting place of his twin brother first, so they camped near the Powder River while Crazy Horse went on. Holy Bull went up into the mountains, and when two days had passed and he had not come down, a scouting party went up to look for him and found him where his brother was buried. Holy Bull was sick; they didn't know how or why, so they brought him back down and the medicine men were called in to doctor him, but it was too late; he got worse and worse and a few days later he was dead. Nobody knows why. They took him back up and buried him by his brother, and then my grandmother and my father and the others followed after Crazy Horse, but by the time they got to Fort Robinson, Crazy Horse was history.

Crazy Horse wanted to be close to that which he held sacred, the Black Hills, and he agreed to go to Fort Robinson with the understanding that he would have his own reservation on Beaver Creek. He was very beholden to the sacred land, and the Beaver Creek he was talking about was on the west side of the Black Hills, not the Beaver Creek between Red Cloud's and Spotted Tail's agencies in Nebraska. Those two were fearful that the government might make him the the overall chief and so they felt threatened, and in the end there was a conspiracy to do away with Crazy Horse. One-on-one I don't think there was any of them that had the bravery to face him; he was quite a man. I've done a lot of research on this and I always believed that a soldier ran a bayonette through Crazy Horse – but it wasn't – it was his own people. Little Big Man was one of them and Woman's Dress was another. I have reason to believe that No Water was among them too. I hate to admit it, but that uncle of mine had revenge in his heart. I remember talking to the older people when I was growing up and I'd inquire, "Is it true that Crazy Horse wasn't killed by the soldiers?" Some of the elders wouldn't answer me, they'd just walk away. Others would say,

He Dog

"It's not well to talk about it." But the more that I got the treatment, the more curious I became, and the worse nose trouble I got! Of course, years later, I found out from some of the ones who were sympathetic to my question, so I accept their statements. If Crazy Horse were to come back to life today he'd be surprised to find how many relatives he has. A lot of people want to be affiliated with him, but when they killed him at Fort Robinson that was the end of the line, there were no direct descendants to carry on. It's difficult to find out just exactly who talks with one tongue or two, but of course, in history things finally float to the surface which have been kept pretty well hidden.

1. High-Back-Bone.

The guardhouse at Fort Robinson outside of which Crazy Horse was mortally wounded, and the markers where he fell.

WILMER MESTETH

"As was the case in all wars, when the Holy Road War began, four Wakicunza were selected to govern the tribe and set forth how the war would be conducted, both operationally and logistically. For the duration of the war these four Wakicunza, more commonly referred to as Shirt Wearers, had absolute power."

A DESCENDANT OF CHIEF RED SHIRT, WILMER STAMPEDE MESTETH IS RECOGNIZED BY MANY AS THE FOREMOST TRADITIONAL SPIRITUAL LEADER ON THE PINE RIDGE RESERVATION. HE IS A RESPECTED EDUCATOR AND LAKOTA HISTORIAN.

The only war in American history that the United States concedes that it lost is what they call Red Cloud's War. We remember it as the Holy Road War, the struggle to close the Bozeman Trail and to protect the buffalo in the Powder River country. In our Lakota language we call the Powder River 'Cahli Wakpá,' the River of Black Dirt. Our ancestors described that area as wijíca, meaning that it was our commissary, in which could be found our staff of life, the buffalo. Cahli Wakpá was synonymous with the buffalo and its meat. That whole area was thick with buffalo, and our people tell stories of how the herds almost covered the hills when the buffalo were migrating and how the earth rumbled beneath their hooves. The Powder River country was so rich that it was coveted by many tribes, the Shoshones, Crows, Assiniboines, Gros Ventres, and Blackfeet, all of whom valued it and were prepared to fight for it, just as the Lakota people were prepared to defend it. The northern Oglalas of Chief Smoke, the Osóta or Smoke people, claimed this territory as their own, and amongst the Titatunwan Oyate, the seven divisions of the Lakota Nation, the Oglalas were the most populous.

A lot of tribes feared the Lakota people because we were very warlike and defeated many enemies: the first were the Kiowas and Crows, followed by the Pawnees, who Bull Bear's people warred upon along the Niobrara River; then it was the Snake People, the Kizuzeza Oyate, the Comanches, who we met in Colorado and Kansas, and then war started with the Sapa Wicása, the Utes. When we ventured into the Bighorn Mountains and the Tetons, hostilities broke out with the Comanches' and Utes' relatives, the Shoshones. In our language we still have terms for all of these sites and stories about the warriors who fell in battle and where they were laid to rest. Those are like sacred places to us today, and the Powder River is among them. The Lakota people did not fight to annihilate their enemies, only to retain control of this country and our hunting grounds. A battle would often set a precedent and the vanquished would surrender their claim to an area, and in this way the Powder River country was ceded to the Lakotas.

Lakota people cherished this area because of the buffalo. The significance of the buffalo goes way back in our history to the ancient times. 'Otokahekagapi' is a word we use to describe the beginning of time, the time of creation. In the Lakota creation account, the buffalo was once a human being. When the people dwelt within the earth, some were coaxed up onto the surface prematurely by Iktomi, the trickster, and Anog-Itewin, the Double-Faced Woman. The Creator had not intended the human beings to emerge upon the surface of the earth when they did and so these humans found it difficult to survive their first four seasons up here. They decided that they would go back into the earth, but the Creator met them at Wind Cave, the doorway, and scolded them for coming up onto the world without His permission. He told them that He was going to punish them, "You wanted to be first on the world and so now you will always be first," He said. "I'm going to turn you into this beast, this buffalo, and when you go forth into the world you will go to the four directions and populate the world. Then when it's time for the human beings to come up onto the world they will hunt you and you will sacrifice your lives because you will be the sustenance of life for the human beings. They will eat your flesh and use your bones for their tools, and use your hides for their clothing and homes. Only when you have fulfilled your task will your spirit become human again, and only then will you cross over into the spirit world on Wanági Canku, the Ghost Road." It is our belief that this is how we are related to the buffalo, and when the human beings came onto the earth the Creator instructed them to hunt this four-legged, Tatánka, and He said, "This buffalo is going to be your food, your medicine, and clothing. This buffalo will be everything to you." And it was, and still is.

Our ancestors listened to the Creator and followed the buffalo everywhere. Our old people said that for some reason the buffalo moved from the Southern Plains to the Northern Plains and that the Black Hills was the crossing point of the migrations. There is a place in the Black Hills we call Pte Tatiyopa, Buffalo Gap, that is this doorway of the Buffalo Nation. When the immigrants came with their wagon trains they disrupted these massive herds and the buffalo were afraid of their trains. The first road that impacted our people and the buffalo was the Oregon Trail, which forced the buffalo from their traditional ranges and meant that to survive we had to follow them, and consequently enter the territory of enemy tribes. Our chiefs were greatly disturbed by the white men because when they came through they had no regard for the ecosystem and no respect for the buffalo, and in our culture the buffalo is everything to us, the buffalo is sacred. We lived how the Creator intended, so who were these white men, these army generals and politicians, to tell us to change our ways? We weren't going to disavow the Creator just so that the white men could get to the goldfields faster by making this Bozeman Trail.

When Edward B. Taylor, the treaty commissioner, and Colonel Henry Maynadier, the commanding officer at Fort Laramie, first raised this issue, our chiefs thought it was strange. They started to refer to this road as canku wakan, 'the holy road,' because it seemed to mean so much to these white men to have it, and they said those who might travel upon it through our country could not be touched, and a man who you cannot touch must be imbued with some mysterious power! What distressed the chiefs was that while Taylor's commissioners were asking for permission, Carrington's Eighteenth Infantry was on the way to take the road and build forts irrespective of what they said. The year before, when Connor built Cahli Wakpá Akícita Oti, the Soldier Fort on Powder River, the Osóta people were very upset and Taylor knew that, so the chiefs figured that was why he hadn't

1880 Oglala delegation to Washington, D.C. Left to right: Red Dog, Little Wound, Red Cloud, American Horse and Red Shirt. John Bridgeman, the interpreter, is standing behind the chiefs.

mentioned wanting to build more forts along the road. Just like the trickster had managed to coax some of the human beings onto the surface of the earth, Taylor coaxed some of the loafer chiefs into giving them permission to take the Bozeman Trail, and coaxed some of the Northern Cheyennes into considering it. The northern Oglalas stepped in and threatened Dull Knife, telling him and his band not to sign any papers agreeing to this road as collaborating with the United States was an insult to their relatives who were massacred at Sand Creek.

To the Lakota people, Sand Creek was a horrific event, and they were angered by what was done to the Cheyennes. It reminded them of when Harney massacred Chief Little Thunder's band on Blue Water Creek in 1855, the year after what we call 'Mazawakantanka Okícize,' the Grattan Fight, brought war between the Lakotas and the United States. A great many atrocities were committed against the Cheyenne people at Sand Creek and our people were horrified. The Lakotas and Cheyennes had been allied ever since the Pawnees captured the Four Sacred Arrows from the Cheyennes, and in 1837 the Lakotas went among those Skidi Pawnees, devastated their village, and retrieved one of the Sacred Arrows for the Cheyennes. We believed that what the army did to the Cheyennes at Sand

Creek was shameful, and so we joined with them to war on the whites in 1865, starting with Camp Rankin near Julesburg, and continuing to Platte Bridge Station. When war over the Bozeman Trail appeared inevitable, Red Cloud advanced his argument for unity and resistance by reminding people of these events, and Connor's expedition into the Powder River country the year before aided this diplomatic effort. The way the northern Oglalas put it to the Cheyennes and Arapahos was that they needed to join forces for the common good, to defend this hunting ground, because they all subsisted off it.

The Lakotas didn't start attacking the wagon trains on the Bozeman Trail until after Carrington passed Fort Reno, and this Holy Road War began. Young men went out on raids to try and prove themselves in the ways of war, but it wasn't only young Lakotas who committed hostile acts; it was also men from the wagon trains who opened fire on friendly bands, and so the freighters and immigrants instigated fights too. History forgets that many Lakota people were afraid of this Bozeman Trail and the other immigrant routes because they feared the sickness that came with the white people, and so many didn't want to go near it. Okícize means 'the battle over the Holy Road,' and our people recognized that the fight would be with the army, not the immigrants. It was at times such as this, the onset of war, that the governance of the tribe shifted from the chiefs to the Wakicunza, and this has never been brought up or recognized in connection to the Holy Road War, or the subsequent 1868 Fort Laramie Treaty. To have any understanding of the Bozeman Trail from a Lakota perspective, it is necessary to have an appreciation for our traditional form of government. As was the case in all wars, when the Holy Road War began, four Wakicunza were selected to govern the tribe and set forth how the war would be conducted, both operationally and logistically. For the duration of the war these four Wakicunza, more commonly referred to as Shirt Wearers, had absolute power. With the endeavor of war, the chiefs acquiesced to the Wakicunza and the chiefs had to abide by the decisions of the Wakicunza.

In the Holy Road War the four Wakicunza were Crazy Horse, Young-Man-Afraid-of-His-Horses, He Dog and Sword, all prominent warriors who, in a comparative context, were elected to head up the War Department. These men were selected not only for their capabilities in war but because they exhibited the characteristics required of a Wakicunza: they were strong-minded, moral people who adhered to one of the principal Lakota values – honesty. A Wakicunza had to have a heart for his people and his decisions had to be for the the benefit of the tribe as a whole. Those were all requirements for a Shirt Wearer, and these four Wakicunza were all presented with a shirt and a pipe, and the responsibilities of a people at war. At the end of the war governmental power reverted back to the chiefs. However, in the case of the Holy Road War, the chiefs entered into treaty negotiations with the U.S. government while a state of war still existed and the Wakicunza were still in power, which could be interpreted as a contravention of traditional Lakota law, which goes some way to explaining why Crazy Horse and some other northern Oglala leaders never recognized the legitimacy of the U.S. government's demands in connection to that treaty. On the other hand, I believe that the chiefs who negotiated and signed it foresaw their future: the buffalo herds were being depleted and mass starvation was starting to take hold; they realized that our whole way of life was coming to a end. The chiefs knew that they could not hold on too much longer and so they opted for what they believed was in the best interests of their people.

When a Wakicunza was chosen the people saw this power in him. When Crazy Horse was a young boy he received this power through a vision quest, and a lot of people witnessed firsthand his power in war. There are stories of Crazy Horse riding against the Shoshones, charging in bravely as the Shoshones loosed their arrows at him, and how those arrows were always deflected. He killed many Shoshones but he never scalped them. Crazy Horse received that power, what we call a 'wotawe,' his war medicine, on that vision quest, and that wotawe protected him. His uncle was named Woptuha, Horn Chips, and he was the one who interpreted Crazy Horse's vision, out of which came the ritual that Crazy Horse had to follow to protect himself before he went into battle. He painted himself a specific way with a lightning bolt and hailstones, and he wore a spirit stone behind his ear. This stone was a spirit interpreter that spoke to him and guided him, and he wore it behind his ear so that he could hear its voice. In his hair he had the body of a red-backed hawk, with a red-tailed hawk braid lock that was part of his war clothing, his medicine. They said that before Crazy Horse went into a battle he would ride up to a high hill, ascend it, then pray and sing his song so that the spirits would recognize him and protect him. This is a sacred song that we still use in our ceremonies, and in this song he calls out to the powers of the four directions, above and below the earth. He calls out to these spirits, and these four spirit stones watch over him, like the one behind his ear. After this he would ride down to his warriors and instruct them to gather dirt from gopher mounds and sprinkle that dust over themselves and their horses. Crazy Horse did that too, and all of this medicine protected him and his warriors in battle. In this Holy Road War, Crazy Horse rode through the infantry lines to deplete their cartridges and draw their fire. They shot at him but they couldn't hit him because his sacred war medicine protected him.

The one we call Cankáhu Wankátuya, High-Back-Bone, taught Crazy Horse the ways of war. High-Back-Bone was a blota hunka, a war leader, and many years ago a prominent warrior would take a young man under his wing and teach him, and this is how Crazy Horse received his military training. High-Back-Bone and Crazy Horse went on many war journeys together against the Crows, Shoshones, Comanches and Utes. Before the Battle of Kills One Hundred, the Fetterman Fight, Crazy Horse and High-Back-Bone advocated a different approach to war. Before the Lakota fought with the white men, when they fought with other tribes, the highest in honor in battle was to count coup, to touch the enemy with an open hand or a coup stick or society lance. That was the bravest deed, what we called the first coup, and the second coup went to whoever killed this enemy. These brave warriors who counted first coup didn't kill their enemy. That was the old way of war among the tribes; they were wars of honor. When the wars began with the soldiers there was no honor in them. The white man had no regard; a lot of times it didn't matter to him if he was killing a man, a woman or a child; that was how the white man fought. It was a different kind of war. Crazy Horse said that counting coup on the soldiers was not enough, and that to defend themselves they could not take pity on the soldiers as the soldiers did not take pity on our people, so the warriors must fight the white man at his own game.

In our language we call the Fetterman Fight 'Opáwinge Wicaktepi Okícize,' the Battle of Kills One Hundred, which came from the winkté, Crazy Mule, who had the power to see into the future. This winkté rode out towards Fort Phil Kearny to find the enemy four times, and when he returned the fourth time he had one hundred soldiers in his hands. Opáwinge Wicaktepi Okícize created a lot of excitement among our warriors. Chief Red Cloud was with several Lakota and Cheyenne chiefs who oversaw this battle, and when the Lakota and Cheyenne warriors annihilated Fetterman's command it was one of the greatest victories our people ever had. They didn't know who this soldier was, this Fetterman, but Crazy Horse brought him out of that fort. Among those powers of war possessed by Crazy Horse was the power to attract the enemy, and that is why he was chosen to lead the decoys. In the height of this battle they didn't know who these individuals were that they were killing; they only knew that they were the enemy and that was enough. It was the same in the Custer fight: they didn't know it was Custer until they discovered his body, but after this fight they didn't recognize Fetterman because they didn't know who he was.

When the last soldier was killed that day the Lakotas wanted to cause fear in the hearts of those who would find their dead comrades, and so they mutilated the soldiers' bodies. They turned some of them facedown to the ground, just as they did with Custer, so that they would never get to the spirit world. They wanted to shame this enemy and to fill them with fear of dying a horrible death like that. That's why they hacked the soldiers' bodies and drove arrows into them, so that when Carrington's men found their dead comrades, they might be afraid to fight against the Lakotas again. Crazy Horse and High-Back-Bone weren't involved in that; Lone Bear, one of their friends who had ridden with Crazy Horse as a decoy, had been mortally wounded and so they were making preparations to take him from the battlefield. Many of our warriors almost froze after that battle. An ice storm came up right after the fight was over, and a lot of them were without food because they had been preoccupied with planning the fight. There was hunger among their families too when they returned to camp, for the same reason.

In our oral history accounts it is told that we lost thirty-five men in the Fetterman Fight, but there is nothing about the story of American Horse killing Fetterman. Chief American Horse was a leader of the Kiyaksa, Chief Little Wound's band, the Bull Bear people. American Horse was a great orator; he once talked for days in a treaty council and put all the people to sleep! But he was a very thoughtful person and before he decided upon something, he considered every option. American Horse looked to the future, and because he had status as a chief, he could sway the other chiefs. He played an important role during the negotiations of the 1868 Fort Laramie Treaty. Way back then there was no such a thing as a 'sellout,' and nobody would ever have considered American Horse or the other chiefs in those terms. The people knew the chiefs as leaders and they listened to the chiefs, so once the chiefs acknowledged that the old ways of life were gone, they accepted that they had to negotiate with the United States government in the best interests of all the people. The well-being of their people was always first and foremost in the chiefs' minds. When they negotiated the 1868 treaty after closing the Bozeman Trail, the chiefs were under the impression that the treaty negotiators held the same status as they did, so they believed that they were making a nation-to-nation agreement that was binding, *in perpetuum*. At that time the chiefs didn't know that U.S. government administrations changed every four years.

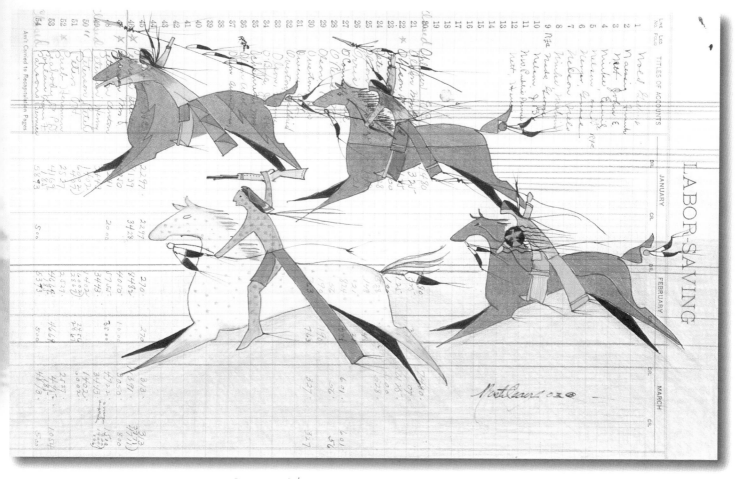

Crazy Horse — by Donald F. Montileaux

I believe our chiefs made that treaty in the utmost good faith, but none of our chiefs spoke English and so they had to negotiate through interpreters; a lot of things were misconstrued through interpretations, particularly what the chiefs' actual intentions were in regards to the treaty. The Lakota people believed that they had fought this Holy Road War to preserve their territory, the buffalo and their way of life. They believed that they had accomplished that by defeating the United States in the Holy Road War, but when they signed the 1868 treaty, the government referred to the Powder River country as 'unceded territory,' and the implication of that was never fully explained to the chiefs. Nevertheless, upon execution and ratification the treaty became law, and thenceforth, from the Lakota perspective, the government never lived up to its obligations. The annuity goods we were supposed to receive were stolen by corrupt officials, government Indian agents, post sutlers and traders, and so an entire black-market economy evolved with the annuity goods we were supposed to receive. Consequently, once the Lakota people were confined to reservations, they were soon in a starving state. Our people were in that condition when the U.S. government came to take the Black Hills, the spiritual center of the Great Sioux Reservation as defined in the 1868 treaty. Chiefs Red Cloud, American Horse, Spotted Tail and the others told the interpreters to tell the government that they were only prepared to lend this land; they were not going to sell it or give it to the government. In effect they were only leasing the mineral rights so that the government could extract gold and silver, but in exchange for that the government would owe the Lakota people the cumulative amount of what they mined for many generations to come. That's how the chiefs stated it to the government, but the interpreters never translated it correctly, and so the chiefs' statements are not on the record. The U.S. government interpreters did not fully represent the chiefs, and so our understanding of this document is buried by malfeasance, but the truth must be brought out. Despite the corruption, it still states that we are the landlords, the owners of this land.

SUSAN BADGER DOYLE

"On all the overland trails, including the Bozeman, accidents and diseases were the major cause of emigrant fatalities, not Indian attacks. I've figured that there were probably less than seventy emigrant deaths on the Bozeman Trail but it's been magnified terribly because of the military defeats and battles."

DR. SUSAN BADGER DOYLE IS AN INDEPENDENT SCHOLAR, AUTHOR, AND HISTORIAN. SUSAN IS THE RECOGNIZED AUTHORITY ON THE EMIGRANT PERSPECTIVE OF THE BOZEMAN TRAIL, AND SHE IS THE EDITOR OF *JOURNEYS TO THE LAND OF GOLD: EMIGRANT DIARIES FROM THE BOZEMAN TRAIL, 1863-1866*.

John Bozeman was an entrepreneur of sorts and he was out to make money any way he could, and guiding emigrants on a more direct route to the Montana goldfields was a likely way. Bozeman had left his family in Georgia, and there is little evidence to suggest that he was supporting them or intended to bring them out West, and his activities in Montana show that he was just interested in the main chance. When mining lost its attraction for him, he dabbled in a lot of things, but success eluded him and so he was looking for another way to make a living when he teamed up with John Jacobs. Like Bozeman, Jacobs had been drawn to the Montana gold rush, but he had more experience of the territory, having lived there for at least ten years. Jacobs was not a likable character, he was rather unreliable and known to be a drinker and a brawler, but from Bozeman's perspective there was something to recommend him – Jacobs had guided wagon trains on the Oregon Trail. Jacobs and Bozeman considered the economic potential of a more direct route to Montana, a cutoff that went from the main Platte overland road to the goldfields, so that emigrants wouldn't have to take the existing trail through Idaho.

In March 1863, Bozeman and Jacobs set out from Bannack, Montana, to make that cutoff, but we don't know their exact route. They went east and they were spotted once on the Bighorn River, significantly, going in the wrong direction. I don't think either Bozeman or Jacobs were mountain men types, even though they presented themselves as such. I don't believe that Bozeman knew the area at all and Jacobs had never been there, but they knew enough to follow Indian trade trails and so they must have thought that they could find a way. Many people think that Bozeman and Jacobs spent some time in the Bighorn Basin scouting a possible route, but they probably realized that for a significant number of people that would have been too dry, although Jim Bridger opened that route a year later. They ended up encountering either some Sioux or Crow, we don't know which, near the Bighorn River in Wyoming, and the Indians confiscated most of their things, and so they limped on down to the Platte River without really exploring this route that they had in mind. Nevertheless, on July 6, 1863, they started out from Deer Creek Station with a train of forty-six wagons and eighty-nine men, some with families, to open a shortcut to the goldfields and the Beaverhead Valley. Before that train even left Deer Creek Station, Bozeman knew that the Indians did not want him crossing the Powder River Basin, but he ignored that and I believe that he omitted telling the people in the train because it would have been bad for business. There is documentation to support that from an Indian agent who was at Deer Creek and who said that some Indians – possibly Northern Cheyennes, as they were known to camp around Deer Creek at that time – went in and told Bozeman that he was not to pass through on the east side of the Bighorn Mountains as they considered that area to be their country.

I think Bozeman and Jacobs had an interesting relationship that was probably not equitable. In Bozeman's mind he was the leader of this group, even though he wasn't the actual guide because he didn't know the area. Whenever Bozeman tried to go through the whole route without a guide he got lost. Interestingly, the emigrants in this wagon train referred to Bozeman, Jacobs and a Latino they hired named Rafael Gallegos, as 'our guides.' Gallegos was actually the guide; he was a local resident of the Upper Platte who probably knew more than Boyer,[1] the other guide Bozeman engaged. Jacobs had his young daughter, Emma, with him; the girl was half Shoshone-Bannock and it was said that he mistreated her. Jacobs didn't guide the train, but he more or less entertained the emigrants with his stories. On July 20, after crossing Clear Creek east of present-day Buffalo, Wyoming, they continued north for about four miles and made camp on Rock Creek, and it was there that a party of Cheyennes confronted the emigrants at their corral and told them to go back. The Cheyennes had some Sioux with them and the emigrants estimated that there were about two hundred warriors, but that was probably a significant exaggeration. All I've ever done is repeat what the emigrants themselves said, but we just don't know. Gallegos favored caution but there were some who wanted to continue and to call the Indians' bluff, and had they done so they probably would have got through. We don't know exactly what Bozeman or Jacobs said – they were relying on what Gallegos told them – and so the emigrants got together and reached a consensus and decided to follow Gallegos's advice, and they turned back. This failed attempt meant that by the end of 1863 there was still no Bozeman Trail, but that was to change during June 1864.

Nevada City

Bozeman pioneered less than a quarter of the Bozeman Trail, and he was actually just one of the four significant openers of the route, the others being Allen Hurlbut, James Sawyers and Jim Bridger. The four of them were responsible for developing various segments of the Bozeman Trail, as during that era, 1863–1868, there were several variant routes. The segment that Bozeman contributed is not known anymore. Jim Bridger was responsible for a greater number of Bozeman Trail miles than the other three combined, and Bozeman's segment was not used after 1864. Bridger is a legendary figure, but virtually nothing is known about Allen Hurlbut. We know that he was an early prospector who had found some mines and that he used that information to lure people onto his wagon train, saying that he thought he could lead them to this so-called lost gold mine, but he never could. Hurlbut had some knowledge of the territory, enough to come down to the Platte and then make his way back to Omaha where he started recruiting people. Of the four trains that departed from Richard's Bridge that summer to follow John Bozeman's proposed shortcut, Hurlbut's was the first to leave, pulling out on June 16 with 124 wagons and 438 people. Hurlbut led his train north to the head of Salt Creek before he intersected Bozeman's 1863 route, Bozeman having left from Deer Creek the previous year, forty miles east of Richard's Bridge, and so Hurlbut is responsible for that part of the trail. Bozeman's train was the second to leave, but his train passed Hurlbut's on Wolf Creek, a few miles south of present-day Ranchester, Wyoming, and ultimately he arrived in the Gallatin Valley first, which explains why the trail is remembered as the Bozeman, not the Hurlbut Trail. Fifteen hundred emigrants and 450 wagons traveled Bozeman's cutoff in 1864. The four trains were named after the respective captains, and the last two of that defining year, the trains of A. A. Townsend and Cyrus Coffinbury, followed the route opened by Hurlbut and Bozeman.

On all the overland trails, including the Bozeman, accidents and diseases were the major cause of emigrant fatalities, not Indian attacks. I've figured that there were probably less than seventy emigrant deaths on the Bozeman Trail, but it's been magnified terribly because of the military defeats and battles. The only Indian engagement on the Bozeman Trail in 1864 involved the Townsend train, and only four emigrants were killed in that, and that was the largest armed conflict between emigrants and Indians in the trail's history. That incident occurred on July 7 on the north bank of the Powder River, a few miles east of Kaycee, Wyoming. According to the emigrants, when they stopped for breakfast a man went off to look for a cow, and at about the same time a party of Cheyennes approached them and, supposedly, demanded to be fed. At that point I guess the prospect of chasing the guy who went looking for the cow became too attractive to some of the younger warriors and so they chased after him in full view of the wagon train. The emigrants then mounted a group to go out after the Indians, they engaged, and then the emigrants raced back to the train. The emigrants regrouped in a defensive position on and around a little bluff near the river, and this, coupled with the fact that the emigrants had some new Henry repeating rifles, really gave them the advantage. After a four-to five-hour siege the Cheyennes disengaged, and that was the only major emigrant wagon train fight along the Bozeman Trail.

I don't know how the Bozeman Trail got the reputation it did for emigrants constantly being attacked by Indians. Even at the time the emigrants didn't really talk about being afraid of Indian attacks, and there were really only signs of uncertainty in 1864. It's known that in the Coffinbury train they had a discussion about how they would act if they met Indians, and at first they said, "We'll kill them all if we see them," but then they reconsidered and said, "We'll leave them alone if they leave us alone." At the time I don't think that there was the perception that Indians would make the journey hazardous, but that became the myth, and I guess we have to blame the existing literature and Hollywood for that. Even today there still seems to be a reluctance to acknowledge what really happened on the Bozeman Trail and who ultimately suffered as a consequence of the Bozeman Trail. I don't know why that is, or why in relatively modern publications about the Bozeman Trail you see the term 'savages' and nobody objects. I hope that we are beginning to realize that when historians tell a story, they generally only present one perspective, even when it's supposed to be factual. Up until now the Bozeman Trail has been a Euro-American story to Americans, and that's what has been presented. Writers

The Madison Range overlooking the final leg of the Bozeman Trail to Virginia City

have been selective in telling the Bozeman Trail story to put the Euro-American perspective in the best light; you rarely hear or read about the soldiers and civilians who wanted to scalp Indians, did scalp Indians, and mutilated their bodies, but that happened.

I would agree that this attitude is probably the residue from Manifest Destiny – it's holding on to that idea of the West, when in reality it was just plain old American imperialism: we came out, we conquered, we imposed our way of life on the whole landscape and we manipulated and exploited the peoples who were here. It's unfortunate that this attitude carries forward to this day, and not just toward the Native people, but to the land itself. I think that Manifest Destiny started it and that is what started American expansion. I think of it as having been carried out by individuals, the individual agents of expansion, who carried these attitudes with them. The emigrants themselves wrote that way, how the Indians would be overrun and that they had to either disappear or be pushed aside because "our civilization is going to come across this whole area." You can see from comments they made in their diaries that the emigrants were aware of the Indians' opposition to the Bozeman Trail, but the tone was, 'We're Americans, we have the right to do this and we don't understand why they're objecting.' They knew – but I don't think they understood just how much – it was affecting the Indians. Would they have cared if they had understood? Probably not. It was American imperialism reflected in individual actions.

There was some positive interaction between emigrants and Indians on the Bozeman Trail, where trains benefited from both trade with the Indians and learning the locations of river crossings. In her diary on the trail in 1866, Nellie Fletcher described a lengthy trade rendezvous with a band of Arapahos on the Bighorn River, but you wouldn't know any of that had happened if you read *The Bloody Bozeman* or some of the other books. Military historians usually don't write about the Bozeman Trail before Carrington's arrival in 1866, and the interesting thing to me is that when they talk about the military period in the Bozeman Trail being from 1866–1868, there really was no Bozeman Trail as such then! After the end of 1866, the Bozeman Trail was never used again in its entirety. During that period it was mainly used as a military road between the forts in Wyoming and Fort C.F. Smith. Some of the writers who have concentrated on the events surrounding Fort Phil Kearny have blurred the emigrant role and the military role and have created the impression that everybody who traveled along the Bozeman was attacked and had to fight their way through, but that just wasn't happening and didn't happen. The Bozeman only became the 'Bloody Bozeman' after the military intervention that started with the 1865 campaign, and escalated with the occupation that began in 1866.

John Bozeman

The military thought that the emigrants were a nuisance, and the emigrants found the military to be incompetent and more of a bother than a help because the military imposed rules upon them that they didn't want to follow. The emigrants knew that the military's presence was necessary, but they didn't realize that the military had actually created the situation that made their presence necessary. Many in the military were often people right off the boat, a lot couldn't speak English and some were very unruly. Some emigrants never mentioned it one way or another, but there was almost an uneasy kind of truce between them. It was symbiotic in some ways and yet neither one respected the other. If there was a homicide on a wagon train the captain would turn to the military, and there are some cases of homicide on the main overland route where the perpetrators were turned over to the military at Fort Kearney. In fact, there were many instances of homicide on the main road, mostly from men fighting over women.

The claims office in Nevada City

On the Bozeman Trail there was a homicide when two teamsters got into a fight, and the one that lived was taken in to Fort Phil Kearny, but generally theft was the most prevalent crime. In the diaries you also find mention of assault and spousal abuse, and it is likely that there was a level of crime amongst these mobile communities that was

Vicinity where John Bozeman was killed near Mission Creek, Montana

149

Nelson Story

proportionate to any community of that size in that era; it's just that they had to deal with it right there on the trail and often they would convene their own little court to do that. Like other land and mineral rush trails, on the Bozeman there were fewer family groups and so there was a greater potential for discord, particularly with the captain if he was real autocratic, but it just depended on the people. Everybody was moving towards the same place, with the same goal, and they were in a hurry to get there, and so tension among the emigrants often came down to personalities.

There had been some severe problems with Indians on the emigrant roads west of South Pass and, as far as the military and various politicians were concerned, General Patrick E. Connor had settled that, which is why they brought him in to take care of the Bozeman and the Northern Plains. Connor had attained status in the military by massacring Paiutes near Bear River in Utah, and he was representative of the 'exterminationist' attitude that was then prevalent in the U.S. military and sections of the government. Basically Connor's whole campaign was a failure: when he fell upon Black Bear's Arapahos on the Tongue River he attacked the one village in the region that was not combative, and consequently he guaranteed the Indian-white conflict that raged over the Bozeman Trail and for years across the Northern Plains. They claim that Connor didn't know that Black Bear's village was not hostile, but he probably did know because Jim Bridger was his guide, and Bridger had close ties with the Arapahos and he was familiar with most of the prominent Indians in the territory. I think Connor's aim was just to get somebody, and that village was sitting there. Although it really was an expensive disaster with far-reaching consequences, while guiding Connor's command Bridger established a new segment of the Bozeman Trail from the North Platte to Clear Creek, and this new route was taken by all subsequent travelers. Connor managed to create a foothold by establishing his fort on the Powder River, which set the scene for what followed.

James A. Sawyers' expedition ran into the Arapahos three days after Connor's attack. Sawyers hit the Bozeman Trail about seventeen miles south of what was then Camp Connor but became Fort Reno, and he was leading a federally funded wagon-road expedition to survey the Niobrara to Virginia City Wagon Road. This was one of the Wagon Road Office's grandiose ideas, but it was totally unfeasible because they chose a terrible route. A lot is made out of Sawyers having prospectors on his train, but the main criticism was his taking people to capitalize on this road, like the Hedges supply train, which was actually a commercial freight train. I think the contract was worth $50,000 and today that's the equivalent of many millions, which is a lot for a dirt road! There are stories about Sawyers taking Red Cloud, Bull Bear and Dull Knife captive after their skirmish on Bone Pile Creek, and that in return for their release they agreed to guide him through the Powder River country, but I think that they are totally untrue. They parlayed after a cease-fire was called, and the Indians agreed to let them continue in exchange for a wagonload of goods. George Bent interpreted during the parlay and wrote an accurate account of the encounter. Sawyers did very little road work but he did recommend an adjustment to the Bozeman Trail, a cutoff from the Bighorn River to the Clarks Fork. Sawyers pioneered that cutoff the following year and that became the final route in that region.

My feeling is that you can't say who was supposed to be in the Powder River country and who was not supposed to be there based upon the 1851 Fort Laramie Treaty. The Sioux, Cheyenne and Arapaho were there, and by 1865 the government knew that they were the dominant tribes in the Powder River Basin, around the Bighorns and up to the Yellowstone River. In the mid-1860s the government wasn't following what the 1851 Treaty Commission had established, and there is a letter from an Indian agent to the Commissioner of Indian Affairs in which he states that the Cheyennes who were camped right around Deer Creek in 1863/64 believed that the government had officially recognized that this area was theirs because of the Harney Treaty of 1856. That treaty was a factor in what was understood at the time, particularly among the tribes, even though it was never ratified. I doubt that the military gave much thought to the animosity the sight of Jim Bridger and Jim Beckwourth would engender among the Sioux, Cheyenne and Arapaho when they saw them guiding Carrington's column in 1866. I don't think that they cared that any goodwill the Arapahos might have had towards Bridger had gone up in flames with Black Bear's village, or that the Cheyennes would have little tolerance for Beckwourth after he assisted Chivington in reaching Sand Creek. There was such arrogance in the military that not only did they not care about the Indians' reaction, they didn't really care who Bridger and Beckwourth were. I'm not sure that the military ever truly listened to Bridger or Beckwourth after they had guided them into the region; had Carrington listened to Bridger, Fort Phil Kearny would have been built in a different location.

Beckwourth is the best-known African-American associated with the Bozeman Trail, but we know from the emigrants' diaries that there were a few other African-Americans on the trail. They aren't referred to by name; the diarists would just write 'Darkey' or 'Jim.' African-Americans aren't commented upon much, so it's possible that they had either learned to cope without calling attention to themselves, or had succeeded in establishing a measure of equality, so they were not remarked upon as being unusual. Captain Tenodor Ten Eyck had an African-American servant named Susan Fitzgerald who was the subject of some debate at Fort Phil Kearny. Carrington disliked her, but that probably had more to do with his disdain for Ten Eyck than the activities he admonished her for, and we don't actually know what Ten Eyck's relationship was with her. She was his servant, she was living with him, and Ten Eyck often wrote about her in his diary. When Anne Butler wrote about prostitutes in the West she included Susan Fitzgerald, but I don't know if she was one or not. Her relationship with Ten Eyck is one of the many controversies that arose during the Bozeman Trail era.

John Bozeman's death continues to be one of the main controversies. I always felt that it was probably Indians who killed him because in Lieutenant George Templeton's diary he mentions some people arriving at Fort C.F. Smith who had supposedly heard the story from the Indians themselves, but they could have just heard a rumor. We really only have Tom Cover's word for what happened on April 18, 1867, as he and Bozeman headed toward Fort C.F. Smith. Would Bozeman have mistaken Piegans for Crows as Cover claimed? And would a Piegan war party have let Cover escape? There are those who say that Cover shot Bozeman out of jealousy because the two of them were in a love triangle with Cover's wife, but I've never considered that to be anything more than gossip. I think the theory that Cover and Bozeman had an altercation over business, and Cover then shot Bozeman to remove him from that equation, is much more plausible. Theoretically, it could be argued that by killing Bozeman, Cover would have assisted Montana's territorial governor, Thomas Meagher, because Meagher wanted the military to end Montana's 'Indian problem' so settlement and commerce would boom, and so reporting that Indians had killed a well-known figure like Bozeman would certainly have helped to justify that, and it is known that Cover and Meagher were in communication. When I asked Merrill Burlingame[2] who shot Bozeman he wouldn't confirm it either way, but people have told me that he really thought it was Cover, and around Bozeman, Montana, there is a strong contingent that believes it was Cover. Pete Story, a descendant of Nelson Story, one of Bozeman's closest friends, is of the opinion that Cover shot Bozeman, and he told me that there were powder burns on Bozeman's body, and that wouldn't make sense if he had been shot from a distance as Cover claimed. I just say that it's controversial, but I believe that the story that he died on his trail at the hands of Indians elevated John Bozeman into legend. I was once asked, "If Bozeman had lived would he have ever been more than a second-rate entrepreneur?" So I looked at his estate list: he left one trunk with a suit coat and a pair of shoes – there was the answer to the question.

When I think of the Bozeman Trail I have images of these emigrants looking for a new life in Montana. Most of them enjoyed the trip and didn't have any problems with Indians or anything else, other than the occasional river crossing or accident. I think I would have liked most of the emigrants that I've met through their writings. When you read somebody's thoughts you feel like you know them, and I could particularly identify with Nelly Fletcher and Margaret Carrington. Nelly Fletcher was very sympathetic to what was being done not only to the Indians, but to the environment. I also adore Davis Wilson and Sam Blythe; they were just two guys having a good trip who didn't have any interest in prospecting. At the same time, I am appalled that the Bozeman Trail led to the way the Indian tribes were treated. The Bozeman Trail really initiated that whole process on the Northern Plains that resulted in reservations, and the degraded lifestyle that Native American people endure on them. It really is a tragedy, but I was asked at my dissertation defense if it could have happened any differently. And I don't know. I really don't. The parallels in human history go on and on and on, but that doesn't make this instance any less tragic. The exploitation of the land, its resources and its peoples is – and continues to be – the story of the West.

1. For the 1863 Bozeman train, John Baptiste Boyer replaced Rafael Gallegos and guided the train back to the main emigrant road. John was the father of Mitch Boyer.
2. The late Merrill G. Burlingame was a professor of history at Montana State University and was the acknowledged authority on John Bozeman.

LEONA BUCKMAN

"Eagle Head and Black Coal were the Arapahos who were chosen to join Crazy Horse and the others in the decoy party. North was sent with the group that attacked the wood train. All told, there were about fifty Arapahos in the Fetterman battle."

LEONA BUCKMAN IS A DESCENDANT OF CHIEF SHARP NOSE AND A GRANDDAUGHTER OF THREE BULLS. LEONA IS A RESPECTED NORTHERN ARAPAHO ELDER, EDUCATOR, AND HISTORIAN.

The Bozeman Trail was a route of invasion. Along with the completion of the Union Pacific, the Bozeman Trail resulted in the end of freedom for the Arapaho people. The roots of our hardships can be traced back to those prospectors and immigrants who first crossed, and then commandeered, that last pristine buffalo range between the North Platte and the Bighorn Rivers. When they first discovered gold in California we felt that we were far enough away from the immigrants to retain a degree of security, but then the gold rush came right into the heart of our traditional territory, to the Rockies in Colorado. When the camp criers carried the scouts' reports of white encroachment, the old people said, "That's what the dreams told, that the spiders would come in like a horde and spin their webs. Then the spiders will be as locusts and devour everything." They knew that they were going to be robbed and that the spiders would take what they owned.

It simply did not make sense to the Arapahos; this is Mother Earth, nobody owns her! But here were people coming in and saying, "I want that. I will buy it or take it." The Arapahos had no idea what they were talking about. I think American history leaves out the parts that are unpalatable, but these settlers and soldiers were, by and large, ignorant of our treaties, our claims and rights. Even if they had been aware, history has taught us that they would not have cared. They felt that they could run roughshod over us, and they hoped that we would die and leave no trace. It seems that some historians have amnesia when it comes to the Bozeman Trail; they seem to forget that the Arapahos, Lakotas and Cheyennes were well aware of what was at stake as they had seen it before with the Oregon Trail – the diseases, the decimation of game, the destruction of the environment and the specter of dependency. Our elders knew what was going to happen, and it was 'shock and awe' to those who were taking the Bozeman Trail. Like the writers today, the immigrants back then forgot that we had been smart enough to coexist in this country for thousands of years before they had even crossed the Atlantic.

My mother told me that many years ago we also came from the east, but not from across the ocean! There were many big trees in that ancestral land and our people built houses out of them. She said we are the Besawoohenanah, the Big Lodges, or Wood Lodge People, and she taught me that we are the ones who were chosen to carry the Flat Pipe. We traveled from there, up around Lake Superior, and into Canada, before coming back south through Montana. It was then that the tribe had to cross a large river, which we think may have been the Missouri. The river was frozen, and among those crossing was a grandmother and her grandson. The grandmother was raising the child and, like all grandchildren, he wanted his own way, so when he saw a horn sticking out of the ice he told his grandmother, "I want that horn." She told him, "No, we cannot stop to get it." He threw a tantrum and so she said, "All right, I'll get it for you." She took out her knife and sawed at the the horn and handed him a piece of it, for the the rest of it was attached to an animal that was under the ice. As she cut the horn the animal started to move and the ice started to break. Half of the people were already across the river and were on their way south, but the others were stranded on the opposite bank when the animal broke the ice and so they could not cross.

Those people remained there, in that area of Montana and Canada, and they are now known as the Gros Ventres. The French called them Gros Ventres, meaning 'Big Bellies,' because when the French asked them who they were they made a sign which looked like a big belly, but it wasn't. The people call themselves the Ruptured Buffalo People, and that was the meaning of the sign. Traditionally, every summer they journeyed to a shrine in the vicinity of the Clark's Fork Canyon, to worship at the healing waters of a sacred lake. In that body of water sits a huge rock that looks like a ruptured buffalo bull, which is how they got their name. My uncle was a Gros Ventre and he told me this story many years ago, and it is true that the buffalo used to migrate up and down that canyon into Yellowstone. In 1877, my great-grandfather, Little Shield, helped guide Chief Joseph and the Nez Perce through that canyon and up into Montana. But one of my other grandpas, Chris Carlos Buckman, was a courier for General Miles.

We Arapahos call ourselves Hononono, the Red Earth People, the Human Beings, and our journey from the east was actually a quest to find the Center Place, the center of the earth. I've heard old people say that we have relatives as far south as the Andes, so we traveled a long way. My mother said that we traveled with the Kiowas for part of this journey, and we arrived on the plains, around the Rockies and in the Powder River country, a good five hundred years before the Bozeman Trail. It was a combination of survival instincts and government duplicity that caused the Arapahos to divide again, into the Northern and Southern branches. One group frequented the area around the Platte River, while the other ranged near the Arkansas River. After Colorado Territory was established, and the city of Denver was chartered after the Pikes Peak gold rush, the U.S. government and the territorial politicians were desperate to remove the Arapahos from that country. The government wanted to exile the Arapahos and Cheyennes to the south of the Arkansas River, which brought about the 1861 Treaty of Fort Wise. Theoretically, by signing the Treaty of Fort Wise the Arapahos and Cheyennes ceded all of the territory that had been recognized as theirs in the 1851 Fort Laramie Treaty, supposedly agreeing to exchange their lands in Wyoming, Colorado, Nebraska and Kansas for a small reservation in Colorado, $450,000 over fifteen years, and a promise to make them farmers. The legality of the treaty and the land cession was highly dubious as only four Arapaho and six Cheyenne headmen signed it, and an article of the treaty stipulated the necessity of acquiring the majority of Cheyennes' and Arapahos' signatures before the status of the tribes' lands could be altered. That treaty disenfranchised many Arapahos who lived in Wyoming and around the Black Hills.

The Treaty of Fort Wise established the Sand Creek Reservation. Many Cheyennes and Arapahos were unaware that the treaty even existed, so they did not leave our country 'between the rivers,' the Platte and Arkansas, where most of the stage lines and overland trails ran, so the territorial politicians and military commanders had to achieve that objective by different means. Extermination became their preferred option. While President Lincoln was freeing the slaves he was letting those who wore the uniform of his army exterminate the Indians. I feel very angry about that, and when he was assassinated and Andrew Johnson came on board, extermination was already in the wind. Johnson became the commander in chief of an army that had no war to fight. A year earlier, on Lincoln's watch, Governor John Evans and Colonel John Chivington needed an Indian uprising in Colorado to fulfill their political ambitions, and the Hungate Massacre gave them the excuse they needed to launch a campaign. Several Arapahos, including Friday and Medicine Man, were blamed for killing Ward Hungate and his wife and two children, but the horse tracks at the scene were all from shod horses, and we never shoed our ponies. Could they have been horses one of our men had stolen? Of course, and this is what Bob North, a white man who lived with the Arapahos, told Governor Evans. North claimed that it was Northern Arapahos under Notee, but I don't believe that. North had his own animosities within the tribe which probably motivated that accusation, and the circumstances the Arapahos found themselves in around Denver in June 1864 were desperate, and not at all conducive to inciting the military and militias. They were weakened to the point of starvation, and verging on defenseless. Gangs of settlers led by thugs like Big Phil the Cannibal would ransack Arapaho camps and rape the women, young and old, with impunity. Near Boulder, the women of Niwot's camp were among his victims. In Denver the townsfolk would sprinkle corn from their horses' nosebags in the streets just to watch starving Arapaho children scurry around and pick it up, and immigrants on the Platte did the same thing. Does this honestly sound like a band who would provoke a military attack? But Evans made sure that would be the result when the Hungates' bodies were displayed in Denver and hysteria broke out. How Chivington arrived at Sand Creek the following November is well-known.

My great-great-grandma survived the Sand Creek Massacre. Her name was Wilda Carson, the daughter of Kit Carson. About thirty years before Sand Creek, Kit Carson had married into the Arapaho tribe. Wilda escaped the massacre because she left the camp with her husband, White Wolf, and the rest of the hunting party that went out just before Chivington attacked. They couldn't take her mother, Singing Wind, and so that woman who had lived with Kit Carson all those years and who had borne him a daughter was slaughtered at Sand Creek. Carson had influence in that territory but chose not to intervene, probably because he had married into money in Taos, New Mexico, and it would have hurt him politically. As Chivington was attacking the Cheyennes and Arapahos, Carson was attacking the Kiowas. White Wolf and Wilda came north as the whites were making the Bozeman Trail, and that's where the White Plumes come from on the Wind River Reservation. We don't think much of Kit Carson and we don't think much of Jim Bridger either. They made their names by being so-called friends of the Indian and yet they both stabbed the Arapahos in the back. Bridger had also married into the tribe and yet he was the one that led General Patrick E. Connor to Black Bear's camp on the Tongue River in August 1865. Bridger had guided Connor's expedition up the Bozeman Trail, knowing that Connor's orders were to kill every male Indian over twelve years old and not to make peace with any Indians.

Little Horse, a Cheyenne Contrary, who had kin among our tribe, tried to warn Black Bear that the soldiers were coming with Bridger, but Black Bear wouldn't listen because he was acquainted with Bridger. The Arapahos are matriarchal, so when a man marries, and then his wife's sisters marry others, all the sisters and their husbands become one big family. That's why Black Bear considered Bridger to be kin, and in the Arapaho way you don't go against kin, but

Bridger did and he abused that trust. It was shameful to them, and because they were Bridger's kin, that shame then reflected upon them, and it was hard to take. A lot of the women fought hand to hand with the soldiers there and that shocked them, but being the matriarch is a powerful thing and she had to know how to take care of herself in every situation. Connor's troops were killing women and children indiscriminately and so the women caught in the crossfire had a choice: to die fighting defending their children, or to die begging for their lives. They chose to fight, a fact even military records corroborate. As the women were fighting the troops, the warriors regrouped and launched a counterattack, and in the end Connor was lucky to escape alive. Connor would have been defeated without his Pawnee scouts, and over and over again, in engagements between the army and the Cheyennes and Arapahos, the Pawnees saved the army and often did most of the damage. The best I can say about the presentation of that site today is that over a period of time we get pretty thick-skinned about atrocities. If folks realized the suffering our Arapaho people endured that terrible day I don't think that they would want a playground for their children there. What mother could want their child to play where other mothers and children were slaughtered?

Non-Indian historians often get the chiefs Black Bear and Medicine Man confused. They were two different people who, interestingly, also married into the tribe. Years ago I was told that Black Bear was actually a Sioux, and Medicine Man was a Cheyenne. Intermarriages were common among the Arapahos, Sioux and Cheyenne at that time. Black Bear and Medicine Man became brothers, so close that I would compare their relationship to that of Shoulder Blade and Sharp Nose, who I am kin to. Shoulder Blade married Wilda Carson's daughter. My grandfather, Three Bulls, told me that they were all with the hunting party that left Colorado before Sand Creek, and that they formed the basis of the band that was harassed throughout the Bozeman Trail era. When they left Colorado, they traveled to the Powder River area over our ancient trails through the Rockies. The old people would talk about that trail that went from our original home, Estes Park, and passed from peak to peak, through the Medicine Bow, until it dropped out onto the Laramie Plains. The trail was high in the mountains because there was water everywhere. The Arapahos have names for every one of those peaks, two of the most significant being our Twin Guides, Longs Peak and Mount Meeker. Laramie Peak and the Laramie Plains were always important to us; Elk Mountain is there and those plains were known as Where-They-Jerk-Plenty-Elk-Meat. Back in 1859, Medicine Man had tried to impress upon Agent Twiss the importance of this area to us, stating that if we were to settle on a reservation we wanted it to be on the Laramie River.

Elements of this band established itself in the Red Wall Country, along the Middle Fork of the Powder, north of present-day Casper. It was while they were there that Arapaho scouts brought in the first reports of Connor and his men on the Bozeman Trail. They were very observant and discovered that some of the troops had been detailed to bury caches of munitions in those sandy hills around the Powder River. They didn't realize that the caches were of rifles, powder and balls until they dug some of them up. This was before Connor had finished building the fort there, so presumably he needed somewhere close by to leave supplies while he went out to try and find Indians to kill. Our young men were told that this army had come to kill us and that they would use these weapons to do it and so they needed to go and find them all, and then destroy them. That's what they did while Connor was attacking Black Bear's people and Red Cloud was harassing Sawyers: they searched out those munitions caches and blew them up. That entire valley was black from the smoke for days. History books say that the Sioux had to persuade us to fight, and yet groups of Arapahos were fighting a guerilla war throughout that time. Along the Powder River, they were right under the army's nose and the army didn't know it until they set fire to those munitions.

A sense of foreboding came across them after this, and one old lady who carried the Flat Pipe told the people to follow her and so they pulled camp. They had heard about Black Bear being attacked, and they had heard about Sawyers and other soldiers all over the country, and the woman with the Flat Pipe knew the soldiers were going to come after them. They had to leave, but at the same time they felt surrounded. She assured the people that she had been told that they could go through the mountains, not over the mountains, but physically

through them. They followed her and that's what happened. The mountain opened for her to walk through and that's the power of this Flat Pipe. Army scouts found their trail but the tracks went just up to the Bighorns and stopped. It was as if they had disappeared off the face of the earth. When they walked through the mountain their footprints were erased and they went through to where present-day Thermopolis, Wyoming is. Our belief in the Flat Pipe goes back eons. It's always been there. It is our holiest bundle, and if we ask it for help in a good way, we'll be helped. A woman carries the pipe and that woman must walk. The pipe cannot be transported on a conveyance. The old people talked about this incident, but I doubt that it is known by anybody outside of the tribe.

Red Horned Buffalo was among the men who came north before Sand Creek and ended up fighting Connor. His wife was killed at Sand Creek but his son, then only a little boy, survived the massacre and was taken captive by Chivington's butchers. Red Horned Buffalo was on his way back south to the Arkansas River in June 1866 when he found Edward B. Taylor and his treaty commissioners at Fort Laramie. He talked to them but I never heard that he signed that treaty. He told them about his son and that he wanted him back, which is why he was headed back south – most Arapahos were unaware of the treaty negotiations at Fort Laramie, but they had heard of the ones taking place on the Little Arkansas. Taylor wanted him to sign on behalf of the Arapahos, but Red Horned Horned Buffalo said, "We have shaken hands with you. We have done nothing bad. Most of our people are on the Bighorn with the whites." What he said is revealing because it showed that the Arapahos clearly differentiated between combatants and noncombatants. The whites he was talking about on the Bighorn were immigrants, and the Arapahos often helped them between the Tongue and Bighorn Rivers on the Bozeman Trail in 1866. The Arapahos were good negotiators and great traders. They were able to travel into different tribal areas to broker peace between different groups and to negotiate terms for trade or hunting access. Often they would settle the issue by gambling, by throwing the dice or sticks, to decide the length of time the terms of an agreement would last. We read about these bitter tribal enemies and yet they were able to negotiate peaceful terms, so it wasn't all black and white. They adopted the same pragmatic approach towards the immigrants on the Bozeman Trail: they wanted to trade with them, not fight them, and maybe peace with the soldiers could come out of that. Once, I heard someone say, "Those Indians would come to the wagons and beg." If they were coming to beg, why were they bringing goods with them to trade?

Red Horned Buffalo tried to explain to Taylor why he couldn't sign for all of the Arapahos, but that if everybody else agreed after the commissioners had talked to them, his band would sign. He continued south and the return of his son was raised as a condition to the southern bands signing the amendments to the Treaty of the Little Arkansas. The military located the boy, he was being exhibited in a circus along with one of two little Cheyenne girls who were also Sand Creek captives. The following April, General Hancock took the boy to Fort Larned and released him to Agent Wynkoop, who then located Red Horned Buffalo's family. Even if Red Horned Buffalo had signed the Fort Laramie Treaty of 1866, it wouldn't have meant anything and the government knew that. One man did not have power over all the people, as the Arapahos, like their allies, had a democratic form of government. Sometimes the U.S. government used Chief Washakie as an example to counter that argument, but the Shoshones said he was full of whiskey when he signed away their land. That 1866 treaty was never a mandate from our people because so few signed it. Even the U.S. Senate failed to ratify it.

Cut Nose and about seven others signed it, but Taylor categorized Cut Nose as a Cheyenne. Because of similar names among the men of the tribes, and the frequency with which men's names could be changed, the whites often confused identities and tribal membership. I think that Bob North was with Cut Nose when he signed, not because he wanted peace with the army, but because he wanted to see what was going on and maybe get a new rifle or blanket out of the commissioners at the same time. North had talked to White Wolf before Sand Creek and he knew the Cheyennes and Arapahos there were not hostile and so he told the authorities that. It is possible that North lost relatives at Sand Creek, or he became enraged because Governor Evans intentionally misrepresented what he had told him about which Indians wanted to fight, which enabled Chivington to carry out the massacre of those that didn't. Whatever it was, North

rejoined the Arapahos. He had both Northern Arapaho and Gros Ventre wives, and the old people said that he was with them so long he became one of them. They called him No Fingers, and I heard about him when I was little. I believe he was a trapper, not a trader, and that he lost his fingers in a trap. He called himself a medicine man but he wasn't regarded as one, and when people talked about him years later they would say Chief North. It is said that he led a raid against some miners in the Powder River country, and that once he rescued an Arapaho woman who had been captured by the Utes. They came to respect him because he proved that he had powers; here was a man who had lost several fingers and yet he was able to do various and sundry things.

North led small parties of Arapahos in a number of skirmishes around Fort Phil Kearny and he was involved in the Fetterman Fight. North, Little Chief, Sorrel Horse, Black Bear and Medicine Man all had a say in the councils before that battle, but it was Eagle Head and Black Coal who had the most prominent roles in the battle. Eagle Head and Black Coal were the Arapahos who were chosen to join Crazy Horse and the others in the decoy party. North was sent with the group that attacked the wood train. All told, there were about fifty Arapahos in the Fetterman battle, the Day of the Hundred Killed. The last battle North fought in was the Hayfield,

Monument in Ranchester, Wyoming, commemorating Connor's attack on Black Bear's village

Site of the Arapahos' counterattack on Sawyers' party at the Tongue River crossing

where he was the Arapahos' leader. For a long time many thought that he had been killed at the Hayfield, but it seems that he was hung in Kansas a couple of years later. I can remember hearing the old men talk about the Fetterman battle in their little meetings, recounting how they all worked together and were assigned different positions, and came in on Fetterman's group from all directions. Most of those old men had served as scouts for the army, and it's ironic that the majority of those who enlisted as scouts with General Crook in 1876 were the ones who fought in the Fetterman battle. The Arapahos never divulged who the decoys were or who did what in the Fetterman battle because they feared that their families would be harmed if the white men found out, so they kept mum and didn't discuss it with outsiders.

Some of those old men were ashamed of being scouts, but at that time they were forced into it. We won the war to close the Bozeman Trail but we lost the peace. Under the terms of the 1868 Fort Laramie Treaty the Northern Arapahos were given the option of remaining in the north and accepting life under the Sioux at the Whetstone Agency, or moving south to be bound by the terms of the Medicine Lodge Treaty that the Southern Arapahos had previously signed. Going south meant abandoning the country that they had just fought to keep, but some saw it as the lesser of two evils and headed for Fort Sill before ending up at Darlington, Oklahoma. Black Bear, Medicine Man and Black Coal kept their people north of the Platte and pressed the government for their own agency, lobbying the military at Fort Fetterman. They wanted a reservation near Casper and they were led to believe that they would be granted one at Glen Rock, Wyoming, and that Fort Fetterman would become their agency. I think the soldiers at Fort Fetterman were willing but the government was not, and so the Northern Arapahos were effectively destitute. In order to survive they had little choice but to raid white settlements along the Sweetwater, hitting Atlantic City and Lander, which resulted in a Wyoming militia being raised. Black Bear did not agree with the raids and so his band did not particpate, yet he was the one the militia killed when they found him and his family on the way to Lander where they were going to trade.

Medicine Man, Black Coal and Sharp Nose moved their people back to Fort Fetterman, and Colonel Woodward agreed to distribute their annuities there as they refused to go to Red Cloud Agency. The Colonel persuaded Black Coal to send a delegation to Washington, D.C., but when they got there, Red Cloud was already there, and he had informed President Grant's staff that he could speak for the Arapahos and Northen Cheyennes, which did not please them. They hadn't wanted to live around a Sioux agency because they didn't want to be absorbed by the Sioux; they wanted to remain independent, and to retain their identity. This experience with Red Cloud in Washington, D.C., strengthened their resolve; they didn't want a chief of another tribe speaking for them, they were very capable of speaking for themselves. They did not want to move to Red Cloud Agency, but the Glen Rock reservation issue remained unresolved, and Medicine Man had died without knowing where his people stood. Black Coal succeeded him as chief, with Sharp Nose becoming subchief, and Sorrel Horse taking the Medicine Man name. Black Coal held out until his people were attacked by the army and their Shoshone scouts on Nowood Creek in July 1874, and although they were not defeated in this so-called Bates Battle, they lost most of their provisions, which meant that they could no longer survive and had no choice but to move to Red Cloud Agency.

They were being confined, like prisoners of war, which they didn't like, but the old men counseled, "You have no choice. If you fight you're going to die. If you fight your families will die. We're going to have to give up peacefully and accept it." It was then, at Red Cloud Agency, that the military put enormous pressure on the Arapaho men to become scouts for them. Their families' lives were at the mercy of the army, the post commander at Camp Robinson, and the Indian agent, so they either risked starvation or enrolled. Most went on General Crook's Powder River Expedition in the fall and winter of 1876, but some were with Terry and Custer as they moved on the Little Bighorn. Years ago I tried to find the records of these Arapaho scouts who went with Custer, but most of them were enlisted as Sioux, presumably because they were registered at Red Cloud Agency. White Bear, White Plume[1] and Whole Buffalo Robe[2] were actually Arapahos who rode into the Battle of the Little Bighorn with Major Reno and survived the siege on Reno Hill. These three were among the Arapaho scouts who later went out with Crook. Only five Arapahos fought with the Sioux and Cheyenne against Custer at the Little Bighorn, and those five were also scouts, but they left Custer's command to scout the trail that led to Sitting Bull's Sun Dance site at Deer Medicine Rocks and never returned. A Sioux rearguard party found them and took them captive, and when they got them into the Sioux camp they wanted to kill them. At that time there was a lot of tension both on and off the reservation between the Arapahos and the Sioux, and my grandmother said that the Sioux would as soon cut their throats as visit with them. Some Cheyennes intervened, including Two Moons, who believed the Arapahos' denials – they were insisting that they weren't scouts – and so the Sioux agreed not to kill them but to hold them captive. When Custer attacked, they fought against him to prove that they weren't his scouts.

Fort Fetterman

Two of these men, Left Hand and Walking Water,[3] returned to Red Cloud Agency and were recruited by General Crook's command. My grandfather, Three Bulls, told me about this. He remembered them coming back. When they were selecting scouts for Crook he wanted to go with them, but he was only thirteen so they wouldn't take him. Crook wanted the Arapahos to find Dull Knife's and Crazy Horse's people. Dull Knife had left Red Cloud Agency that July, after the Little Bighorn, and because he was the most prominent chief to have made his getaway, they had to recapture him. Without one of my grandpas, Chief Sharp Nose, they might not have found Dull Knife. Those were very hard times, with hard choices; nobody wanted to join the spiders, but if they hadn't they would have had to watch their families suffer even more. Years later, when I was a little girl, my mother would send me to the store, and often there would be an old man there. I'd watch to see what he was carrying, to see if his can had a gumdrop in the spout, and if it did I knew he'd have money. My mother called him the 'pension person' because there wasn't any term for it in Arapaho. This old man had been a scout for Custer and his pension was from the army. We nicknamed him Ja Boo Shotgun, but I think it was Left Hand, and once a month when he got his money we all got gumdrops.

Black Coal and Sharp Nose believed that cooperating with the army would ultimately benefit the Arapahos, because only the spiders – the army and government – had the authority to let them stay in Wyoming on their own reservation. They did not want to stay at Red Cloud Agency and they didn't want to move to Oklahoma. They told the army, "You've got to protect us and our families because you forced us to work with you." They had impressed General Crook, particularly Sharp Nose, who he made a First Sergeant, so the army agreed to protect them and let them return to Fort Fetterman. A combination of military assistance, and the diplomatic skills of Black Coal and Sharp Nose when they met President Hayes, secured the Northern Arapahos a home in Wyoming. The governor of Wyoming suggested that they move to the Wind River Reservation with the Shoshones, which all but the Shoshones agreed to. When the army and the Indian agent escorted the Arapahos to Wind River, the Shoshones asked, "Why are you bringing those people?" They said, "Because they have worked with us and we've agreed to take care of them through the winter. We have a place reserved for them near Casper and in the spring we'll take them there." The Shoshones agreed, but spring 1878 has lasted until the present time. As it was, cupid settled the issue. Cupid shot arrows at an Arapaho girl and a Shoshone boy who came together. Chief Washakie said, "I do not want to lose my child and if you Arapahos leave my child will go with you. I would rather keep my child with me, so you are welcome to stay."

Our traditional ways were then outlawed when they confined us to the reservation, and we could neither speak our language nor practice our religion until we regained that right in 1978 under the American Indian Religious Freedom Act. Many of the socioeconomic problems that face the Arapahos today are a consequence of the Bozeman Trail.

1. Listed with Reno as White Cloud.   2. Listed with Reno as Whole Buffalo.   3. Also known as Waterman.

ISAAC DOG EAGLE

"My grandfather, Sitting Bull, received his name in the Powder River country after he counted his first coup in battle there, sometime around 1845."

ISAAC DOG EAGLE IS A GREAT-GRANDSON OF CHIEF SITTING BULL. ISAAC IS A RECOGNIZED AUTHORITY ON SITTING BULL'S LIFE AND LEGACY IN HUNKPAPA LAKOTA HISTORY, AND HE HAS CONTRIBUTED TO NUMEROUS DOCUMENTARIES AND BIOGRAPHIES ABOUT SITTING BULL.

Memories become clouded with the passage of time, and many do not remember that the Powder River country was once Hunkpapa territory, but I have not forgotten. My grandfather, Sitting Bull, received his name in the Powder River country after he counted his first coup in battle there, sometime around 1845. Twenty-one years later, Sitting Bull was not involved in what the white men call 'Red Cloud's War' because, at that time in 1866, the Hunkpapas were confronted by a similar dilemma to that which faced those tribes on the Powder River, only our problem was along the Missouri River. Sitting Bull always said, "Leave me alone and I will protect my people. I will feed them," and while the war to close the Bozeman Trail was being waged that is exactly what he was doing around the Missouri, from the battle at Killdeer Mountain in July 1864, through to leading Hunkpapa resistance against forts Buford, Stevenson and Rice. Those three forts had been built in the center of what, by then, was recognized as our country, and so Sitting Bull and the Hunkpapas felt the same way about those forts as Red Cloud and the Oglalas felt about the three forts on the Bozeman Trail. When Sitting Bull said "Leave me alone and I will protect my people," he was talking about protecting and preserving our way of life. Those forts, which provided a foothold for the white man and westward expansion, were a threat to that "Leave me alone and I will protect my people" maxim.

Even though he had all of these other issues to take care of, Sitting Bull did participate in the opening exchanges of the struggle to close the Bozeman Trail. By 1865 Sitting Bull was the leader of the Midnight Strong Hearts, an elite group of fighting men from the most prestigious warrior society, the Strong Hearts, and it was in that capacity that he led and organized the fall 1865 campaign to drive the military columns of Cole and Walker out of the Black Hills and away from the Powder River. These troops were not particularly effective but they were well armed, and so a series of skirmishes were fought. Basically, Sitting Bull harried the soldiers until the main fight happened around September 5, 1865. They pretty much fought the troops to a standstill, and with the weather and their inexperience of conditions in our country, these soldiers were not in a position to continue their war on us. Ironically, Bull Head was among those who gained honors in this fight. White Bull, my grandfather's nephew, fought against Cole and Walker, and years afterwards he was quoted as saying Sitting Bull was "sort of a coward" in those fights. A lot has been made of that, mostly by those who have tried to discredit Sitting Bull. The truth is that what White Bull said was misinterpreted and taken out of context; all he was trying to explain was that, in those particular fights, Sitting Bull did not engage in the kind of combat he was known for, and there are two reasons for that: firstly, his role was to organize his men, to communicate how they should fight these soldiers; Sitting Bull was getting older and the role of a warrior changes with age. And secondly, Sitting Bull's mother, known both as Her-Holy-Door and Mixed Day, advised him to be more cautious in battle. "You've got all of these other responsibilities, so do not be so brave," she counseled.

Her-Holy-Door was right because by then he had a whole gamut of things to take care of on behalf of the tribe, including the political and social welfare of the tribe and, of course, his own family responsibilities – Sitting Bull was a husband, a father and a son. Years later Sitting Bull's youngest wife, Four Robes, was also known to some as Her-Holy-Door, and she was the wife who gave birth to most of his children. Sitting Bull himself was born on the Grand River, just south of present-day Bull Head. The Hunkpapas used to call that area Many Caches because there are a lot of little caves there that have been formed where the gumbo has been weathered, and so those

Chief Sitting Bull

natural stores were good places to keep food, which made the area a popular location to camp. Certain writers claim that Sitting Bull was called Jumping Badger as boy, but he wasn't. His nickname was Hunkesni, but in the English language there is no literal translation. If you think about a porcupine, how it moves and its attributes, that is hunkesni, but in English that has been interpreted as 'slow.' Hunkesni was his name for a long time, and then his father gave him the name Sitting Bull. People from outside of our culture often become confused by our names and the way we give and change names. Sitting Bull's father was called Returns Again, but at the time that he gave his son the name Sitting Bull, he himself was known as Sitting Bull, after which he took the name Jumping Bull. After Sitting Bull's dad was killed in battle against the Crows, Sitting Bull gave his adopted Assiniboine brother the name Jumping Bull. It is that Jumping Bull that people are familiar with. When Sitting Bull had his vision foretelling victory before the Greasy Grass, the Battle of the Little Bighorn, Jumping Bull was one of his attendants.

Some years earlier a mighty buffalo bull had appeared to Returns Again and had given him four powerful names – Sitting Bull, Jumping Bull, Bull-Standing-with-Cow and One Bull. Those names were given to him alone for his own use, and so he could confer those names upon whomever he pleased. So, Returns Again took the name Sitting Bull, before bestowing it upon his son, and taking Jumping Bull for himself. He gave the other two names to the sons of Sitting Bull's sister, Good Feather Woman. Bull-Standing-with-Cow fought in the Powder River country in 1865 and in the Fetterman Fight of 1866. At the time of that battle Bull-Standing-with-Cow received another name, Big-in-the-Center, but he is better known as White Bull. Sitting Bull was not the overall chief in 1865/66, but he was destined to be given that role, although that did not occur until the chiefs had been tested and Four Horns, Sitting Bull's uncle, nominated him to become overall chief. Even so, being leader of the Midnight Strong Hearts, his voice was never ignored, and when they returned from fighting Cole and Walker in the fall of 1865 to find a peace conference taking place at Fort Sully he was not in favor of participating. Look at it from Sitting Bull's perspective: In September he's trying to protect the sacred Black Hills from a military invasion and yet by October there are these other white men here wanting to make peace! Well, who were these white men speaking for? All of the white men? Those he had just been in combat with? Who? I go back to "Leave me alone," that's what Sitting Bull's whole philosophy was. Aside from that he did not think it appropriate for the Hunkpapas to be called to talk peace in enemy territory. At that time Fort Sully was in what could have been considered Mandan, Hidatsa and Arikara country.

Sitting Bull just wanted to preserve his way of life. He had never been impressed by white men or their military. He had observed them at Fort Pierre and didn't care for the conduct of their traders, and then when General William S. Harney marched into our country after massacring Little Thunder's Sicangus in Nebraska, he watched as Harney tried to appoint a chief over all of the Hunkpapas. This wasn't our way. It was the same when the soldiers built Fort Randall. Sitting Bull tolerated some white men, mostly traders who came and then left. He wanted to be left alone, he did not want to be around white men or become one. I feel like that too. I have to live with white men and so I tolerate them. And that's what Sitting Bull represented. When he said, "Leave me alone," he wanted to avoid what happened to us. Take Standing Rock for example: we were bombarded by missionaries, we were bombarded by the United States military, and we were bombarded by the white man's boarding schools. And what happened? We nearly lost everything. They nearly beat us to death, is what it amounts to.

Because so much that has been written about Sitting Bull has been made up, it might be hard for people to believe that after the 1865 Fort Sully peace conference failed to convince the Strong Hearts, it was Sitting Bull who took the initiative in trying to make peace with the soldiers. In the spring of 1866 he rode to Fort Rice with that intention, and when he got there, he paused for a few moments on a hill that overlooked the fort. Today there is a farm house on that hill where he stopped. Within minutes of arriving there the soldiers fired at him, and that's when he turned away from any thought of making peace

Top: Plate 34 from Sitting Bull's own ledger, the chief's drawing depicting his capture of a horse on the Bozeman Trail in 1865

with the whites. That's when he said, "Let's get these soldiers out of our country," and resolved to close Fort Buford and Fort Rice as Red Cloud and his people went after Fort C.F. Smith and Fort Phil Kearny. Sitting Bull's campaign against Fort Buford was like the one against Fort Phil Kearny; he even managed to take the fort's sawmill in December 1866. There is a story about Sitting Bull sending a message to the soldiers at Fort Buford, telling them that he was going to wear a red shirt in battle so that they would be able to identify him, but that story is totally untrue! It was fabricated like so many others, and like so many of the quotes attributed to Sitting Bull that have been made up. Historians should look at the sources, and a lot of these things originate from military reports or traders, not from Sitting Bull's family. There is criticism of Stanley Vestal's book on Sitting Bull, but he is the only author who actually came to Standing Rock to talk to us. I went to the University of Oklahoma to view some of his materials, and I found three small boxes of documents that are not translated into English, and those were the research materials I was interested in.

While all of this was happening at Fort Buford, Sitting Bull's nephew, White Bull, was fighting on the Bozeman Trail. White Bull said that none of Sitting Bull's Hunkpapas took part in the Fetterman Fight, and that is true, but there were some Hunkpapas, a handful or so. Red Horn is the name that has been associated with the Fetterman Fight but I believe that it was the younger Bear's Ribs. The possibility is there; Bear's Ribs was a Hunkpapa and his father was the man Harney had appointed chief at Fort Pierre in 1856, but that Bear's Ribs, his father, was killed by two Itazipco[1] Lakotas at Fort Pierre in 1862 because they thought he was selling out to the white men. Although it was quite rare at that time, names were passed on, which is how the son then received the name Bear's Ribs. This son was respected by some, but he did not have the stature or following of Four Horns or Sitting Bull, so his opportunities for honors were limited in our country, which may explain why he went to fight at Fort Phil Kearny. It was Mitch Boyer, an army scout, who came up with the name Red Horn in the inquiry they held into the Fetterman Fight. The Red Horns were from our part of the country at the time of that fight, but the Red Horns were mostly Yanktonais who had come to us after the 1862 Minnesota rebellion. I'm pretty sure that it was Bear's Ribs at the Fetterman Fight, and that he had a few Yanktonais there with him. To confuse matters, there was a Hunkpapa chief known as Red Horn, but he wasn't at Fort Phil Kearny.

There are so many misnomers. For instance, my name, Dog Eagle, is supposed to be His-Horse's-Eagle, but they changed it to Dog Eagle because it was easier for them on the tribal rolls. Chasing Hawk is another; the old man's name was Circling Hawk, and he was one who fought alongside Sitting Bull in that Bozeman Trail era. The war to close the Bozeman Trail did impact us, and if you look at the 1868 treaty you will see that Man-That-Goes-in-the-Middle was among the Hunkpapas that signed it. Man-That-Goes-in-the-Middle is better known as Gall, and Four Horns and Sitting Bull had asked Gall to go to Fort Rice after Father DeSmet had brought them word of it. Gall signed at Fort Rice in July 1868. It was after this, probably within a year, on Rosebud Creek, that Four Horns' campaign to make Sitting Bull chief of the Hunkpapas was realized. Sitting Bull not only became overall chief of the Hunkpapas, but all of the Lakotas who wished to live by his "Leave me alone and I will take care of my people" philosophy. Bull Head had been one of those. Bull Head fought beside Sitting Bull to close the Bozeman Trail in 1865, and he fought at the Rosebud and at the Greasy Grass. But in the end the U.S. government did its job well and recruited Bull Head and others from Sitting Bull's camp, and from the Yanktonai camp, for Agent McLaughlin's Indian police on Standing Rock, after they had made us prisoners of war.

In his orders to Bull Head, dated December 14, 1890, McLaughlin wrote, "You must not let Sitting Bull escape under any circumstances," and to us that means 'Bring Sitting Bull back dead or alive.' Before dawn on December 15, Bull Head knocked on the door of Sitting Bull's cabin and Shave Head said, "Brother, I came to get you." Sitting Bull didn't struggle, he just asked for some clothes. Now, if you dress someone, you honor him by dressing him. Bull Head was helping Sitting Bull dress, but his intention was not to honor him, it was to hurry him up. Sitting Bull even said, "You don't have to honor me in this way." When they led him outside, Bull Head was on his left side and Shave Head on the right, with Red Tomahawk behind Sitting Bull. Red Tomahawk was not a Hunkpapa, he was Yanktonai. They had got Sitting Bull a little way out when his wife began singing an encouragement song for him. Sitting Bull stopped to listen to her song, to hear what words she was singing for him. In the books they say he resisted arrest, but he was just listening to that song. Tensions were high and Catch-the-Bear, a staunch supporter of Sitting Bull, came forward to defend him. In the struggle that followed, Catch-the-Bear shot at Bull Head, then Bull Head shot Sitting Bull in the torso, and then Red Tomahawk shot Sitting Bull in the head. This all happened in Little Eagle, and today we hold our Sun Dance there, not on the actual spot, but in that area where they took Sitting Bull's life.

1. Itazipco, 'Without Bows,' are the Teton band commonly referred to as the Sans Arc in popular literature.

163

DOUGLAS SPOTTED EAGLE

"Though Little Horse wore the Sacred Buffalo Hat in the charge, Little Wolf was still the Cheyennes' leader in the Fetterman Fight. Crazy Horse was running with the Elk Horn Scrapers then and Little Wolf's people taught Crazy Horse this way of life."

DOUGLAS SPOTTED EAGLE IS THE CURRENT KEEPER OF ÉSEVONE – THE SACRED BUFFALO HAT – FOR THE CHEYENNE NATION. DONNA SPOTTED EAGLE ASSISTS DOUGLAS IN THIS SACRED DUTY. DOUGLAS IS SECOND CHIEF OF THE BOWSTRINGS MILITARY SOCIETY, AND HE IS A DIRECT DESCENDANT OF CHIEF MAGPIE, A VETERAN OF THE WASHITA, ROSEBUD, AND LITTLE BIGHORN BATTLES. DOUGLAS FOLLOWED IN THAT WARRIOR-TRADITION, AND HE WAS AWARDED THE PURPLE HEART IN VIETNAM.

Douglas: Trying to translate Cheyenne to English is hard, and it is difficult to fully explain to non-Cheyennes the importance of the Sacred Buffalo Hat in our culture, but Her importance cannot be overstated. There are two branches of the Cheyenne Nation, the So'taa'e and the Tsetsehésestahase, and each was given a Sacred Bundle in which the health, prosperity, renewal and very survival of the Cheyenne people are invested. Our two great prophets, Erect Horns and Sweet Medicine, who might be described as emissaries of the Creator, brought to us the Sacred Buffalo Hat and the Sacred Arrows. Erect Horns brought the Sacred Buffalo Hat to the So'taaeo'o, and with this Sacred Bundle came the power and knowledge for our life-renewing ceremonies, like the Sun Dance and the Massaum. What befalls Her – the Sacred Bundle – befalls the people. If She is abused, if She is not cared for correctly in accordance with the traditional teachings, turmoil and death can wreak havoc among our people. The role of the Keeper of the Sacred Buffalo Hat goes all the way back to when Erect Horns first brought Her to the So'taaeo'o, and those responsibilities have not altered. How the Keeper takes care of Her affects the people, and how the Keepers conduct themselves reflects upon the people. It has always been this way and it was no different during the era of the Bozeman Trail.

The hardships we suffered as a consequence of that era were prophesied. Half Bear was the Keeper throughout that period, right up until the 1868 Fort Laramie Treaty was signed. In the months that followed, sometime in 1869, Half Bear passed on. Half Bear's son, Coal Bear, would probably have become Keeper, but the military societies felt that he was too young, and so an interim Keeper was chosen. This man, Broken Dish, had been acquainted with Half Bear and was familiar with the responsibilities of being Keeper, but, despite that knowledge, when it was time for him to relinquish those responsibilities he refused. It is up to the military societies to decide who should be Keeper, and, four years on, they felt Coal Bear had matured and designated him to be Keeper. In the end they had to remove the Sacred Bundle from Broken Dish, but unbeknownst to them at the time, Broken Dish's wife had abused Her. Whether this was out of spite or hurt I don't know, but she removed one of the horns from the Sacred Buffalo Hat, and then turmoil came upon the people: freedom gave way to confinement, the theft of our land, assimilation, and attacks upon our way of life.

As Keeper you have to accept that you may care for the Sacred Bundle for the rest of your life, or She may be removed from your care tomorrow. My wife and I experienced turmoil that is not too dissimilar to that back then. A couple of times people have wanted to come and take the Sacred Bundle by force, but that is not our traditional way. If somebody wants to protest the manner in which the Keeper is conducting himself, a meeting of the military societies must be called and the issue decided there. We notified the societies when we learned of this threat to Her, and the Bowstrings and Crazy Dogs came to guard Her. If it had been back in the Bozeman Trail era there might have been some shooting going on; some of the young society members were getting mad at the individual who had come to take Her, but the older society people calmed them down.

Donna Spotted Eagle

Chief Magpie

Donna: It was really sad because the day that happened two Cheyennes were in a car wreck in Busby, and that's where the individual who wanted to take Her is from. The day after everything happened it was really windy at our place, and the previous Keeper and his wife came over and she said that usually happens when something is wrong.

Douglas: Just like in Half Bear's day, the military societies have the last word. The Keeper can make recommendations to keep the bundle in his family, like with Coal Bear, but the Keeper's son should complete the ceremonies and know this way of life. I completed my ceremonies, and I'm also a combat veteran. Then as now, they want someone who has seen life-and-death situations as a warrior, somebody who has been out into the world and is educated, and somebody who is So'taa'e. Unlike Broken Dish, the previous Keeper didn't defy the societies, he followed protocol, and when the societies offered the Sacred Bundle to our care, my wife and I were scared. I didn't think I was qualified to be Keeper, but we do our best. It is a hard way of life, and we take it a day at at time.

Today the Bowstrings and the Crazy Dogs are the societies that stay close to the Sacred Bundle. The Bowstrings are called the 'wolf soldiers' because the wolf taught them their ways and the wolf songs, but at the time of the Bozeman Trail it was the Elk Horn Scrapers who were close to the Sacred Bundle. The Elk Horn Scrapers were very well organized then, a strong society that included some of the most respected warriors in the tribe. The Elk Horn Scrapers were the principal society in the Fetterman Fight. Little Wolf, the Sweet Medicine Chief, was the leader of the Elk Horn Scrapers, but he did not lead the Cheyennes' charge against Fetterman; they gave that honor to Little Horse. I heard that Little Horse led the charge at Platte Bridge the year before and so this Fetterman Fight was not the first time that he'd led the Cheyennes into battle. Little Horse was a Contrary, not an Elk Horn Scraper, and I believe that he was wearing the Sacred Buffalo Hat in both of these battles. Contraries have a lot of powers, and people must have seen those in him and observed him as a warrior, so when he asked the Keeper if he could wear Her, he said yes. Little Horse had to go through ceremony before wearing Her and he probably vowed something, either to dance in the Sun Dance, or to fast, or in this situation he probably vowed to help the tribe conquer the enemy. The only time Little Horse had contact with the Sacred Buffalo Hat was directly before the fight, when the warriors were making their final preparations and the medicine man appointed to care for Her in the Keeper's absence put the Sacred Buffalo Hat on him. Half Bear, the Keeper, would have appointed a medicine man to carry the Sacred Bundle on the expedition, and although I don't know who that was, I know that he traveled with the other men so that the Sacred Bundle would be protected and not lost. Being a Contrary, Little Horse traveled by himself, and so it was too risky for the Sacred Bundle to be with just him and the appointed guardian. The Sacred Bundle includes the Turner, but the Keeper had to retain the Turner in the main camp. The Turner wards off bad spirits. It has to be treated and presented in a prescribed manner, and then its power will deflect any negativity the enemy may direct towards the people, and as the Keeper has responsibilities to all of the people, the Turner must stay to protect the people.

Donna: There was an occasion much earlier in our history than this, when a warrior called Two Twists asked to wear the Sacred Buffalo Hat in battle, and it was the Keeper's wife who said no. Two Twists had vowed to die and she didn't think it was right for him to take Her under those circumstances; she didn't want Her to be bloodied. This is an example of the responsibilities of the Keeper's wife, and it's the same now. In today's life, if I felt that my husband wasn't worthy or was doing something wrong, I could tell the societies to come after him. I think that the Keeper's wife has always played a real important role.

Douglas: Though Little Horse wore the Sacred Buffalo Hat in the charge, Little Wolf was still the Cheyennes' leader in the Fetterman Fight. Crazy Horse was running with the Elk Horn Scrapers then, and Little Wolf's people taught Crazy Horse this way of life and gave him medicine which helped him to be a great warrior. Young-Man-Afraid-of-His-Horses was another Lakota who ran with them, but they didn't get along with all of the Sioux. On the way to this Fetterman Fight, Lame Deer spoke to them in a manner that they didn't appreciate, and a decade or so later that came back on him because by then some of those Cheyennes were scouts for the army, and they hadn't forgotten it, so they fought against Lame Deer. There were some disagreements, the same as today, and it was not as straightforward as people think. Over the years, some people have tried to diminish Little Wolf's role in the Fetterman Fight, but you have to analyze those accounts and where they came from. A lot of the old people who shared that information back then were members of the Kit Fox Military Society and there was a great rivalry between the Kit Foxes and Elk Horn Scrapers; in fact there is rivalry between most of the societies. Also, a lot of these men who talked to writers at the turn of the century were Tsetsehésestahase, not So'taa'e, but it may be that the main reason for devaluing his contribution was the stigma Little Wolf carried after he killed Starving Elk, a fellow Cheyenne.

Donna: In a sense I think that's true. In those days people were adamant about adhering to Cheyenne traditional law, and a Cheyenne who takes another Cheyenne's life is automatically banned. That person is shunned, they're nobody. Long after it happened, I believe that whenever Little Wolf's daughter went into town she covered her face with a veil, because when something like that happens the shame falls on all of the family.

Douglas: Little Wolf was still a great leader. He didn't just turn up at the Fetterman Fight and leave before it started! He was the leader there, he organized the warriors, and his lieutenants were Crazy Head, Lame White Man and Wild Hog. Without him the warriors wouldn't have fought with the discipline they did, and people don't understand that. It's hard to become a leader, and Little Wolf was the Sweet Medicine Chief. It takes a lot of years to be respected in that way. After the Starving Elk incident, when Little Wolf took himself into exile, people still followed him. They knew there was a reason for why that happened – they didn't condone it, but they understood it. In those days a man couldn't fraternize with somebody else's wife, and for years Starving Elk had done that with Little Wolf's wives. When he turned his attention to Little Wolf's daughter he couldn't take it anymore, and that, with the influence of alcohol, brought about the shooting. Little Wolf moved away to Muddy Creek, the same place they camped before the Fetterman battle. People that know history still respect Little Wolf, but people that just listen to rumors have no idea.

Donna: I have respect for Little Wolf. With Dull Knife he brought us back from Oklahoma. He walked a long way for us and I don't view Little Wolf any less than Dull Knife. As the Sweet Medicine Chief, Little Wolf was the Keeper of the Sweet Medicine Chiefs' Bundle, but after the Starving Elk incident the people believed that the Chiefs' Bundle was tarnished. There was a general feeling of unease towards the bundle and nobody seemed willing to take it, and so my grandfather, Grasshopper, took the Chiefs' Bundle and cared for it for many years. Eventually his son, Frank Grasshopper, buried the original Sweet Medicine Chiefs' Bundle in the Kirby Hills area. My aunt was just a little girl then and she did not witness the burial, but later she was shown where it was buried. It is said that Frank Waters was given the Sweet Medicine Chiefs' Bundle, but he did not receive the original bundle, he was given a replica. The replica was considered to be a renewed bundle and the purpose was to ensure that the Sweet Medicine Chiefs' Bundle would still be represented within Cheyenne culture.

Douglas: The Cheyennes and Arapahos started the resistance against the Bozeman Trail. In 1864 it was a small party of about twenty Cheyennes who tried to turn a big wagon train back on the Powder River.[1] It was hard for them because they didn't speak English, but they tried to tell the immigrants to go around or to go back where they came from but they wouldn't, so the shooting started. The Cheyennes didn't have any guns and so they set the prairie on fire to stop the immigrants from following them to their village. These immigrants had more men and were well armed. Historians sometimes forget that in that era the Cheyenne warriors didn't have rifles, they only had about four muskets between the four hundred fighting men the tribe could muster! It was that way in the Fetterman Fight; there they used mostly bows and arrows and spears. I've heard it said that Fetterman's men weren't very well armed and that they only had muskets; maybe so, but they all had one, and they killed a lot of people in the Civil War with that gun. The reason that they tried to detour that wagon train was because our ceremonies were being held in that area and they didn't want those immigrants crashing through there.

The So'taaeo'o have an ancient, sacred connection to the country the Bozeman Trail bisected. In the Bighorn Mountains there is a Massaum Ceremonial Lodge on Medicine Mountain, the site they call the Medicine Wheel. The So'taaeo'o, we're simple people, but we had the Massaum ceremony before running across the Tsetsehésestahase, and when the two came together that ceremony was performed by the entire tribe. The So'taaeo'o had the Sacred Bundle and the Tsetsehésestahase had the Sacred Arrows, and each taught the other their ways. Ceremonially it's the same concept now, but with their union some of the symbolism changed. The Sun Dance was originally a So'taaeo'o ceremony. The set up of the Sun Dance today is very similar to what it has always been, other than there are some different dancers who participate in different paints. Some of these animal paints came out of the Animal Dance – the Massaum – when elements of that ceremony were absorbed into the Sun Dance. The U.S. government attempted to outlaw the Massaum and the Sun Dance, which contributed to the Massaum's decline, but it just takes people to revive it, people who know the songs and are willing to make that sacrifice.

The Sun Dance is a ceremony of renewal, of rebirth, and reenacts how Erect Horns and the Sacred Woman brought the Sacred Bundle to our people. The Sun Dance Lodge is constructed and arranged in terms of what Erect Horns saw when he entered Bear Butte and received the covenant. From that time forward, in any of our ceremonies, there has always been a woman there to complete the ceremony, just as the Sacred Woman accompanied Erect Horns. In the Sun Dance, the Keeper camps behind the Sun Dance Lodge and brings the medicine, the things that are in the Sacred Bundle that are used in the ceremony. When we renew the Sacred Bundle in the spring, the Sun Dance Priest will be there to inspect what is needed for the Sun Dance and then those items will be attended to and prepared for ceremony. For example, the bundle contains enemy scalps; there used to be nine but now there are six, from the Crow, Shoshone, Ute, Pawnee, Blackfeet and Arikara, and if any of the scalps needs repairing, the Sun Dance Priest takes that responsibility. As the Sun Dance begins, in accordance with the ancient tradition, the Crow scalp is placed upon a pole and members of the military societies race on horseback to count the first coup on it. Father Peter Powell earned the respect of the old people and they opened the Sacred Bundle for him, and the description he gives of Her in his books is pretty accurate. I think it would be inappropriate to elaborate, other than to say that the horn Broken Dish's wife took from Her was returned and is back on.

I think it was a combination of security concerns that inhibited the people and prevented them from renewing the Sacred Bundle for so long after the Battle of the Little Bighorn; not only did they have to be wary of enemy tribes but also the whites who had first started coming into our country on the Bozeman Trail, carrying the Catholic faith with them. After the victory in the Rosebud battle, before the Little Bighorn, Coal Bear renewed the Sacred Bundle. There are a lot of famous pictographs of the village at the Little Bighorn and the Sacred Bundle's lodge features prominently in them; it is the yellow and black lodge, the new lodge that was made for the bundle when She was renewed. Yellow and black is bald eagle paint, so it is likely that it was bald eagle paint that Coal Bear had danced in the Sun Dance. Each Keeper, and each family, has their own paint and he probably made it that way for protection, because you use those paints for protection. Today it is the same, and when the lodge is renewed, if the people wish to be blessed they walk across the new lodgeskin.

Donna: My grandmother, Augusta Medicine Wolf, was at the Little Bighorn battle. She was a little girl then, and when the soldiers attacked, her parents hid her in a bush. While she was hiding, horses started jumping over her – it was the cavalry when they came down to the river, near the Cheyenne camp.[2] There was a lot of noise, and then she said it just went quiet, so she came out. That time was very significant to our people, particularly the Rosebud battle, The-Fight-Where-the-Sister-Saved-Her-Brother. What Buffalo Calf Trail Woman did for her brother, Chief Comes in Sight, really plays a significant role in the Cheyenne way of life and the responsibilities Cheyenne women have, and it is all connected to the Sacred Bundle.

Chief Magpie holding one of the carbines he captured at the Battle of the Little Bighorn.

Douglas: The spirit of the girl who saved her brother is in the Sacred Bundle. This bundle is very sacred and we do our best to protect Her and preserve the ways of our people. Throughout our history, up to the Bozeman Trail era, the Little Bighorn, and to the present, every aspect of the Cheyenne way of life has related to the Sacred Bundle. It is still that way today.

1. The Townsend train.
2. Medicine Tail Coulee.

169

TIM LAME WOMAN

"My family are Chief Little Wolf people and I am a grandson of Wild Hog, and this we do not forget. To us, the Bozeman Trail was the road of Manifest Destiny, it was the beginning of the end of our freedom as it brought the colonizer into the heart of Northern Cheyenne country."

TIM LAME WOMAN IS A DIRECT DESCENDANT OF WILD HOG. FOLLOWING IN THE TRADITION OF HIS ANCESTORS, TIM IS A HEADSMAN OF THE ELK HORN SCRAPERS, THE CHEYENNE MILITARY SOCIETY THAT WAS HONORED FOR THEIR ROLE IN FETTERMAN'S DEMISE.

There are those outside of our culture who are under the impression that we Cheyennes and other tribes have lost what amounts to our historical archives, and that we are now as reliant upon the white man's books as we are on his commodity foods. Those who think that are living under a misapprehension: just because we don't commonly volunteer our historical register does not mean that we do not know. Our elders are the keepers of our archives and they remember. That is how it is in our culture: we remember; people only started to forget when they became lazy, and that happened when they didn't have to remember because they could write it down. My family are Chief Little Wolf people and I am a grandson of Wild Hog, and this we do not forget. To us, the Bozeman Trail was the road of Manifest Destiny, it was the beginning of the end of our freedom as it brought the colonizer into the heart of Northern Cheyenne country. When you look around at our reservation today, you see the consequences of the Bozeman Trail in the problems faced by our people, from high unemployment and poverty, to alcohol, substance abuse and dependency.

Our elders say that Northern Cheyennes and Northern Arapahos were the first to begin the resistance movement against the whites coming into our country along the Bozeman Trail. It was a group of Northern Cheyennes and Northern Arapahos that first stopped Bozeman and Jacobs in on Rock Creek in 1863, near present-day Buffalo. It is told that these two white men had a young Indian girl with them and that she was the main reason that they let them live, so maybe Bozeman studied Lewis and Clark and followed the Sacajawea precedent. Then in the spring of 1864 they did the same thing; they turned Bozeman's party back, making them pay a toll in goods and clothes for trespassing. Later that same year, along the Powder River in July, twenty or so Northern Cheyennes, mostly Kit Fox Military Society men, tried to send the Townsend wagon train on a different route, but, not unlike what happened to the Lakotas near Fort Laramie in 1854, because of a wayward cow a battle ensued. The Cheyennes were outnumbered and outgunned but they created enough of a diversion to keep the immigrants from finding their camps. Although dime-store historians have tried to perpetuate the myth that the Cheyennes and Lakotas attacked every wagon train on the Bozeman Trail, the truth is that this was the most serious encounter between our people and immigrants on the Bozeman Trail. It was the invasion of the bluecoats that gave rise to the 'Bloody Bozeman.'

When we speak about terrorism today, we identify the terrorists' desire to change our entire way of life as being one of their fundamental objectives. They are fanatics, the architects of unconscionable acts against noncombatants, but it would serve our society well to remember what was perpetrated on this continent by the Jihadis of their day. Manifest Destiny was imbued with cultural Darwinism and fueled by the conviction that Judeo-Christian belief was the superior faith of the superior race. Today the Jihadis want to blow us up because they consider us to be infidels, just as the nineteenth-century Jihadis like Sherman, Sheridan, Chivington, St. George Cooke, and on and on down the line to the Wisharts and Templetons, wanted to exterminate us – the Cheyennes and our allies – because they believed us to be heathen, unenlightened savages who stood in the way of their perceived God-given right to make this 'wilderness' bloom. But this wilderness just happened to constitute the land base of our nations. How many times did they advocate extermination? Check the record: 'extermination' was their term, not mine. To them we were 'unbelievers,' the definition of 'infidels,' and we were to be 'exterminated' or to become 'believers' like them.

They wanted to change our entire way of life, and they did at places like Sand Creek, where under the American flag and a white flag, they piled the bodies of women and children whose breasts they'd cut off and genitals they'd cut out; they did through germ warfare, introducing diseases to us along immigrant trails to which we had no immunity – in 1849/50 cholera halved the Cheyenne population; they did by starving us and then kidnapping our children to 'Kill the Indian and Save the Man' at their boarding schools; and they did by making us the longest-serving prisoners-of-war in history, leaving us to decay in abject poverty on these reservations where levels of disease are up to eight times higher than the national average. This isn't a matter of being anti-American, this is fact. My grandpa, Wild Hog, served the United States as a scout, and in our culture we honor all of our Cheyenne veterans who have sacrificed, from the Tongue River to the beaches of Normandy, from Iwo Jima to Hamburger

Hill, right up to the Persian Gulf. It is not unpatriotic to say that we, the Cheyenne Nation, along with our allies, whose economies and populations were devastated as a result of war with the United States and a subsequent invasion, are entitled to reparations to reconstruct our nations. How much was spent to rebuild Germany and Japan? What is being spent to rebuild the former Yugoslavia, Iraq, and Afghanistan?

In 1866 my great-great-grandfather, Chief Little Wolf, and my grandpa, Wild Hog, were leaders in what might be classified as the Cheyennes' Department of Homeland Security. The Cheyennes and Arapahos were the first to resist the Bozeman Trail because our ancestors knew only too well the consequences of these immigrant roads, having seen the destruction of our southern relatives who had already been exposed to the Oregon, Santa Fe, and Smoky Hill Trails. Little Wolf, our Sweet Medicine Chief, was the chief headsman of the Elk Horn Scrapers Military Society, and Wild Hog was a little chief of the Elk Horn Scrapers, making him one of the society's four headsmen. Today I have the honor of being a headsman of the Elks. Wild Hog was married to one of Little Wolf's daughters, and so through kin and military rank, he served as Little Wolf's lieutenant. Wild Hog was the chief's right-hand man. Our old ones described Wild Hog as being the Northern Cheyenne equivalent of Crazy Horse, and when we finally committed to the war to close the Bozeman Trail forts, Wild Hog featured prominently in the strategic planning of the campaign alongside Crazy Horse, Little Wolf and Hump. The winter of 1865/66 was a starvation winter, and so the old people had advised against continuing the war against the whites until we had enough supplies; they said we starved that winter because fighting the whites throughout 1865 limited our ability to hunt.

Dull Knife's people were following this advice from their elders when they visited Carrington as he was establishing Fort Phil Kearny. I think our ancestors' participation in the war was in the balance until Dull Knife went to sign the 1866 Fort Laramie Treaty in October and saw Chivington doing business there, and then Carrington's credibility was called into question after Little Moon and his family were surrounded by ninety soldiers at Fort Phil Kearny who had slaughter in mind. Carrington had given Little Moon permission to camp by the fort, and even though the colonel intervened, our people never forgot it. That's the Cheyenne way: No surrender! Add to that some two thousand immigrants and twelve hundred wagons carving up our country on the Bozeman Trail, grazing the land out with their livestock, and leaving buffalo and elk to rot after shooting them for sport, and something had to be done to protect our future generations. On December 21, 1866, our grandfathers sent a message: No more!

If anybody needs convincing that Little Wolf and Wild Hog planned the Fetterman Fight decoy tactics with Crazy Horse and Hump, they only need to look at the strategy for the attempted Punished Woman Creek fight on their epic journey home from Oklahoma in 1878. The main Cheyenne men in the Fetterman Fight were Little Wolf, Wild Hog, Little Horse, Crazy Head and Lame White Man. Basically, Little Wolf was like the Cheyennes' general in the fight, and he had Crazy Head join the attack on the infantry at the north end of the ridge, while concurring with Lame White Man that the rest of the infantry, the men with Fetterman, would try and get back down the road toward the fort to at least get into a position where reinforcements might reach them, which is why Lame White Man swept around to the south to cut them off. Little Wolf and Wild Hog focused on the remnants of the cavalry who became trapped about halfway between the two points. Little Wolf gave the orders against these dismounted cavalrymen in the rocks, but it was Wild Hog who led the actual fighting and whose actions were responsible for their demise and for stopping them

Wild Hog's son, Bird Wild Hog

reuniting with Fetterman's men. This Fetterman Fight was really the Elk Horn Scrapers' victory, as the Elk Horn Scrapers claimed sixty kills out of the eighty-one soldiers who died in the battle. It was after this battle that the Elk Horn Scrapers embraced the name 'Blue Soldiers' because the Elk Horn Scrapers took the soldiers' coats that day. It was Chief Little Wolf, Wild Hog and the other Elk Horn Scrapers who burnt Fort Phil Kearny to the ground after the 1868 treaty was signed and the soldiers left.

Even though the military gave up the Bozeman Trail in 1868, its influence upon our lives didn't end. The Battle of the Little Bighorn and that whole era of conflict was a consequence of the Bozeman Trail. After Custer broke the 1868 treaty by marching into the Black Hills in 1874, the Bozeman Trail became the staging post for the army's new war against our people, a war that they once again manufactured through corruption, duplicitous economics and political expediency. They sued for peace when they were losing the war to close the Bozeman Trail, but the 1868 treaty bought them just enough time to finish the railroad, and so then they wanted to prosecute their 'final solution' to the 'Indian problem.' Fort Ellis, Fort Fetterman and Cantonment Reno, all Bozeman Trail posts, were major launching pads for the U.S. Army in the campaign of 1876. Wild Hog was there at the Rosebud and at the Little Bighorn, and in his name I was proud to have contributed to the completion of the Indian Memorial at the Little Bighorn – it took us a lot of walking and a lot of talking, but it's progress. We got the 'Custer Battlefield' renamed the 'Little Bighorn Battlefield,' and now we have a memorial.

For all that, our reservation is still surrounded by towns that are named after war criminals who, if judged by today's standards, would be on trial in the Hague. Be it in Bosnia or here on the Plains, one man's butcher is another man's hero. Some might include Miles City on that list, but in fairness General Miles lobbied for the Northern Cheyenne people and helped us to secure the Tongue River Reservation. Revisionists have written that the Cheyenne scouts who went against the Nez Perce with Miles were shunned by other Cheyennes, but in my research I haven't found that to be true. Who were the Nez Perce to the Cheyennes? The Nez Perce were a tribe with nice horses from over the mountains who were allies of our enemies, the Crows. The reality is that had these men not agreed to become scouts and cooperated with Miles, the chances are that the Northern Cheyennes would not have held the Tongue River Reservation. Wild Hog scouted for the military and his wife Lydia, Chief Little Wolf's daughter, drew his military pension of $2 per month in Sheridan. Wild Hog and Little Wolf had a bond with that area, their beloved Bighorn Mountains, and even today you can feel it when you stand at Little Wolf's campsite on Muddy Creek and realize that he camped there because of the view of the Bighorns. I too have always been drawn to that area.

It was so hard for Wild Hog's and Little Wolf's people to leave in 1877, and the pain they felt can clearly be seen in the sacrifices they made to return. When the Cheyennes were

Wild Hog, center-left, sitting next to the interpreter, George Reynolds, during the trial preliminaries in Dodge City, Kansas, in April 1879. Wild Hog's codefendants are, left to right: Tangle Hair, Strong Left Hand, Old Crow, Porcupine, Noisy Walker, and Blacksmith.

at Red Cloud Agency there was never any consensus to go south to Oklahoma; only Standing Elk agreed to go, and the army just used that as an excuse to ethnically cleanse our people from our homeland. They endured great hardship in Indian Territory, and the combination of heat, malaria, starvation and heartbreak from being ripped from their homes was taking its toll in lives, until Little Wolf announced that they were going home, but that he didn't want to make the ground at the agency bloody. Ultimately, 284 of our relatives, all but 87 being women and children, were pursued by thousands of soldiers and settlers. They were guided and protected by their spirituality, Chief Little Wolf carried the sacred Sweet Medicine Bundle, and more than once this spiritual power saved them and rendered them invisible to the army, once giving them the appearance of a herd of buffalo lying on the plains. Little Wolf did not want to separate from Dull Knife and he advised against it, but Dull Knife was ailing and thought he might find help at Red Cloud's agency. Little Wolf said that parting made his heart like stone, and he asked Wild Hog to go with Dull Knife and his people to interpret for them and to use his strength to protect them. It was as if Little Wolf had foreseen what would happen, and when Dull Knife's people were apprehended on Chadron Creek and disarmed, Wild Hog only had a bow and arrows.

When they were taken to Fort Robinson it was tolerable at first, but then Dull Knife's son went looking for his missing wife, which resulted in a heavy guard. Wild Hog, Tangle Hair, Dull Knife, Porcupine and Strong Left Hand were instructed that they had to go back south but they refused, and so Wessels, the soldier chief, tried to starve and freeze them into submission. After a few days of cold and hunger, Wessels called for Wild Hog and asked if they were now ready to

The barracks at Fort Robinson where Morning Star's (Dull Knife's) people were imprisoned without food, water or fuel

go back south, but Wild Hog told him that this was part of their traditional homeland and that the consensus was that they would rather die here. Wild Hog pulled out a knife and attempted to pierce his heart, for in our way there is no surrender. In the scuffle, Wild Hog and a soldier, Lieutenant Cummings, were injured, and then, cut and bloody, Wild Hog was put in irons with Old Crow and Strong Left Hand. That night, January 9, 1879, with Wild Hog bleeding in chains and their strength waning through malnutrition, the young men amongst Dull Knife's people decided to break out. They had managed to retain some arms by dismantling them and disguising various parts as jewelry and children's toys, and so they hastily reassembled what they could and fought their way out. It is said that the sound of the soldiers' bullets cutting them down as they ran was like canvas being torn. Nearly half of them, sixty-four, were slain in the escape, but the military society men ensured Dull Knife's safety. After the carnage, Wild Hog was informed that he was going to be sent for trial in Kansas, but he looked around at the blood of his relatives and tried to take his life again, as did his wife. The post surgeon reported that Wild Hog tried to sacrifice himself so that his wife and children would be allowed to go to Pine Ridge and would not be sent back to Indian Territory.

Among those sent to Kansas with Wild Hog, were Tangle Hair, Old Crow, Strong Left Hand and Porcupine. They were charged with ravishing white women, stealing horses and killing settlers. Wild Hog was appointed as spokesman for the group and testimony in the *State of Kansas v. Wild Hog et al.* began. Wild Hog addressed the court and explained that they hadn't killed or ravished anybody, and that their circumstances had required them to stay as far away from settlers as possible. As to the horse he rode, he said it was his own. In outlining their defense, Wild Hog used the treaties and the articles therein as the cornerstone of his rebuttal, a precedent Indian people have followed in litigation from that day forth. "When you took me and my brothers away from Fort Robinson in chains," he said. "We were all bloody. Then I looked around the fort and the snow was all red with the blood of my people. I wish to ask today who is going to go on trial for killing my relatives?" he asked. The court had no answer, but the verdict was not guilty. Wild Hog passed away on the Pine Ridge Reservation. On our sacred mountain, Bear Butte, and in our sweat lodges, and during our Sun Dances, the spirits of our ancestors come to us. "Sacrifice for your children and the future generations, as we sacrificed for you. Protect them and this way of life," they say. One day we hope to bring Wild Hog home to our land, the homeland we continue to fight for and protect for those future generations.

Chief Little Wolf's grave in Lame Deer

JACK BAILEY

"Overall there were tensions, and yet there were still good relationships between some of the settlers and some of the Cheyennes. My grandmother was seven years old when the family came over from Ireland and she played with the little Cheyenne kids and learned to speak fluent Cheyenne."

JACK BAILEY'S ANCESTORS WERE AMONG THE FIRST CATTLEMEN IN MONTANA TERRITORY. JACK'S GREAT-GRANDFATHER THEN SETTLED ON THE ROSEBUD, AND FROM THEN UP TO THE PRESENT, THE BAILEYS' FAMILY HISTORY HAS BEEN INTERWOVEN WITH THAT OF THE NORTHERN CHEYENNE – FROM TWO MOONS AND WHITE BULL, TO JOHN STANDS-IN-TIMBER, TO THE SACRED DEER MEDICINE ROCKS JACK STRIVES TO PROTECT.

First it was the Bozeman Trail and then it was the railroad that opened up this territory to settlement. Montana was still a territory when both my grandmother's side and my grandfather's side of our family came in the 1880s. My great-grandfather's family came directly from Ireland in 1883. Jack Lynch, my great-grandfather's brother, had been running Marcus Daly's cattle ranch up in the western part of the territory. Marcus was Jack's cousin and, as sometimes happens among family, they had a falling out, and so Uncle Jack moved down to the Rosebud, and Marcus Daly paid for the cattle that started the Lynch family cattle ranch. My great-grandfather discovered that there was land open for homesteading in this area at that time, and so he made a legal homestead and came in here to the Rosebud in 1883. It was poverty that brought them to Montana; in Ireland they had suffered from the effects of the potato famine and, being Roman Catholics, had also endured religious persecution. St. Labre Mission opened a year after they arrived and it gave their kids the chance to have an education and to follow their religious training without persecution.

The other side of the family were down in Kansas at this time. Henry Bailey's father died of pneumonia, which left him with a young sister and an ailing mother to take care of. Henry's uncles had already moved to Montana and set up as hunters on the Rosebud, and so he decided to follow them. Before they could make the trip they needed a little money, but there wasn't a job anywhere. Finally, Henry got a job on the railroad, which he said was just the lowest work that you could get. The workers were buggy and diseased but he stayed at it for a month to get enough money to come, and then he packed his mother and little sister up in a wagon, spent his last $1.87 on oats for his horses, and came to the Rosebud in 1887. Coming from Kansas, I'm sure they must have heard of Nelson Story's exploits on the Bozeman Trail.[1] It was twenty-one years after Nelson Story that Henry Bailey made the journey from Kansas to Montana, but in those early days people who came out here all had something in common: they were pretty independent. Just think of a 16-year-old boy with his mother and sister coming up to Montana with a team and wagon and a cow herd. When Nelson Story drove his thousand head of longhorns up in 1866 his party had the benefit of safety in the numbers. For some people Nelson Story is just a name from history now, but I'm sure he was quite a character in his day – he had to be!

I don't think the Story cattle drive on the Bozeman Trail would have been that bad. They were well armed, they had cattle they could eat if it got tough, and they must have had good, experienced scouts that found their water and navigated the trails. George Herendeen was on the Story cattle drive, and he went on to make his reputation as a scout in Montana and Dakota Territory. Like many others, the Bozeman Trail brought Herendeen his first experience of the Sioux and Cheyenne, but he got plenty more. Herendeen was back and forth through the Rosebud from then until the Battle of the Little Bighorn. He started scouting for the army on the west end of the Bozeman Trail, at Fort Ellis, and came east along the Yellowstone with Major Eugene Baker's command to scout another trail, this time for the Northern Pacific surveying crew. Somewhere around present-day Billings they ran into some of the northern bands of Oglala Sioux, and some say that was the first post-Bozeman Trail battle between the Army and the Sioux. The Sioux who fought Herendeen and Baker had declined the government's invitation to sign the 1868 Fort Laramie Treaty, and Herendeen met some of these warriors again at the Little Bighorn. Custer brought the Seventh Cavalry right through our property here on the way to the battle, and Herendeen was with him. When they got here they found the site of Sitting Bull's vision of soldiers without ears falling like grasshoppers into the Sioux and Cheyenne encampment; they had found the site of the great Sun Dance that had been held in front of the Cheyennes' sacred Deer Medicine Rocks. Herendeen survived the Battle of the Little Bighorn because Custer sent him and many of the other scouts with Reno.

Two years before the battle Herendeen had participated in the Yellowstone Wagon Road & Prospecting Expedition that again brought him to the Rosebud. The land then was a lot like it is now, other than on the occasions that it may have been overgrazed, such as during the buffalo migrations. When Sitting Bull and Crazy Horse came through before the Custer battle they must have brought close to twenty-eight thousand head of horses up the Rosebud, so the

Montana pioneer's homestead

country must have been somewhat denuded that year. The valley was not open meadows like we know it now, it was all trees and brush and swamps, but the brush was wild rose bushes, and they say it was a beautiful place when it was all in bloom in the spring. The purpose of the Yellowstone Wagon Road & Prospecting Expedition was to prospect between the Rosebud and the Powder River, to survey for a townsite at the mouth of the Tongue River, and to scout a freight road from the Rosebud area over to Bozeman to expand commerce in the territory and make Bozeman City more prosperous. All of this was to have an impact in the following decade on both the Indians and the settlers around the Tongue and the Rosebud.

A lot of the Northern Cheyennes who had been forced to surrender had gone in to either General Miles at Tongue River Cantonment, or to General Crook's staff at the Red Cloud Agency. It was from Red Cloud Agency that Little Wolf's and Dull Knife's people were sent to Oklahoma, which then lead to the Cheyenne exodus back north. Little Wolf brought his band back to the Rosebud and the Yellowstone, Two Moon's and White Bull's bands were already here, and the survivors of Dull Knife's band were eventually allowed to transfer from Pine Ridge to Fort Keogh. General Miles was instrumental in the Cheyennes receiving a reservation in this area, and in 1883 the U.S. government was formulating what became the 1884 Executive Order that created the Cheyennes' Tongue River Reservation. At first it didn't seem that the reservation would include the land here on the Rosebud where our family lived, but then they set the northern boundary here because it was forty-five miles or so from the railroad. Had they not done that, every other section would have been railroad land, and so they had to get beyond that to establish the reservation. When the problem reached something of a crisis point – in that to have a viable reservation land base the government had to relocate legal and illegal settlers, compensate landowners and appease the railroad – they thought that because the Crows had such a large reservation they should buy part of that land back and give it to the Cheyennes, but after Mr. McLaughlin studied the situation he soon found out that the Crows didn't have anything good to say about the Cheyennes, and the Cheyennes didn't have anything good to say about the Crows, and so he recommended that they not do that, and so they moved back here instead. When the reservation boundaries were settled, our family was moved off the reservation to just over the northern boundary where we are today.

Little Wolf's, Two Moons' and Dull Knife's people had been living back on the Rosebud, and Lame Deer Creek, since 1882, and with the establishment of the reservation imminent, General Miles gave George Yoakam, a young private from Fort Keogh, the job of teaching the Cheyennes how to become farmers. I don't think that our family had very much to do with him because he spent most of his time in the Ashland area, but I expect that they knew of his reputation because he was supposed to be a controversial character. Yoakam became something of a champion of the cause to have the Cheyennes settled in the Tongue River valley and Rosebud Creek areas, which put him at odds with a lot of the ranchers here and the stockmen around Miles City. In 1883, a rancher called Jesse Haston gathered a lot of the area's stockmen together to form an alliance with the Wyoming Stock Growers Association to try and stop the Cheyennes from being settled in the Tongue River valley and the Rosebud. Haston said there were probably one hundred thousand head of cattle there and that there was little or no game for the Cheyennes to hunt, and so he and many others felt that the Cheyennes would rustle these cattle to survive. I actually think that the entire issue was misrepresented. The local people did sign a petition asking the government to remove the Cheyennes, but the main issue wasn't what the stockmen were saying; it goes back to the purpose of the Bozeman Trail and the Yellowstone Wagon Road & Prospecting Expedition that Herendeen was on. In 1883, just like in 1866 and 1874, the politicians and businessmen wanted to free up trade all through the area, from the Tongue River to the Gallatin Valley and the country in western Montana. Ever since the Bozeman Trail, attempts had been made to incite the Indians and to get them on the warpath so that there would be an excuse to send the army in to move the Indians out for good, so that east-west commercial routes could be opened through the country. I think that the businessmen and the politicians just tried to use the stockmen's issue as an excuse. The government wasn't taking care of its responsibilities; the government has a hard time taking care of its responsibilities now and it was worse then.

The stockmen did have some cattle killings. One time my grandad went out and found two of his cows with their throats slit and just their tongues cut out. When he told me the story, my grandad didn't know of any reason why the Indians did that, but I understand it now. In later days the Cheyennes told us that they used to do that because the white men had killed all the buffalo and just took their tongues. There was tension here then, and some settlers and some Cheyennes were shot, but there is a lot more to that than meets the eye. The Cheyennes were not being fed very well and there was a lot of crooked work in the Indian Service and the government. A lot of times they pointed at the settlers and said they were the ones who were causing the problems, but I really think a lot of it was the government. They were not taking care of their responsibilities to the Indians and so the Indians were going hungry. My grandmother had a story about one of her old Indian friends who was just so hungry for meat that she had to kill her cat and eat it. That's hunger. Black Wolf was the first Cheyenne to be shot, which happened during an incident at Alderson's ranch in the spring of 1884, and the level of tension more or less stayed the same until 1890. In that spring a rancher named Robert Ferguson was found dead, and near his body was a beef carcass. Three or four Cheyennes were arrested, but there was the suggestion that the murder was set up to look like the Cheyennes had done it so that there would be pressure to remove them. Then that September a member of our family, Hugh Boyle, was killed, and most all of the settlers then wanted the Cheyennes to move out.

Hugh Boyle had gone to get the milk cow in and he rode up on two Cheyenne boys who were butchering the cow. When he accosted them they shot and killed him, and then hauled him away up the canyon and hid him in the shale slide. I think Grandpa Bailey was one of those who went to look for him with my great-uncle, Hugh Lynch. They found his bloody cap or some such thing, and they found blood where they'd butchered the cow, but they couldn't find anything from there. I believe they then sent for the old scouts from Fort Keogh to come up and they were able to find the tracks and locate his body. In the meantime, the government had sent a case of rifles to the settlers, and the settlers all banded together at one homestead while the Cheyennes left the agency and hid in the hills. American Horse informed Agent Cooper that Head Chief and Young Mule had killed Hugh Boyle, and the government wanted the two Cheyenne boys to turn themselves in. Two Moons said that they couldn't do that because it was against the boys' religious principles, and he said that they would rather die fighting. An agreement was reached in that the two Cheyenne boys would ride against the soldiers at Lame Deer, which they did. On September 13, which was ration day at the agency, they ran down off the hill that today rises above Dull Knife College, and they rode back and forth in front of the soldiers and Indian police until they were shot down. When he was on his death bed old man Lynch forgave the Cheyenne boys that killed Hugh Boyle; he said that nobody should be starved into such a state of desperation. Not too long ago, Herman J. Viola, Philip Whiteman and myself were all sitting at the table drinking coffee, and Herman thought it was marvelous that a relative of Head Chief's and Young Mule's, and a relative of Hugh Boyle's, could sit together at the table and have coffee.

Overall there were tensions, and yet there were still good relationships between some of the settlers and some of the Cheyennes. My grandmother was seven years old when the family came over from Ireland and she played with the little Cheyenne kids and learned

Rock Creek, near present-day Buffalo, Wyoming, the vicinity of Nelson Story's skirmish with Lakotas in October 1866. Bozeman and Jacobs had been turned back by Cheyennes in the same area three years earlier.

Left to right: Jack Bailey, John Stands-in-Timber, and Father Peter Powell at the Deer Medicine Rocks

to speak fluent Cheyenne. Later she became an interpreter and taught the Indian kids at St. Labre; she taught the old type of Cheyenne which is not as abbreviated as it is now. Yellow Robe was one of her friends, as were a lot of the old scouts that worked for General Miles. Yellow Robe and his family took the Bailey name and his descendants are still known as Baileys. When I was a kid I remember the old scouts saying, "We're going to go to church on Sunday and we'll see everybody after church," and my grandmother would always go along and meet with them because it was a great honor to have them gather there for worship and socializing. I think our family got along with the Cheyennes because there was commonality that they could relate to: the problems the Cheyennes were having were probably not too different from the problems our family had experienced in Ireland – the denial of religious freedom and government oppression. I think it was natural for them to develop a good relationship, and the old Cheyennes would go back and forth from our family's place to the Tongue River. Something else that they had in common was hardship. Once when it was about twenty or thirty degrees below zero, a young Cheyenne couple knocked on the cabin door of my great-uncle, George Snider. They were all just sitting around talking when this young Cheyenne man asked if he could bring his wife inside to get warm. They said, "Sure, come in and use the kitchen." It was evident that the young man's wife was going to give birth in the next few hours, and so they got water and rags for them, and then never heard another thing. When they arose the next morning everything was all cleaned up and the Cheyenne couple had gone. The woman had given birth to her baby and then they had left in that bitter cold.

Grandpa Bailey told of once having a difficult time in temperatures like that. One of his uncles had asked him if he would go to Miles City with him to move a furnace from there to the lower Rosebud where they were going to build a school. That uncle only had an Indian pony and a thin mule, and at first it was all well and good, but when they loaded the furnace on the wagon and headed back to the Rosebud, the pony and the mule were so thin that they couldn't pull the wagon with the furnace in it up hill. They could pull it downhill, and so Grandpa Bailey and his uncle had to pull the furnace up every hill from Miles City to the Rosebud, and it took them three days . "You know, I told my uncle," he said, "if that's the way you go to town in Montana, I don't want to go very often!" But then there was the other side of going to Miles City; there was an organ-grinder in a bar there and grandpa said that when this organ-grinder's monkey died he just threw it in the garbage. Grandpa was with Two Moons and they were behind this bar when they saw the dead monkey. Two Moons had a stick and he turned the monkey over this way, then he turned him over that way, and he was studying him. Grandpa asked Two Moons, "What do you think that is, Two Moons?" And Two Moons said, "I don't know. A long time ago maybe a Chinaman and a cat got together!" It wasn't an easy life and so they needed a sense of humor.[2] At sixteen my grandfather was too young to be a regular hand for a cow outfit, but Frank Robertson let him be the horse wrangler in the Old Diamond outfit that ran cattle from the Bighorn Mountains to the Yellowstone River and the Bighorn River. Grandad would tell about trailing cattle down to the railroad, and how they sat out on the flats holding these large herds of cattle until the trains came. They didn't sleep, they sat up all night by the fire and changed guards every two hours. In those days people were out with the cattle all day and all night.

The Cheyenne people have always been a part of my life. I have a son that is a member of the Kit Fox Military Society, and all of our children have Cheyenne names. My brothers and sisters and myself were all given Cheyenne names too. When I was a small boy George American Horse decided to make me an authentic Cheyenne bow and arrow, and I just couldn't wait for him to get that made. He showed me just how to make this bow, how he had to bake it for four days, how to put the feathers on the arrows, and how to make the sinew string and put it on. That's still a very fond memory of mine. The Hiwalkers are another family we have known for years. John Stands-in-Timber was Belle Hiwalker's brother, and John and I became good friends when, as a Cheyenne tribal historian, John used to come to the Deer Medicine Rocks. I also came into being friends with Many Bad Horses because he was married to a Hiwalker. Back in 1952, when the Crow Tribe decided to give St. Labre three buffaloes for meat because the mission had a lot of orphans and kids in boarding school who needed feeding, Father Christopher asked if we would like to go and get those buffalo on top of the Bighorn Mountains. We managed to get the buffalo and I gave the hide to Hiwalker, and he made a nice travois and put this buffalo hide cover on it. He sold it to the Cheyenne Tribe, and at about that time, the movie of Mari Sandoz's book *Cheyenne Autumn* came out, and they sent the travois to Europe with Carol Baker to promote the movie and it never did come back! Then, still in the 1950s, my buffalo skull was used by the Cheyennes in some ceremonies at Bear Butte that they hadn't done for years, and since that time it has been used twice in the Sun Dance.

In those days the Cheyennes wanted the Deer Medicine Rocks to be a place you went to if you needed help; you didn't just casually visit the rocks to show your friends the petroglyphs. It's only in the last few years that the older people have found it acceptable for visitors to see the rocks without a spiritual reason. The older people decided that showing outside people the rocks would communicate a positive side of their tradition, and so they have allowed it, but before that we didn't really let people come in. I feel that we have a responsibility to the older people. I think they should be given respect, in the same way that we try to respect the rocks and try to keep the rocks from being damaged in any way. I think the Deer Medicine Rocks should be kept in a natural state, without any cement sidewalks or visitors' center. There are a lot of old cultural things that outside people don't understand. One of them is that the Cheyennes are traditionally a very socialistic people; they did everything for the good of the band rather than for themselves. Traditionally, to be a big man among the people, you had to kill a lot of buffalo and give them all away – it wasn't about how many buffalo you could kill and keep for yourself. In the same way, if you stole a lot of horses you gave a lot of them away. In today's society, Cheyennes will still tear down a person who tries to accumulate too much because they think that person is stingy, and people from the outside don't understand that.

I don't think most outside people could really believe the poverty that there is on the Northern Cheyenne Reservation today. There is a lot of despair: suicide rates are really high; unemployment is really high; drugs and alcohol are big problems; and diabetes is one of the worst health problems. I don't know if the federal government has any idea or not. Despite that, I think that some of the young people are doing fine and that there are some great young people. I'm beginning to see some kids that I think are going to go somewhere, and I hope I'm right. Today I think the stockmen and the Cheyennes get along pretty good. Wherever you go, wherever you have different groups of people, beliefs and customs, there will be some disagreements, but in general I think we get along. The Cheyenne people and the stockmen want to protect our land and the water from mining processes and other activities that could ruin both. People should pay attention to our history. At the time of the Bozeman Trail some were after gold at any price, and today it's coal, gas and oil. We should learn from the things in the past, and if we don't there's something wrong with us.

Marker on the Little Bighorn Battlefield where Stands-in-Timber's grandfather, the great Elk Horn Scraper warrior Lame White Man, was killed in action on June 25, 1876

1. Nelson Story trailed approximately one thousand head of longhorns from Fort Worth, Texas, up to the Bozeman Trail. Kansas cattlemen objected to him running Texas stock through that territory, and so he was forced to detour via Fort Leavenworth.

2. Two Moons made this comment in the context of the times. Even though his point of reference for Chinese people was ostensibly negative – associating them with constructing the railroads that decimated the buffalo – it is still unlikely that he intended this comment to be a racial slur.

RICHARD TALL BULL JR.

"After Sand Creek, Tall Bull understood that to keep that oath they had to shut down the overland trails and stop the railroads, and so he led the Dog Soldiers north to the Powder River country, striking Julesburg, the South Platte River Road, and the Oregon Trail, on the way to the Bozeman Trail."

RICHARD TALL BULL JR. IS DESCENDED FROM THE GREAT DOG SOLDIER CHIEF TALL BULL AND THE NORTHERN CHEYENNE CHIEF, OLD CROW. RICHARD IS A CHEYENNE CULTURAL INTERPRETER AND EDUCATOR

On my father's side we are descended from Tall Bull, the Dog Soldier chief, and on my mother's side from Old Crow, one of the chiefs who went to Washington, D.C., in 1873 with the Northern Cheyenne delegation. I am Southern Cheyenne from Oklahoma, but I have lived on the Northern Cheyenne Reservation since the late 1960s. When we moved north it was like walking into the midst of all the history that happened here, and that's when I began talking to the old people about the Cheyennes, our history, and culture. That is how I learned, but those old people I talked to are gone now. One of the things that I asked them about was the four original military societies that Sweet Medicine brought to the Cheyennes: the Kit Foxes, Elk Horn Scrapers, Buffalo Bulls[1] and the Dog Soldiers. When Sweet Medicine first brought these societies the Chiefs' Council had not yet been organized, and so the Cheyennes looked to the Dog Soldiers for leadership, and even after the Chiefs' Council was in place, if the chiefs couldn't decide upon a particular issue they would send it to the Dog Soldiers and let them make the decision. Of all the Cheyenne societies the Dog Soldiers are probably the most widely known, in part because of the aura that surrounds them and the reputation that proceeded them into the history books. Tall Bull is a good example of that; he got blamed for a lot of stuff, but my dad said that Tall Bull wasn't responsible for much of what they accused him of, but the white people knew he was a Dog Soldier head chief and that brought a certain notoriety.

Long Chin was the recognized leader of the Dog Soldiers before Tall Bull. Long Chin and Tall Bull were half-brothers, Long Chin being about fifty-three years old in 1854 when the Dog Soldiers absorbed Buffalo Chief's band, the Flexed Legs People, and took their place in the Council of Forty-four. This is when the Dog Soldiers became a distinct band among the Cheyennes, in addition to being a military society. At this time, Tall Bull and White Horse were the same age, twenty-six years old, and although they were very young to sit on the council, they were entitled to do so because they were the third and fourth headsmen of the Dog Soldiers, and so they took the two seats next to the band's head chiefs, Long Chin and Buffalo Chief. Ten years later, when the Cheyennes were massacred on Sand Creek in the south, and the Bozeman Trail opened in the north, Tall Bull and White Horse were the Dog Soldiers' head chiefs and Bull Bear and Little Robe were the headsmen. The Dog Soldiers were the Cheyennes' equivalent of the Marines. Today the armed forces take an oath to protect the United States, and the Dog Soldiers were the same way: they had taken an oath to protect their people and it was their duty to be the first to go into battle. To uphold that oath they had to try and stop the white people from taking the Cheyennes' land, for with the immigrants came diseases, then hunger because they destroyed our food sources, and then war because the army followed when the Dog Soldiers and the other military societies tried to stop the whites crowding the Cheyennes out. After Sand Creek, Tall Bull understood that to keep that oath they had to shut down the overland trails and stop the railroads, and so he led the Dog Soldiers north to the Powder River country, striking Julesburg, the South Platte River Road, and the Oregon Trail, on the way to the Bozeman Trail.

Tall Bull's approach was to meet the threat wherever it was, and the Dog Soldiers got a reputation for themselves, and whether it was good or bad they did it. In 1865 the trails along the Platte and Powder Rivers were the biggest threat and so they went there. Traditionally that was Cheyenne country; the Northern Cheyennes laid claim to all of that land the 1851 Fort Laramie Treaty defined as 'unceded Indian Territory.' No white person was supposed to go across there, but that's where they brought the Bozeman Trail through and the Cheyennes knew that signalled devastation, more disease and the slaughter of the buffalo in the Powder River country. The 1851 treaty reserved the land between the Platte and Arkansas Rivers as Cheyenne and Arapaho territory. Before that treaty, the Cheyennes once came upon a small group of Indians between those two rivers. These Indians were sickly, they were diseased, and the main tribe had left them. The Cheyennes nursed them back to health and told them, "You can go back to your tribe now," but they didn't want to go. "No, our tribe has abandoned us and so we're going to stay with you," and that's how the Southern Arapahos joined the Cheyennes. The Dog Soldiers roamed around between those two rivers, in Colorado, Nebraska and Kansas, as well as south-central Wyoming and clear into Texas. The heartland of the Dog Soldiers was the Smoky Hill country and the buffalo ranges around the Republican River, but at the time of Sand Creek and the Bozeman Trail they didn't perceive themselves to be separate from the Northern Cheyennes, as they had that oath to uphold, and they had ties in that north country. After Sand Creek, Tangle Hair replaced Little Robe as one of the Dog Soldiers' headsmen. Little Robe's father, a chief of the Scabby Band, was slaughtered at Sand Creek, after which Little Robe took his place on the Council of Forty-four and became a peace advocate. Tangle Hair became one of the most prominent men among the Northern Cheyenne.

The allied campaign of the Lakotas, Cheyennes and Arapahos in 1865 gives an insight into the other bands that generally united with the Dog Soldiers. Among the Cheyennes, the So'taaeo'o camp led by Black Shin ran with them. Black Shin's son-in-law was Gray Beard, and Gray Beard was Roman Nose's best friend, which is why Roman Nose

Tall Bull's own ledger art depiction of Wolf-with-Plenty-of-Hair relieving him during battle with the Wolf Men, the Pawnees. Having staked himself to the earth in the face of the enemy, a Dog Soldier could not retreat from that vow, and only a fellow Dog Soldier could free him.

was also associated with the Dog Soldiers, so much so that the whites regularly mistook him for a Dog Soldier chief. The Oglala Sioux of Whistler and Pawnee Killer hung with the Dog Soldiers, and it was during this period that the Sioux, particularly the Oglalas, and the Dog Soldiers started to get mixed up through intermarriages. A lot of Northern Cheyennes were already mixed up with the Sioux because after the 1851 treaty they decided to stay in their own country, in that 'unceded Indian Territory,' parts of which they shared with the Sioux, and vice versa. The boundaries of Sioux country under that treaty went from the Missouri to the Platte and north to the Bighorn River, in the center of which is the Black Hills and Bear Butte, and so the Northern Cheyennes and the Sioux cohabited there. When the Cheyennes came together after Sand Creek and went north to resist the Bozeman Trail, little cultural differences had started to appear due to the Northerners' interaction with the Sioux, and the Southerners' exposure to the whites between the Platte and the Arkansas.

Over the next decade or so, those differences became more pronounced; the Cheyenne dialect in the north changed a little because they had to accommodate three other languages in camp, the main one being So'taa'e, but also Northern Arapaho and Sioux. The Cheyennes between the Platte and Arkansas Rivers, the Heévaha-taneo'o – the Rope Men or Southern Cheyennes – didn't have as much exposure to the So'taa'e dialect or Sioux, and so

I think that is why the language sounds different in the north and south. In fact, they make fun of me when I talk Cheyenne up here! Then their appearances altered; the Southern Cheyennes were around white people more and so they had access to more trade goods, cloth and white man's clothes, whereas the Northern Cheyennes were around the Sioux and so they adopted some of their styles of dress, and so when they traveled south to visit they still wore buckskin clothes, and some of the Southern Cheyennes thought they looked wild! That Sioux influence is prevalent; a long time ago the Sioux told the white men we were the Sahíyelas or Shyennas, which is why they called us Cheyenne. And then look at Chief Morning Star; most people call him Dull Knife, which was his Sioux name. His brother-in-law was an Oglala, a relative of Red Cloud's, and he called him Dull Knife because once, when they went hunting, his knife was so dull he couldn't cut open a deer, and so Dull Knife became his nickname.

Tall Bull worked with Dull Knife and Red Cloud in the Powder River country when they confronted Sawyers and some of Connor's men in 1865. The chiefs had chosen the Dog Soldiers to 'soldier' that camp on the Little Powder, and Bull Bear was selected as crier, and so when they went against Sawyers' party, Bull Bear went with Red Cloud and Dull Knife to parlay with Sawyers. Tall Bull's role in that engagement was purely operational: he had the responsibility of signalling the attack and he was there as the field commander, not a negotiator – he did his job and then Bull Bear and the others went down to talk. Red Cloud was accepted as the leader that day because he initiated the action. Red Cloud wanted to do that and so he announced it. "Okay, we'll back you," was the response from Tall Bull and the others, and that's how the people were back then, they didn't bicker about who was in charge because everybody had a role to play. You can compare that with our Sun Dance today; whichever society the Pledger belongs to are the people that are in charge of that Sun Dance. The other societies hang back, but if they are asked to help by the Pledger's society brothers they will help knowing that they're not in charge. A lot of things that you read in books about that time are inaccurate, but the facts are preserved in our oral history. You hear a lot about the Dog Soldiers, but all of the other societies were in there too, each given specific responsibilities ranging from combat, to social and logistic organization, to protecting the camp while others went to fight the soldiers. A book will probably say that this was Red Cloud's camp, or Dull Knife's camp, or Little Wolf's, or Tall Bull's, or whichever famous chief that author knows – but there were many other chiefs there. It was common for them to designate a particular leader to be their spokesman, and so he is the one that gets his name in the history books. It wasn't any one man's camp; there was a united Cheyenne camp, a Northern Arapaho camp and a Sioux camp.

Tall Bull's self-portrait

Tall Bull and the Dog Soldiers went back south in the fall of 1865 after the Cheyennes had headed east from the Powder River towards Bear Butte. The Cheyennes call Bear Butte 'Noaha-vose,' and they've tried to translate that into English but there's no real translation for that. Sweet Medicine was taken to Bear Butte by the spirits and guided to a cave on the north side of the mountain. That cave is blocked off now, but Sweet Medicine went into that cave and came out with the Sacred Arrows. When the Dog Soldiers reached Turkey Creek – Solomon's Fork – they stayed there in the heart of their territory. The Dog Soldiers didn't go back north in 1866 to fight Fetterman because they had to confront other threats south of the Platte, like the survey crews and construction of the Kansas Pacific. Tall Bull tried to stop those trains, and this is when the white people really started to take notice of him; they read reports of what he said at treaty conferences and they considered him to be defiant, but if you look at the documents of the Treaty of the Little Arkansas you will see his signature, dated April 4, 1866. That was a statement of intent; Tall Bull wanted peace but then the government attempted to amend the treaty and take the Dog Soldiers' homelands without their consent. It wasn't the Dog Soldiers who broke that treaty, it was the U.S. government and military, Generals Hancock and Custer. Even after Hancock's campaign against the Dog Soldiers in 1867, Tall Bull

HERE LIE THE REMAINS
OF TWO MOONS
CHIEF OF THE
CHEYENNE INDIANS WHO
LED HIS MEN AGAINST
GENERAL CUSTER
IN THE BATTLE OF
LITTLE BIG HORN
JUNE 25, 1876.
ERECTED BY
W. P. MONCURE
INDIAN TRADER

Chief Two Moons' resting place in Busby on the Northern Cheyenne Nation

Summit Springs Battlefield

still sought peace and participated in the Medicine Lodge Treaty Council where he reiterated his position, that the Dog Soldiers wanted to be left alone, they wanted peace, and they wanted to roam around their country as their ancestors did.

Whichever way the government interpreted it, Tall Bull never agreed to give up the buffalo ranges around the Republican River or to relinquish the Smoky Hill country, but soon his people were being pushed out by the settlers, their trails and the railroads. This is when they started to camp away from the main tribe of Southern Cheyennes because they had not agreed to confinement on a reservation or to give up their lands in Kansas. In this period, many of the so-called Dog Soldiers' raids started out as peaceful requests for food. They didn't usually just attack a farmhouse or ranch, they went to ask for food because the game in their country had been depleted by the settlers and hide hunters, and by the buffalo hunters like Buffalo Bill Cody, who were employed by the railroads to supply buffalo meat to the construction crews. When the white people saw the Dog Soldiers approaching their houses they often shot at them, and if they killed or wounded a Dog Soldier their homes would then be raided in retaliation. That's how a lot of the trouble started, and very often incidents like this didn't involve men like Tall Bull or White Horse – it would be young guys who wanted to make a name for themselves and gain recognition as warriors. Tall Bull mainly focused on the big battles.

Tall Bull's sacred shield imbued with the power of the sun, the crescent moon, the Four Sacred Persons, and the buffalo bull from which he was given his name.

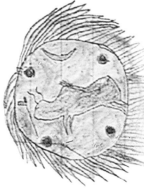

I'm not too much into the battles because of the controversy you can get into. Take the Fetterman Fight; you might talk to somebody that was told what happened by a warrior who fought on the north end, but then, when you're talking to somebody else, they might say that your version isn't true because they heard something different, most likely from a warrior who fought on the south end! The old people I talked to rarely spoke about the battles. I think it was pretty hurtful for them to talk about those wars like that. I heard two stories about that fight; one involved the Sioux half-man, half-woman called His Crazy Mule, who could predict the future. This man was blind but he was the one they sent out for guidance and who brought them the hundred soldiers in his hands. Some people have said that he was a Cheyenne but he wasn't, he was definitely a Sioux, and the confusion has arisen because the Northern Cheyennes had a famous medicine man who was also called Crazy Mule and who was also involved in ceremonies leading up to this Fetterman Fight. The other thing I heard was about Two Moons; that on the morning of the fight he went into

Fort Phil Kearny to scout it out, to see if it could be taken without losing too many lives. And so Two Moons went in there and asked for help; I think he told them that he needed shells to go hunting. Some people say that it was the white people who built Two Moons up after the Northern Cheyennes were placed on the Tongue River Reservation. Writers and historians back then gave him a lot of attention because he fought in the Battle of the Little Bighorn, and it was during those reservation days that he became recognized as a chief. At the time of the Bozeman Trail he was a pretty regular guy, but I think he made his name and became a little chief of the Kit Foxes after he went into the fort that morning. In talking to these old Cheyennes, I never heard anybody say, "Well, I went over there and stuck seven arrows into this soldier or that soldier"; they never talked to me about anything like that.

Little Wolf had far more influence than Two Moons; he was the headman of the Elk Horn Scrapers and the Sweet Medicine Chief over all of the Cheyennes. I was told that Little Wolf burned down Fort Phil Kearny because he was mad at the government because he had been deceived by the treaty commissioners during the 1868 Fort Laramie Treaty negotiations, and he only found out that they had misled him after he had signed the treaty. Little Wolf was told that the Northern Cheyennes would keep their traditional country in the north and that the soldiers would leave the three forts on the Bozeman Trail and that Fort Phil Kearny would become their agency. When he signed the treaty nobody told him that it didn't say that, it said that by signing he was agreeing to be bound by the terms of the Medicine Lodge Treaty, a treaty that had little to do with him or the Northerners, but everything to do with Tall Bull and the Southerners. About eight months after Little Wolf burned Fort Phil Kearny, Tall Bull was killed at the White Butte, what the white people call 'Summit Springs.' White Horse and Tangle Hair then became the head chiefs of the Dog Soldiers and both went north, to the Northerners and the Sioux, but White Horse came south again within a year or so. Tangle Hair stayed with the Northern Cheyenne and he was one of the headmen who made the journey back home from Indian Territory with Little Wolf and Dull Knife. I agree that the Bozeman Trail was the primary invasion route; it was like the first domino that fell. Then came the Battle of the Little Bighorn, and then the Northern Cheyennes were sent to Indian Territory and Little Wolf and Dull Knife had to risk everything to lead them back. The dominoes continued to fall, which is why the people are in this situation here today.

1. Also known as the Red Shields.

Chief Crazy Head in later years

ROBERT C. WILSON

"If the Native Americans had had as many soldiers as the whites this would not be the western United States now. The only reason the U.S. military prevailed is because they had more men and more guns."

BOB WILSON IS THE CURATOR, INTERPRETER, AND ASSISTANT SUPERINTENDENT AT FORT PHIL KEARNY STATE HISTORIC SITE, AND THE PROJECT MANAGER AT FORT FETTERMAN. BOB CREATED THE INTERPRETIVE DISPLAYS AT BOTH FORTS, AND AT THE FETTERMAN AND CRAZY WOMAN SITES.

A lot of people want history to be black and white, and the answers to their questions to be yes or no. There are very few yes or no answers because history is a compilation of human stories, and human beings are far more complex than that. The Bozeman Trail is one of those human stories, and it is not black and white, it is filled with diverse personalities whose actions and personal stories were bound together by time and circumstance to create the whole. In a sense the physical route known as the Bozeman Trail embodies that; people often ask, "Where's the Bozeman Trail?" with the expectation that it's like a modern highway that goes from A to B over a prescribed course; but the Bozeman Trail is not like that; it's a combination of several different routes that changed several times, and within those changes there were a lot of detours brought about by practical necessity. Historically that was part of the problem with the overland trails. When the Native Americans were considering giving their approval for the Bozeman Trail they envisaged it to be a single road, but then came the realization that a fifty- or a hundred-mile swath through the area would be the upshot, not one trail. The same thing had happened with the Oregon Trail; the Native Americans stepped forward and said, "Yes, you can have a trail through our lands," but they were not expecting the wide tract on either side of the trail to be damaged, which adversely affected the wildlife, vegetation and everything else.

People chose the Bozeman Trail over the Bridger Trail because the Bozeman Trail had better grass, better water and better wood, and was a slightly quicker route to Virginia City. I don't imagine that John Bozeman and John Jacobs thought about the Indian perspective at all, as long as the emigrants went to Virginia City little else mattered to them. The American emigrants who were taking the Bozeman Trail to Montana felt that America was theirs from coast to coast and that the indigenous people were just in the way; they were going to Virginia City and if the Indians got in the way they would just push them out of the way. The American emigrants traveling the Bozeman Trail to Montana believed in "Manifest Destiny," that it was their right to conquer and civilize the North American continent and its inhabitants. If one uses the boundaries established by the Fort Laramie Treaty of 1851, the Bozeman Trail was located only in those lands of the Crow, a nation which remained allied with the U.S. government during the entire length of the Plains Indian Wars. That said, the Lakota and Northern Cheyenne occupied these lands, opposing the trail and the damage it would bring. They stopped and turned back the very first train brought up the trail by John Bozeman, and harassed many others. The emigrants knew that there would be a chance of hostilities if they used the trail. They chose to ignore the threat, and instead to petition congress and the military for soldiers to protect and support their travels. However, facts like the end of the Civil War, cuts in the defense budget, and this war being fought on the Indians' home turf did not help the military. The decline in emigrant traffic, and the coalition of opposing tribes, contributed to the eventual closure of the trail. The Bozeman Trail went through the last, best hunting grounds of the Plains Indians, and it is unlikely that any amount of negotiating or treaty making would have convinced the Native Americans that they would be compensated for the damages they knew would result. They knew what to expect from their experiences with the Oregon Trail, and so the Lakota and Cheyenne would never have let the new trail in. Probably the only reason the Crow allowed it was to get help from the soldiers to force the other tribes out.

General Patrick E. Connor would be categorized by some as a proponent of extermination. There are always two sides to the story and there are always two extremes, and Connor was one of the extremes. Connor was not representative of all of the white policy makers at the time, and not every military officer favored exterminating the Indians as a final solution, he was just one extreme element. There were some officers that were good, some who were bad and some who found themselves in situations

Contact: One of Bob Wilson's original pieces of art depicting the clash of cultures on the Bozeman Trail

beyond their control. Connor marched into the Powder River Basin to prosecute a punishment expedition against the Lakota and Cheyenne in response to the tribes' post–Sand Creek raids along the North and South Platte Rivers, during which they sacked Julesburg and fought the Battle of Platte Bridge. Connor's command was two thousand strong, and included two columns under Colonel Nelson Cole and Lieutenant Colonel Samuel Walker. Connor sent Cole and Walker to apprehend the hostiles via the Missouri River and the Black Hills, while he concentrated on the Powder and Tongue Rivers, but none of them were prepared for what they would encounter. Some historians believe that the three columns were meant to converge at a preordained time and location, but from what I understand that was never their intention as they all felt that their respective columns were strong enough to take care of whoever they might encounter.

Connor directed his men to attack and kill every male Indian over twelve years old and to reject any peace overtures. Connor didn't care what Indians he ran into; he was on duty up here to punish some Indians and he didn't care whether they were Crow, Cheyenne, Arapaho, Shoshone or Lakota – an Indian was an Indian as far as he was concerned. As it was, he attacked Black Bear's Arapaho village on the Tongue River on August 29, 1865. Smoke from the village was spotted from roughly where the Fetterman monument now stands, and so Connor moved his command down Prairie Dog Creek and rode through the night to hit the village at dawn. Jim Bridger was Connor's guide and I don't know what his thoughts were about the attack, but it is possibile that Bridger knew it wasn't a hostile village and that he told Connor. Bridger didn't have any influence over Fetterman and Brown fifteen months later so we shouldn't presume that he had very much influence over Connor; he was under the command of an officer who had the authority to shoot him on the spot if he didn't do what he told him to. If the officer said, "Show me where that village is," the guide did it. How many times during the Plains Indian Wars did an officer send somebody ahead to an Indian village to ask, "Are you friendly or hostile?" Chivington knew that Sand Creek wasn't a hostile village, but that didn't mean anything. Men like Chivington and Connor were among the extremist element who believed that any Indians were fair game, that they were wildlife to be exterminated, and it's not a pretty picture of America's past. At the same time, it behooves us to remember that not everybody in the military thought that way. People are people, good and bad, whatever race they are.

According to the historians' criteria, for something to be accepted as fact it has to come from three different sources. However, as an interpreter I take into account the reality of the situation: if somebody is attacking my home, my village, I am going to fight until all hope is lost. Based upon that and the written record, there is no reason to disbelieve what Captain Palmer reported about the troops shooting indiscriminately and killing women and children, and that the Arapaho women fought alongside the warriors and engaged the soldiers in hand-to-hand combat. I'm sure it's possible that Arapaho history corroborates that. I agree with the theory that the Arapahos regrouped and were forcing Connor to retreat from the field until his artillery halted their counterattack. Actually, if the Arapahos hadn't regrouped quite as fast as they did, I think they would have had Connor. If the Arapahos had retreated a little bit further, Connor's men would have become even more stretched out and that might have presented the Arapahos with the opportunity to use the decoy tactic as an offensive option. Because they responded so quickly, Connor was able to retreat back towards the village as they regrouped and started pushing him back. My understanding is that after the fight the Arapahos followed the column and took most of their horses back that Connor's Pawnee scouts had cut from the village pony herd. After Connor moved out of the vicinity, Colonel James Sawyers' wagon road expedition soon moved in, and the Arapahos attacked them, and a protracted engagement unfolded through the valley between present-day Ranchester and Dayton.

The area designated as the Connor Battlefield in Ranchester, Wyoming, is probably not the actual battlefield. No archeological evidence exists that identifies that as the site of the Arapaho village and battlefield, and when the playground and recreational facilities were constructed there, they never came across anything. Connor burned that village, made a pyre out of the Arapahos goods and food stores, and killed horses, but there's no evidence of that at the site. There is some thought that the battlefield was further downstream and, with that in mind, the playground and campsite being there doesn't bother me, but if it was firmly identified as being the battlefield then I would agree with those who consider it to be insensitive. Many of the western Indian battlefields need better interpretation, more-sensitive interpretation, and a more balanced perspective on both sides. At the Fetterman site, at Crazy Woman Creek, and at some of the other battlefields managed by Wyoming State Parks we are trying to make that effort, but securing the Native American perspective can be very difficult.

Connor's expedition basically didn't accomplish any of his goals. For something like $40,000,000 you would have expected a better return from Connor than creating more enemies than he defeated, which is all he achieved by attacking the Arapahos. Both Cole's and Walker's columns struggled throughout the campaign; they were harassed by Sitting Bull's Lakotas before they returned to the Powder River and were harassed by Red Cloud's Lakotas and some Cheyennes when they arrived. They simply were not prepared for the West. They lost over two hundred horses and mules, losing eighty horses on a picket line in one night; nowadays that is just astounding to most of us, as is the fact that they had to feed their horses twelve gallons of grain a day, but one should remember that these were unprocessed grains and the horses were heavily worked. That would kill an American horse today. It was a very expensive failure and it was pretty egotistical of Connor to name the fort he left after himself. In American military etiquette you don't name a fort after a living officer, you name it after a deceased officer, and so they renamed it Fort Reno after Jesse Reno. It became very expensive to run the forts on the Bozeman Trail, and the high expense of keeping the trail open to the military at the same time as the post–Civil War army was being cut back may have contributed to the decision to abandon the forts so quickly.

I don't believe that there was factionalism between the Galvanized Yankees and the Union volunteer troops who were on Connor's expedition. To put it bluntly, a Confederate and a Union soldier in that situation probably looked at it as two white guys fighting a red guy. They weren't fighting the Civil War out here, they were fighting to save each others' lives. Connor left Companies C and D of the Fifth U.S. Volunteers to man the new post, and these Galvanized Yankees were fairly competent men until the Civil War ended and some problems with discipline arose; desertion was high and they developed a bad attitude about being kept in the Powder River country. That was true not only of the Galvanized Yankees, but also of the Illinois Volunteers and the regular Union troops who had volunteered for the Civil War but ended up on the western frontier – when the Civil War ended they all wanted out. We do have an account of a Galvanized Yankee who had been captured at Stone Mountain, and when he was sent out here he was put in charge of the artillery. When Carrington arrived this man turned the guns over to him, and Carrington then probably utilized his expertise before he was released with the other troops. I think Carrington definitely took note of the condition of the men he found at Fort Reno and what they had been through, but there just wasn't that much he could do about it. He was given orders to occupy the post and then to move north and build other posts, so he left Company B at Fort Reno and appointed Captain Joshua Proctor post commander. Carrington took all the horses at Fort Reno to mount the infantry, and I think he did a pretty good job of managing the resources available to him in a manner that was consistent with his orders.

Before he left Fort Reno, Colonel Carrington issued new regulations for emigrant traffic on the Bozeman Trail. The trains that suffered casualties were generally the ones that were traveling under a slack wagon master. Carrington's analysis was that a tight, well-captained wagon train with roughly fifty armed men should easily have been able to make it through on the Bozeman Trail, no matter what the force of Native Americans was that confronted them. Carrington was adamant that the trains should be tight, that stragglers shouldn't be tolerated, and that travelers shouldn't be allowed to wander off by themselves, but he was dealing with a bunch of independent Americans who often didn't want to be told what to do. The stretch between Brown Springs and Fort Reno was one of the most perilous after Carrington arrived to build the forts. On July 22, 23 and 24, 1866, the Cheney, Horner and Dearborn trains were all attacked, probably by the same party of Lakotas that had forced Lieutenant George Templeton's detachment to corral on Crazy Woman Creek on July 20. Templeton was in command of a military train heading from Fort Laramie to what would become Fort Phil Kearny, before continuing on to what was to be Fort C.F. Smith. For the military and the emigrants the section between Fort Reno and Crazy Woman Creek was

General Patrick E. Connor

191

the worst one-day stretch on the Bozeman Trail for lack of water. It's almost twenty or thirty miles, and so when they came into Crazy Woman they had to camp there for water, and that's partially why it was a good ambush point. The Indians knew that the soldiers had to camp there, and there are only certain draws down to the creek where you can cross, and the soldiers had to follow those paths.

Once again, the fight on Crazy Woman Creek goes back to the fact that they were not doing what Carrington instructed all of the trains to do, to stay tight up. In the military, be it an infantry column marching or a wagon train, there is always a tendency to bow out and then chain, and then bow out and then chain, but what you want to do is to keep it tight and the same length all the time. Here, Templeton and Lieutenant Daniels were way out in front when the train came to Crazy Woman Creek that morning. They rode down that big, long draw that leads into the creek, and then they dropped down into that real soft, sandy spot that's like an old creek bottom – and that's where the Indians attacked them. Daniels was killed while chasing buffalo on the creek bottom in advance of the train. The train was strung out in that bottom and so they retreated partway back way up the hill. As soon as they could, they moved to a higher, better position and formed the wagons into a square and closed in. That was a normal nighttime corralling technique, to interlock the tongue into the next wagon and to use it as both a corral and a defensive position. A train coming south from Fort Phil Kearny under Captain Burrowes happened upon them, and they were able to hold their position. Burrowes was for turning the train back to Fort Reno, but by that time Chaplain White and a private named Wallace, who had snuck out of the train to get help from Fort Reno, were on their way back with reinforcements.

The military wanted to form squares when wagons were corralled. At the Crazy Woman Fight the Indians did not ride around and around the wagons, they made a couple of charges at the corral and that was it. The idea that Indians circled corralled wagons is one of the fallacies of the John Wayne movies. There were probably only about two thousand warriors among the tribes on the Plains and so they were not in a position to take a lot of casualties, and therefore they tried to minimize casualties by attempting to draw the military into fighting them under conditions that best suited the style of combat they were skilled in. There was a limited number of warriors and there were only certain leaders that were respected and followed, and so I'm sure that up and down the Bozeman Trail, and

right through until 1876, the military was running into those same warriors and leaders. The Indians fought and won in situations that conformed to their strengths, and they lost in situations that didn't. When the Fetterman Fight and the Wagon Box Fight are compared to the Last Stand and Reno's entrenchment during the Battle of the Little Bighorn, the Little Bighorn fights are virtually replicas of the two from Red Cloud's War. The Fetterman Fight is a running battle – it's almost a buffalo hunt like the one that ended on Last Stand Hill. That was the type of battle that best suited Plains Indian warfare, whereas engaging troops who were in an entrenched position did not. When the soldiers were dug in they could stand and fight a European-style battle and at least hold their own, and that's what happened at the Wagon Box Fight and on Reno and Benteen Hill. At Fort Phil Kearny, I think the Indians realized after the skirmish on December 6, 1866, that if they could get the soldiers away from the fort and over the ridge they could defeat them. On the other hand, the soldiers were safe in the fort – that was their firebase – but just as in Vietnam, if they left that firebase and the enemy was in the area of operation, there were problems.

During Red Cloud's War, particularly after the Fetterman disaster, some attributed the defeat to the Indians' superior firearms. Based upon archeological evidence, we can identify a minimum of thirty-eight firearms used by the Indians in the Fetterman Fight, but I would expect there were more. Mostly they were pistols and smooth-bore

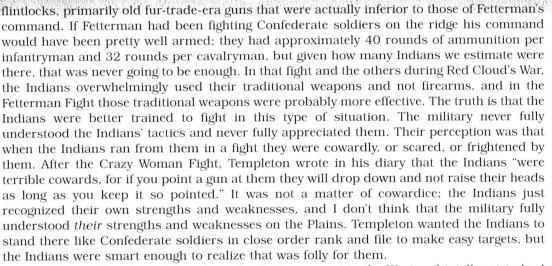

KILLED ON THIS SPOT JULY 20ᵀᴴ 1866, BY SIOUX INDIANS

flintlocks, primarily old fur-trade-era guns that were actually inferior to those of Fetterman's command. If Fetterman had been fighting Confederate soldiers on the ridge his command would have been pretty well armed; they had approximately 40 rounds of ammunition per infantryman and 32 rounds per cavalryman, but given how many Indians we estimate were there, that was never going to be enough. In that fight and the others during Red Cloud's War, the Indians overwhelmingly used their traditional weapons and not firearms, and in the Fetterman Fight those traditional weapons were probably more effective. The truth is that the Indians were better trained to fight in this type of situation. The military never fully understood the Indians' tactics and never fully appreciated them. Their perception was that when the Indians ran from them in a fight they were cowardly, or scared, or frightened by them. After the Crazy Woman Fight, Templeton wrote in his diary that the Indians "were terrible cowards, for if you point a gun at them they will drop down and not raise their heads as long as you keep it so pointed." It was not a matter of cowardice; the Indians just recognized their own strengths and weaknesses, and I don't think that the military fully understood *their* strengths and weaknesses on the Plains. Templeton wanted the Indians to stand there like Confederate soldiers in close order rank and file to make easy targets, but the Indians were smart enough to realize that was folly for them.

Time and again, soldiers from the East came out to the West and totally misjudged the situation. They were in a completely different environment that they did not understand, and I don't think that they really caught onto it until after the Indian Wars. If the Native Americans had had as many soldiers as the whites this would not be the western United States now. The only reason the U.S. military prevailed is because they had more men and more guns. If a student studying world history wanted to know the difference between the history of the U.S. Army during the period of Manifest Destiny and that of other conquering armies, I would say that it is in the way we initially recorded U.S. history, and the way we are now revisiting it. In the histories of all great civilizations, when wars are fought and a people defeated and nearly annihilated, it has usually been done and recorded as being done for some just or greater cause. This was so in our initial historical record of the conquering of the West. It is now being revisited and it is not always a pleasant trip, but by revisiting our mistakes we will become a greater culture, and can now hopefully learn more from those cultures we so nearly destroyed. It won't be any different when the next populous and technologically superior culture marches across this country in a thousand years; it is human nature to take from somebody else and to try and justify it in some way. For now, I don't see the United States government giving the Black Hills back to the Lakota, Cheyenne, Crow or whoever else claims to have been there first, I think the ownership will stay exactly as it is. I don't see a solution, but at some point I contend that another culture will come and push out the people who occupy this land now. That's man. Taking from each other is the curse of the human race; it's never going to stop. There is no beginning and there is no end.

Inscription from the marker remembering the fight at Crazy Woman Creek

POSTSCRIPT

by Harold Salway & Herb Pavey

On April 10, 1868, a handful of U.S. President Andrew Johnson's most illustrious officers stood waiting at Fort Laramie. For company the Indian-fighters had an equal number of their ideological antagonists, the nation's principal peace advocates, but neither group had any Indians to threaten or make peace with. Generals Sherman, Terry, Harney and Augur had been dispatched with Commissioner of Indian Affairs N. G. Taylor, Senator J. B. Henderson, General John B. Sandborn and S. S. Tappan to negotiate and conclude a peace treaty with the Lakotas, Cheyennes and Arapahos who had succeeded in constricting the Bozeman Trail militarily, until it was no longer a viable immigrant road or supply route. The Peace Commissioners waited, and in May Chief Little Wolf was among the Northern Cheyenne delegation who signed the treaty, the same month that the first Oglalas signed. The Commissioners were expecting Red Cloud, but their expectations were based upon misunderstandings and misinterpretation, a negative precedent that, to this day, continues to undermine the nation-to-nation relationship between the Sioux Nation and the United States.

Red Cloud arrived at Fort Laramie on November 4, 1868, and it was left to General William Dye, the post commander, to explain the articles of the Fort Laramie Treaty of 1868 to Red Cloud. The Lakotas listened, discussed what they understood to be what Dye had said, and Red Cloud signed the treaty in good faith and in accordance with how he interpreted what had been presented to him. We won the war, but the peace was taken from us along with our land. To the Lakota, Cheyenne and Arapaho who signed it, the 1868 treaty was sacrosanct; it was a solemn commitment that had been made before the Creator, but to the political and commercial forces in the United States it was a real estate deal that could be bought, sold or abandoned as the will of the influential demanded. In this book we have tried to present an insight into those diverse perspectives in an attempt to nurture understanding, healing and progress between our peoples. Serle Chapman drew upon his own experiences and knowledge, along with the knowledge and experiences of his relatives and friends among the Cheyenne, Lakota and Arapaho people, to share our perspective. At the same time, he went back inside himself to bring a Euro-American view to this critical period of history we share.

What Red Cloud heard was that the United States wanted peace, and the 1868 Fort Laramie Treaty appeared to concede all that the Oglalas and their allies had fought for. The forts were abandoned, the army marched away from the Powder River country, and the U.S. acceded to

Chief American Horse and Chief Red Cloud

26 million acres west of the Missouri River, including our sacred Black Hills, to be the Great Sioux Nation. This land mass was ostensibly all of what is now western South Dakota, designated for "the absolute and undisturbed use and occupation" by the Lakota people. The Bozeman Trail had cut through the 34 million acres north of the Platte River and east of the summit of the Bighorn Mountains that the 1868 treaty classified as "unceded Indian territory." With the signing of the treaty, no white people were permitted to settle there, and the Lakotas and Cheyennes could continue to hunt buffalo and live in accordance with our traditions for as long as the buffalo ranged across that area. Even before the treaty was ratified by the U.S. Senate, mining interests in Wyoming had threatened to break the treaty, and it was a short five years before the U.S. government followed their lead and invaded the Black Hills in 1874. The 1868 treaty stipulated that no cession of lands held in common on the Great Sioux Reservation would be valid unless at least 3/4 of the adult male Lakota population occupying, or with interests to, the Great

194

Sioux reservation, signed such an amendment. The land cession that followed had no legitimacy as they did not adhere to that condition.

The 1868 Fort Laramie Treaty was a treaty of peace, not a treaty of land cessation or otherwise, and it was developed between one sovereign and another: the Sioux Nation and the United States. The 1868 treaty, like all treaties between Indian nations and the United States, was analogous to the supreme law of the land, as noted in Article VI of the United States Constitution. The treaty established a finite process of cooperation and responsibility that influences the affairs of both nations, but the U.S. government has continually impugned the integrity of the 1868 Fort Laramie Treaty by congressional acts to supplant that relationship as sovereign, by land encroachment and the exploitation of natural resources, through to physical oppression – resultant from which is our contemporary situation. Today we live in a dual system, both under the Indian Reorganization Act (IRA) and according to our traditional ways. The IRA governments were established as models of the U.S. constitution and government, and we all know how corrupt the federal system can be. Corruption permeates throughout the institutional processes when the decision makers are corruptible, and today our administrations suffer from that. We deal with this on a daily basis, and with the frustration of this duality where we search to find the best approach to better the lives of our people, while remaining a distinct social political entity. This duality has created generations of Lakota people who don't know where they fit, and in response I have attempted to develop methodologies to reinvigorate our traditional presence by establishing a Council of Elders to participate and advise in tribal council meetings from the traditional Lakota perspective, and to bring Lakota eloquence of delivery into the legislative arena. As tribal president you run into this wall of frustration, and the cumulative effect is oppression and suppression from the federal government which manifests itself as poverty and depression amongst our people.

The three poorest counties in the United States are on Sioux reservations in South Dakota, one of them being Shannon County, the largest county on the Pine Ridge Indian Reservation, "the Oglala Lakota Nation." Our unemployment rate hovers at around 85 percent, over 30 percent of our people are homeless, we have devastating levels of alcohol and substance abuse, and diabetes is becoming pandemic among our people. Amidst this crippling poverty, our people have the lowest life expectancy of any ethnic group in the United States, the highest rate of teen suicide, and the highest infant mortality rate. One of the primary reasons we see such deplorable conditions and statistics here is due to a lack of funding, and subsequently a lack of investment. However, our leaders need to evaluate what natural resources we already protect as caretakers of this geographical area. Our reservation sits upon the deepest pool of the highest grade crude oil on the North

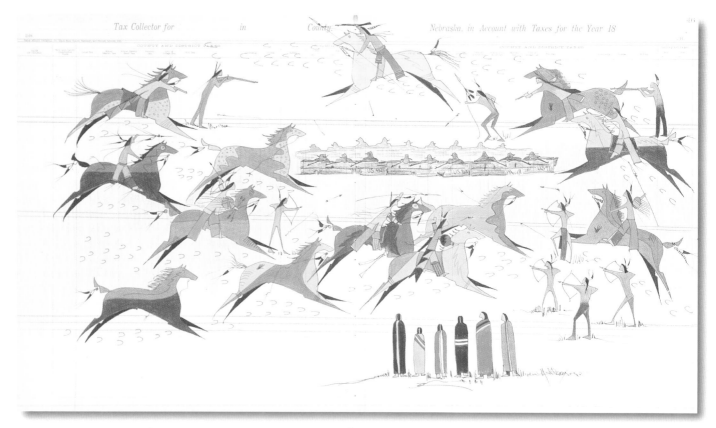

The Wagon Box Fight — *by Donald F. Montileaux*

American continent; we have zeolites so high in value that they are only exceeded by those found in Turkey; and we have sand and gravel deposits in abundance, so we have some potential here. Having such a high volume of natural resources is one of the reasons why I believe my people will not allow any type of humiliation through corporate exploitation.

When my administration brought President Clinton to our nation in 1999, the crux of my effort was to have him recognize the 1868 Fort Laramie Treaty, and to persuade the U.S. government to allow us to develop an economic model that is tailored specifically from our perspective. The IRA government system has so far suppressed any attempt to revitalize or empower traditional government. Our people are durable and we are still here fighting for our land and treaty rights. For all Lakota tribal presidents and elected representatives, protecting the Black Hills land claim and the status of dockets 74-A and 74-B should be paramount. In 1980, the U.S. Supreme Court decreed that, "A more ripe and rank case of dishonorable dealing will never, in all probability, be found in our history," after hearing the treaty claims of the Great Sioux Nation and ruling that the U.S. had violated the 1868 treaty when it unlawfully invaded and seized the Black Hills. Following the U.S. Supreme Court's decision, the Indian Claims Commission awarded our people $100 million. We rejected the money and reasserted that the Black Hills, our Holy Land, is not for sale at any price. With accruing interest that award now exceeds $500 million, but to put that sum into context, on the day that award was made, it was calculated that one mine in the Black Hills had plundered in excess of $14 billion in gold and silver dating back to 1876 – an operation that, under the 1868 treaty, was established illegally. We have been fighting for years to tell the U.S. government that we don't want money, we want our land back, and it is imperative to remember that along with our land comes our governance of people, which duly comes with the oversight stewardship responsibility of nationhood, which maintains sovereignty. The treaty that closed the Bozeman Trail is still at the center of our struggle today.

Harold Salway has served two terms as President of the Oglala Lakota Nation. Before being elected president, he held the offices of Vice President and Fifth Member.

Herb Pavey

Upon learning of my involvement in the publishing of this book, the usual question asked is: How did a former Chicago city slicker, retired technologist, and adventure junky get caught up in chronicling the history of the western United States? The answer is in what Harold Salway explained. My own knowledge of history of the West, like that of most Americans, was limited to a homogenized version taught in our schools, and the Hollywood lore of cowboys and Indians. It wasn't until I was given the opportunity to participate in the reenactment of the crossing of the Bozeman Trail that I learned just how many of the tales of the west that drew me here are, in fact, fraudulent. While it's easy to be comfortable with the fairy tale version of the history of pioneers and Native people, I was bound, after one illuminating visit with Serle Chapman, to learn more myself, and to help those who had the knowledge to find a platform so that others could hear and learn. I learned that there were many more stories to be told, and I wanted to help myself and others understand what really occurred.

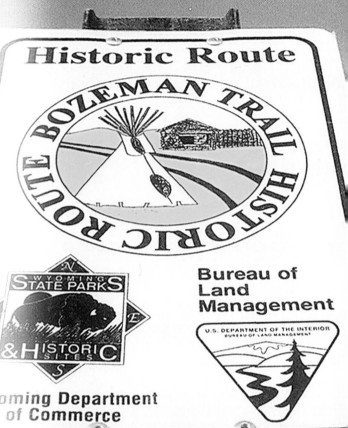

In the early stages of contemplating the publishing of this book it seemed appropriate to delve into the multiple perspectives of the participants of this period. I encouraged Serle to make *Promise* bridge the gap for the reader by providing the different perspectives of the early pioneers, the military and Native people. I expect this has helped you, as it has myself, to be able to understand those perspectives from a single book. During the creative process, I was honored to meet with pioneer descendants, tribal historians, spiritual leaders, and the keepers of sacred bundles. Being able to listen to these people tell their history was an experience I will never forget, and I grew to appreciate the people who are considered to be 'the keepers of the stories and songs.'

The overriding reason for my participation in the production of *Promise* is to encourage others to take off their blinders and to see our history and its ramifications as they manifest today. Native people are the only classification of people in this country who, through their respective tribal governments, have a sovereign relationship with the U.S. government that guarantees them a place to live and health care for their lifetime. Yet Native people have the largest disparity in health status, economics and education of any group of people in this nation. We must acknowledge and understand why this has happened to the Native people of America, and we need to take action to undo the harm that we, as a country, have turned a blind eye to. I hope that this book reaches the hands of many people so that its profit can be used to improve the quality of life of Native people and ensure that there are healthy "keepers of the story" for many years to come.

Herb Pavey is the Executive Director of Pavey Western Publishing.

Ben Kern's Bozeman Trail reenactors who retraced the trail in 2001

ACKNOWLEDGMENTS

Thanks are due to many, for when a book makes it onto a shelf the author is just one of the people who worked to put it there.

It is unlikely that *Promise* would exist if Rich Holstein had not asked me if I had ever thought about writing and photographing a book on the Bozeman Trail. I hadn't, so I did, and *Promise* is the result. I thank Rich for asking the question, for his optimism, and for calling Herb Pavey.

Belief isn't easy to find in this age of having to see it to believe it, but who can ever really see it if they don't first believe? I gratefully acknowledge Herb and Patti Pavey for believing and seeing.

As always, I am indebted to Sarah Gilbertson-Chapman for coordinating this project with the same strength and resolution she has brought to my previous books and to my life.

With gratitude to all of the interviewees, advisors, models and contributors without whom there would be no *Promise*. For John Parker, Susan Badger Doyle, Ron Medicine Crow, George and Rachel Magpie, Jack and Carol Bailey, Bill Neal, Alex and Percy White Plume, and Mark Hertig – your combined generosity of spirit made it easy when it could have been difficult. Many thanks to all of the landowners who let me wander onto their properties, particularly the Plainfeather family from Fort C.F. Smith who were as gracious on this occasion as on the first.

With appreciation to my good friend Harold Salway. To Rob Williams, Ingrid Estell and Beth Parker at Mountain Press. To Bo Bowman, Patrick Hui, the Sheridan Library Wyoming Room librarians, the Sheridan Holiday Inn, Judy Blair of Blair Hotels, the Reptile Gardens (Rapid City) and Ironside Bird Rescue (Cody).

Thanks to: Coi Drummond-Gehrig, Chester Cowan, Cindy Brown, Bonnie Morgan, Nancy Sherbert, Belinda Hall, Lesley Shores, Debra Neiswonger, John Powell, Angelika Tietz, Vyrtis Thomas, Pat Fullmer, Tammy Benson, David Burgevin, Dorothy Neuhaus, Sharon Silengo, Rick Young, John Gavin, Arlene Ekland-Earnst, Kitty Deernose and all at the Little Bighorn.

For Jude Carino whose enthusiasm reminds me that this is all worthwhile. For John Trudell – inspiration and wisdom in this reality of many realities. For my brothers Douglas Spotted Eagle and Paul DeMain whose advice keeps me centered; and to my sisters Marley Shebala and Karen Testerman who do the same. For Henri, Jackie and Montoya: Nea-ese!

For Darlene Nichols, the most courageous person I know.

This is how it all began and will someday begin again.

Photography Credits

ALL PHOTOGRAPHY © BY SERLE L. CHAPMAN EXCEPT WHERE INDICATED BELOW.

Dog Man, pg. *xiii*, © by Sarah Gilbertson-Chapman.

Black Elk, pg. 101, © by Bill Groethe.

Fetterman Disaster Club, pg. 121, © by Mark Hertig. Courtesy of Agate Fossil Beds National Monument.

Jack Bailey, John Stands-in-Timber and Father Peter Powell, pg. 180, by Emmie D. Mygatt, © by the Foundation for the Preservation of American Indian Art and Culture.

Serle Chapman, pg. 200, © by Alistair Devine.

Wagon train at dawn, pg. 2; lowering the wagons, pg. 29; Bozeman Trail reenactors, pg. 197, all © by Rich Holstein.

Yucca, pg. 4; gumbo lily, pg. 7; running buffalo, pg. 14; swallowtail, pg. 23; Indian paintbrush, pg. 32; tanager pg. 90, all © by Guy W. Tillett.

Archive Photographs & Art

AUTHOR'S COLLECTION
Quanah Parker © 1892 by Lanney, pg. *ix*.
Set-t'ainte's shield (1895 lithograph), pg. *xiii*.
Fetterman Fight by Don Montileaux, pg. 64.
Crazy Horse by Lorence Bjorklund, pg. 83.
Spotted Elk, Young Little Wolf, and Wild Hog by Grabill, 1887, pg. 174.
Crazy Horse by Don Montileaux, pg. 145.

BUFFALO BILL HISTORICAL CENTER
William F. Cody in Paris, 1899, pg. *vi*. BBHC, Cody, Wyoming (P.6.367).

COLORADO HISTORICAL SOCIETY
Plates from *Cheyenne Dog Soldiers: A Ledgerbook of Coups and Combat* © Colorado Historical Society.
Plate 113, 'A Dash for the Fort,' by Big Crow, pg. 68.
Plate 139, 'The Bravest Coup,' by Tomahawk, pg. 72.
Plate 85, 'A Stand at the Village,' by Red Lance, pg. 75.
Plate 131, 'A Surprise Encounter,' by Brave Wolf, pg. 77.
Plate 82, 'Taking the Soldier Wagon,' by White Horse, pg. 109.
Plate 34, 'Wolf with Plenty of Hair rescues Tall Bull,' pg. 184.

DENVER PUBLIC LIBRARY
Denver Public Library, Western History Collection.
Satanta by W. Soule, X-32385, pg. *xi*.
Bosse, Left Hand, White Wolf, X-32364. Chiefs at Camp Weld pg. *xviii*.

William Tecumseh Sherman. Unknown. Pg. 40.
Jim Beckwourth. Unknown. Pg. 46.
Spotted Tail by D.F. Barry, B–201. Pg. 62.
Red Cloud by A. Gardener, X-31824. Pg. 70.
Two Moons by Richard D. Throssel, X-32029. Pg. 81.
American Horse, B-166. Pg. 93.
Black Coal, X-32374. Pg. 97.
Low Dog by D.F. Barry, B-805. Pg. 104.
Short Bull by D.F. Barry, B-567. Pg. 105.
Fetterman Fight by John Guthrie, X-31541. Pg. 118.
Red Cloud (in felt hat), X-31326. Pg. 123.
Medicine Crow by Edward S. Curtis, X-34122. Pg. 131.
White-Man-Runs-Him by Richard D. Throssel, X-31261. Pg. 134.
Red Cloud delegation, Z-2299. Pg. 142.
Chief Red Shirt, X-31528. Pg. 143.
Sharp Nose, X-32358. Pg. 155.
Arapaho group, X-32346. Pg. 156.
Sitting Bull profile, Nate Salsbury Collection, NS-102. Pg. 161.
Sitting Bull by D.F. Barry, B-69. Pg. 162.
Wild Hog and group, X-32021. Pg. 173.
Red Cloud and American Horse, B-729. Pg. 194.
Red Cloud, B-852. Pg. 214.

LOIS BRILL DIXON COLLECTION
Washita Battlefield Commemoration, pg. *xvii*.
Chief Magpie holding a carbine from the Little Bighorn, pg. 169.

FORT LARAMIE NATIONAL HISTORIC SITE
KKa-73(485) George Templeton, pg. 38.
KKa-32(486) Captain William J. Fetterman, ca.1865, pg. 49.
KKa-37(173) U.S. Grant pg. 61.
© Fort Laramie National Historic Site, National Park Service.

KANSAS STATE HISTORICAL SOCIETY
Jim Bridger, pg. 50.

LITTLE BIGHORN BATTLEFIELD NATIONAL MONUMENT
Mvc-104s.jpeg: William Sherman, circa 1865 (catalog No. 14592).
Mvd-105s.jpeg: Mitch Boyer, circa 1875 (catalog No. 174).
Courtesy of Little Bighorn Battlefield NM Western National Parks Association.

JOE MEDICINE CROW COLLECTION
Iron Bull, pg. 132.
Medicine Crow, pg. 133.

MONTANA HISTORICAL SOCIETY
John Bozeman, pg. 149.
Nelson Story, pg. 150.
Bird Wild Hog, pg. 172.
Crazy Head, pg. 187.
Montana Historical Society, Helena.

NATIONAL ARCHIVES AND RECORDS ADMINISTRATION
Henry B. Carrington, 111-BA-867, pg. 43.

NATIONAL ANTHROPOLOGICAL ARCHIVES, SMITHSONIAN INSTITUTION
Little Wolf and Dull Knife # 270A, pgs. 73 & 88.
Cat. no. 82-15200, shield purported to have been Crazy Horse's, pg. 83.
Spotted Wolf and Crazy Head #268, pgs. 90 & 104.
Sitting Bull's ledger drawing # 3199-D-34, pg. 162.
Magpie #230, pg. 166.

NEBRASKA STATE HISTORICAL SOCIETY PHOTOGRAPH COLLECTIONS
He Dog by John A. Anderson, pg. 74.
Lame White Man, November 1873, pg. 96.
No Water, Black Hills Peace Treaty 1876, pg. 138.
He Dog, pg. 139.
Fool Bull by John A. Anderson, pg. 198.

NEWBERRY LIBRARY
Little Wolf at Fort Laramie circa May 1868 by Alexander Gardner, pg. 111.
Courtesy Edward E. Ayer Collection, the Newberry Library, Chicago.

STATE HISTORICAL SOCIETY OF NORTH DAKOTA
0160-010, White Bull, pg. 85.

OKLAHOMA STATE HISTORICAL SOCIETY
Mrs. Amos Chapman, Mary Long Neck # 2554. Pg. *vii*.
Mrs. Amos Chapman holding Benjamin Chapman # 20738.N31. Pg. *xii*.
Amos Chapman #14980. Pg. *xii*.
Archives & Manuscripts Division of the Oklahoma Historical Society.

UTAH STATE HISTORICAL SOCIETY
General Patrick E. Connor, pgs. 36 & 191.
Used by permission, all rights reserved.

UNIVERSITY OF WYOMING
Henry B. Carrington, pg. 57.
Courtesy of the American Heritage Center, University of Wyoming.

W.H. OVER MUSEUM
White Bull (Ice) by Stanley J. Morrow, pg. 108.
Courtesy W.H. Over Museum, Vermillion, South Dakota.

WYOMING STATE ARCHIVES
1908 Reunion at Fort Phil Kearny #9938, pg. *xvi*.
Lt. George W. Grummond #5731, pg. 53.
Captain Ten Eyck Neg #9545, pg. 119.
Colonel Carrington #10466, pg. 120.
1908 Fetterman monument dedication #10208, pg. 121.
Wild Hog #479, pg. 105.
Wyoming State Archives, Dept. of State Parks and Cultural Resources.

Contributors

BILL GROETHE

Bill is one of the most respected photographers in the western United States. In a career spanning seven decades, Bill has produced some of the West's truly enduring images, including his 1948 series of Lakota veterans who fought at the Battle of the Little Bighorn, one of which, his portrait of Black Elk, is featured in *Promise*. Bill was among those who first encouraged Serle Chapman to pursue photography. A collection of Bill's work is showcased in his book, *A Journey of Visions*.

RICH HOLSTEIN

Rich's three images in *Promise* mark his publishing debut, the shots having been taken during Ben Kern's 2001 Bozeman Trail reenactment. www.richholstein.com

DONALD F. MONTILEAUX

Through his art, Don is a modern-day Oglala Lakota storyteller. Don created three original ledger pieces for *Promise*, and his work is prominently displayed in galleries and museums throughout Lakota country and the American West. Don considers that his mission as an artist is to portray the history and culture of the Lakota people in an honest way, "to illustrate our people as human beings who lived, made love, raised children, and hunted buffalo." www.montileaux.com

KEVIN RED STAR

Kevin is quite simply one of the Masters, and his works chronicling Crow culture adorn museums, galleries, and private collections around the world, including the Smithsonian Institution, the Heard Museum, the Eiteljorg Museum, the IAIA, the Buffalo Bill Historical Center, the Pierre Cardin collection in Paris, and China's Shenyang National Art Museum. www.kevinredstar.com

GUY TILLETT

Guy is a South Dakota-based wildlife artist, photographer, author and educator. Guy's book, *Ovis, North American Wild Sheep*, achieved critical acclaim and is one of the bestselling titles of its genre. His photography has appeared on the covers of several outdoor and sports magazines, including *Bowhunter*, *Turkey Call*, *Wild Sheep*, and *South Dakota Conservation Digest*. Guy contributes special reports to the *Rapid City Journal*, and he and his wife Kathy have supported Serle Chapman throughout his career.

Fool Bull

ABOUT SERLE CHAPMAN

The author of six successful titles, Serle Chapman received a 1996 'Book of the Year' accolade in Europe for his first book, *The Trail of Many Spirits*, and his second, *Of Earth and Elders: Visions and Voices from Native America*, achieved outstanding international reviews. Chapman's work has been highlighted on national TV and radio, and one of the world's premiere arts complexes, London's Barbican Center, described him in their 'Written America' series as "a critically acclaimed writer and one of the world's leading photographers." His photography is on permanent display at various museums and visitors' centers in North and Central America, including the Biosphere Reserve in Mexico.

In the capacity of both author and photographer, Chapman's work has appeared in numerous national and international publications, including *The Times* (London), *The Guardian/Observer* (London), *The Daily Express* (London), *The Mail on Sunday* (London), *The Navajo Times*, *Indian Country Today*, *The Lakota Times*, *Aboriginal Voices* (Canada) and various U.S. city and statewide newspapers. His work for the Inter-Tribal Bison Cooperative featured in *Audubon Magazine* and he has been recognized in both *The Washington Post* and *Le Monde*. His first U.S. royalties from *The Trail of Many Spirits* were donated to the Head Start program located in Martin, near the Pine Ridge Indian Reservation, and his author royalty from *Of Earth and Elders* was committed to the American Indian College Fund. Following the publication of *Of Earth and Elders*, in recognition of his literary efforts and philanthropic activities in Native America, Chapman received a letter of commendation from President Nelson Mandela.

We, The People, Volume 2 of his *Of Earth and Elders* sequence, is described as "a stunning visual and literary portrait of indigenous existence past and present." Chapman's portraiture in *We, The People* was acclaimed by critics as "a contemporary equivalent to the work of Edward S. Curtis." Former President of the United States Bill Clinton contributed the foreword remarks to *We, The People*. Chapman has undertaken extensive public speaking engagements in the U.S. and Europe, being invited to lecture at both Oxford University and Cambridge University. Chapman's antecedents include the legendary frontier scout, Amos Chapman, the husband of Long Neck Woman, a granddaughter of Chief Black Kettle. Chapman is a son of the respected Cheyenne educator Dr. Henrietta Mann, and his tribal heritage also includes lineage to the ancient Kalderaš.

Chapman's books have been published in different languages on three continents.

The author's trusty assistant, Jim, who accompanied Serle throughout the process of photographing and researching PROMISE. *Jim may be one of the only dogs to have traversed the length of the Bozeman Trail twice in contemporary times!*

"A critically acclaimed writer and one of the world's leading photographers."

www.gonativeamerica.com   www.serlechapman.com

A Letter Home

1. Common to the gold rush era, 'rag towns' were hastily organized camps that, in short order, often developed into towns, the longevity of which was inextricably linked to the duration and productivity of the respective mining operation from which it was spawned.

2. 'Old Bedlam,' the oldest existing military building in Wyoming, housed bachelor officers posted at Fort Laramie and its name is reflective of the parties held by its occupants, generally after payday.

3. A reference to Atlanta before Major General William Tecumseh Sherman's Georgia campaign and 'march to the sea.' After blockading and bombarding Atlanta through August 1864, Sherman's forces defeated those of Confederate General John Hood at Jonesboro on September 1, resulting in Hood's retreat from Atlanta. "If the people raise a howl against my barbarity and cruelty," Sherman wrote to Union Army Chief of Staff, Major General Henry Halleck. "I will answer that war is war and not popularity seeking." Two years earlier, Sherman had expressed the view that, "The only way to win the war is to reconquer the South in the same manner that the army has been beating the Indians for years. The destruction of the Indian villages was the key."

4. General John Pope's General Order No. 27 required a train to have a minimum of twenty wagons and thirty armed men before it would be allowed to proceed. At the time, Pope was Commander of the Department of the Missouri.

5. Prior to the Bozeman Trail, goldseekers heading for Virginia City took the circuitous Lander Road, a cutoff west of South Pass to Fort Hall, which required prospectors to travel west and then turn back east to reach Montana's goldfields. Today, Fort Hall, located in Idaho, is the tribal headquarters of the Shoshone-Bannock Nation.

6. A scornful term for Union troops.

7. Robert Burns, Scotland's national poet, whose lifestyle, opinions, and provocative works challenged the dominant Calvinist attitudes of his day.

8. Montana's first territorial capital. The gold rush to Bannack began in 1862. It was in Bannack, in early 1863, that John Bozeman and John Jacobs formulated a plan to explore a shorter route to Montana's goldfields, the result being the Bozeman Trail.

9. A 'booshway' is a mountain man of some repute.

10. A derogatory name for an Anglo-American who had an American Indian wife. The term 'squaw' is highly offensive, being a corruption of a word of Algonquin origin, which translates to profane slang for female genitalia. Without exception, the term was used in reference to American Indian women in letters and literature from and about the frontier, and its use throughout this passage is purely for reasons of authenticity and to communicate the attitudes of the day with the hope that, over a century on, more people will appreciate how offensive it is and that eventually it will fall from popular usage.

11. The 'tame' antelope at Fort Laramie was partial to bread and butting all and sundry.

12. John Ross, Principal Chief of the Cherokee Nation during the tragedy and aftermath of the Trail of Tears, is believed to have had Scots ancestry. It is said that Stand Watie, a Cherokee, but political foe of Ross, was the last Confederate general to surrender to the Union.

13. Predominantly Oglala and Brulé Lakotas, the people here were often referred to as 'Loafers' or 'Hang Around the Fort Indians,' and were the first Lakotas to fall victim to the pernicious cycle of dependency that was fostered by the agency – and subsequently the reservation – system promulgated by the U.S. government. The Wagluhke, or 'Loafers,' eventually became a recognized band among the Oglala Sioux.

14. The unratified Fort Laramie Treaty of 1866. Red Cloud and many other prominent leaders among the Oglala and Mniconju Lakotas left the treaty conference upon learning that Colonel Carrington was on his way to garrison the Bozeman Trail before the tribes had agreed to 'sell the road.' The questionable positive representation of the treaty by the President of the Commission and Superintendent of Indian Affairs, Edward B. Taylor, and a fellow negotiator, Fort Laramie's post commander, Colonel Henry Maynadier, contributed to Colonel Carrington's difficulties.

15. Colonel Henry B. Carrington's seven hundred strong Second Battalion of Eighteenth Infantry; the much admired regimental band, plus 226 wagons, over 1000 head of livestock, mowing machines, two sawmills and an array of construction materials contributed to 'Carrington's Overland Circus.'

16. From Mattes, *The Great Platte River Road*. The 1852 diary of Jane D. Kellogg recounts the horrors of cholera epidemics, and Ezra Meeker described the Platte as looking like a battlefield, so numerous were the graves of cholera victims. In *Plagues and Peoples*, William McNeill contends that Irish emigrants brought the disease to North America. A Lakota winter count for 1849/50 designates the year as 'Many Died of the Cramps,' and in the same year the Southern Cheyennes lost half of their tribe to the disease.

17. A widely held but erroneous belief among the emigrants.

18. The woman was Susan Hail.

19. Mni Aku Win, Brings Back Water, was the daughter of Chief Spotted Tail and Appearing Day. From his own reminiscences, it would appear that the officer was Eugene F. Ware. Legend has it that Mni Aku Win died of a broken heart, so strong was her desire to marry Ware. Mni Aku Win asked her father to lay her to rest in the post cemetery at Fort Laramie and Colonel Maynadier consented to Spotted Tail's request, her funeral taking place around March 9, 1866, with elements of Lakota and military ceremony.

20. Snakebites were just one of the maladies whiskey, regarded as something of a cure-all, was thought to aid.

21. Between 1866 and 1867, Bridger's Ferry was the most important 'jumping-off' place on the Bozeman Trail. In 1865, the government had supplied Jim Bridger with the materials to construct the cable ferry across the North Platte, which he operated until departing with Colonel Carrington's expedition as chief guide and interpreter.

22. Pancakes.

23. Rawhide Buttes are located near Lusk, Wyoming, and the 'Legend of Rawhide' is annually recognized in the town. This was a common story among emigrants, which likely had different locations attributed to it.

24. The scalp belonged to an emigrant named Mills, a member of A.A. Townsend's 1864 train. Near present-day Kaycee, Wyoming, at the confluence of the Powder River and the South Fork, on July 7 a small party of Cheyennes, mostly Kit Fox society members, approached the Townsend train and tensions rose when inquiries were made as to the whereabouts of Mills, who had left the train to look for a cow, followed by a search party. A fight ensued, in which the Cheyennes skirmished with the search party and then besieged Townsend's train for some six hours. The train of Cyrus Coffinbury found Mills' scalp dangling from a cedar tree on July 21. The Townsend Fight was arguably the most significant engagement fought between emigrants and American Indians on the Bozeman Trail.

25. It is believed that Mrs. Eubanks was captured in a Cheyenne raid along the Little Blue River, east of Fort Kearny, Nebraska, on August 9, 1864. She ended up in the possession of Two Face, a Lakota, who delivered her and her child to Fort Laramie in May 1865. Mrs. Eubanks detailed a catalog of abuse, in which it was alleged that Two Face had participated. Colonel Moonlight duly ordered Two Face be hung along with Blackfoot, another Lakota accused of sexual assault. The charges against the two were never substantiated, but on May 26 they were hung and their decomposing bodies were left as a warning to others.

26. Many on the frontier favored the deployment of territorial militias over the return of the army, believing that if a bounty of $100 per Indian scalp was introduced the 'Indian problem' would soon be over.

27. The Bloody Angle at the Battle of Spotsylvania Courthouse in May 1864 saw some of the most intense fighting of the Civil War; in twenty four hours of combat each side suffered some seven thousand casualties, the trenches said to have been knee-deep in bloody mud.

28. Yucca was known as soap weed due to the plant being used by American Indians as a natural cleanser.

29. A 'wrapper' was a full-length one-piece, dress designed for the rigors of daily chores and the road.

30. John C. Frémont was the son-in-law of influential expansionist Senator Thomas Hart Benton. Frémont led a U.S. Topographical Corps of Engineers expedition to South Pass, Green River, and Wind River, Wyoming, in 1842, and became an icon of Manifest Destiny.

31. Accidents of this nature were relatively common on the Bozeman Trail, and along with disease and drowning, they accounted for more casualties on the overland trails than Indian attacks.

32. Historically, the Dry Fork had been a major trade route and thoroughfare for the Lakota, Cheyenne, Arapaho, Crow, and Shoshone.

33. The 'elephant' was a common metaphor for emotional and physical breakdown on the overland trails, hence the phrase 'seen the elephant.'

34. This is a description of a Mniconju Lakota of some standing; his face paint tells of his exploits in war, representing his coups and scalps, and the stick in his hair symbolizes his ability with a gun. The 'thin plait' is a scalp lock, and the paint on his feathers relates to enemies killed in battle. In his diary, Lieutenant George Templeton records a Lakota wearing an army blouse after Lieutenant Daniels had been killed in the Crazy Woman fight of July 20, 1866.

35. The scars on his breast are from participation in the Sun Dance, and the 'xylophone of bones' is a hair pipe breast plate. Red lines on a horses muzzle indicate coups, handprints tell of killing an enemy in hand-to-hand combat, horseshoes represent the number of horses taken in a raid, and zigzags are lightning bolts, symbolizing speed and the power of the West from where the thunders come. This description fits an Oglala Lakota.

36. Few emigrants appreciated that it was the custom of the tribes in the region to offer strangers a gift as a token of hospitality, which is what they expected the emigrants to do when they were passing through their country. Consequently, most emigrants make mention of Indians begging, as this is how they interpreted it. Before the army arrived to garrison the Bozeman Trail, the most common exchanges between emigrants and Indians concerned 'tolls' of food the Indians expected the emigrants to pay to travel the road.

37. See note 27.

38. Both were notorious POW camps in the Civil War.

39. The grave of Mansel Cheney was eight miles from Fort Reno on the Dry Fork, Powder River. Cheney was killed during an engagement with Lakotas on July 22, 1866.

40. On August 17, 1866, a party of Lakotas entered the corral at Fort Reno and drove off seventeen mules and seven cavalry mounts.

41. Established on August 14, 1865, during General Patrick E. Connor's failed punitive Powder River Expedition, Fort Connor was renamed Fort Reno in honor of Major General Jesse L. Reno, who was killed while leading Union forces to victory in the Battle of South Mountain, September 14, 1862.

42. A Confederate term for an area of confinement.

43. Of the two thousand people and twelve hundred wagons that traveled the Bozeman Trail in 1866, a large proportion were freighters in what was categorized as the 'second rush.' The freighters were intent on profiting from the miners, emigrants, and where they could, the military.

44. Both were common insults of the day: 'here's your mule' was directed at the cavalry by the infantry, and 'pumpkin rinds' was ostensibly a Union jibe directed at lieutenants.

45. Lieutenant Thaddeus Kirtland was a cousin of Colonel Henry B. Carrington, and before continuing up the Bozeman Trail to establish Fort Phil Kearny, Carrington left Kirtland's Company B at Fort Reno, appointing Captain Joshua Proctor to post commander. On June 30, 1866, Colonel Carrington issued new regulations for emigrant traffic on the trail.

46. Both were derogatory Union terms for Confederate soldiers. Connor had left Companies C and D of the Fifth U.S. Volunteers to man the post, the men being 'Galvanized Yankees,' former Confederate prisoners.

47. The Indian scouts were Ho-Chunks (Winnebagos) of Company A, Omaha Scouts. Jim Bridger held the Ho-Chunk scouts in high esteem.

48. Yellow Eagle, a brother of Man-Afraid-of-His-Horses, coordinated many of these forays in July and August; Man-Afraid-of-His-Horses was one of Red Cloud's closest allies in the fight to close the Bozeman Trail. Freighters of the Kirkendall train were engaged by Lakotas on July 24, 1866, near Clarks Springs. A military train under the command of Lieutenant George Templeton was forced to corral under attack from Lakotas on Crazy Woman Creek, July 20, 1866. The skirmish near Buffalo Springs involved the Burgess party and occurred on July 22, 1866, resulting in the aforementioned death of Mansel Cheney, an uncle to Perry Burgess.

49. 'Somebody's darling' was a term commonly used for the dead.

50. The officer was Lieutenant Napoleon H. Daniels. Daniels had been scalped, a finger removed, was probably sodomized with a stick, and had over twenty arrows fired into his body. The wounds were inflicted to make it difficult for him to shoot and ride in the next life.

51. On November 15, 1864, James Laughlin Orr, a Union soldier under General Sherman's command in Atlanta, wrote, "Many buildings had already been burned. The railroad depot completely destroyed. Homes were pulled down or burned. All personal property that could be consigned to the flames was destroyed." Sherman had ordered the forced evacuation of Atlanta in September, with civilians shipped north in railroad cars or sent to a transfer station near General Hood's lines. The 'bummers' were companies detailed to 'forage,' of whom Captain George Pepper commented, "They appear to be possessed of a spirit of pure cruelty and cursedness." 'Anything to preserve the Union' was a popular Northern phrase.

52. The water was alkaline.

53. Between 1812 and 1868 some 500,000 travelers crossed South Pass. The Oregon, California and Mormon Trails all rolled over South Pass. In 1854 John Hockaday, a mountain man, proposed developing an emigrant road out of an Indian trail in the South Pass area. Shortly thereafter, under the direction of F.W. Lander, the government soon had a new wagon road, the Lander Road. See note 5.

54. Squanto was a Patuxet Indian whose incredible odyssey began when English mariner George Weymouth persuaded him to travel to England in 1605. Sir Ferdinando Gorges became his 'guardian' until, in 1614, he returned with John Smith. While mapping the coastline, Smith named Squanto's home 'Plymouth.' One of Smith's captains, Thomas Hunt, then took Squanto and some thirty other Indians as slaves and sold them in Spain but in 1619 he escaped to England and Gorges facilitated his return to 'Plymouth,' only to find that his tribe had been decimated by smallpox. Later, after the Pilgrims had endured their first winter in Squanto's Patuxet homeland, Squanto settled with the Pilgrims and they described him as "a special instrument sent of God for their good."

55. Opothle Yahola was the recognized leader of the Union faction of the Creeks, a group that quickly encompassed Seminoles, Chickasaws, Kickapoos, Shawnees, Delawares and Comanches, plus a number of African-Americans, some of whom were Creek slaves, others

being escapees from Confederate states. Slave owners were common among the Cherokees and Creeks and the Civil War brought further turmoil to the tribes who had already suffered removal. John Ross attempted to keep the Cherokees neutral but his hand was forced by the duplicitous treaties negotiated by Albert Pike, Jefferson Davis's treaty commissioner, with the tribes in Oklahoma and Texas. Stand Watie's participation in the Confederate victory on August 10, 1861, at Wilson's Creek led to Ross committing to the Confederacy, and realized his worst fear, that of civil war breaking out between the Five Civilized Tribes and their neighbors amidst the backdrop of the Civil War being fought by the North and South. After a series of skirmishes, Opothle Yahola's alliance was defeated at Hominy Creek on December 26, 1861, and the survivors who didn't freeze to death regrouped in Kansas and eventually formed into 'jayhawking' regiments.

56. A necessary element in blacksmithing.

57. A derisory term for a fort.

58. Wetting wagon wheels helped to stop shrinkage and the loosening of metal tires.

59. 'Bloody flux' was a colloquialism for dysentery.

60. She is describing the Bighorn Mountains. The mountain sheep after which the Crows named them were likely Rocky Mountain Bighorns.

61. Clear Creek, near present-day Buffalo, Wyoming. John Gavin, Director of the Jim Gatchell Museum in Buffalo, affirms that "a major catalyst for development of the Bozeman Trail was the abundance of fresh water via Clear Creek."

62. It was essential to keep the wagon train together to deter attack, something Colonel Carrington placed great emphasis upon.

63. Irrespective of whether the authors were from the North or South, a review of both military and civilian correspondence from the 1860s indicates that African-Americans were more often than not referred to by what are now unacceptable racist insults. For example, on his march to the sea, General Sherman commented, "Damn the niggers, I wish they could be kept at work," as some 25,000 freedmen rallied to his banner. The phrase, "I'd rather shoot an abolitionist than a Johnny any day," was not uncommon among the Union army, and several celebrated Union military heroes preferred to sacrifice rank rather than command African-American troops after the Civil War; George Armstrong Custer refused a lieutenant colonelcy with the Ninth Cavalry, a renowned black regiment.

64. Altercations between travelers on the Bozeman Trail were not unheard of, as documented by William K. Thomas in his diary entry for July 23, 1866; and from a military perspective, Lieutenant George Templeton makes mention of such in his diary on October 9, 1866. The works of Susan Badger Doyle are the definitive points of reference for emigrant diaries on the Bozeman Trail.

65. A legendary figure of the West who also seems to have shared this common belief was Doc Holliday; just like those who traveled the Bozeman and other trails, Holliday thought the dry climate and mountain air might aid his struggle against tuberculosis.

66. In August 1866, Colonel Carrington established a permanent lookout position atop Pilot Hill, near Little Piney, east of the fort. Nine flag signals were adopted to communicate what was, or wasn't, happening in the surrounding area. To the irritation of many at the post, the Lakotas began mimicking the signals.

67. Before Carrington's command departed from Fort Kearny, Nebraska, General Sherman had encouraged the officers' wives to travel with their husbands and to keep diaries of their experiences, giving them the impression that they would not be in harm's way.

68. Colonel Carrington had intended to name the new post Fort Reno, but having retained the original Fort Reno, which he had initially planned to abandon, the new fort was named after General Philip Kearny, a Union hero who died at the Battle of Chantilly in 1862.

69. John Bozeman was from Georgia.

70. "I well remember how the wolves howled and made the night hideous, and we could hear them scratch at the stockade posts," recounted Sergeant Frank Fessenden, a member of the regimental band at Fort Phil Kearny, following the death of Bandmaster Curry. Ostensibly the wolves were attracted to the post's slaughter yard located near Little Piney. The Lakotas observed the habits of the wolves and subsequently utilized wolf skins for strategic advantage when approaching the fort after dark.

71. The sutler's area.

72. Liquor.

73. From the Gaelic *beinn*, ben is a Scottish appellation for a mountain or peak.

74. The laundress, Susan Fitsgerald, was known as either 'Colored' or 'Black Susan,' and she was Captain Tenodor Ten Eyck's 'servant.' Colonel Carrington once stated that Susan, "must observe better behavior or she will not be tolerated in the garrison." Apparently, her misdemeanors included baking pies that were made from government supplies, and then sold back to the soldiers for "half a dollar or more." In his 1865 diary, Captain Ten Eyck referred to his previous servant, Dick, as "my negro boy."

75. After inspecting Fort Phil Kearny between August 27 and 30, 1866, General William Hazen, Assistant Inspector General, Department of the Platte, commented, "the best stockade I have seen excepting one in British America built by Hudson Bay Company."

76. Judging from their diaries, the regimental band made a favorable impression with many of the emigrants.

77. Chaplain David White, the 'Fighting Parson,' enlisted in the Union's 107th Illinois Infantry and participated in General Sherman's Georgia campaign, most notably in the engagements around Atlanta.

78. Mr. and Mrs. James Wheatley. Along with his colleague, Isaac Fisher, James Wheatley was killed in the Fetterman Fight of December 21, 1866.

79. Private Allando Gilchrist and civilian photographer Ridgway Glover were among those who met such a fate. Upon her arrival at Fort Phil Kearny, Frances Grummond Carrington witnessed such a scene.

80. Pierre Gazeau, a.k.a. 'French Pete,' had established a trading post of sorts near the junction of the Bozeman and Mormon Trails to capitalize on emigrant commerce. Gazeau, his Lakota wife and five associates then preceded Colonel Carrington's command to the site of Fort Phil Kearny. On July 16, while camped on Peno Creek (now Prairie Dog Creek, near present-day Banner, Wyoming), Gazeau was questioned by a party of Lakotas who were seeking intelligence on Colonel Carrington and his command. Red Cloud led the interrogation and was unconvinced by Gazeau's responses, and similarly unimpressed by the conduct of Cheyenne leaders Black Horse and Dull Knife who were in the camp and had also recently interacted with Colonel Carrington. Until then the Lakotas had tolerated Gazeau as, due to his marriage to a Lakota woman, he was considered by some to be a relative. However, after some debate the Lakotas judged him to be guilty of perfidy and on July 17 killed him and all in his party with the exception of his wife and children.

81. James A. Sawyers of Sioux City, Iowa, led the only civilian train on the Bozeman Trail in 1865. As General Patrick E. Connor attempted to prosecute his punitive campaign against the Lakota, Cheyenne and Arapaho, Sawyers followed behind on his government-funded wagon-road expedition. On August 15, Sawyers men were attacked on Bone Pile Creek, southwest of present-day Gillette, Wyoming. After fighting the expedition to a standstill, Lakota and Cheyenne leaders, including Red Cloud and Dull Knife, parlayed with Sawyers, George Bent acting as interpreter. After a toll was agreed, Sawyers was allowed to pass, but on September 1 he was attacked on the Tongue River by Arapahos whom Connor had attempted to massacre three days earlier, the fight causing Sawyers to corral for twelve days while awaiting reinforcements from Connor. Sawyers disbanded the 1865 expedition in Virginia City, but he recorded that a cutoff could be made from the Big Horn River west to Clarks Fork that would save travelers on

the Bozeman Trail some twenty miles. On July 29, 1866, during his second expedition, Sawyers forged his proposed cutoff, and from that point forth emigrant traffic for the 1866 season followed Sawyers amend to the Bozeman Trail.

82. The first sign means 'friend,' and the second indicates that he is Cheyenne.

83. Colonel Carrington first issued this 'paper' to Black Horse on July 16, 1866, and several copies were hastily written and distributed to other Cheyennes, including Dull Knife and Little Moon.

84. Some of the Cheyennes allied with, but not including, Black Horse, followed the lead of the Arapahos under Red Horned Bull, and kept up a lively trade with emigrants on the Bozeman Trail between the Tongue and Bighorn Rivers in 1866.

85. The 'thin plait' is a scalp-lock. The 'charm' would have been the man's personal medicine bag, containing elements of great power and protection. Among the Northern Cheyenne, the Notamé-ohméseheestse, white represents the east (SE); red, south (SW); yellow, west (NW); black, north (NE). Among the Heévaha-taneo'o, the Southern Cheyenne, green and blue may be substituted for white and red respectively.

86. Thomas Jefferson 'peace medals' were distributed by Lewis and Clark; with successive presidents, new editions followed and they were much admired and often handed down from generation to generation.

87. The fork, here described as resembling a pennant, is a quintessential design feature of Cheyenne leggings.

88. A breechclout. For Cheyenne men, traditionally both the breechclout and its string are significant masculine symbols.

89. Parfleche.

90. This style of lance is often referred to as a coup-stick, but in this instance it symbolizes the man's membership in the Elk Horn Scrapers military society, once known as the Crooked Lances among the Southern Cheyenne. While the importance and qualities associated with eagle and hawk feathers are well known, those of the sandhill crane are not; among the Cheyenne the sandhill crane is respected for its courage, and its cry is said to strike fear into the hearts of its enemies. In addition, the grizzly claws on the shield embody the bear's strength, power, and indomitable spirit. The black crescent moon, with its 'horns' pointing upwards, is a symbol that can be interpreted in several ways, according to the medium in which it is presented. In this instance, being as it appears on a shield, it is important to recognize that the designs on shields have enormous significance to those who carry them, the images being representations of a sacred nature to which there is ceremony and defined procedure. Here, the crescent has dual meaning, it represents the strength of the Cheyenne Nation, being a depiction of a great Cheyenne gathering of military societies, and it also calls on the spirit of the moon to protect its owner through the darkness. Cheyenne military leaders such as Tall Bull and White Bull Robe had shields that featured a crescent moon.

91. Both suggest that the man was a Northern Cheyenne.

92. Due to their earlier interaction with white men, and consequently exposure to Anglo trade goods, the Southern Cheyennes commonly used cloth, of which red was popular, to wrap their braids. At this time, the Northerners still largely used otter pelts or hide, which indicates that the man described here was influenced by the Southerners during the Platte and Powder River campaign of 1865.

93. Women's leggings in the Tsetsehéstahase style that became the norm.

94. The elder is wearing a traditional So'taaeo'o dress. By 1866 this style was rare and generally only worn by So'taaeo'o elders with the Northerners.

95. A frame structure used to transport items that was dragged by a horse or dog.

96. Matches were popular trade items.

97. Parfleche or rawhide containers.

98. The Cheyenne speak an Algonquian dialect with regional differences between the Southerners and Northerners. The Lakotas speak a Siouan dialect. The Romany (gypsies) speak Indic dialects.

99. Ammonium carbonate; sal volatile.

100. The grave of George Pease, an emigrant from Chambersburg, Pennsylvania.

101. Lieutenant George Templeton notes in his diary how Hugh Kirkendall's partner, Mr. McGee, was buried in an old gun box, McGee having commented that it should be saved as "it would make a good coffin for some one."

102. Several emigrant diaries mention game that had been shot for sport and left near the road, Mary Foreman Kelly's reminiscences being among the most revealing.

103. The man was James Pierson Beckwourth. The Cheyennes and Arapahos knew Jim Beckwourth as Medicine Calf and, despite his ruining many of their people with alcohol, they treated him well until, late in years, Beckwourth was recruited by Colonel John Chivington to guide his 'Bloodless Third' to Sand Creek and infamy. Born into slavery in Virginia circa 1798, his white father manumitted him in 1824 and in the fall of that year he was engaged with General William Ashley's Rocky Mountain Fur Company, traversing South Pass, Wyoming, with Ashley in winter 1824/25. Beckwourth briefly held a trading post among the Blackfeet, taking the first of his numerous Native wives, before his relations with the Blackfeet turned sour and he found himself in the employ of William Sublette in 1827/28. It is claimed that at this time, while attending the 'big doin's' on Bear Lake, Utah, a fellow mountain man, Caleb Greenwood, supposedly convinced a band of Crows that Beckwourth was a long-lost-son of Big Bowl, and thenceforth the legend says that the Crows accepted Beckwourth and allegedly gave him the names Morning Star and Bloody Arm, along with recognition as a minor chief. However, Crow history remembers Beckwourth quite differently; he was never a chief of any kind, he gave himself his Crow names, and he went to the Crows seeking recognition, unlike in the Caleb Greenwood yarn. The only name the Crow knew Beckwourth by was Deer, occasionally translated as Antelope. Despite his many exploits, real and imagined, which included guiding for the U.S. army in the Seminole War, to being among the California 'Bear Flaggers,' to discovering Beckwourth Pass through the Sierra Nevadas, Beckwourth sought to retain an association with the Crows, from whom he profited greatly and among whom he died, in the lodge of Iron Bull. Although his name was remembered by many, Beckwourth's race was often forgotten, even his biographer failed to mention that this legend of the West was African-American.

104. The fort was named for General Charles Ferguson Smith, a U.S. officer who won distinction during the Mexican War.

105. Lieutenant George Templeton's diary exposes this attitude.

106. The Bighorn Canyon.

107. The Pryor Mountains.

108. Pryor Gap is now known as Devil's Gap, and the spring referred to is Millard Springs.

109. Rock Creek Crossing near present-day Joliet, Montana. Emigrants on the Bozeman Trail commonly left notes scrawled on whatever was available to warn those following of possible danger.

110. The Beartooth Mountains.

111. Sandborn Hill, which overlooks the Stillwater River, near present-day Absarokee, Montana.

112. This technique was occasionally employed by early travelers on the Oregon and California Trails.

113. The grave of the Thomas/Schultz party is located south of the Yellowstone River, beside Interstate 90, east of Graycliff, Montana.

114. The Crazy Mountains.

115. Jim Bridger initiated use of the Yellowstone Ford in 1864, the ford unsurprisingly carrying his name for a period thereafter. John Bozeman began operating the nearby ferry in 1866.

116. Several emigrants made mention of these messages in their diaries.

117. "I heard that the privates of White Antelope had been cut off to make a tobacco bag out of," testified Captain L. Wilson, First Colorado Cavalry, during the 1865 army and congressional inquiries into the Sand Creek Massacre. In addition to his scrotum, White Antelope's nose, ears, scalp, and fingers were cut off by Major Sayr, Lieutenant Richmond and their troops. The body of testimony reveals that White Antelope was not the only victim to suffer that day; among others, First Lieutenant James Cannon recounted how the genitals of Cheyenne women were taken for use as hat bands and covers for saddle-bows. In this regard, Sand Creek was not an isolated incident, the practice of using American Indian body parts for miscellaneous accessories being more prevalent than many care to recognize.

118. After Jack McCall shot Wild Bill Hickok, aces and eights became known as 'the deadman's hand.'

119. Redskin is a highly offensive term that originated when Dutch and British colonists first put bountys on 'redskins,' the bounty hunter having to present the skin of his victim to receive payment. Later, the heads of victims, and then scalps, were accepted as proof for payment in New Amsterdam.

120. Supplying this grisly demand was not just the work of bounty hunters. In a letter to author Cyrus T. Brady, Fort Phil Kearny's post surgeon, Samuel Horton, described how after the Wagon Box Fight, "Soldiers brought back to the fort the head of an Indian for a scientific study of Indian skulls!" This habit was not peculiar to the Plains; after the January 18, 1863, murder of the Chiricahua Apache chief, Mangas Coloradas, near old Fort McLean, a volunteer sentry, Daniel Connor, reported that the chief was decapitated and the flesh boiled from his skull in a cooking pot before it was sold to a phrenologist 'back East.' By 1868, the surgeon general of the U.S. army ordered army personnel to procure Indian crania for the Army Medical Museum, following which the heads of 4,000 American Indians were taken from battlefields, graves, and burial scaffolds. Similarly, the frontier military and militias were not averse to collecting American Indian scalps; in another letter from Brady's collection, R.J. Smyth, a teamster with Colonel Carrington's command, documented how after the Wagon Box Fight, "many of our men carried away with them scalps, etc., taken from the bodies of dead Indians near the corral." Prior to his demise in the Fetterman Fight, Captain Fred Brown is widely quoted as saying he wished to take Red Cloud's scalp. Others, such as Riley Miller, an Andersonville survivor and veteran of South Dakota's Home Guard, made their livelihoods from exhibiting their gruesome collections. With Omaha Charlie, Miller opened a 500-piece sideshow, their posters advertizing the main attraction as a, "Mummified Indian Papoose, the Greatest Curiosity Ever on Exhibition." The baby had been dried and set in a glass box. The 1990 Native American Graves Protection and Repatriation Act (NAGPRA) was created to address these issues, the impetus for the legislation coming after a group of Northern Cheyennes visited the Smithsonian Institution's 'Cheyenne Collection' in 1986 and discovered that 18,500 of their relatives' remains were laying in the museum's draws.

121. Road agents were a menace on the Bozeman Trail. These highwaymen ranged from hard-bitten criminals from earlier gold rushes who had rejected prospecting in favor of bushwhacking, to corrupt officers of the law such as Nevada City sheriff Henry Plummer. George Ives, one the trail era's most celebrated and infamous road agents, was hung in Nevada City on December 21, 1863, and his apprehension, trial and execution precipitated the Vigilante Compact, signed by members of the Committee of Vigilance, two days later. With little faith in law enforcement, and the Ives success behind them, the vigilantes organized to counter the road agents and for a time Virginia City's first stone building was utilized by the group, becoming known as 'Kiskadden's Vigilante Barn.' George Thexton later remodelled the barn into his 'Blacksmith and Wagon Shop.'

122. Bozeman Pass.

123. Kelly Canyon.

124. Mount Ellis.

125. Tom Cover was among the six prospectors who discovered gold at Alder Gulch on May 26, 1863. Tom Cover's mill in Bozeman City was variously known as Cover's Mill, Coover's Mill, and Couvier's Mill. Cover was present when John Bozeman was killed in April 1867, east of Mission Creek on the Yellowstone, near present-day Livingston, Montana. At the time, Cover and Bozeman were embarking on a business trip to the Bighorn, hoping to secure grain and beef contracts from the military at Fort C.F. Smith before moving on to Fort Phil Kearny. According to Cover, they were approached by a small party of Indians Bozeman believed to be Crows, but Cover later wrote that the five men were Blackfeet, one of whom shot Bozeman twice in the chest. Cover received a bullet wound to the left shoulder and claimed that the assailants disengaged after he shot one of them. In a letter to Montana's then acting Governor, General Thomas Meagher, Cover identifies the date of the incident as April 20. The veracity of Cover's account remains open to debate, not least because it is the only account.

MODELS

Jerry Percival

Wyatt Stanley

Casey Mott

Bruce Berst

Jasmine Pickner

Nupa White Plume

Dean Spotted Eagle Jr.

Rita Lovell

The staff at the Sheridan Holiday Inn were honored when Serle Chapman made the Holiday Inn his home-away-from-home while researching and photographing *Promise: Bozeman's Trail to Destiny*. Original photos from *Promise* are on display in the lobby of the hotel. Sheridan's rich western heritage is centered around the Bozeman Trail and we invite you to experience its history, while still enjoying the modern comforts of the Hoilday Inn. We look forward to seeing you on your next visit to Wyoming.

Hundred-Soldiers-Killed-Fight

1. The Fetterman Fight, December 21, 1866. In Cheyenne history, the battle is known as The-Hundred-Soldiers-Killed-Fight or The-Battle-of-One-Hundred-in-the-Hands. The Northern Arapaho and Mniconju Lakota refer to it as One-Hundred-White-Men-Killed, and the Oglala Lakota record it as The-Battle-of-Kills-One-Hundred.

2. Vé'ho'e is the Cheyenne name for both 'white man' and 'spider.' 'Ve'hó'e' is plural. Many believe that, in relation to Caucasians, the term 'vé'ho'e' was introduced by Sweet Medicine in his prophesy that foretold of the arrival of Euro-Americans: *Ne-to'se-ho'e hvo'estanéhe'tovovo. 'Vé'ho'e' ne-to'se-hetovo. Eto'se-maha-ve'senohe.* "You are going to encounter a person. 'Vé'ho'e' you're going to call him. He is going to be all sewed together." The last sentence is thought to be a reference to both the covered wagons and dress of the emigrants.

3. The 'shiny round-things' are buttons. In Cheyenne, honé'komo means 'button,' the literal translation being 'clothes-round-thing.'

4. The Cheyennes are categorized as an Algonquian people. Cheyenne history is divided into four periods: the Ancient Time, the Time of the Dogs, the Time of the Buffalo, and the Time of the Horse. In the Ancient Time, the Cheyennes lived to the northeast, probably in Canada, until an epidemic to which they had no immunity swept through the tribe, causing them to vacate the region. The location of this ancestral area is most likely between the Great Lakes and Hudson Bay, after which they moved south of the Lake of the Woods, and into Minnesota. Anthropologists believe this movement to be consistent with the pattern of Algonquian migrations from east to west. In 1880, Black Moccasin stated that the Cheyennes reached the Missouri River around 1676. The Rev. Rodolphe Petter recorded several interviews with Cheyenne elders in the early 1900s in which they recounted living near lakes and fish being their staple food. In addition to Cheyenne oral history, documented references can be found in the works of Father Peter Powell, George Bird Grinnell, and the Rev. Rodolphe Petter.

5. Hotóhkeso, 'Little Star (person)' – 'Oglala Lakota.' Traditionally, the Cheyennes only counted first, second and third coups, and if during that sequence a non-Cheyenne ally counted coup on the same victim, that coup was not recognized by the Cheyennes, but was of course recognized by whichever tribe that ally belonged to – in this instance the Little Stars.

6. Ésevone, the Sacred Buffalo Hat, is commonly referred to as 'Is'siwun' in existing literature. Similarly, Maahótse, the Four Sacred Arrows, are referred to as the 'Mahuts.' These largely phonetic interpretations have, over the past quarter-century, been amended by Cheyenne linguists. Therefore, where possible, throughout this account of The-Hundred-Soldiers-Killed-Fight, the spelling of Cheyenne terms adheres more closely to those presented in the Northern Cheyenne Bilingual Education Program. Many believe that a definitive, English-Cheyenne dictionary is yet to be developed, some favoring a return to the phonetic approach as being a more accessible way for non-Cheyenne speakers to learn the language.

7. The French frontiersman, Sieur de La Salle, is thought to be the first white man the Cheyennes encountered. The meeting took place on February 24, 1680, at Fort Crèvecoeur, near present-day Peoria, Illinois. However, La Salle's countryman, explorer Louis Joliet, recorded a band on the eastern shore of the Mississippi that may have been Cheyenne, circa 1673.

8. The Sand Creek Massacre, November 29–30, 1864, in which Colonel John M. Chivington, Commander of the District of Colorado, led some seven hundred troops of the First Colorado Cavalry, the Third Regiment Colorado Cavalry, the First New Mexico Volunteers, and the Fort Lyon Colorado First, in a brutal assault on the peaceable village of Black Kettle and Left Hand. Etched into the pages of infamy, Chivington's troops made good on his desire "to be wading in gore" and slaughtered 109 Cheyenne and Arapaho women and children, plus 28 of the 35 men who had been in the camp. "Black Kettle raised the American flag, and raised a white flag. He was supposed to be killed, but was not. They retreated right up the creek. They were followed up and pursued and killed and butchered. None denied that they were butchered in a brutal manner and scalped and mutilated. . . . They were cut to pieces in almost every manner and form." Samuel G. Colley, Indian Agent, *The Chivington Massacre*, testimony, p. 29. The Cheyenne term for Sand Creek is Dry Creek; however, to minimize confusion, Sand Creek is used throughout this account of The-Hundred-Soldiers-Killed-Fight.

9. Little Bear, a survivor of the massacre, recounted the grandmother blinded by her own scalp. Little Bear's recollections appear in Hyde, *Life of George Bent*. During the 1865 army and congressional inquiries into the Sand Creek Massacre, First Lieutenant James Cannon testified that the genitals of Cheyenne women were taken for use as hat bands and covers for saddle-bows. "All manner of depredations were inflicted on their persons; they were scalped, their brains knocked out; the men used their knives, ripped open women, clubbed little children, knocked them in the head with their guns, beat their brains out, mutilated their bodies in every sense of the word." John S. Smith, interpreter, *The Chivington Massacre*, testimony, p. 42.

10. Ho'óhomo'e, 'Inviter' – 'Sioux.'

11. Vano'é-tane, 'Sage Person' – 'Northern Arapaho.' Hetane-vo'e – 'Cloud Man' or 'Arapaho' (Southern).

12. Big Crow was wearing a silver pectoral, and the horse's bridle was Mexican in style and mounted with silver. In Cheyenne, vo'kome-ma'kaeta is 'silver,' the literal translation being 'white-metal.'

13. This attack on Fort Rankin and Julesburg occurred on January 7, 1865. Captain Nicholas J. O'Brien was commander of the thirty-seven man detachment of Seventh Iowa Cavalry that was decoyed by Big Crow and his party. O'Brien lost fifteen soldiers and four civilians in the engagement.

14. The dog-faced man was William M. Hudnut, a messenger for the Holladay Overland Mail Express Company. Hudnut was with the stage when it was attacked by Dog Soldiers and, upon arriving at Julesburg Station, he changed horses and set out for Fort Rankin. Hudnut failed to convince Capt. O'Brien to provide an escort for the stage in the midst of the action on January 7, 1865. Hudnut then returned to the stage station while O'Brien attempted to relieve a wagon train but, in short order, both were soon retreating to the fort with the Cheyennes in pursuit, O'Brien shouting to those within earshot at the stage station to flee and save themselves, hence Hudnut's desperate ride to the fort.

15. The allied Cheyenne, Lakota and Arapaho forces returned to Julesburg on February 2, 1865, and set the town ablaze. In the interim period they had successfully undertaken some thirty engagements on targets around the North and South Platte Rivers. On January 27, 1865, General Robert B. Mitchell gave the order to create "ten thousand square miles of prairie fire." The tactic was ineffective and the tribes virtually paralyzed the Overland Stage and South Platte River Road to Denver during this campaign.

16. Notamé-ohméseheestse, 'Northern Eater,' or just Ohméseheestse, 'Eater' – both terms are used for 'Northern Cheyenne.' The Cheyenne Nation, the Tsetsehésestahase, is comprised of ten divisions, one of which is the Ohméseheestse. The Ohméseheestse is the predominant division of Northern Cheyennes. At the time of the Hundred-Soldiers-Killed-Fight, the So'taa'e were a distinct division primarily residing in the north alongside the Ohméseheestse. Today the So'taaeo'o are generally associated with the Northern Cheyenne, although there are So'taaeo'o among the Southern Cheyenne, and were at the time of the Hundred-Soldiers-Killed-Fight; for example, Black Shin's people. In 1959, Fire Wolf, a respected So'taa'e Buffalo and Sun Dance priest, told Father Peter Powell that the alliance between the So'taaeo'o and Tsetsehésestahase, the

Cheyennes now ostensibly categorized as Southern Cheyenne, began near present-day Pipestone, Minnesota. By 1833, the Year the Stars Fell, the two tribes' ancestral roots were intertwined. The So'taaeo'o are often called the 'Buffalo People' and they brought Ésevone, the Sacred Buffalo Hat, to the Cheyenne, along with the sacred ceremonies associated with Her, such as the Sun Dance. In existing literature, So'taaeo'o generally appears as 'Suhtai' and Tsetsehésestahase as 'Tsistsistas.'

17. This is a traditional So'taa'e hairstyle.

18. Robert 'Bob' North. North was a trapper and trader who had Northern Arapaho and Gros Ventre wives. It is believed that North lost some fingers in a trapping accident. In 1863, North was engaged by Colorado Governor John Evans to cajole the allied Cheyenne-Arapahos to attend a treaty council on the Arkansas River. Evans was later implicated in the Sand Creek Massacre, while North elevated himself to a medicine man of the Northern Arapaho. The Northern Arapaho never considered North to be a medicine man, but they welcomed his abilities on the battlefield and he became a legitimate war leader in the tribe. In the months proceeding his association with Evans, North led a party of Northern Arapahos in an attack on a mining camp near the mouth of the Powder River, in which ten prospectors were killed. North may have provided the authors of dime novels with the inspiration for the 'crazed white man' character who ends up living with Indians, the Indians duly interpreting his insanity to be 'medicine' – a popular stereotype in Hollywood Westerns.

19. The incident occurred on or around December 22, 1864, at the Denver Opera House.

20. Among the Northern Cheyenne, the Southern Cheyenne are called Heévaha-taneo'o, meaning 'Rope Person.' It is possible that this is a post-reservation term, a reference to the Southern Cheyennes being 'tied' to Oklahoma, or it could be derived from a traditional rope-making process employed by the Southern Cheyennes that is related to their abilities as horse catchers. Either way, it is likely that the narrator of the Hundred-Soldiers-Killed-Fight would have used the term, being as his recollections are set some years after the battle.

21. From southeast to northeast, the Four Sacred Persons are Essenetah'he, Sovota, Onxsovon and Notamota.

22. Near present-day Kaycee, Wyoming, at the confluence of the Powder River and the South Fork on July 7, 1864, a band of Northern Cheyennes approached the wagon train of A. A. Townsend and tensions rose when inquiries were made as to the whereabouts of an immigrant named Mills who had left the train to look for a cow. Townsend dispatched a search party and a fight then ensued between the Cheyennes and the search party. The Cheyennes, who in the main were members of the Kit Fox military society, numbered no more than twenty-five men, none of whom possessed firearms. Under the leadership of Last Bull, they besieged Townsend's train for some six hours before disengaging and then setting fire to the prairie. The immigrants later speculated that the Cheyennes were trying to "burn them into the river," when in actuality they were attempting to stop the immigrants, who were better armed and supplied, from pursuing them and finding their camps where ceremonies were being held. The Townsend fight was arguably the most significant engagement fought between immigrants and Indians on the Bozeman Trail.

23. Platte Bridge Station, later renamed Fort Caspar in honor of Lieutenant Caspar W. Collins. Hóxovoho'o means 'bridge' in Cheyenne, the literal translation being 'across-walking-thing.' In view of that, as a compromise between accuracy and literary style, throughout the Hundred-Soldiers-Killed-Fight account Platte Bridge is referred to as the 'walking-across-logs.'

24. 'Thunder wagon' or 'wagon gun' was often used to describe a cannon. At Platte Bridge Station the thunder wagon was a model 1841 twelve-pound mountain howitzer. Má'xe-ma'aetano'e, 'cannon,' translates to 'big-iron-gun.'

25. Sósoné'e – 'Shoshone.' Contrary to Western folklore, the Northern Cheyennes did not call the Shoshones 'Snakes' in the 1800s; that designation was reserved for the Shoshones' relatives, the Comanches, who are still known as the Se'senovotsé-taneo'o – 'Snake People.'

26. Voohéheve, Chief Morning Star, is more commonly known as Dull Knife. Morning Star's brother-in-law was a member of the Itésica band of Oglala Lakotas which, at the time, was led by Chief Red Cloud. As the name suggests, Dull Knife was a quip, but his brother-in-law's joke stuck and from then on, among the Oglala Lakotas, Chief Morning Star became Dull Knife.

27. Major Martin Anderson was in command at Platte Bridge Station, the 96-man garrison being comprised of the Eleventh Kansas Cavalry, Eleventh Ohio Cavalry, Third U.S. Volunteers, and several Shoshone scouts. By the morning of July 26, 1865, Anderson's command had increased to 119 officers and men, Captain Henry C. Bretney having arrived the night before. At approximately 7:30 A.M. Lieutenant Caspar W. Collins crossed Platte Bridge with 25 cavalrymen to escort Sergeant Amos Custard's approaching wagon train to the post. The Battle of Platte Bridge, July 26, 1865, began when Collins' men reached the waiting Cheyennes.

28. Lieutenant Caspar W. Collins was the officer shot in the head. Several stories exist in Cheyenne history about Collins' horse; Slow Bull took the horse, but such was its temperament that had it not been a fine-looking horse it would have been discarded.

29. It is believed that five of Collins' detail were killed and eight wounded. Under the command of Captain James Greer, the infantry, armed with Spencer repeating rifles, held Platte Bridge.

30. Allegedly, Lieutenant Caspar W. Collins spent much of the winter of 1863/64 with the Oglalas, at which time he supposedly became acquainted with Crazy Horse. Both Agnes Wright Spring and Mari Sandoz made reference to this in their respective works, *Caspar Collins . . .* and *Crazy Horse*, and Stephen Ambrose repeated it in *Crazy Horse and Custer*. Contemporary Oglala tribal historians believe Collins' interaction with the Oglalas has been exaggerated and that the manner in which his relationship with Crazy Horse is documented owes more to romanticism than fact.

31. In his youth Roman Nose was known as Bat. He was given the name Hook Nose as he rose to prominence, which Euro-Americans later recorded as Roman Nose.

32. The twenty-four soldiers were of the Eleventh Kansas Cavalry under the command of Sergeant Amos Custard. The wagon train consisted of five wagons, two of which were corralled. Custard and his men defended their position for approximately four hours before Roman Nose decided to end the siege by "emptying the soldiers' guns." None of Custard's detail survived.

33. In this context, to 'wipe their tears' meant that they wished to avenge the deaths of their friends and relatives, which on this occasion they did along the Platte River.

34. The Medicine Lodge is more commonly known as the Sun Dance, Hoxéhe-vohomo'ehestotse.

35. Stone Forehead is erroneously called 'Medicine Arrows' in a body of existing literature which primarily relates to the occasion on which he emptied ashes onto George Armstrong Custer's boots and warned him that if he ever made war upon the Cheyennes again he would be killed, which he duly was at the Little Bighorn. When the Cheyennes selected Stone Forehead to be their spokesman relative to the 1851 Fort Laramie Treaty, the commissioners recorded his name as Man-Who-Walks-with-His-Toes-Turned-Out.

36. Last Bull was well known for his scouting ability; for example, Last Bull warned of Colonel Joseph Reynolds' approach prior to his March 17, 1876, attack on Old Bear's camp on the Powder River. However, by then Last Bull's overbearing demeanor and aggressive behavior had diminished his credibility among all but the Kit Foxes and his warning was ignored.

37. Colonel James A. Sawyers' column for this government-sponsored wagon road expedition was comprised of Companies C and D, Fifth U.S. Volunteers, plus a 24-man detachment of First Dakota Cavalry, in total 143 troops. In addition, 53 civilian 'scouts' accompanied Sawyers' fifteen wagons, which were supplemented by

forty private wagons, and the Dakota Cavalry's twenty-five wagons.

38. The fight took place on Bone Pile Creek on August 15, 1865. The 'white-man buffalo,' vé'ho'e-otóvaao'o, are cattle.

39. William Bent was a prominent trader and later Indian Agent who established Bent's Old Fort and Bent's New Fort trade centers on the Arkansas River in present-day southeastern Colorado. Named Little White Man by Chief Yellow Wolf, William Bent married Owl Woman, daughter of White Thunder, who at the time was Keeper of the Sacred Arrows. William and Owl Woman had four children, two daughters and two sons, but she died while giving birth to Julia Bent in 1847. William then married Owl Woman's sister, Yellow Woman, who bore him another son, Charles. Of William's three sons, George and Charles eventually lived with their mothers' people, and George married Magpie, a niece of Chief Black Kettle, and somehow survived the Sand Creek Massacre. Chief Yellow Wolf was killed in the massacre. Yellow Woman was killed near the Bozeman Trail by Pawnee scouts under General Patrick E. Connor on August 16, 1865.

40. Among the Cheyenne, George Bent was known as Hóma'e, 'Beaver.' His nickname among the people was Tex. The literal translation of cowboy in Cheyenne is 'Texas white man.'

41. Óoetaneo'o, 'Crow-people' – 'Crows.'

42. Established on August 14, 1865, during General Patrick E. Connor's failed punitive Powder River Expedition, the then Fort Connor was renamed Fort Reno in honor of Major General Jesse L. Reno, who was killed while leading Union forces to victory in the Battle of South Mountain, September 14, 1862.

43. The Wolf Men, Ho'néhe-taneo'o, were the Pawnees under General Connor.

44. On August 29, 1865, General Patrick E. Connor's forces attacked Medicine Man's and Black Bear's village of Northern Arapahos on the Tongue River in the vicinity of present-day Ranchester, Wyoming. The Northern Arapahos launched a successful counterattack and drove Connor from the field before later recovering many of the ponies that Connor's Pawnee scouts had taken in the initial attack.

45. The Little Missouri was a traditional hunting site where, as its Cheyenne name suggests, antelope were harvested by driving them between two 'wings.' People concealed themselves aside the winged fences until the antelope were sufficiently close to the covered pit towards which the wings funneled them. Ordinarily, a spiritual leader who had been gifted with the power to hunt antelope in this way would conduct the appropriate ceremonies prior to the hunt.

46. Throughout this account of the Hundred-Soldiers-Killed-Fight, the Hunkpapa Lakota are referred to as 'northern Sioux.'

47. The Second Missouri Light Artillery, the Twelfth Missouri Cavalry, and the Sixteenth Kansas Cavalry were among the dual two-thousand-strong columns of General Patrick E. Connor's Powder River Expedition. These two columns were commanded by Colonel Nelson Cole and Lieutenant Colonel Samuel Walker, and in addition to a battery of howitzers the troops were armed with repeating Spencer carbines. Nevertheless, the Hunkpapas under Sitting Bull harried the columns, primarily Cole's, between September 1 and 5, 1865.

48. Both Cole's and Walker's columns struggled throughout the campaign, their difficulties exacerbated by a storm of icy rain and sleet on September 2 that left 225 of their already starving horses and mules dead.

49. Most agree that Roman Nose's Fight took place on September 5, 1865. Sitting Bull's Hunkpapas were also present for what amounted to several sporadic engagements.

50. Ané'kohomó'hestotse, 'pecking-thing' – 'fork.' White Bull, Roman Nose's spiritual adviser, instructed him never to eat any food that had touched metal. Unbeknownst to Roman Nose, before the Battle of Beecher Island, he ate food at a Lakota feast that had been prepared using a fork. He did not have the opportunity to undertake the necessary purification ceremonies before the battle and knew he would be killed. Roman Nose passed away on the morning of September 18, 1868, from a wound he had sustained in action the previous day at Beecher Island.

51. Throughout the Hundred-Soldiers-Killed-Fight account the Mniconju, Sihasapa, Itazipco, and Oohenunpa Lakota divisions are categorized as Greasy Foam River Sioux, meaning the Sioux from around the Missouri River, as the Cheyenne considered this to be the area from which they hailed. High-Back-Bone was Mniconju. The Missouri River, É'ometaa'e, is variously translated as 'greasy' or 'fatty' river, a designation that may be traced back to the first time the Cheyenne came to the Missouri, on which occasion it is said that the banks of the river were strewn with drowned buffalo. The buffalo, the river, and the subsequent cooking of the buffalo and the foam from the cooking pot are the elements melded together to form the name Greasy Foam River.

52. During the 1865 Powder River Expedition, Lieutenant Colonel Samuel Walker estimated that the combined Lakota and Cheyenne forces he encountered possessed no more than "four or five good muskets."

53. Between 1849 and 1850 the Cheyennes lost approximately 50 percent of their population to 'cramps,' cholera brought into Cheyenne territory by immigrants – more specifically, 'Forty-niners' on their way to the California goldfields. This dramatic and tragic loss devastated the traditional ten-band Cheyenne tribal structure.

54. The 1851 Fort Laramie Treaty, called the 'Big Issue' by the Cheyennes. 'Long Meadows' was the name given to the area around Horse Creek, Nebraska, where the treaty was signed.

55. Horse River is Horse Creek, where the 1851 treaty was negotiated. On occasion, the Laramie River was also known as Horse River among some Cheyennes; either way, both Horse Creek and the Laramie River empty into the North Platte (Moon Shell) River with Fort Laramie standing between them.

56. The preliminary negotiations for the 1866 Fort Laramie Treaty council were conducted by telegraph. The post commander, Colonel Henry Maynadier, and the participating chiefs gathered in the telegraph office at Fort Laramie while Superintendent of Indian Affairs Edward B. Taylor wired them from Omaha. The upshot was that the chiefs agreed to reconvene for face-to-face discussions on June 1. With Taylor presiding and Maynadier cheerleading, the Cut Nose party signed the unratified 1866 treaty on June 28.

57. Several accounts attempt to implicate Turkey Leg in the Plum Creek Massacre in Nebraska Territory on August 8, 1864, and the subsequent hardships endured by the captive immigrants Nancy Morton, Laura Roper, Danny Marble, Lucinda Eubanks and her two children. However, Turkey Leg is the victim of mistaken identity – it was three years after the Plum Creek Massacre, on August 6, 1867, west of Plum Creek Station, that a party of men from Turkey Leg's camp attacked and derailed a Union Pacific Railroad freight train. Wolf Tooth, a veteran of the Hundred-Soldiers-Killed-Fight, and later the Battle of the Little Bighorn, participated in this action. Eleven days later, again near Plum Creek Station, Turkey Leg was present when men from his camp engaged a detachment of forty Pawnee scouts under the command of Major Frank North. The Cheyennes were armed only with traditional weapons, while the Pawnees carried Spencer repeating carbines, and after a running fight the superior arms of the Pawnees prevailed. Seventeen Cheyennes were killed in action and three taken captive before they disengaged.

58. Hotóva'a – 'buffalo (bull)'; mo'éhe – 'elk.' Some two thousand immigrants, prospectors and freighters in twelve hundred wagons with accompanying livestock traveled along the Bozeman Trail in 1866.

59. Véhoné-ma'kaeta, 'chief-metal' – 'gold.'

60. This incident took place near Buffalo Gap in the Black Hills in early April 1866.

61. It was not uncommon for immigrant routes to be called 'holy' due to the treaty negotiators' insistence that those traveling upon them could not be touched, inferring that

when the treaty was signed the road itself had some form of power. This was interpreted literally by some, but with an amount of irony by others.

62. The Townsend Fight, July 7, 1864.

63. Wolves was a common name for scouts, and when news was to be reported it was generally preceded by a distant wolf howl, a signal that the scouts had information of importance. The wolf had many attributes that, in a sense, made the animal a mentor for those who were chosen to be scouts.

64. Cheyenne history records that scouts from Black Horse's band first sought to pass a message to Colonel Henry B. Carrington on Clear Creek near present-day Buffalo, Wyoming, but they were unsuccessful. In all probability the Colonel was unaware of this attempt.

65. The Black Horse–Morning Star party made contact with Colonel Carrington on July 14. After apprehending nine deserters from Carrington's command, with the assistance of French Pete, Black Horse pressed one of the deserters into service as a messenger. Joe Donaldson, a teamster, was sent back to Piney Creek with a message for Carrington requesting he dispatch his black-white man with his reply. The black-white man was Carrington's interpreter, Jack Stead, who the Cheyennes also knew as Buffalo Cow Teat. Although it has never been confirmed, Stead himself was likely indigenous, possibly belonging to a Romany tribe in Britain before taking to sea and ending up in the Rockies. Stead formed a trade association with the Pawnees, raised the ire of the Lakotas, and then managed to marry a Cheyenne woman with whom he was seen at Fort Laramie – hence the Cheyennes' familiarity with him.

66. Colonel Carrington was the Little White Chief, and the meeting occurred on July 16, 1866, at the site of Fort Phil Kearny.

67. The talking paper was Carrington's written instruction to "military officers, soldiers and emigrants" that the bearer of the note "must be treated kindly." The meat from the sharp-nose-dog (eskoséesé-hotame – 'pig') was pork, the sweet-water (ve'kee-mahpe) was sugar and the pounded-fine-powder (penoheo'o) was flour.

68. Mowing machines and construction tools.

69. The regimental band.

70. Crow Standing Off Creek was named after a battle in 1820 between a party of approximately thirty Cheyennes and a larger force of Crows. The fight lasted for two days before the Crows prevailed, the Cheyennes having 'stood off the Crows.' In some accounts the Cheyennes killed were Crazy Dogs, in others they are identified as Elk Horn Scrapers. Two scouts and one combatant are thought to have survived. The Crows lost in excess of twenty men.

71. Jim Beckwourth was among the worst of these. Beckwourth was despised not only for acting as a guide for Colonel John Chivington at Sand Creek, but because of the carnage he caused among the Cheyennes when he introduced alcohol to trade conferences in order to rob the Cheyennes of hard-earned robes. Beckwourth boasted of this practice in his autobiography.

72. The prominent Oglala leader here referred to as Black Twin was actually called Holy Bald Eagle, but Black Twin has been recorded so many times that it is used here to avoid confusion. Black Twin had a twin brother, unimaginatively referred to as White Twin in most published sources, but whose name was Holy Buffalo. Johnson Holy Rock is a grandson of the twins, both of whom played a prominent part in closing the Bozeman Trail (see Chapman We, The People). The incident with the Oglalas and Black Horse et al. occurred on the evening of July 16, 1866. At the same time, Pierre Gazeau, a.k.a. 'French Pete,' was questioned by the Oglalas who were seeking intelligence on Colonel Carrington and his command. Red Cloud led the interrogation and was unconvinced by Gazeau's responses. Until then the Lakotas had tolerated Gazeau as, due to his marriage to a Lakota woman, he was considered by some to be a relative. However, after some debate the Lakotas judged him to be guilty of perfidy and on July 17 killed him and all in his party with the exception of his wife and children.

73. Survey crews for the Kansas Pacific Railroad were active by the summer of 1866. Tall Bull's Dog Soldiers were vehemently opposed to the construction of this railroad through the heart of traditional Tsetsehésestahase hunting grounds.

74. The so-called Hang-Around-the-Forts. At Fort Laramie, these people were predominantly from Oglala and Brulé Lakota bands. Often referred to as Loafers, they were the first Lakotas to fall victim to the pernicious cycle of dependency that was fostered by the agency system – and subsequently the reservation system – promulgated by the U.S. government. The Wagluhke, or 'Loafers,' eventually became a recognized band among the Oglala Sioux. 'Ordinary-people,' xamáa-vo'estaneo'o, means 'Indian.'

75. Morning Star signed the 1866 Fort Laramie Treaty on October 11. The treaty was never ratified.

76. The incident occurred on September 27, 1866.

77. Óxaxová-maheo'o, 'cut-open-house' – 'sawmill.'

78. Jim Beckwourth.

79. Jim Bridger guided General Patrick E. Connor's forces to the Arapaho village on Tongue River, August 29, 1865.

80. Chivington had business interests at Fort Laramie in the form of contracts with the quartermaster and sutler's store.

81. Maahé-o'hé'e – 'Arrow Creek (Pryor Creek).' The Arapaho chief of Crow descent was Night Horse, and the battle took place circa 1861.

82. Otaasé-taneo'o – 'Nez Perce (Pierced-nose-person).'

83. Their sister hung herself and her body was found near present-day Birney, Montana.

84. Crazy Horse's war pony was badly wounded in the engagement of December 6, 1866. The pony died soon after, which is why Crazy Horse rode his brother's fastest pony in the Hundred-Soldiers-Killed-Fight. Biologically, Little Hawk was Crazy Horse's half-brother.

85. At 1 P.M. on December 6, 1866, a party of Lakotas attacked a wood train approximately four miles west of Fort Phil Kearny. Colonel Carrington ordered Captain William J. Fetterman to relieve the wood train and to drive the Lakotas over Piney Creek where, theoretically, between the Sullivant Hills and Lodge Trail Ridge, the Lakotas would be intercepted by Carrington's men, along with Lieutenant George W. Grummond. The officers were unaware of the presence of a larger force of Oglala and Mniconju Lakotas, aided by about ten Northern Arapahos, who were concealed some five miles distant over Lodge Trail Ridge, waiting in the broken ravines for the decoy party to bring the troops to the vicinity of the Bozeman Trail. According to Fetterman he "took command of the cavalry numbering about thirty men" with Lieutenant Horatio Bingham, Second U.S. Cavalry. Shortly thereafter Captain Fred Brown and Lieutenant Alexander Wands, Eighteenth U.S. Infantry, "and a couple of mounted Infantry" joined Fetterman. Carrington stated that he had "twenty one mounted infantry, their orderlies and Lieutenant Grummond." All appeared to be going to plan until, as Fetterman described it, after a pursuit of five miles "in a valley through which passes the 'Bighorn Road' the Indians offered us battle. In the most unaccountable manner the cavalry turned and commenced a retreat." Lieutenant Bingham started his cavalrymen back towards the fort, in the direction from which Colonel Carrington was approaching. Bingham was soon joined by Lieutenant Grummond who, before the Colonel's men had completed their descent of Lodge Trail Ridge, had advanced and then moved forward at a gallop in the direction of four Lakotas on the Bozeman Trail. "I moved rapidly forward on the Big Horn road," wrote Grummond, "accompanied by Lieutenant H.S. Bingham and followed by Sergeant G.R. Bowers and two men of my command. . . . About forty Indians were in our front and retreating rapidly before us." The waiting Lakotas allowed Bingham and Grummond to pass through their lines, anticipating that the other troops would soon follow, whereupon the attack could be executed. However, both Fetterman's and Carrington's remaining men had already been engaged and they skirmished with separate parties of Lakotas before Carrington

advanced in sight of Fetterman and the Lakotas besieging the captain scattered. Although the Lakotas' primary decoy and ambush plan failed, had it not been for Carrington coming into view it is likely that Fetterman and his men would not have survived, which, consequently, would have left the colonel similarly vulnerable. But it was Grummond who reported what was arguably the most significant encounter of the day: "About two miles from where I left the Colonel we overtook one Indian; Lieut. Bingham with his revolver wounded his horse; the Indian then jumped off, turned to the right towards some high bluffs about two miles off running very fast. Lieut. Bingham firing his last shot at him (and I having no weapon but my sword) we drew our swords and gave chase. We came up to him after a run of about one and a half miles and tried to cut him down but he was so active dodging our blows and running under our horses it was no easy matter. While there engaged Lieut. Bingham raised his head and looked around and cried out to me 'We are surrounded.'" Grummond and Bingham had fallen for the decoy ploy. Grummond survived but Bingham and Bowers didn't. Oglala historians have identified the Indian Grummond followed, the one he tried to "cut down" but couldn't because he "was so active dodging our blows and running under our horses." The Indian was Crazy Horse. Among the Oglalas there was nobody more distinctive in appearance than Crazy Horse, which may go some way towards explaining Lieutenant Grummond's reaction when he saw him again on December 21, 1866.

86. Blue Feather's grandson, William Tall Bull, was until his passing 'living history' on the Northern Cheyenne Reservation. William Tall Bull made an immense contribution to the students who attended his programs at Dull Knife Memorial College, and one of his greatest passions was that future generations of Cheyennes would know the authentic history, culture and remarkable heritage of the Cheyenne people. Bill Tall Bull was generous with his time and knowledge, a fine teacher and an honorable man.

87. The antelope horn imbued the pony with the speed and agility of the antelope.

88. Fort Rankin and Julesburg on the South Platte. Platte Bridge Station on the North Platte.

89. The term 'Iron Bellies' described both the Spanish and, after independence, Mexicans, and was a reference to the body armor worn by soldiers of both armies. The armor was sought after by some Cheyennes; the great chief Alights on the Cloud was known for his 'iron shirt.' In the context of this piece, the narrator is emphasizing how few guns the Cheyennes had, and that those they did possess were outdated flintlock or percussion trade muskets. By 1866 the muskets were supplemented with a few six-shot revolvers, though acquiring appropriate ammunition for the Colts and Remingtons was a major problem. Archeological fieldwork at the Fetterman battle site indicates that the allied Lakota-Cheyenne-Arapaho force used thirty-eight different firearms in the engagement (see *Reflections* – Robert Wilson).

90. See note 45.

91. Vo'kome-ma'kaeta, 'white-metal' – 'silver.'

92. On December 19, 1866, the Oglala and Mniconju Lakotas made another attempt to draw troops from Fort Phil Kearny beyond Lodge Trail Ridge and into an ambush. The Lakotas' tactics were similar to those employed on December 6: a party attacked the wood train and disengaged when the troops appeared, at which time a smaller group made their presence known and attempted to decoy the troops. The plan met with less success than on December 6; Colonel Carrington sent Captain James Powell to relieve the wood train with orders to "heed the lessons of the 6th. Do not pursue Indians across Lodge Trail Ridge." Powell followed the Colonel's orders and achieved the objective without incident.

93. His Crazy Mule, the Mniconju Lakota winkté, is often confused with the Cheyenne spiritual leader Crazy Mule. The identity and tribal affiliation of the winkté/hé'e-ma'haeso remains a point of conjecture among tribal historians, but the body of evidence suggests that this person was the Mniconju Lakota, His Crazy Mule. Had the individual been Northern Cheyenne, it would have

been Pipe Woman, and it is known that it was not. Pipe Woman dressed like an old man, and when he died in 1868 he was the last hé'e-ma'haeso among the Northern Cheyenne.

94. Hé'e-ma'haeso, literally meaning 'woman-old man', often appears as 'Héemaneh' in existing literature. 'Winkté' is a comparative Lakota designation.

95. This is why the battle is remembered by some as the 'One-Hundred-in-the-Hands.' Black Shield, the Mniconju Lakota chief, was also a Shirt Wearer at the time of the Hundred-Soldiers-Killed-Fight. Although he is more commonly known as Iron Plume, Iron Shield or American Horse, virtually every other account of the Fetterman Fight refers to him as Black Shield so, to avoid confusion, that is the name used here. Black Shield was mortally wounded at Slim Buttes on September 9, 1876, from where testimony exists as to his fortitude. After Captain Anson Mills' attack at Slim Buttes, Black Shield apparently sat through the night with one arm across his belly to stop his entrails from falling into his lap; it is said that he never once complained or gave any indication that he was in pain. Short Buffalo, a brother of He Dog and a fellow Oglala veteran of the Fetterman Fight and the Battle of the Little Bighorn, said Slim Buttes became known as The-Fight-Where-We-Lost-the-Black-Hills. The Brulé Lakota Ghost Dance advocate, Short Bull, was also on Fetterman Ridge.

96. During the Special Investigating Commission's inquiry into the Hundred-Soldiers-Killed-Fight – then referred to as the Fetterman Massacre or Fetterman Disaster – Mitch Boyer stated that Red Horn was the leader of the Hunkpapas he believed participated in the fight. Isaac Dog Eagle, a grandson of Sitting Bull's, suggests that it was not Red Horn but the younger Bear's Rib who led the few Hunkpapas that fought in the battle. Bear's Rib's band included several Yanktonais among whom Red Horn was a common name, hence the confusion – added to which there was a Hunkpapa leader on the Missouri who, for a period of time, was known to some by the name Red Horn. General William S. Harney had attempted to appoint Bear's Rib's father 'Chief of the Hunkpapas' during his questionable treaty conference with the Lakotas of the Missouri at Fort Pierre in March 1856. Chief Bear's Rib was killed by two Lakotas, Mouse and One-Who-Limps, at Fort Pierre on June 6, 1862, the two being representative of the popular feeling at the time that by his adherence to the wishes of the whites, Bear's Rib was placing the Lakotas in jeopardy. After his slaying, his son carried his name and, for the majority of his tenure, his philosophy, with the exception of one brief interlude: the Hundred-Soldiers-Killed-Fight. In 1866, Bear's Rib was eclipsed among the Hunkpapas by the likes of Sitting Bull, Four Horns, Black Moon, Gall et al., and these men were then engaged in a parallel campaign to that being waged on the Bozeman Trail, their struggle being against forts Buford, Stevenson and Rice along the Missouri. Therefore, Bear's Rib was unable to play a prominent role on the Missouri and, possibly under pressure to save face, turned his attention to the Powder River country in the fall of 1866.

97. A flintlock trade musket.

98. Oglala, Northern Arapaho, and Northern Cheyenne historians consulted for this project estimate the combined force that participated in the Hundred-Soldiers-Killed-Fight at approximately 850 men: six hundred Lakotas, two hundred Cheyennes, and fifty Northern Arapahos. In his July 27, 1867, testimony to the Special Investigating Committee, Mitch Boyer claimed "there were 1800 Indians on the ground *but only half of them engaged in the fight*." The tribal historians consulted for this project state that this 850-man force was larger than that which fought at the Rosebud on June 17, 1876, and was of a comparative size to that which defeated Lieutenant Colonel George A. Custer at the Little Bighorn eight days later. All concurred that the main winter camp on Tongue River was far larger than that at the Little Bighorn, estimates for the latter – supported by as yet unpublished oral history accounts – being in accord with the conclusions drawn by Greg Michno in *Lakota Noon*, much of which was based upon previously published Lakota and Cheyenne accounts of the Battle of the Little Bighorn.

99. Vé'ho'é-maahe, 'white man arrow' – 'cartridges/powder/ball.'

100. General Nelson A. Miles began making peace overtures towards the Cheyennes in February 1877, following the Battle of Tongue River. It is said that after the battle, due to their impoverished condition, several Cheyennes thought it was time to consider surrendering to Miles. A party of Cheyennes that became known as Two Moons' band concluded their surrender in April 1877. In actuality Two Moons was not the leader of this group; Crazy Head and Old Wolf were. Although the majority of the Elk Horn Scrapers were opposed to surrendering to Miles, White Bull and his family accompanied this group. White Bull became the first man among them to enlist as a scout for General Miles, followed by Brave Wolf and twenty-eight others. On May 7, 1877, White Bull played a prominent role in Miles' battle with Lame Deer's Mniconju Lakotas on Muddy Creek. Many are of the opinion that had these men not acted as scouts for Miles, the Northern Cheyennes would not have secured their reservation on the Tongue and Rosebud.

101. A chief should embody the qualities of the sun, and 'like the sun' was commonly used to describe respected chiefs.

102. Little Wolf probably acquired the saber in an engagement along the Platte River, post-1851; these skirmishes were in response to violations of the 1851 Fort Laramie Treaty. Little Wolf gave his nephew, Young (Laban) Little Wolf, both his war bonnet and saber after Young Little Wolf had distinguished himself in battle against the Shoshones and white men. Young Little Wolf was a veteran of the Wagon Box and Little Bighorn battles. (See *Reflections* – Douglas and Donna Spotted Eagle, for discussion of the Sweet Medicine Chiefs' Bundle).

103. The attack on the wood train directed by High-Back-Bone began at approximately 11 A.M. on December 21, 1866. Both the Cheyennes and Lakotas referred to the general area of the pinery, and the road back and forth to the fort, as Pine Woods.

104. "A case-shot dismounted one," wrote Colonel Carrington in his post-Hundred-Soldiers-Killed-Fight report, referring to the howitzer fire directed at the decoys, the Kit Foxes, and the wolves whom he had spotted across Big Piney Creek.

105. A capote: a long, hooded coat made from a trade blanket.

106. The pony Crazy Horse rode in the battle was a bay – 'e-vo'neova.'

107. Following his success on December 19, Colonel Carrington had intended to give Captain James Powell command of the relief column, but he acquiesced to Brevet Lieutenant Colonel William J. Fetterman's request for the duty, Fetterman having cited superiority of rank over Powell. In his report of January 3, 1867, Carrington stated that he gave Fetterman "the men of his own company that were for duty and a portion of Company C, 2nd Battalion, Eighteenth U.S. Infantry. Lieutenant G.W. Grummond, who had commanded the mounted infantry requested to take out the cavalry. He did so." The Colonel continued, "My instructions were therefore explicit. I knew the ambition of each to win honor. . . . Hence my instructions to Brevet Lieutenant-Colonel Fetterman: Support the wood train, relieve it, and report to me. Do not engage or pursue Indians at its expense. Under no circumstances pursue over Lodge Trail Ridge. To Lieutenant Grummond I gave orders to 'report to Brevet Lieutenant-Colonel Fetterman, implicitly obey orders, and not leave him.' Before the command left I instructed Lieutenant A.H. Wands, my regimental quartermaster and acting adjutant, to repeat these orders. He did so. Fearing still that the spirit of ambition might override prudence, as my refusal to permit 60 mounted men and 40 citizens to go for several days down Tongue River Valley after villages had been unfavorably regarded by Brevet Lieutenant-Colonel Fetterman and Captain Brown, I crossed the parade, and from a sentry platform halted the cavalry and again repeated my precise orders." Fetterman's command consisted of eighty men, including two civilians, Isaac Fisher and James Wheatley, and Fetterman's cohort, Captain Fred Brown, who, apparently desperate to "bring in the scalp of Red Cloud," went, according to the Colonel, "without my consent or knowledge." Brown rode to his death on a pony borrowed from the Colonel's son. "With eighty men, I can ride through the entire Sioux Nation" is the quote most often attributed to Fetterman. Ironically, Fetterman's nemesis, Colonel Carrington, played a part in his fallen officer's widely repeated boast; in his speech at the 1908 dedication of the battlefield monument, Carrington specified "eighty men" as the number Fetterman thought he needed. The Colonel's second wife, Francis Grummond Carrington, repeated the "eighty men" assertion in *My Army Life*, although it seems far more likely that the Colonel's first wife, Margaret, came closer to quoting Fetterman in *Absaraka*. Apparently, after only two days at Fort Phil Kearny, Fetterman expressed the opinion that "a company of regulars could whip a thousand, and a regiment could whip the whole array of hostile tribes." In a letter dated July 30, 1866, Colonel Carrington informed General Litchfield that, under the circumstances that then prevailed, the effective strength of a company at Fort Phil Kearny was eighty men.

108. To be 'talked about' was to be ridiculed and shamed as a coward.

109. Lieutenant George W. Grummond is described as the 'pony soldier on the white horse' throughout this account of the Hundred-Soldiers-Killed-Fight.

110. They were moving north on the Bozeman Trail, passing where the monument now stands. The 'land shaped like the blade of a knife' is often referred to as 'massacre ridge.'

111. The infantry were dressed in greatcoats.

112. The cavalry were armed with seven-shot Spencer repeating carbines (Model 1860 .52 caliber or Model 1865 .50 caliber. The infantry and mounted infantry carried Springfield muzzle-loaders (Model 1863 rifle-musket .58 caliber).

113. Fire Thunder, then only a teenager, was in the camp of Big Road when the battle occurred. Fire Thunder shared a comprehensive account of the Hundred-Soldiers-Killed-Fight with other Oglalas of the Itésica band in the proceeding years. Fire Thunder recollected the decapitation of the young Oglala boy, he himself having been in the opening exchanges of the battle in the same area. Fire Thunder became a friend of the celebrated Oglala holy man, Black Elk. Black Elk was only three years old at the time of the Fetterman Fight, but his father, who then also carried the name Black Elk, gained a great deal of praise and honor for his bravery in the battle. Black Elk Sr. received a severe leg wound in the fight, an injury that left him partially crippled for the rest of his life. In the immediate aftermath of the Fetterman Fight, when military personnel were attempting to ascertain who participated in the battle, Black Elk, Sr. was often called 'Black Leg' by those who relayed the story of the fight. The name Black Leg thus become synonymous with the battle due to a combination of the reference to the leg wound Black Elk Sr. sustained, plus errors in translation and general misinterpretation.

114. This man was probably Eats-Meat, a Mniconju Lakota. Stanley Vestal's interviews with White Bull (Sitting Bull's nephew, not the Cheyenne man also known as Ice) have been widely quoted and provide valuable insights into the battle from a Mniconju Lakota perspective. Eats-Meat is one of the men mentioned in Vestal's materials. A significant proportion of what White Bull shared with Vestal is corroborated herein – independently – by those who contributed to the Hundred-Soldiers-Killed-Fight account. Low Dog, one of the principal Lakota combatants in the Wheatley/Fisher sector, was part Northern Cheyenne. A veteran of several battles, including the Little Bighorn, at the time of the Hundred-Soldiers-Killed-Fight he was approximately nineteen years old.

115. Wheatley and Fisher were using sixteen-shot Henry repeating rifles.

116. Pilot Hill.

117. "At 12 o'clock firing was heard towards Peno Creek, beyond Lodge Trail Ridge. A few shots were followed by constant shots, not to be counted. Captain Ten Eyck was immediately dispatched with infantry and the remaining cavalry, and two wagons, and orders to join Colonel Fetterman at all hazards," reported Colonel Carrington. Fetterman had left the post at approximately 11:15 A.M. and Grummond followed around 11:30 A.M.

In the Hundred-Soldiers-Killed-Fight account, "the sun must have been going to the center when the shooting came back" indicates that it was approaching noon when the decoys appeared with the troops; and "the sun was not much past the center" when the fighting ceased suggests the battle did not last very long, probably between thirty and forty minutes. "About noon it was known from the firing that a desperate battle was going on in the valley beyond the ridge," wrote Ten Eyck. "The Colonel at once sent me with a relieving party of about 75 men, with his own mounted orderly. We moved as rapidly as possible in the direction of the firing, following the road, the route over the mountains being almost inaccessible for men on foot. The firing ceased shortly after we left the post and was not heard again."

118. Eli S. Ricker stated that American Horse visited him in August 1906, at which time he commenced interviewing him. Ricker subsequently presented an account of the Fetterman Fight that is attributed to American Horse, in which American Horse apparently claimed to have killed Captain Fetterman. Ricker's transcript then became the basis for the popularly held belief that American Horse did indeed kill Fetterman, the theory having been given credence by its appearance in Hebard and Brininstool, *The Bozeman Trail*, and several publications since. Each publication has supported and contributed to the theory's near acceptance as fact, not unlike the momentum that carried the yarn about Rain-in-the-Face and Tom Custer at the Battle of the Little Bighorn, and countless other tales from Custer Hill. But reevaluation and closer scrutiny reveals questions as to the reliability of the Ricker/American Horse claim: There were issues of translation from Lakota to English, and issues of interpretation. Ricker interspersed shorthand throughout his notes, some portions of which are so indecipherable that 'best guesses' have been inserted. The passage attributed to American Horse pertaining to the Fetterman Fight includes significant discrepancies when analyzed alongside other, corroborated accounts – both Indian and military – of December 21, 1866. For example, Ricker has American Horse claiming that the decoy party consisted of "American H. and 9 other Oglala warriors"; that the soldiers were trapped by "thousands of Indians"; and that "in one hour and a half every soldier was killed." All of these statements are inaccurate, and that alone is enough to create reasonable doubt. Some are of the opinion that American Horse identified Fetterman by recounting the insignia on the officer's uniform, but the interview was conducted forty years after the battle, and American Horse had been through incredible upheaval and trauma in the interim and was an elderly man in 1906. The errors noted previously do not indicate that American Horse's memory was unaffected by time and circumstance. And then there is the 'smoking gun,' where Ricker's text reads "American Horse himself ran his horse at full speed directly on to Col. Fetterman knocking him down! He then jumped down upon him and killed the Colonel with his knife." On December 21, 1866, the slopes leading up to the rocks where Fetterman and his men were killed were, by all other accounts, hard and icy, and according to White Bull "no place for horsemanship" – three of the four being sufficiently steep when the ground is good to make running a horse at full speed into the rocks difficult. Riding a horse among the large rocks where the troops were gathered would have been quite a feat at the best of times, let alone when it was icy and when, as corroborated oral history accounts clearly state, Fetterman's troops were overrun by men on foot. So mounted, not only were there the icy conditions, the slopes and large rocks to negotiate, there were also masses of men on foot to get through, past or over. American Horse was also mounted on a pony that would have been played out, having been ridden hard to and from the fort in the decoy phase, a distance of some eight to ten miles. Oral history accounts identify Big Nose as the only decoy who changed mounts, the other decoys, including Crazy Horse, all engaging in the battle around the Wheatley/Fisher area and Cavalry Knob, some distance north of where Fetterman's body was found. That Fetterman was found with his throat cut, the wound Assistant Surgeon Horton identified as the cause of death, is not particularly persuasive in terms of validating Ricker's American Horse transcript – the Sioux were often referred to as 'cut-throat Indians' or 'throat cutters,' a reference to the practice of leaving such a mark on a dead enemy; the sign used by many to identify the Sioux in sign language involves a throat-cutting motion. It could be argued that it would have been more surprising had American Horse not recalled cutting an adversaries throat, whoever it was. In *Fifty Years on the Old Frontier*, James H. Cook contends that Red Cloud confirmed that American Horse killed Fetterman, but one of Red Cloud's grandsons, Alfred Red Cloud, denies his grandfather gave any such confirmation and asserts that Red Cloud family history makes no mention of American Horse killing Fetterman (American Horse married into the Red Cloud family). However, Alfred states that Red Cloud family history does support the notion that American Horse did kill an officer in the battle, but that this happened before Fetterman and the troops in the rocks (where the monument now stands) were killed. The incident occurred where, as previously stated, all of the decoys who were not debilitated by injury engaged in the fight; and the officer that American Horse killed was the leader of the cavalry – the man who nearly reached the creek and then fought a rearguard back up the hillside. In Ricker's text, American Horse recollects "One of the Indians who was killed, having a very brave heart, succeeded in riding into the midst of the soldiers shooting right and left." The two incidents most commonly cited in oral history accounts that would support this are the charge of Eats-Meat into the Wheatley/Fisher group, and Big Nose's charge into the dismounted cavalry, both of which occurred at the opposite end of the field to where Fetterman died, nearer to the vicinity of Grummond's demise. In *The Fetterman Massacre*, Brown writes that when Carrington found Grummond's body "the lieutenant's head was almost severed from his body." So it is documented that both Fetterman and Grummond sustained similar lacerations to the throat. Allowing for the fact that on December 21, 1866, American Horse would not have known that Captain Fetterman was a breveted lieutenant colonel, or that Grummond was a lieutenant, and therefore would not have used either 'colonel' or 'lieutenant' in any statement about either officer, Ricker wrote that American Horse "then jumped down upon him and killed the Colonel with his knife." The so-called 'Fetterman Disaster Club,' on display at Agate Fossil Beds National Monument, should probably be renamed the 'Grummond Disaster Club.' Had the traces of blood and hair that were said to be on that club *actually still been on it* – as some have claimed – then it is possible that DNA evidence could have settled the issue. However, anybody who has seen the Fetterman Disaster Club would be hard-pressed to find anything on it. The portion of the Ricker/American Horse narrative that appears on page 93 was selected because those extracts are supported by other, independent accounts.

119. Oglala history supports the testimony of Assistant Surgeon Samuel Horton who, on July 25, 1867, concluded that Grummond's head had been smashed with a club "and his legs were slightly scorched by fire." Horton was post surgeon at Fort Phil Kearny at the time of the battle.

120. Probably Sergeant James Baker, Company C, Second U.S. Cavalry.

121. This was Sitting Bull's nephew, White Bull. White Bull was a Mniconju Lakota, at that time known as Big-in-the-Center, having previously been called Bull-Standing-with-Cow. White Bull was a veteran of not only this battle, but later the Battle of the Rosebud and the Battle of the Little Bighorn. He should not be confused with the Northern Cheyenne holy man, White Bull, who is mentioned several times in the Hundred-Soldiers-Killed-Fight account and accompanying notes. In other published works, White Bull the Northern Cheyenne holy man is sometimes referred to as Ice. The Northern Cheyenne holy man's son, Noisy Walking, was fatally wounded at the Battle of the Little Bighorn, the teenager being hit in close proximity to where Lame White Man was killed.

122. The accounts of White Elk and Little Wolf, shared with George Bird Grinnell and George Bent respectively, at first appear to be contradictory in regards to the horse Big Nose rode. However, Cheyenne historians consulted for this project agree that there is no contradiction as Big Nose was the only decoy who is known to have

changed mounts during the battle. He rode to the fort and back on the black horse, then changed mounts and rode Little Wolf's white horse on the battlefield. White Elk said the black horse survived, which it did, and Little Wolf said his white horse was killed, which it was. It seems unlikely that Little Wolf would not have accurately recounted the details of his brother's death, and in the process of doing so there would have been few language barriers between Little Wolf and George Bent as both were Cheyenne speakers, the differences in dialect not being sufficient to result in significant misinterpretation.

123. These two men were probably Bugler Adolph Metzger, Company C, Second U.S. Cavalry, and Captain Fred Brown, Eighteenth U.S. Infantry. "A soldier with a horn (Metzger, with his bugle) went galloping down the wagon road on a gray horse and behind him was a soldier who had an upside down head (Brown was bald) who was hanging on to him." This observation, preserved in oral history, correlates with a scenario outlined by Deanna Umbach Kordik in *Portraits of Fort Phil Kearny*. Brown had been fighting in the Wheatley/Fisher area but his body was found with Fetterman. Men from Ten Eyck's detail, those who first saw the troops' bodies, suggested that the bugler was found with Fetterman and Brown, but some historians believe that Metzger was found near the Wheatley/Fisher area.

124. Little Horse fought at a distance of twenty to forty feet from the troops. Although not widely credited, Little Horse also had a prominent role in the Battle of the Little Bighorn, fighting on Custer Hill when the so-called 'Last Stand' ended. Oral history testimony indicates that Little Horse was the likely slayer of Tom Custer.

125. It is said that John Stands-in-Timber explained this many times. Stands in Timber covered the topic in his book with Margot Liberty, *Cheyenne Memories*.

126. Where the monument is now located.

127. Lame White Man was killed in action June 25, 1876, in the Battle of the Little Bighorn. In narratives relating to the Hundred-Soldiers-Killed-Fight and the Battle of the Little Bighorn, Lame White Man is identified by no fewer than nine other names: Bearded Man, Black Body, Dull Knife, Moustache, Mad Hearted Wolf, Mad Wolf, Rabid Wolf, Walking White Man and White Man Cripple. Lame White Man was John Stands-in-Timber's grandfather, and is the great-grandfather of Elva Stands-in-Timber.

128. "Fetterman and Brown had each a revolver shot in the left temple. As Brown always declared that he would reserve a shot for himself as a last resort, so I am convinced that these two brave men fell each by the other's hand," wrote Colonel Carrington in his official report of the battle, dated January 3, 1867. Carrington's wife at Fort Phil Kearny, Margaret, gave a similar description in her book *Absaraka*. The majority of the Colonel's report seems to be accepted as being accurate, other than in regards to Fetterman's death. Debate has ensued since as to how Fetterman died, and whether or not he obliged Brown, or Brown killed himself. There exists the previously examined Ricker/American Horse interview that some choose to believe, but oral history accounts that correlate with each other when compared, unequivocally state that some soldiers in the location where Fetterman and Brown were found did shoot each other – or at least attempted to – but that the number did not exceed five or six. In his report Carrington said Horton was of the opinion that out of the entire command "not more than six were killed by balls." In his July 25, 1867, testimony, Assistant Surgeon Samuel Horton said Brown's body showed "a hole made in his left temple by a small pistol ball, the latter most probably caused his death." Few if any Cheyennes or Northern Arapahos in the battle carried such a firearm, though some Lakotas did, but it seems unlikely that such a precise wound would have resulted from an enemy combatant in the heat of such a battle. If Brown had killed himself, the likelihood is that the bullet hole would have been in his right temple, unless he was left-handed. Of Fetterman's injuries, Assistant Surgeon Horton stated his "body showed his thorax to have been cut crosswise with a knife, deep into the viscera; his throat and entire neck were cut to the cervical spine, all around. I believe that mutilation caused his death." Horton does not mention any bullet wounds to either of Fetterman's temples, but neither does he categorically

state that such a wound did not exist. That Fetterman's throat was cut is hardly a matter for dispute, but, medical science being what it was in 1866, it is unlikely that Horton could have proved that the wound to Fetterman's throat had not been inflicted *after* death. It is reasonable to assume that Colonel Carrington saw Fetterman's and Brown's bodies, but, as gruesome as they must have been, is it reasonable to conclude that he would make such an error when it related to his officers, or that he fabricated his report? If he had wanted to discredit these men it seems doubtful that he would have eulogized them, which he did on occasion. The colonel certainly attempted to vindicate himself in the months and years following the battle, including what some might consider to be creative additions to Frances's *My Army Life* and his 1908 memorial dedication speech. So did "these two brave men fall each by the other's hand"? Or was it a calculated misrepresentation? Or was it a simple error on the colonel's part? Assistant Surgeon Horton said the bodies made such a "terrible sight" they would "never be forgotten by those who saw them." So could the Colonel really have forgotten the details of what he saw? If it was possible, maybe the only way to definitively end the debate would be to exhume Fetterman's and Brown's bodies and to let contemporary forensic science provide the answers.

129. Bugler Adolph Metzger and Sergeant James Baker were both covered with buffalo calfskin capes after the battle in recognition of their valor. It is widely accepted that Metzger fought to the end armed only with his bugle.

130. It is possible that the soldier with the stripes described here is either Corporal Kelly or Corporal Horrigan, both of Company C, Second U.S. Cavalry.

131. In his report of January 3, 1867, Colonel Carrington listed the mutilations, from "eyes torn out" to "entrails taken out and exposed" to "punctures upon every sensitive part of the body, even to the soles of the feet and palms of the hand." Assistant Surgeon Samuel Horton wrote "every man was stripped of all his clothing, but with few exceptions, when bloody stockings remained on their feet. All the bodies were more or less mutilated." Years later, after learning the purpose of the mutilations, Carrington concluded "the key to the mutilations were startling and impressive. Their idea of the spirit land is that it is a physical paradise; but we enter upon its mysteries just as in the condition we hold when we die."

132. Fort Phil Kearny was torched in 1868 as the Hard Face Moon gave way to the Big Hard Face Moon. At the Hayfield Fight, August 1, 1867, near Fort C.F. Smith, Crazy Mule led the Cheyennes and Bob North led the Arapahos. Cheyenne oral history does not correlate at all with the military reports in regards to the casualties sustained by the Cheyennes. It is recalled that only one Cheyenne died from wounds sustained in the fight and that the most significant thing that occurred was Crazy Mule receiving a minor bullet wound to his neck, after which people lost faith in his bulletproof power. At the Wagon Box Fight the following day, White Bull led forty Cheyennes, mostly young men like Young Little Wolf and Wolf Chief. The only Cheyenne killed in the Wagon Box engagement was Sun's Road.

133. 1868.

134. Upon the death of Half Bear it was felt that his son, Coal Bear, was too young for such a responsibility, although it had been agreed that he should become the Keeper. Broken Dish was temporarily given the responsibilities of Keeper, but, when the military societies deemed it time for him to relinquish Ésevone so that Coal Bear could become Keeper, Broken Dish's youngest wife, Standing Woman, and to some degree Broken Dish himself, were reluctant to let Ésevone go. In an act of defiance, desperation, grief or a combination of the three, Standing Woman removed one of Ésevone's horns, thus unleashing a catalog of pain and misfortune. The mutilation of Ésevone happened circa 1872. Today Ésevone is healed.

I look at our Lakota people today, struggling to survive in this poverty they consigned us to, and I think of what my great-grandpa, Chief Red Cloud, said: "They made us many promises, more than I can remember, but they kept only one. They promised to take our land, and they took it."

CHIEF ALFRED RED CLOUD

Mahpíya Lúta

214

WILDLIFE

Bozeman's Trail to Destiny